Windows Forensics

Understand Analysis Techniques for Your Windows

Dr. Chuck Easttom
Dr. William Butler
Jessica Phelan
Ramya Sai Bhagavatula
Sean Steuber
Karely Rodriguez
Victoria Indy Balkissoon
Zehra Naseer

Apress®

Windows Forensics: Understand Analysis Techniques for Your Windows

Chuck Easttom
Plano, TX, USA

William Butler
Maryland, MD, USA

Jessica Phelan
Austin, TX, USA

Ramya Sai Bhagavatula
Houston, TX, USA

Sean Steuber
Kansas City, MO, USA

Karely Rodriguez
Bonney Lake, WA, USA

Victoria Indy Balkissoon
Lake Mary, FL, USA

Zehra Naseer
Eastvale, CA, USA

ISBN-13 (pbk): 979-8-8688-0192-1
https://doi.org/10.1007/979-8-8688-0193-8

ISBN-13 (electronic): 979-8-8688-0193-8

Managing Director, Apress Media LLC: Welmoed Spahr
Acquisitions Editor: Jessica Vakili
Development Editor: Laura Berendson
Editorial Assistant: Smriti Srivastava

Cover designed by eStudioCalamar

Cover image designed by Freepik (www.freepik.com)

Distributed to the book trade worldwide by Springer Science+Business Media New York, 1 New York Plaza, Suite 4600, New York, NY 10004-1562, USA. Phone 1-800-SPRINGER, fax (201) 348-4505, e-mail orders-ny@springer-sbm.com, or visit www.springeronline.com. Apress Media, LLC is a California LLC and the sole member (owner) is Springer Science + Business Media Finance Inc (SSBM Finance Inc). SSBM Finance Inc is a **Delaware** corporation.

For information on translations, please e-mail booktranslations@springernature.com; for reprint, paperback, or audio rights, please e-mail bookpermissions@springernature.com.

Apress titles may be purchased in bulk for academic, corporate, or promotional use. eBook versions and licenses are also available for most titles. For more information, reference our Print and eBook Bulk Sales web page at http://www.apress.com/bulk-sales.

Any source code or other supplementary material referenced by the author in this book is available to readers on GitHub. For more detailed information, please visit https://www.apress.com/gp/services/source-code.

If disposing of this product, please recycle the paper

This book is dedicated to forensic analysts and students of forensics.

Table of Contents

About the Authors

Dr. Chuck Easttom is the author of 42 books, including several on computer security, forensics, and cryptography. He is also an inventor with 26 patents and the author of over 70 research papers. He holds a doctor of science in cybersecurity, a PhD in nanotechnology, a PhD in computer science, and four master's degrees.

Dr. William Butler is Vice President of Academic Affairs and Executive Director of the Center for Cybersecurity Research and Analysis (CCRA) at Capitol Technology University (located in Laurel, Maryland). Before this appointment, Bill served as the Chair of Cybersecurity programs for eight years.

Jessica Phelan is a computer science graduate student at Vanderbilt University. She is currently doing research in natural language processing at the University of Texas at Austin.

Ramya Sai Bhagavatula is a cybersecurity enthusiast and holds a Security+ Certification from CompTIA. She is currently working as an AI engineer for a medical organization, Baylor Genetics, where she is using her AI expertise to work with genomic data to bring out valuable insights and predictions. She has previously worked for NASA as a Deep Learning Research Intern, where she developed deep learning models to effectively predict severe climate patterns. She was also a lead Data Analyst Intern at an arts organization, Houston Arts Alliance, where she was involved in analyzing in-depth patterns and providing recommendations for their future art grants. Through her dedication to continuous learning and professional development, she pursued her master's in Data Analytics at the University of Houston and is currently pursuing her second master's in Computer Science at Vanderbilt University. She is also 3x Microsoft Certified in AI and Data Engineering. She aspires for her future career path to involve cybersecurity, quantum computing, and AI. In her free time, she loves to volunteer at local organizations to raise awareness about computer science among underprivileged school students. She has also received the Presidential Volunteer Service Award for her volunteer services.

Sean Steuber holds a BS in Engineering from the University of Alabama and an MS in Computer Science from Vanderbilt University and has eight years of professional computer science experience.

Karely Rodriguez is a first-generation DACA recipient and a woman pursuing STEM. She earned a Bachelor of Science in Computer Science and minored in Mathematics at the University of Washington and has continued her education in achieving a Master of Computer Science from Vanderbilt University.

 **Victoria Indy Balkissoon** is working in the Naval Enterprise Research Data Science (N.E.R.D.S.) team at NAWCTSD Orlando where she currently works on developing software applications and data science solutions for the US Navy. She is also currently pursuing a master's degree in Computer Science at Vanderbilt University.

 **Zehra Naseer** holds an MS in Computer Science from Vanderbilt University.

About the Technical Reviewer

 **Dylan Waggy** is a Senior Advisor and Incident Response Analyst with over eight years of experience at a leading American multinational technology company. Armed with a bachelor's in Digital Forensics, he holds certifications in Certified Forensic Computer Examiner (CFCE), Cloud Forensics Responder (GCFR), and Reverse Engineering Malware (GREM). Dylan has successfully contributed to over 300 federal crime cases, assisting law enforcement entities. He has also played a crucial role in establishing digital forensics and incident response teams for Fortune 500 companies. Passionate about proactive and retrospective protection, Dylan takes pride in fortifying organizations against both internal and external threats. His work reflects a commitment to elevating the standards of digital forensics and incident response in today's dynamic cybersecurity landscape.

Acknowledgments

The authors of this book would like to thank the wonderful team at Apress publishing, including the technical reviewer. Without their help, this book would not be possible.

Introduction

Windows is a ubiquitous operating system. As a forensic examiner, you will likely encounter Windows machines quite frequently. Certainly, many forensics tools can extract data from a Windows computer, even if the user of such tools is not well versed in Windows. However, it is important that you fully understand the Windows operating system. This is necessary first so that you can properly understand and interpret the information that such tools provide. Secondly, a thorough knowledge of Windows is important because no tool is perfect. Any tool may miss something. Only by having a solid understanding of the Windows operating system can you identify such gaps and seek the evidence through alternative means.

This book begins with an overview of the Windows operating system. This will provide you a foundational understanding to base the rest of the book on. Then in Chapter 2, you will learn forensic concepts. This includes legal standards such as the Daubert vs. Dow Chemicals case and Federal Rule 702, as well as the scientific method. Subsequent chapters will then go through different portions of Windows including the Windows Registry, Shadow Copy, and related topics. You will also learn to use Microsoft PowerShell to accomplish forensics tasks.

This book is designed for two audiences. The first is the student that is learning forensics. This could be in a university setting or less formal setting. As the book assumes no prior knowledge of either forensics or Microsoft Windows, it can be used by a beginner. The second audience is the professional forensic examiner that requires a more in-depth understanding of Microsoft Windows forensics. This book will provide a depth that will give you a thorough understanding of how to do Windows forensics.

Throughout the book, you will be introduced to forensic tools. These will include commercial tools such as OSForensics as well as open source tools such as Autopsy. The coverage of tools will allow you to actually conduct a detailed forensic examination of a Microsoft Windows computer.

CHAPTER 1

Introduction to Windows

Introduction

It is certainly possible to perform Windows forensics without a deep understanding of the operating system. That is, however, a serious mistake. The various automated forensics tools, many of which you will see in this textbook, can provide you evidence, but they cannot interpret the evidence for you. Furthermore, the automated tools cannot always catch everything. To be a truly competent Windows forensic examiner, you must have an understanding of the operating system itself. The goal of this chapter is to provide you a working knowledge of the Windows operating system and a strong foundation for learning more. To be able to truly perform forensics on any system, you need a deep understanding of that system.

What Is an Operating System?

Before delving too deeply into the Windows operating system, it is helpful to first explore what an operating system is. An operating system (OS) is the underlying software that provides a computer user with all the basic services of resource management on the machine, including a file system structure for data storage and a means of communicating with all the various computer hardware. The operating system controls input and output (I/O) from disk storage (hard drives, solid-state drives, etc.), and other computer components. It is also the job of the operating system to make sure programs running on the computer do not interfere with each other when competing for system resources. This involves memory and resource management.

© Chuck Easttom, William Butler, Jessica Phelan, Ramya Sai Bhagavatula, Sean Steuber, Karely Rodriguez, Victoria Indy Balkissoon, Zehra Naseer 2024
C. Easttom et al., *Windows Forensics*, https://doi.org/10.1007/979-8-8688-0193-8_1

The core of any operating system is referred to as the kernel. The kernel is the core of the operating system. A process is an executing instance of a program. The kernel ensures that processes are allocated the necessary resources and are executed without interfering with each other. There are three types of kernel. With a monolithic kernel, all the system services run along with the main kernel thread in a single memory space. This makes them fast but potentially less secure, as a bug in one service can affect the entire system. A microkernel will manage the core system services like networking, file system drivers, etc., as separate processes, usually in user space. This can provide increased system stability and security but might be slower due to the additional overhead of communication between the kernel and the service processes. A hybrid kernel is a mix of monolithic and microkernel designs.

Most modern operating systems support multitasking. Multitasking is the ability of an operating system to simultaneously support two or more running programs. When multitasking, it seems to the user that both programs are running simultaneously even though they are not. The computer simply switches control between the programs, giving the illusion they are running at the same time. For example, imagine you printed a file while browsing the Internet, streaming music, and checking your email. It may appear as though all these programs are running simultaneously, but in reality, the computer runs the software in between sending packets of data to the printer.

One common way to accomplish multitasking is called preemptive multitasking, sometimes referred to as time slicing, which is a process that allows multiple programs to share control of the operating system. For example, two or more programs can share the CPU for processing information, but no single program can totally take charge of a computer system. All programs running in preemptive mode are allowed to run for a set period of time, called the time slice, by an operating system process known as the scheduler. At the end of the time slice, a process is interrupted so the next process in line can run. This way, all the processes on the computer can share the CPU fairly. Since each time slice is quite brief, a few milliseconds, it appears the system is performing tasks simultaneously.

History of Windows

Microsoft Windows was released as just a graphical user interface (GUI) for the MS-DOS (Microsoft Disk Operating System) operating system. Windows itself was not actually an operating system. In fact, versions 1.0 to 3.11 were simply GUIs on top of MS-DOS.

Windows 1.0 was released in 1985 but received very little notice from the public. Windows 2.0 and 2.1 were released in 1987 and 1988, respectively, but were still not widely popular. Windows 3.0 was released in 1990, then 3.1 in 1992. Most of the public began to use Windows with version 3.1. It became quite popular.

Windows NT was released in 1993 and was a separate product from the consumer Windows versions. Windows NT was designed to be used in a work environment, on a local area network. While the interface looked quite similar to the consumer version, the internals were different. There were workstation and server versions of Windows NT.

Windows 95 marked a shift in the consumer version of Windows. While not entirely a stand-alone operating system, it was not simply a GUI either. Furthermore, Windows 95 was 32 bits (at least most of it). The fusion of the GUI with the operating system has continued throughout subsequent versions. The general outline and description of various versions is given here:

> **Windows 1.0 (1985)**: The first version of Windows was essentially a graphical shell for MS-DOS, allowing users to run programs in a graphical environment. It introduced basic features like scroll bars, windows, and icons.

> **Windows 2.0 (1987)**: Improved on the first version with better graphics support and overlapping windows. It was during this era that Microsoft introduced the Excel and Word programs.

> **Windows 3.0 and 3.1 (1990–1992)**: These versions marked the true beginning of Windows' dominance. They supported 16 colors and improved the interface significantly. Windows 3.1, in particular, saw widespread adoption.

> **Windows 95 (1995)**: A major milestone, Windows 95 introduced the Start menu, Taskbar, and the concept of "plug and play" hardware. It also integrated MS-DOS with Windows more tightly.

> **Windows 98 (1998)**: Built on Windows 95 but with additional support for new technologies like USB, DVD, and ACPI.

> **Windows ME (Millennium Edition) (2000)**: Aimed at home users, it was not very well received due to its instability and was quickly overshadowed by its NT-based counterparts.

Windows 2000: Part of the NT family, it was geared more toward business users, known for its stability and security.

Windows XP (2001): One of the most successful versions, combining the consumer-friendly interface of the 9x series with the stability of the NT line. XP remained popular for many years, even well beyond its intended life cycle.

Windows Vista (2006): Introduced Aero graphics, improved security, and a new search function. However, it faced criticism for heavy resource requirements and compatibility issues.

Windows 7 (2009): Addressed many of Vista's issues and was praised for its performance, user interface, and enhanced security features.

Windows 8 (2012): Represented a significant overhaul, introducing a touch-centric interface and the Metro design language. However, the removal of the Start menu and focus on touch were controversial.

Windows 8.1 (2013): An update to Windows 8, it brought back the Start button and made several adjustments based on user feedback.

Windows 10 (2015): Aimed to address the criticisms of Windows 8, reintroducing a Start menu and supporting both touch and traditional PC users. It was positioned as a service, with regular updates.

Windows 11 (2021): The latest version as of this writing, Windows 11 introduced a redesigned Start menu, improved window management features like Snap Layouts, and a focus on security and performance.

These are just the client systems. The server operating systems is given in the following brief paragraphs:

Windows NT 3.1 Advanced Server (1993): This was the first version of Microsoft's server operating system, building on the Windows NT architecture, which was designed for robustness and security.

Windows NT 3.5 Server (1994): An update to the original NT system, it included performance improvements and support for new hardware.

Windows NT 3.51 Server (1995): This release focused on interoperability with NetWare networks and included the first version of the web server, Internet Information Services (IIS).

Windows NT 4.0 Server (1996): A major upgrade with a new user interface aligned with Windows 95. It included IIS 2.0 and brought in the concept of domains and user accounts for managing network resources.

Windows 2000 Server (2000): Introduced Active Directory, a directory service for managing domains, users, and resources. It also brought in improved support for web services and scalability.

Windows Server 2003 (2003): This version improved Active Directory and included better default security, IIS 6.0, and support for .NET framework. It was also the first server OS to drop support for older Windows 9x clients.

Windows Server 2003 R2 (2005): An update to the 2003 version, it included enhancements like a common log file system and improved branch office performance.

Windows Server 2008 (2008): Introduced Server Core, a minimal installation option for reduced maintenance and attack surface. It also included Hyper-V for virtualization and improved security and management features.

Windows Server 2008 R2 (2009): This was the first Windows Server OS exclusively for 64-bit processors. It improved upon virtualization with Hyper-V 2.0 and included features like DirectAccess and BranchCache.

Windows Server 2012 (2012): A major release with a focus on cloud computing, it introduced a redesigned user interface based on Windows 8, a new version of Hyper-V, and a new file system (ReFS).

Windows Server 2012 R2 (2013): Included enhancements to Hyper-V, storage, networking, and included the return of the Start button in the UI.

Windows Server 2016 (2016): This version focused on cloud and container support, introducing Docker compatibility, Nano Server for lightweight environments, and enhanced security features like Shielded Virtual Machines.

Windows Server 2019 (2018): Continued the focus on hybrid cloud environments, with improved Kubernetes support, Windows Admin Center for management, and enhanced security features.

Windows Server 2022 (2021): The latest version as of my last update, focusing on advanced multilayer security, hybrid capabilities with Azure, and a flexible application platform.

The File System

Operating systems interact with the file system to access files. A file system refers to the method of organizing files on a storage device. It is an indexing system used by the operating system to keep track of all files on the disk. The file system maintains a file table of all areas on the disk, and it tracks which areas are being used for data and which are free and available at any given time. A file table is a component of a file system used to organize files on a storage device.

Microsoft uses NTFS, New Technology File System. One major improvement of NTFS over FAT was the increased volume sizes NTFS could support. The maximum NTFS volume size is $2^{64}-1$ clusters. NTFS also introduced the Encrypted File System (EFS). This allows the end user to easily encrypt and decrypt individual files and folders. There are several individual files that are key to this file system. Two of the most fundamental are the MFT (Master File Table, some sources call it the Meta File Table) file and the cluster bitmap. The MFT describes all files on the volume, including file names, timestamps, security identifiers, and file attributes such as "read only," "compressed," "encrypted," etc. This file contains one base file record for each file and directory on an NTFS volume. It serves the same purpose as the file allocation table does in FAT and FAT32. The cluster bitmap file is a map of all the clusters on the hard drive. This is an array of bit entries where each bit indicates whether its corresponding cluster is allocated/used or free/unused.

Unlike FAT/FAT32, NTFS is a journaling file system, which means it records actions so they can be undone. NTFS uses the NTFS Log ($Logfile) to record information about changes to the volume. With the advent of NTFS, file names can be 1 to 255 characters in length, including the path. You can use uppercase and lowercase (case-aware, but not case-sensitive). You can use spaces and periods. You cannot use these characters:

   / \ : * ? " < > |

With Windows 2000, Microsoft added reparse points to NTFS. Reparse points provide a mechanism to extend the functionality of the file system and are used to implement several advanced features in Windows. A reparse point is essentially a type of data attribute that can be associated with a file or directory, instructing the file system to treat that file or directory in a special way. There are three types of reparse points:

1. **Junction Points**: Similar to Unix hard links, they allow directories to be aliased at another location in the file system. These are the most common.

2. **Symbolic Links**: Introduced in Windows Vista, they are more flexible than junction points and can point to files or directories and work across local and network paths.

3. **Volume Mount Points**: Allow a volume to be mounted at a directory rather than a drive letter.

Since Windows Vista, NFTS has supported what is called Transactional NTFS (TxF). Developers can use this to write transactions that either succeed completely or fail completely, much like database transactions. TxF allows for grouping a series of file operations into a single transaction. This transaction is atomic, meaning either all operations in the transaction are completed successfully or none of them are applied. This is crucial for maintaining data integrity. Transactions are isolated from each other. Changes made in one transaction are not visible to other transactions until they are committed.

The NTFS boot sector contains values described in Table 1-1.

Table 1-1. *NTFS Boot Sector*

Byte Offset	Field Length	Typical Value	Field Name		Purpose
0x00	3 bytes	0xEB5290	x86 JMP and NOP instructions		This causes execution to continue after the data structures in this boot sector.
0x03	8 bytes	"NTFS" Word "NTFS" followed by four trailing spaces (0x20)	OEM ID		This is the indicator that this is an NTFS file system.
0x0B	2 bytes	0x0200	BPB	Bytes per sector	The number of bytes in a disk sector.
0x0D	1 byte	0x08	BPB	Sectors per cluster	The number of sectors in a cluster.
0x0E	2 bytes	0x0000	BPB	Reserved sectors, unused	
0x10	3 bytes	0x000000	BPB	Unused	This field is always 0.
0x13	2 bytes	0x0000	BPB	Unused by NTFS	This field is always 0.
0x15	1 byte	0xF8	BPB	Media Descriptor	The type of drive. 0xF8 is used to denote a hard drive.
0x16	2 bytes	0x0000	BPB	Unused	This field is always 0.
0x18	2 bytes	0x003F	BPB	Sectors per track	The number of disk sectors in a drive track.
0x1A	2 bytes	0x00FF	BPB	Number of heads	The number of heads on the drive.
0x1C	4 bytes	0x0000003F	BPB	Hidden sectors	The number of sectors preceding the partition.
0x20	4 bytes	0x00000000	BPB	Unused	Not used by NTFS.

(continued)

Table 1-1. (*continued*)

Byte Offset	Field Length	Typical Value	Field Name		Purpose
0x24	4 bytes	0x00800080	EBPB	Unused	Not used by NTFS.
0x28	8 bytes	0x00000000007FF54A	EBPB	Total sectors	The partition size in sectors.
0x30	8 bytes	0x0000000000000004	EBPB	$MFT cluster number	The cluster that contains the Master File Table.
0x38	8 bytes	0x000000000007FF54	EBPB	$MFTMirr cluster number	The cluster that contains a backup of the Master File Table.
0x40	1 byte	0xF6	EBPB	Bytes or Clusters per File Record Segment	The number of clusters in a File Record Segment.
0x41	3 bytes	0x000000	EBPB	Unused	This field is not used by NTFS.
0x44	1 byte	0x01	EBPB	Bytes or clusters per index buffer	The number of clusters in an index buffer.
0x45	3 bytes	0x000000	EBPB	Unused	This field is not used by NTFS.
0x48	8 bytes	0x1C741BC9741BA514	EBPB	Volume serial number	A unique random number assigned to this partition.
0x50	4 bytes	0x00000000	EBPB	Checksum, unused	
0x54	426 bytes		Bootstrap code		The code that loads the rest of the operating system.
0x01FE	2 bytes	0xAA55	End-of-sector marker		This flag indicates that this is a valid boot sector.

There is a great deal of information in the boot sector, as you might expect. All of this is used in the booting of the system. Figure 1-1 is a screenshot of the boot sector of an NTFS volume as viewed in OSForensics.

```
                          00                08                0123456789ABCDEF
0x0000000000000000   EB52904E54465320  2020200002080000   .R.NTFS    .....
0x0000000000000010   0000000000F80000  3F00FF0000080000   .......?......
0x0000000000000020   0000000080008000  FF2FC0D101000000   .........../.....
0x0000000000000030   00000C0000000000  0200000000000000   ................
0x0000000000000040   F600000001000000  70E422DA1623DAA4   ........p."..#..
0x0000000000000050   00000000FA33C08E  D0BC007CFB68C007   .....3.....|.h..
0x0000000000000060   1F1E686600CB8816  0E0066813E03004E   ..hf......f.>..N
0x0000000000000070   5446537515B441BB  AA55CD13720C81FB   TFSu..A..U..r...
0x0000000000000080   55AA7506F7C10100  7503E9DD001E83EC   U.u.....u.......
0x0000000000000090   18681A00B4488A16  0E008BF4161FCD13   .h...H..........
0x00000000000000A0   9F83C4189E581F72  E13B060B0075DBA3   .....X.r.;...u..
0x00000000000000B0   0F00C12E0F00041E  5A33DBB900202BC8   ........Z3... +.
0x00000000000000C0   66FF06110003160F  008EC2FF061600E8   f...............
0x00000000000000D0   4B002BC877EFB800  BBCD1A6623C0752D   K.+.w......f#.u-
0x00000000000000E0   6681FB5443504175  2481F90201721E16   f..TCPAu$....r..
0x00000000000000F0   6807BB1668521116  68090066653665366   h...hR..h..fSfSf
0x0000000000000100   5516161668B80166  610E07CD1A33C0BF   U...h..fa....3..
0x0000000000000110   0A13B9F60CFCF3AA  E9FE01909066601E   ..............f`.
0x0000000000000120   0666A11100660306  1C001E6668000000   .f...f.....fh...
0x0000000000000130   0066500653680100  681000B4428A160E   .fP.Sh..h...B...
0x0000000000000140   00161F8BF4CD1366  595B5A665966591F   .......fY[ZfYfY.
0x0000000000000150   0F82160066FF0611  0003160F008EC2FF   ...f............
0x0000000000000160   0E160075BC071F66  61C3A1F601E80900   ...u..fa........
0x0000000000000170   A1FA01E80300F4EB  FD8BF0AC3C007409   ............<.t.
0x0000000000000180   B40EBB0700CD10EB  F2C30D0A41206469   ............A di
0x0000000000000190   736B207265616420  6572726F72206F63   sk read error oc
0x00000000000001A0   637572726564000D  0A424F4F544D4752   curred...BOOTMGR
0x00000000000001B0   20697320636F6D70  726573736564000D    is compressed..
0x00000000000001C0   0A50726573733230  43747726C2B416C742B   .Press Ctrl+Alt+
0x00000000000001D0   44656C20746F2072  6573746172740D0A   Del to restart..
0x00000000000001E0   0000000000000000  0000000000000000   ................
0x00000000000001F0   0000000000008A01  A701BF01000055AA   ..............U.
0x0000000000000200   070042004F004F00  54004D0047005200   ..B.O.O.T.M.G.R.
0x0000000000000210   0400240049003300  300000D400000024   ..$.I.3.0......$
0x0000000000000220   0000000000000000  0000000000000000   ................
0x0000000000000230   0000000000000000  0000000000000000   ................
0x0000000000000240   0000000000000000  0000000000000000   ................
0x0000000000000250   000000000000E9C0  009005004E005400   ............N.T.
0x0000000000000260   4C00440052000700  42004F004F005400   L.D.R...B.O.O.T.
0x0000000000000270   5400470054000700  42004F004F005400   T.G.T...B.O.O.T.
0x0000000000000280   4E00580054000000  0000000000000000   N.X.T...........
0x0000000000000290   0000000000000000  00000D0A416E206F   ............An o
0x00000000000002A0   7065726174696E67  2073797374656D20   perating system
0x00000000000002B0   7761736E27740066  6F756E642E205472   wasn't found. Tr
0x00000000000002C0   7920646973636F6E  6E656374696E6720   y disconnecting
0x00000000000002D0   616E792064726976  6573207468617420   any drives that
0x00000000000002E0   646F6E27740D0A63  6F6E7461696E2061   don't..contain a
0x00000000000002F0   6E206F7065726174  696E672073797374   n operating syst
0x0000000000000300   656D2E0000000000  0000000000000000   em..............
0x0000000000000310   000000000000009A  02660FB7060B0066   .........f.....f
0x0000000000000320   0FB61E0D0066F7E3  66A35202668B0E40   .....f..f.R.f..@
0x0000000000000330   0080F9000F8F0E00  F6D966B801000000   .........f......
0x0000000000000340   66D3E0EB089066A1  520266F7E166A386   f.....f.R.f..f..
0x0000000000000350   02660FB71E0B0066  33D266F7F366A356   .f.....f3.f..f.V
0x0000000000000360   02E8A204668B0E4E  0266890E26026603   ....f..N.f..&.f.
0x0000000000000370   0E860266890E2A02  66030E860266890E   ..f..*.f....f...
0x0000000000000380   2E0266030E860266  890E3E0266030E86   ..f....f..>.f...
0x0000000000000390   0266890E460266B8  90000000668B0E26   .f..F.f....f...&
0x00000000000003A0   02E89009660BC00F  84BFFD66A3320266   ....f......f.2.f
```

Figure 1-1. *NTFS boot sector*

The Windows Master File Table (MFT) contains all the information about files in the file system. The first 27 entries are metadata about NTFS. The sequence number and purposes are listed in Table 1-2.

Table 1-2. *MFT*

Segment Number	File Name	Purpose
0	$MFT	Describes all files on the volume, including file names, timestamps, stream names, and lists of cluster numbers where data streams reside, indexes, security identifiers, and file attributes like "read only," "compressed," "encrypted," etc.
1	$MFTMirr	Duplicate of the first entries of $MFT, usually 4 entries (4 kilobytes).
2	$LogFile	This is a transaction log of file system metadata changes.
3	$Volume	This file contains information about the volume, including the volume object identifier, volume label, file system version, and volume flags (mounted, chkdsk requested, requested $LogFile resize, mounted on NT 4, volume serial number updating).
4	$AttrDef	This is a table of MFT attributes that associates numeric identifiers with names.
5	.	Root directory. Directory data is stored in $INDEX_ROOT and $INDEX_ALLOCATION attributes both named $I30.
6	$Bitmap	Each individual bit indicates whether its corresponding cluster is used (allocated) or free (available for allocation).
7	$Boot	This file is always located at the first clusters on the volume. It contains bootstrap code (see NTLDR/BOOTMGR) and a BIOS parameter block including a volume serial number and cluster numbers of $MFT and $MFTMirr.
8	$BadClus	A file that contains all the clusters marked as having bad sectors.

(continued)

Table 1-2. (*continued*)

Segment Number	File Name	Purpose
9	$Secure	Access control list database that reduces overhead having many identical ACLs stored with each file, by uniquely storing these ACLs only in this database (contains two indices: $SII *(Standard_ Information ID)* and $SDH *(Security Descriptor Hash)*, which index the stream named $SDS containing actual ACL table).
10	$UpCase	A table of unicode uppercase characters for ensuring case-insensitivity in Win32 and DOS namespaces.
11	$Extend	A file system directory containing various optional extensions, such as $Quota, $Objld, $Reparse, or $UsnJrnl.
12–23	Reserved for $MFT extension entries. Extension entries are additional MFT records that contain additional attributes that do not fit in the primary record.	
24	$Extend\$Quota	As the name suggests, this contains information about disk quotas. Contains two index roots, named $O and $Q.
25	$Extend\$Objld	This contains link tracking information. Contains an index root and allocation named $O.
26	$Extend\$Reparse	This contains reparse point data (such as symbolic links). Contains an index root and allocation named $R.
27–	Beginning of regular file entries.	

Windows Details

In the following subsections, you will learn a great deal about Windows. This will include administrative and user tasks as well as understanding the underlying structure and components of Windows.

Windows Timestamps

When collecting data from a device, you will find date-timestamps. It is important that you understand what these actually mean. As an example, the following date-timestamps in Windows have specific meaning:

- **File Created**: This date-timestamp usually shows when a file or folder was created. When a file is moved onto a different volume using the Windows command line or drag-and-drop feature, the File Created date-timestamp of the new copy is set to the current time. When a file is moved onto a different volume using the Cut and Paste menu options, the File Created date-timestamp does not change; however, the Last Accessed will change.

- **Modified**: The last time some change was made to the file. This is usually most important to forensic analysis.

- **Last Accessed**: This date-timestamp represents the most recent time a file or folder was accessed by the file system. It need not be opened to be accessed. That means that even an antivirus scan might trigger this date-timestamp, making it less informative for forensics.

- **Entry Modified Time**: In NTFS, this timestamp indicates when the metadata of the file (like its location on the disk, size, etc.) was last changed.

Windows timestamps are typically stored in a format known as FILETIME, which represents the number of 100-nanosecond intervals since January 1, 1601 (UTC). This choice of start date aligns with the Gregorian calendar reform. The raw timestamps are stored in Coordinated Universal Time (UTC) and are converted to the local time zone for display purposes based on system settings. It's important to note that these timestamps can be altered or manipulated, so they are not always a foolproof method of tracking file history. Additionally, different file systems and operating system versions might handle timestamps slightly differently.

Windows Active Directory

Active Directory (AD) is a special-purpose database that is used to handle all the entities on a Windows domain. That includes services, computers, and users. The Active Directory database consists of objects and attributes. Objects and attribute definitions are stored in the Active Directory schema. The specific services that Active Directory provides are listed here:

Domain Services: AD stores information about members of the domain, including devices and users, and verifies their credentials and rights. A user can use the same username and password to log in to any computer in the domain.

Lightweight Directory Services: This is a lighter version of AD Domain Services, suitable for situations where a full domain controller is not required, such as directory-enabled applications.

Certificate Services: This allows the AD to create, manage, and store certificates used in software security systems using Public Key Infrastructure (PKI).

Directory Federation Services: This provides Single Sign-On (SSO) to authenticate a user in multiple web applications in a single session.

Rights Management Services: This helps to protect sensitive data by establishing policies for who can access or modify it.

Group Policy: In AD, group policy objects are used to define security settings and configure software settings. It allows administrators to implement specific configurations for users and computers within the organization.

Organizational Structure: AD allows the creation of a hierarchical structure of organizational units (OUs), which can mirror an organization's functional or business structure.

Replication and Trusts: AD allows the replication of data between domain controllers and trusts between different domains in a network.

DLLs and Services

A DLL, which stands for "Dynamic Link Library," is a fundamental concept in Windows programming. These libraries are an essential part of the Windows operating system and its ecosystem. A DLL is a type of shared library, meaning it provides code and data that can be used by multiple programs simultaneously. This helps in reducing the size of the programs and the memory footprint on the system. DLL files typically have the extension .dll, although they might also end in .ocx (for libraries containing ActiveX controls) or .drv (for older system drivers).

Unlike static linking, where code is written into the executable at compile time, dynamic linking refers to the process where an executable file references external code or data. The actual linking happens at runtime, which means the executable code can use different library versions without needing to recompile. Executable programs (EXEs) call functions stored in a DLL just like they call their internal functions. The difference is that the DLL's code is stored separately and not in the executable file itself. DLLs can be linked when a program is loaded (load time dynamic linking) or while it is running (runtime dynamic linking). The latter is used for functionalities that are needed only under certain conditions, hence saving memory by not loading them otherwise.

DLLs provide a way to modularize applications so that functionality can be updated and reused more easily. Multiple programs can use the same DLL file simultaneously, which saves memory and reduces redundancy in the system. Updating a DLL doesn't require recompiling or relinking the applications that use it, as long as the functions it exposes remain consistent. Different programming languages can create and call DLLs, making them versatile for various software applications. Many standard Windows functionalities are implemented in system DLLs. Software might use DLLs for adding features or extensions.

However, there can also be issues with DLL's applications depending on specific DLLs. If a DLL is missing or an incorrect version is installed, it can prevent the application from running correctly. "DLL Hell" is a term that refers to problems caused by the installation of different software versions that use different DLL versions, potentially overwriting newer versions with older ones and causing applications to fail. Malicious programs can exploit DLLs by replacing them with harmful versions or by tricking applications into using them, leading to security vulnerabilities.

A Dynamic Link Library (DLL) file in Windows has a structure that is similar to an executable (EXE) file. This structure is based on the Portable Executable (PE) format, which is a file format for executables, object code, and DLLs used in 32-bit and 64-bit versions of Windows operating systems. In the following paragraphs, more technical details on DLLs will be provided.

Every DLL starts with a small DOS header, mainly for backward compatibility. It contains the magic number "MZ" (after Mark Zbikowski, one of the developers) at the beginning of the file. Following the DOS header, the file contains a PE header, which is the main header for the Windows executable format. This header contains information critical for the Windows loader. There is also a signature that identifies the file as a PE format file. The file header also contains general information about the file, such as the architecture (32-bit or 64-bit), the number of sections, and timestamps. The optional header is rather poorly named. Despite its name, this header is essential for executables and DLLs. It contains information needed for the runtime execution of the file, like entry points, required Windows version, and sizes of various data structures. The specific sections in the DLL, after the header, are listed and briefly described here:

> **.text**: Contains the executable code
>
> **.data**: Stores the initialized global and static variables
>
> **.rdata**: Holds read-only data, like string literals and constants
>
> **.bss**: Contains uninitialized global and static variables (Block Started by Symbol)
>
> **.idata**: Holds the import data, including functions and variables imported from other files
>
> **.edata**: Contains the export data, which are functions and variables that can be used by other files
>
> **.rsrc**: Stores resources like icons, menus, and dialog boxes
>
> **.reloc**: Contains relocation information, used if the DLL is loaded at an address different from its preferred base address

DLLs also have an export and import table. The export table lists the functions and variables that the DLL makes available to other modules. Each entry includes the name or ordinal of the export and its address. The import table lists the functions and variables that the DLL uses from other DLLs. This table is used by the loader to resolve addresses at load time or runtime.

Windows Services are another part of Windows that the user usually won't see and interact directly with, but are quite important to the operating system. Services run in the background and do not have a user interface. They can operate whether a user is logged in or not. They are designed to run for a long time without interruption. Services can be configured to start automatically at boot or can be started manually as needed. They are managed through the Service Control Manager (SCM), which is a part of the Windows operating system. The SCM is responsible for starting, stopping, and interacting with service processes. Services can be controlled (started, stopped, paused, resumed) using the Windows Services console (services.msc), command-line tools like sc and net, or programmatically via APIs. The services window is shown in Figure 1-2.

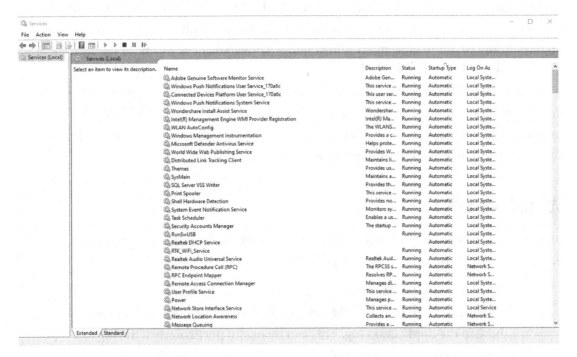

Figure 1-2. *Windows Services*

Swap File and Hyberfil.sys

The Windows swap file formerly ended in an .swp extension and is typically found in the Windows root directory. The swap file is a binary file. You can use any hex editor to extract relevant information of possible evidentiary value. This used to be a file with an .swp extension; in more recent systems (XP and beyond), it is a pagefile.sys.

The size of swap files is usually about 1.5 times the size of the physical RAM in the machine. Swap files contain remnants of whatever programs the user has been working with. In other words, the user might have been working with an Excel spreadsheet, not saved it, but part of it is still in the swap file. This brings up an important forensic fact. SWAP files are not erased when the system shuts down. They work on a queue system, which means data is not erased until that space is needed again. You can examine this file's contents with any standard hex editor. Some forensic analysts like to use a favorite general-purpose tool, such as scalpel.

Hiberfil.sys is a memory file that can be converted to an image file and processed with volatility or even simple string searches. Within this file, there may be password artifacts from applications that were recently run. Starting with Windows 8 and moving on to Window 10, there have been some changes in hyberfil.sys, swapfile.sys, and pagefile.sys.

Starting with Windows 8, the pagefile.sys is there all the time, but the hiberfil.sys is only there if you have fast startup enabled in Windows 8. Also, by default, Windows 8 uses a hybrid shutdown which causes a hyberfil.sys to be generated, but it only has the kernel and files needed to boot, so will be smaller.

Windows Logs

Windows stores a number of logs. Some of these might be important for forensic investigations. It is important to understand what is in each log:

- **Application Log**: This log contains various events logged by applications or programs. Many applications will record their errors here in the application log. This can be useful particularly if the log is on a server that has a database server like SQL Server installed. Examining this log can give clues that someone has been attempting to compromise the database.

- **Security Log**: The most important things you will find in the security log are successful and unsuccessful logon attempts. This log also records events related to resource use, such as creating, opening, or deleting files or other objects. Administrators can specify what events are recorded in the security log. Logon auditing can be turned off but never should be.

- **Setup Log**: The setup log contains events related to application setup. This will show new applications installed on the machine. Obviously, most viruses and spyware won't write to the application log. However, this can let you know if new applications have been installed, which might either have a security flaw or be Trojan horses.

- **System Log**: The system log contains events logged by Windows system components. This includes events like driver failures. This particular log is not as interesting from a forensics perspective as the other logs are.

- **ForwardedEvents Log**: The ForwardedEvents log is used to store events collected from remote computers. This log is important in a networked environment. However, the various systems must be configured to populate this log; it won't occur by default.

- **Applications and Services Logs**: Applications and Services logs are a new category of event logs. These logs store events from a single application or component rather than events that might have systemwide impact. This can reveal problems with a specific application or Windows component. This is not as interesting from a forensics perspective as the other logs are.

You can view logs with the event viewer. Simply type event into the search bar. You will see something like what is displayed in Figure 1-3.

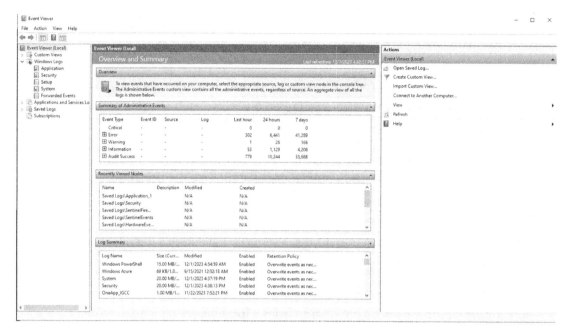

Figure 1-3. *Windows Event Viewer*

Windows Log Entries

There are a very large number of log entry codes. It simply is not possible to know them all. Fortunately, Microsoft and other sources provide a number of online resources.[1,2,3] There are a few that will frequently require a bit more investigation. Those are listed here:

>1102 Audit log was cleared.

>4741 A computer account was created.

>4742 A computer account was changed.

---

[1] https://learn.microsoft.com/en-us/windows-server/identity/ad-ds/plan/appendix-l--events-to-monitor

[2] www.ultimatewindowssecurity.com/securitylog/encyclopedia/default.aspx

[3] https://learn.microsoft.com/en-us/windows/security/threat-protection/auditing/basic-audit-logon-events

4782 The password hash of an account was accessed.

4728 A member was added to a security-enabled global group.

4720 A user account was created.

4767 A user account was unlocked.

4902 Changes to the Audit Policy such as using Auditpol.exe.

It is critical to understand that the preceding list is just exemplary. There are hundreds of codes you may find in the audit log. It will be necessary to search for the meaning to log entries that appear unusual to you. So how do you know they are unusual? If the entry is proximate to the time in which another forensically interesting artifact was created or modified.

Windows Command Line

The Windows command line is a text-based interface that allows a user to issue commands by entering text at the command prompt. It operates much like the shell in Unix/Linux or the terminal in MacOS. Under normal circumstances, the command window has a black background with white text. However, this window has been modified to make it easier to read in this text. There are numerous commands one can execute from the command line. With every command, there will be flags that modify its behavior. Make certain you try the command /? in order to see the help information which lists the various flags for that command. We won't be covering the most basic commands in this section; it is assumed you probably already know these, but if you do not, please ensure you are familiar with the commands in Table 1-3.

Table 1-3. *Basic Windows Commands*

Command	Purpose
cd	Change director
cls	Clear the screen
sir	Lists contents of a directory
mkdir	Creates a folder/directory
rmdir	Deletes a folder/directory
del	Deletes a file
tree	Shows the current directory as a tree
prompt	Changes the default prompt. For example: *prompt this is my computer*
title	Changes the title on the command prompt window
clip	Copies item to the clipboard
ping	Pings an IP address or domain name
sfc	System file check; checks to see if all system files are OK

A few commands that are often forensically interesting are described here.

netstat: It is short for "network status" and lets you know any live connections on the machine. If someone is currently accessing the computer, it will show in netstat, or if the computer is accessing some remote resource. You can see this command in Figure 1-4.

```
Administrator: Command Prompt

Microsoft Windows [Version 10.0.19045.3693]
(c) Microsoft Corporation. All rights reserved.

C:\Windows\system32>netstat

Active Connections

  Proto  Local Address          Foreign Address        State
  TCP    10.0.0.32:52265        1drv:https             ESTABLISHED
  TCP    10.0.0.32:54059        10.0.0.35:8008         ESTABLISHED
  TCP    10.0.0.32:54061        10.0.0.35:8009         ESTABLISHED
  TCP    10.0.0.32:54183        rw-in-f108:imaps       ESTABLISHED
  TCP    10.0.0.32:54212        93:https               ESTABLISHED
  TCP    10.0.0.32:54230        162-254-195-71:27028   ESTABLISHED
  TCP    10.0.0.32:54242        162.159.61.4:https     ESTABLISHED
  TCP    10.0.0.32:54568        rq-in-f188:5228        ESTABLISHED
  TCP    10.0.0.32:54729        52.109.20.96:https     ESTABLISHED
  TCP    10.0.0.32:54730        52.109.20.96:https     ESTABLISHED
  TCP    10.0.0.32:54731        52.109.20.96:https     ESTABLISHED
  TCP    10.0.0.32:54732        52.109.20.96:https     ESTABLISHED
  TCP    10.0.0.32:54734        52.109.20.96:https     ESTABLISHED
  TCP    10.0.0.32:54735        52.109.20.96:https     ESTABLISHED
  TCP    10.0.0.32:54737        52.109.20.96:https     ESTABLISHED
  TCP    10.0.0.32:54738        52.109.20.96:https     ESTABLISHED
  TCP    10.0.0.32:54739        52.109.20.96:https     ESTABLISHED
  TCP    10.0.0.32:54763        rs-in-f95:https        ESTABLISHED
  TCP    10.0.0.32:54767        20.10.31.115:https     ESTABLISHED
  TCP    10.0.0.32:54775        a23-45-119-135:https   LAST_ACK
  TCP    10.0.0.32:54776        a23-45-119-135:https   LAST_ACK
  TCP    10.0.0.32:54777        a23-45-119-135:https   LAST_ACK
```

Figure 1-4. *Netstat*

As you can see, all the connections shown in Figure 1-4 are local, private IP addresses. This is actually quite normal. Your various systems on your home network are talking to each other.

Assoc files are associated with a particular extension. It can be informative to know what those associations are. In Figure 1-5, you can see the assoc command. Notice that .7z is associated with WinRar. The .7z file extension is for the 7-zip compression utility, but on this system, it is associated with the WinRar compression software.

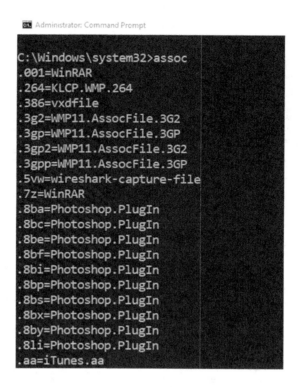

Figure 1-5. *Assoc*

fc: That stands for file compare. For example, if you have a configuration file that you believe has been altered and you have a previous copy you know to be good, you can use fc to compare the two. It will output only the differences. This is shown in Figure 1-6.

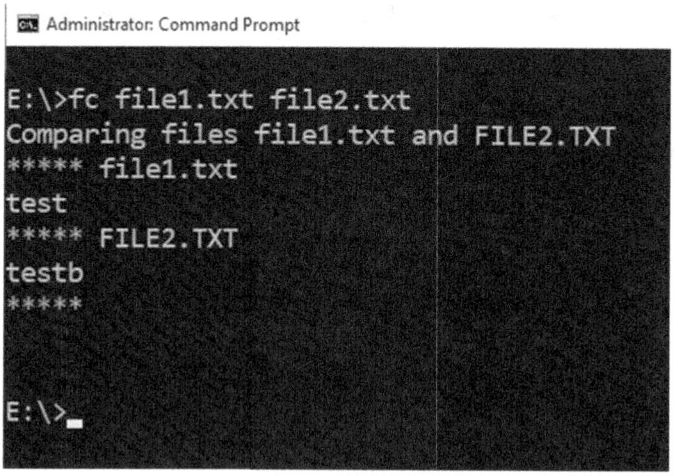

Figure 1-6. *The fc command*

A very useful command in forensic examination is recover. This command will attempt to recover the readable portions of a corrupt file:

Net Sessions: Any currently running network sessions

Openfiles: Shows currently open shared files. Must run as administrator

Net File: Similar to openfiles

The previous three commands are all shown in Figure 1-7.

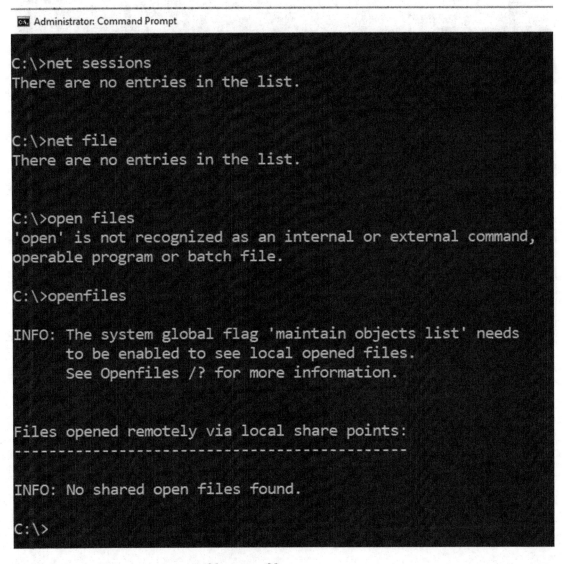

Figure 1-7. *Net sessions, net file, openfiles*

The chkdsk command checks the drive to determine if it is corrupt or functioning as expected. You can see the chkdsk command in Figure 1-8.

```
Administrator: Command Prompt

E:\>chkdsk
The type of the file system is NTFS.
Volume label is New Volume.

WARNING!  /F parameter not specified.
Running CHKDSK in read-only mode.

Stage 1: Examining basic file system structure ...
  728576 file records processed.
File verification completed.
 Phase duration (File record verification): 5.67 seconds.
  217 large file records processed.
 Phase duration (Orphan file record recovery): 0.00 milliseconds.
  0 bad file records processed.
 Phase duration (Bad file record checking): 0.85 milliseconds.

Stage 2: Examining file name linkage ...
  6476 reparse records processed.
  847928 index entries processed.
Index verification completed.
 Phase duration (Index verification): 59.10 seconds.
  0 unindexed files scanned.
 Phase duration (Orphan reconnection): 699.22 milliseconds.
  0 unindexed files recovered to lost and found.
 Phase duration (Orphan recovery to lost and found): 0.96 milliseconds.
  6476 reparse records processed.
 Phase duration (Reparse point and Object ID verification): 16.90 milliseconds.

Stage 3: Examining security descriptors ...
Security descriptor verification completed.
 Phase duration (Security descriptor verification): 15.09 milliseconds.
```

Figure 1-8. *The chkdsk command*

The cacls command will provide the access list for a given file. You can see this in Figure 1-9.

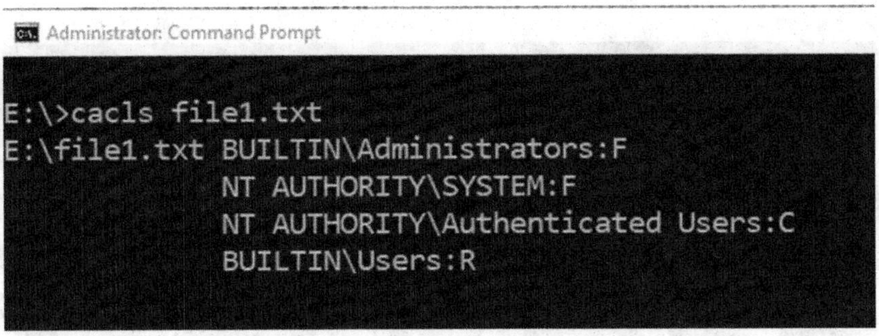

Figure 1-9. *The cacls command*

The findstr command is quite interesting. It searches a file for a specific pattern. The help command for this is rather extensive, as there are many options. To illustrate this command, a file was created with the following content:

> Forensics is very interesting. In this book you will learn a great
> deal about Windows forensics. This will help you become better at
> forensics.

Then the findstr command was used to search all text files for that string. The results can be seen in Figure 1-10.

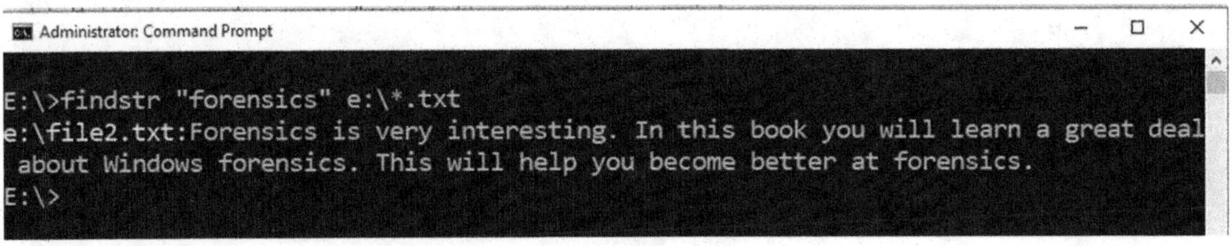

Figure 1-10. *The findstr command*

The getmac command gets the mac address for network cards on the device. This can be seen in Figure 1-11.

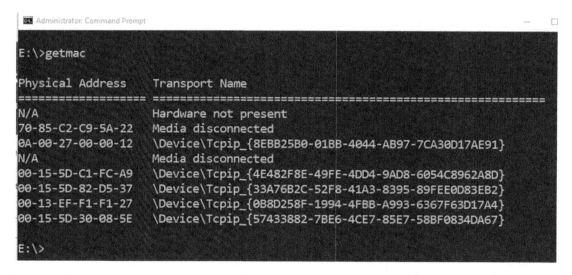

Figure 1-11. *The getmac command*

The ipconfig command gets all the network settings and is shown in Figure 1-12.

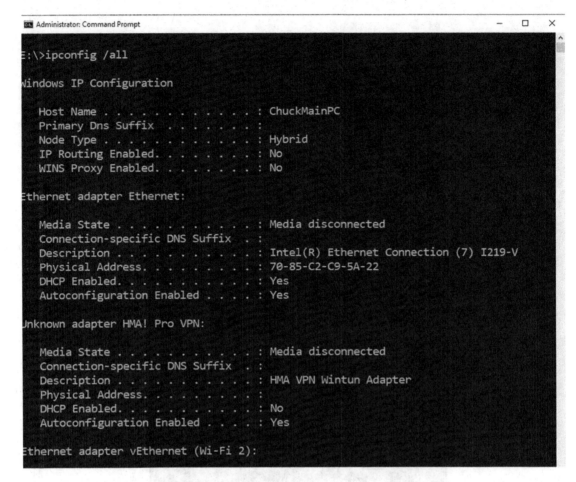

Figure 1-12. *The ipconfig command*

The mode command is a less common command, but can give you important information. You can see that command in Figure 1-13.

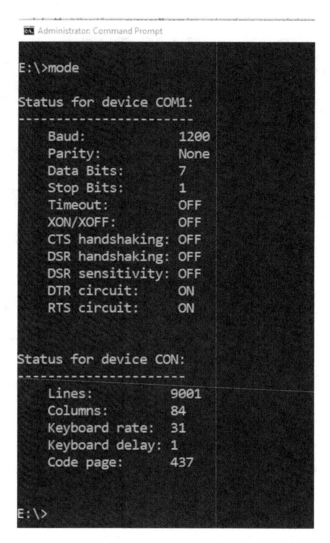

Figure 1-13. *The mode command*

The msinfo command is interesting because when you type it in, it actually launches a Windows graphical utility. However, it provides a wealth of information about a system, as can be seen in Figure 1-14.

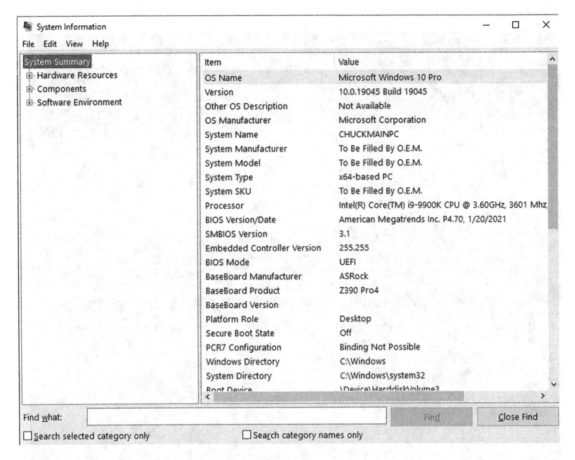

Figure 1-14. *The msinfo command*

The systeminfo command is another command that provides a tremendous amount of details regarding the system, as you can see in Figure 1-15.

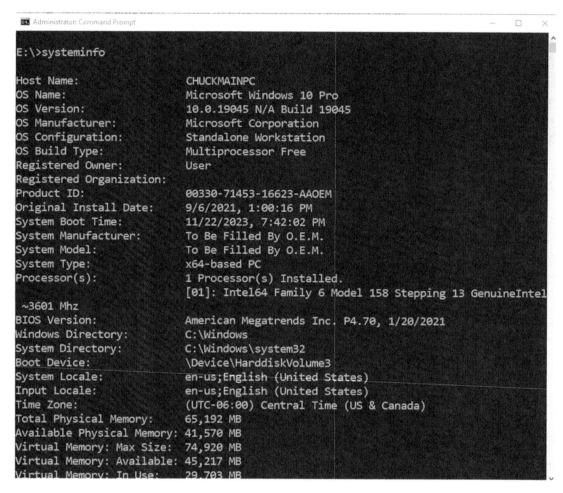

Figure 1-15. *The systeminfo command*

It is not possible to cover every Windows command-line command in one chapter. However, we have covered some of the more important commands. There are numerous online resources for learning more about Windows command-line commands.[4,5,6]

---

[4] https://learn.microsoft.com/en-us/windows-server/administration/windows-commands/windows-commands

[5] https://phoenixnap.com/kb/cmd-commands

[6] www.lifewire.com/list-of-command-prompt-commands-4092302

Windows Defender

Windows Defender works directly with web browsers to protect the computer from spyware. Originally introduced to interface with Internet Explorer 7, it scans files as they are downloaded to the computer through the Internet browser, identifies what appears to be spyware, and allows the user to decide what action to take. The possible actions are ignore, allow, quarantine, and always allow. *Quarantine* isolates and stores the suspected spyware file, allowing the user to install it later if it is found not to be spyware. Windows Defender is fully integrated with the operating system for Windows 10 and Windows 11. It is actually now subsumed as part of the Windows Security panel, shown in Figure 1-16.

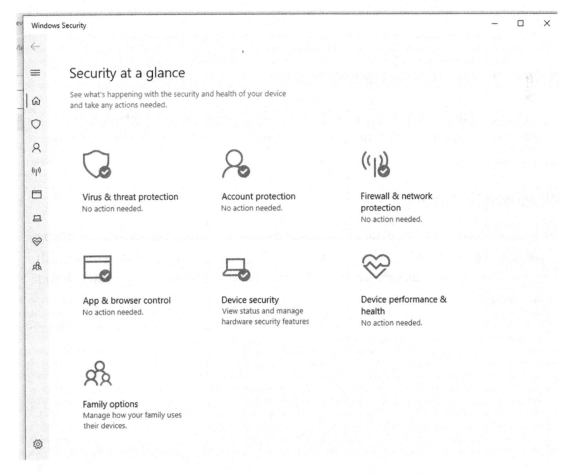

Figure 1-16. *Windows Security panel*

Windows Control Panel

The Windows Control Panel is the starting point for all the graphical utilities in the Windows operating system. The control panel is shown in Figure 1-17.

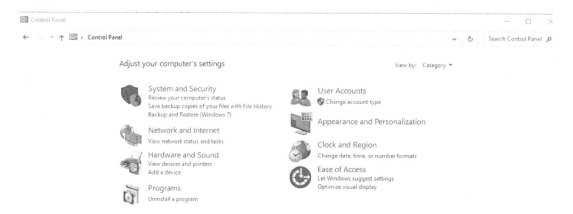

Figure 1-17. *The Windows Control Panel*

In this chapter, a few specific items in the control panel will be touched upon. However, you should be quite comfortable navigating the control panel and using the utilities found in it.

Windows Recovery

The System Recovery feature has been changed from previous versions of Windows by introducing two new wizards: *Refresh* and *Reset*. However, these are now replaced with recovery drive, system restore, and reset PC. The recovery options for Windows 10 and 11 are shown in Figure 1-18.

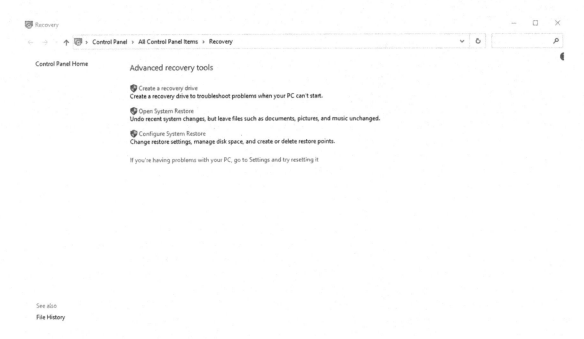

Figure 1-18. *Windows recovery options*

The recovery drive is used for major issues such as hardware failure. The steps are rather simple.

In the search box on the taskbar, search for Create a recovery drive and then select it. You might be asked to enter an admin password or confirm your choice.

System and Security

It is from here that you will be able to get to items such as the firewall, power options, backup and restore, as well as other important tools. You can see Windows System and Security in Figure 1-19.

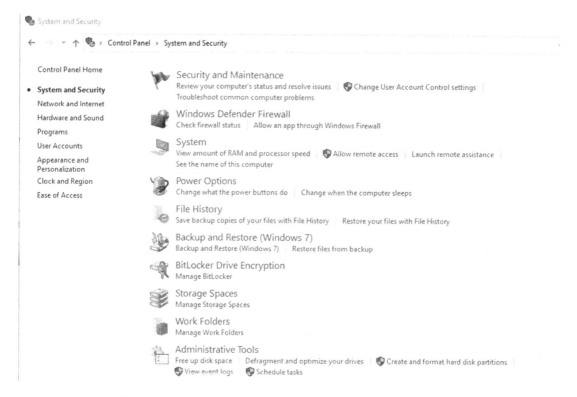

Figure 1-19. *Windows System and Security*

Hardware and Sound

This section of the control panel allows you to configure hardware options, drivers, power options, and more and is shown in Figure 1-20.

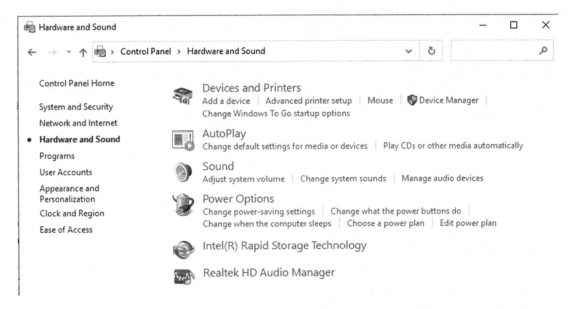

Figure 1-20. *Hardware and Sound*

From this screen, you will not only do trivial tasks such as set up sound settings, but you will also add printers, update device drivers, and related administrative tasks.

Certmgr

When you type certmgr at the search bar, you will launch a utility as shown in Figure 1-21.

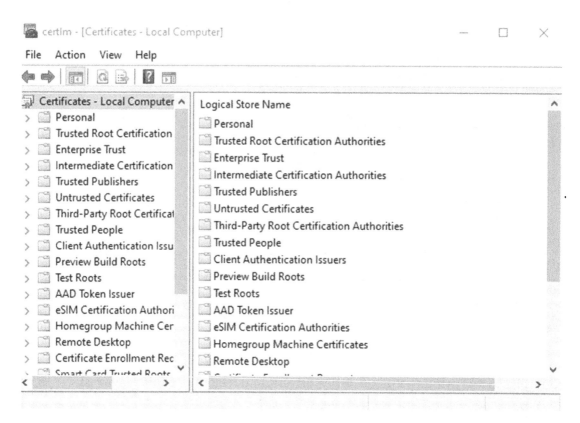

Figure 1-21. *Windows Certmgr*

The Windows Certificate Manager stores all the various certificates your system is aware of and trusts. You can also check here to see if there is a certificate you don't think should be there.

Windows Boot Sequence

This section serves as an introduction to the Windows boot sequence. A *boot sequence* is the step-by-step process of bringing a computer to an operational state. This involves a combination of hardware and software control to initialize hardware and load operating system files.

Warm and Cold Booting

When the boot sequence is initiated, it is called *booting the computer*. There are two styles of booting a computer: cold boot and warm boot. A *cold boot*, also called a *hard boot*, means that the electrical power switch is used to turn on the computer. A warm boot, or *soft boot*, is used to restart a computer that is already running. A warm boot can be initiated by a software program as part of a typical installation, such as installing a game, by using the [Ctrl][Alt][Delete] keyboard combination, or by selecting *Start ➤ Power ➤ Restart*.

POST

All computers start with a power-on self-test. The *power-on self-test (POST)* is a simple diagnostic program that is initiated when electrical power is applied to the computer system. It is common to all operating systems, including macOS and Linux. The POST does a quick system check to determine if all major hardware components, such as the CPU, RAM, keyboard, mouse, video system, and storage devices, are in proper working order. The devices checked may vary slightly from computer to computer depending on the firmware.

The test it performs is not as sophisticated as diagnostic software, but it will check for major problems. When the POST is finished, it usually makes one "beep" sound to let you know that the POST is complete, and everything is in working order. If an error is detected during the POST, an error code is usually displayed on the screen, and a series of beeps is heard that match the code. The codes and beep pattern vary according to the different BIOS or UEFI chip manufacturers, and a list of error codes and beep codes can often be obtained from the website of the manufacturer. The boot process for Windows 10/11 is summarized in the following steps:

- Firmware performs the POST.

- Firmware boot loaders bootstrap the UEFI environment (think mini-OS).

- Run any SoC (system on a chip) vendor, Microsoft, or OEMs UEFI level applications.

- UEFI finds the boot location via the GUID partition table (GPT).

- UEFI launches the Windows Boot Manager (bootmgr).

- Windows Boot Manager reads the BCD file and displays the boot menu.

- Windows Boot Manager starts the Windows Boot Loader (winload. exe) when Windows 10 or Windows 11 is selected or if started automatically.

- The Windows Boot Manager loads ntoskrnl.exe and hal.dll into memory and scans the Registry for device drivers to load. It then passes control to the kernel.

- The kernel loads the device drivers and hal.dll and initializes the computer settings using the values stored in the system registry.

- The kernel starts the Session Manager (smss.exe), which creates the system environment.

- The operating system switches to graphics mode and the winlogon. exe file is loaded, thus starting the Logon Manager (winlogon.exe).

The Logon Manager allows the user to begin the logon process. At this point, the boot process has ended, and the user is presented with the graphical user interface of the Windows desktop.

BitLocker

BitLocker Drive Encryption is an encryption feature that is available as part of many versions of the Windows OS. BitLocker encrypts the entire volume, including the system files required for startup and logon, rather than just data files. BitLocker ensures that data remains encrypted even when the operating system is not running. For example, if someone removes a hard drive and then attempts to access the data from another computer using a different operating system or software utility, BitLocker prevents the data from being accessed because the data remains encrypted.

BitLocker is transparent to the user after it is activated. It is designed to be used with a computer that has a Trusted Platform Module (TPM) or firmware that can read a USB flash drive. The TPM is a microchip that ensures encryption is intact throughout the boot sequence of the computer. If the TPM is missing or has changed, the user is required to supply a password to access the encrypted data. If BitLocker is configured on a system that does not have a TPM, a startup key is required when it is first configured.

A typical startup key is a software program loaded on a USB flash drive. The software program contains the encryption key used to access the encrypted drive. For Windows 7, BitLocker was a downloadable option. In Windows 10 and 11, it is a bundled option only available with Pro and Enterprise editions.

BitLocker To Go is an enhanced version of the BitLocker application first introduced in Windows 7 that allows encryption of USB storage devices. As the name implies, you can encrypt files on a USB drive, remove the drive, and take it to another computer. Microsoft provides the BitLocker To Go Reader as a free download that allows a user to read the contents of an encrypted flash drive. BitLocker To Go, when enabled, is automatically added to the USB flash drive or storage media by default. Starting with Windows 10, the Used Space Only encryption feature allows removable devices to be encrypted in seconds rather than minutes in most cases. If you type BitLocker into the search bar, you will launch the Bit Locker control panel shown in Figure 1-22.

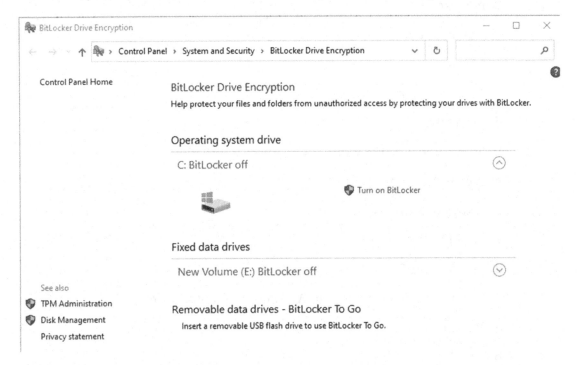

Figure 1-22. *BitLocker*

This is a very simple-to-use interface, making it quite easy to turn on or off BitLocker and to use BitLocker To Go.

Conclusions

This chapter provided you with a general overview of the Windows operating system. The better you understand Windows, the better you can perform forensics. The goal is to be an expert at forensic techniques, but also an expert in the technology you are examining. What you see in this chapter is meant as a baseline. It would be worthwhile to deepen and broaden your knowledge of Windows as much as you can in order to be an effective forensic examiner for Windows systems.

Test Your Knowledge

1. Which of the following is most similar to Unix hard links in Windows?

   a. Mount points

   b. Shortcuts

   c. Junction points

   d. Firm links

2. What is found in $MFTMirr

   a. A complete copy of $MFT

   b. A copy of the first entries of $MFT

   c. Volume Shadow Copy

   d. ACL for $MFT

3. What is the main header for the Windows executable format?

   a. PE header

   b. DOS header

   c. MFT header

   d. MZ header

4. What command-line command will show you who has access to a given file?

   a. permissions

   b. getmac

   c. cacls

   d. mode

5. A computer restart is also known as a _____.

   a. Soft boot

   b. Cold boot

   c. Hard boot

   d. Short boot

CHAPTER 2

Forensics Concepts

Naseer Zehra, zehra.naseer@Vanderbilt.Edu
Chuck Easttom, Ph.D., D.Sc. william.easttom@Vanderbilt.Edu

When people envision digital forensics, they often imagine tracing down hackers and saving the world. In reality, there is so much more to digital forensics. In this chapter, we will be diving into the subset of digital forensics known as Windows forensics. As digital crime and physical crime containing digital footprints increase, so does the need for Windows forensics. Being the most popular operating system, understanding how to perform the Windows forensics process is an essential tool in a skilled forensic examiner's belt. The chapter begins with differentiating between digital forensics, computer forensics, and Windows forensics. Then the process of Windows forensics is broken down, and relevant laws are introduced. The chapter also provides guidance on writing a digital forensics report and testifying as an expert witness.

In this chapter, we will cover the following:

- Importance of Windows forensics

- Computer forensic process

- Relevant laws to computer forensics

- Writing a forensics report

- Testifying as an expert witness

Why Windows Forensics?

Before you dive deep into the techniques and tools of Windows forensics, it is important to understand what it is and why it is important. In order to do that, we will take a step back and take a look at computer forensics first. When picturing computer forensics, an analyst sitting in a dimly lit room with a lighted keyboard clicking away to find the

© Chuck Easttom, William Butler, Jessica Phelan, Ramya Sai Bhagavatula, Sean Steuber,
Karely Rodriguez, Victoria Indy Balkissoon, Zehra Naseer 2024
C. Easttom et al., *Windows Forensics*, https://doi.org/10.1007/979-8-8688-0193-8_2

location of a kidnapping may come to mind. Popular shows like *NCIS* or *CSI* draw the interest to the topic of computer forensics without discussing what exactly it is. These programs frequently give a very inaccurate portrayal of digital forensics.

Computer forensics applies traditional forensic principles to recover, analyze, and present data extracted from a computer as evidence. In the same way traditional, physical forensics aims to shed light on the circumstances surrounding a crime with physical evidence, computer or digital forensics may provide insight into the execution of a cybercrime via the extracted digital evidence.

The first instance of cybercrime occurred in 1834, prior to the invention of the Internet. In this incident, the offenders stole financial market information by accessing the French telegraph system (Arctic Wolf, 2016). In recent decades, cybercrime has seen exponential growth. Among the early cybercriminals was a prominent hacker known as Kevin Mitnick, who gained unauthorized access to several computer systems of major corporations and government agencies. Mitnick was involved in hacking schemes that ranged from stealing computer codes from Nokia to wiretapping the National Security Agency (NSA). The FBI caught up with Mitnick by obtaining a log of Mitnick's online activities, recovered from a compromised computer. Extracting the digital evidence using computer forensics, the FBI gathered information regarding the files and commands he had accessed and ran. The evidence included the stolen passwords and proprietary software, which was used to build a case and eventually convict Kevin Mitnick.

In recent years, a wide range of cybercrimes have become common. This includes phishing attacks, online financial scams, malware, and more. Perhaps the fastest growing threat is ransomware. One example of ransomware is Black Basta. This is ransomware that was first discovered in April of 2022. One of the distinctions that make this ransomware notable is that there are variants for Linux as well as Windows. But our focus is on the Windows variation. When Black Basta is on a Windows domain controller, it begins by creating a group policy to disable Windows Defender and other antivirus software. This is a particularly pernicious aspect of the virus. Another destructive aspect of this malware is that it both steals data and then encrypts the computer files on the affected computer, demanding ransom. The offenders will begin leaking stolen data if the ransom is not paid.

Cybercrime has now become a $1.5 trillion industry; rather than running as one-man shows as it once did, organizations are structured like legitimate corporations (*Hyper-connected web of profit emerges, as global cybercriminal revenues hit $1.5 trillion* *annually*, 2018). With the big explosion of cybercrime in 2010, digital forensics is needed now more than ever to collect evidence that is permissible in a court of law for prosecution.

Computer forensics, Windows or otherwise, also has been applied outside of cybercrimes. There are two notable examples:

> **Dennis Rader (2005)**: The famous "BTK" serial killer was on the run for more than 30 years, and after years, he reemerged and took another victim in Kansas, following which he sent a floppy disk to the police with a letter on it. Upon forensic investigation, the investigators found a deleted Microsoft Word file. The metadata recovered showed that the last person to edit the file was authored by "Dennis" along with a link to the Lutheran Church where Dennis Rader was a deacon. Ironically, Rader had sent a floppy disk to the police because he thought it could not be traced. This was incorrect; the police traced the floppy disk to his church computer, and that computer indicated it had been used by someone named "Dennis."

> **Philip Markoff**: When one woman was killed and another attacked after meeting individuals through Craigslist, Boston was on high alert. Fortunately, law enforcement had their suspect within a week of the murder, thanks to digital forensics. Investigators tracked the IP address from the emails used in the Craigslist correspondence to an unlikely suspect: 23-year-old medical student Philip Markoff. Without the digital trail of evidence, who knows how prolific Markoff could have become.

Windows Forensics vs. Computer Forensics

Windows forensics and computer forensics are terms that are often used interchangeably; however, Windows forensics is actually a subset of computer forensics. Computer forensics is defined by the National Institute of Standards and Technology (NIST) as "the application of computer science and investigative procedures and involving the examination of digital evidence – following proper search authority, chain of custody, validation with mathematics, use of validated tools repeatability, reporting, and possibly expert testimony" (Joyce, 2022). By extension, we can define the term

Windows forensics as the discipline that combines computer science and investigative procedure in the examination of digital evidence collected from computers running a Windows operating system that follow the outlined processes and validations earlier. In our discussion of Windows forensics, we will be using other technical terms that you should familiarize yourself with:

- **Chain of Custody**: A process that tracks the movement of evidence through its collection, safeguarding, and analysis life cycle by documenting each person who handled the evidence, the date/time it was collected or transferred, and the purpose for the transfer (Jansen and Ayers, 2004)

- **Computer Forensics**: The application of computer science and investigative procedures and involving the examination of digital evidence – following proper search authority, chain of custody, validation with mathematics, use of validated tools repeatability, reporting, and possibly expert testimony (Joyce, 2022)

- **Data Volatility**: A measure of how fast data disappears from a system

- **Digital Evidence**: Information that has been processed and assembled so that it is relevant to an investigation and supports a specific finding or determination

- **Digital Forensics**: The process used to acquire, preserve, analyze, and report on evidence using scientific methods that are demonstrably reliable, accurate, and repeatable such that it may be used in judicial proceedings

- **Forensic Image**: The bit-by-bit, sector-by-sector direct copy of a physical storage device, including all files, folders, and unallocated free and slack space

- **Operating System**: The system software that manages computer hardware and software resources and provides common services for computer programs (Barker et al., 2015)

- **Windows Artifact**: Digital traces left behind on a Windows operating system that can be used in computer forensic investigations

- **Windows Forensics**: The discipline that combines computer science and investigative procedures in the examination of digital evidence collected from computers running a Windows operating system that follow proper search authority, chain of custody, validation with mathematics, use of validated tools, repeatability, reporting, and possibly expert testimony

So why is Windows forensics specifically important? The Windows operating system is the most common of the operating systems in use. In 2023, it was reported that around 74% of the computers in the world have a Windows operating system (Taylor, 2023). Out of the computers running a Windows operating system, the Windows 10 version is the most popularly used, as 71.11% of users had Windows 10 (*Desktop windows version market share worldwide*, 2023). This is one reason why a strong background in Windows forensics is essential for forensic analysts.

The Windows operating system stores different types of evidence related to user activity on its system. The gathering of such evidence is crucial during forensic investigations. The digital traces left behind on a Windows operating system are known as Windows artifacts or Windows forensic artifacts. They can help provide valuable information into events occurring on a computer, such as user activity, system configuration, and network activity. In order to gather information properly, it is important to know where different files are located.

Scope of Windows Forensics

The scope of computer forensics extends beyond cybercrime. Two main types of investigations where Windows forensics is applicable include criminal investigations and civil investigations. Investigations of cybercrime are covered under the umbrella of criminal investigations, which involves a crime occurring against a state. Windows forensics can be applicable to physical crimes committed. As technology is increasingly integrated into our daily lives, we tend to depend on it for even the simplest of tasks. With the invention of the computer and the World Wide Web, we rely on our computers for communication, to gain knowledge, to keep track of our schedules, to make transactions, etc. This leaves a digital trail of where we go and what we do on a day-to-day basis. Evidence gathered from Windows computers like email can speak to communications for drug trade or shellbags can vouch for certain pornographic content being consumed.

Criminal investigations are not the only place wherein digital forensics is applied. Digital forensics is frequently a component of civil investigations as well. Unlike criminal investigations, civil investigations deal with disputes that occur between parties, such as cyber-intrusion and misuse of intellectual property. For instance, if a company's proprietary product is accessed and suddenly leaked, Windows forensics can be used to determine the users with privileges. Those users' activity can be searched and determined if sensitive files were exported or communicated to outside the company.

Windows forensics is used by many different parties. Due to the popularity of the Windows operating system, Windows forensics is used by most forensic analysts. Parties such as government agencies, law firms, data recovery firms, insurance companies, etc., all contain a forensics department.

Relevant Laws

Anyone who is interested in learning about or pursuing a career in Windows forensics needs to be introduced to its legal implications. Whenever evidence is being gathered for use in a case or trial, there is a strict process that must be followed for said evidence to be admissible in court. Even when internal investigations are being conducted, depending on corporate policies, forensic analysts must not step out of bounds of what they are authorized to collect. With the speed that technology advances, it seems that there is always a lag with the development of laws and policies governing technology. Due to the relative novelty of computer forensics, many existing laws, legal precedents, and practices related to the field are changing. Laws protecting the privacy of personal data are being increasingly passed, as personal data is increasingly digitized. The US Department of Justice's Cyber Crime website is a good source to keep track of new laws as they emerge. There are three areas of law related to computer forensics that are good to know: Constitutional Law(s), Statutory Law(s), and Federal Rules of Evidence.

The Fourth Amendment, a significant law found in the US Constitution, provides "the right of the people to be secure in their persons, houses, papers, and effects, against unreasonable searches and seizures, shall not be violated, and no Warrants shall issue, but on probable cause, supported by the Oath or affirmation, and particularly describing the place to be searched, and the person or things to be seized" (US Const. amend. IV). In 2014, the Supreme Court determined in *Riley vs. United States* that the warrantless seizure of digital evidence conducted from a search on cell phones violated the Fourth Amendment and was therefore inadmissible in court. This ruling extended the provisions of the Fourth Amendment to include digital evidence found on computers and other devices.

The next category of law we will look at is the US Statutory Laws as they are related to computer forensics. First up, the *Electronic Communications Privacy Act (ECPA)*, also known as the wiretap law, limits how law enforcement can intercept electronic communications and how the evidence can be used in court. Implemented in 1986, the statutory law applies the protections to email, phone communications, and data stored electronically.

Another important law to review is the *Computer Fraud and Abuse Act (CFAA)*, which criminalizes the act of intentionally accessing a computer without authorization. The statutory law was intended to reduce the cracking of computer systems and to address federal computer-related offenses. If you recall our earlier mention of Kevin Mitnick, you won't be surprised to learn that he was convicted as a result of this statute. So how are these two laws related to Windows forensics? Well, violations of either of these statutes by performing unauthorized analysis of emails and/or computers could constitute a federal felony, punishable by a fine and/or imprisonment just like Mitnick.

Understanding the US Federal Rules of Evidence as it relates to computer forensics and digital evidence is important. Additionally, knowing the rules of evidence for authentication, reliability, and best evidence is helpful. Evidence generally should be authentic, complete, reliable, and clear. The US Federal Rules of Evidence can be used to determine whether digital evidence can be used in courts.

Relevant Standards

There are numerous standards that are relevant to digital forensics. These standards can provide guidelines for how to conduct a cyber investigation. Being at least generally familiar with these is critical for every forensic examiner.

SWGDE: Scientific Working Group on Digital Evidence

ASCLD: The American Society of Crime Laboratory Directors

RFC 3227: Order of evidence collection

ISO/IEC 27037:2012: Good practice methods and processes for forensic capture and investigation of digital evidence

ISO/IEC 27041: Guidance on the assurance aspects of digital forensics

ISO/IEC 27042: Covers what happens after digital evidence has been collected, that is, its analysis and interpretation

ISO/IEC 27043: Covers the broader incident investigation activities, within which forensics usually occur

ISO/IEC 27050: Concerns electronic discovery

In addition to these general standards sources, there are specific digital forensics steps that have been outlined by various organizations. You will probably notice that there is some overlap with these. A few prominent step-by-step guides are discussed in the following subsections.

European Union

The European Union posts specific guidelines to assist in conducting a digital forensics investigation. Among those guidelines are five principles that establish a basis for all dealings with electronic evidence:

Principle 1 – Data Integrity: You must ensure that the data is valid and has not been corrupted.

Principle 2 – Audit Trail: Similar to the concept of chain of custody, you must be able to fully account for the evidence. That includes its location as well as what was done with it.

Principle 3 – Specialist Support: As needed, utilize specialists. For example, if you are a skilled forensic examiner but have limited experience with a Macintosh computer, get a Mac specialist should you need to examine a Mac.

Principle 4 – Appropriate Training: All forensic examiners and analysts should be fully trained and always expanding their knowledge base.

Principle 5 – Legality: Make certain all evidence is collected and handled in a manner consistent with all applicable laws.

Obviously, these are only binding on digital forensic examiners in the European Union. However, it should be clear how these are applicable to any digital forensic examiner, regardless of jurisdiction.

FBI Forensics Guidelines

The US Federal Bureau of Investigation performs a great many forensic investigations and has established guidelines. In the case of any cyber incident, even before it has been determined if this matter will lead to court, the FBI recommends that the first responder preserve the state of the computer at the time of the incident by making a backup copy of the system including any logs.

When preserving logs, it is important you get all the relevant logs. That can include router logs, server logs, firewall logs, etc. It is important that all evidence be secured and chain of custody be documented. Whenever possible, make a forensic image of the target system.

Another important step is to document the specific losses suffered due to the attack. Losses typically include the following:

- Labor cost spent in response and recovery. (Multiply the number of participating staff by their hourly rates.)

- The cost of the equipment if equipment was damaged.

- The value of the data if any was lost or stolen. How much did it cost to obtain that data, and how much will it cost to reconstruct it?

- Any lost revenue, including losses due to downtime, having to give customers credit due to inconvenience, or any other way in which revenue was lost.

Windows Forensics Process

Now that we have defined what Windows forensics is, we will explore what performing a Windows forensic investigation entails. There are different ways to break it up, but for our purposes, we will identify the process of acquiring digital evidence as a set of three stages: collection, analysis, appropriate presentation.

During the collection stage, the responsibility of maintaining the chain of custody and preserving data integrity must be upheld. With the appropriate warrants and documentation, allowing for the collection of devices as evidence, the Windows computers are identified. The chain of custody of these devices must be maintained from the moment of seizure to its presentation in court. The chain of custody tracks the movement of the evidence and documents each person that handles it, the date and time of collection, and the reason for its transfer (Jansen and Ayers, 2004). Once the evidence is appropriately transported to the forensics team, the team is responsible for the integrity of the data on the device. There should be a secure place allocated for the evidence, where it will remain safe and only accessible to the delegated individuals. Drives should not be inspected directly; instead, a forensic image should be created and used for forensic analysis. A forensic image is also known as a forensic copy and will be discussed later in Chapter 3, but for an idea, it is a direct copy of a physical storage device. There are times when the forensics team must be involved in the collection of the evidence. This mainly occurs when there is a fear that moving the computer will result in a loss of vital information. The data is acquired live, with the intent of copying as much information as possible.

In Windows forensic analysis, it may be daunting to navigate through such a large amount of data, especially if you are unsure of what you are looking for. There are many tools available to simplify the process, but it is important to have a working knowledge about where information could be hiding. For instance, Windows has a database called the Windows Registry that holds a wealth of information about a system, including user accounts, installed software, and system settings. Analysis of these Windows artifacts can lead to identification of changes made to a system, including the installation of malware or other malicious software. When conducting Windows forensic analysis, the focus is running an in-depth analysis on the Windows operating system and the Windows system artifacts. A common analysis done on the Windows system is the search of files for specific crime-related word lists. The incidences and counts for each of these words are then outputted. Other analysis methods include steganography analysis, which is the practice of discovering concealed files, messages, images, or videos within other files, images, or videos.

The result of a Windows forensic investigation is generally presented in a couple of different ways. While performing the Windows forensic process, the procedure is carefully documented in a digital forensics report. Sometimes, when an expert witness's testimony is required, the findings of the Windows forensic investigation are presented in a deposition or in court. In the coming sections, we will dive into the aspects of writing a digital forensics report and testifying as an expert witness.

The Scientific Method

As a forensic examiner, your role is to provide sound scientific evidence. That makes it imperative that, in addition to being familiar with tools, you need to understand the scientific method and how to apply it. Let us begin with a general overview of how science works. One always begins with a hypothesis. Contrary to popular misconception, a hypothesis is not a guess. It is a question that is testable. If a question cannot be tested, then it has no place in science whatsoever. Put another way, a hypothesis is a testable educated guess. Once one has tested a hypothesis, one has a fact. For example, if I suspect that confidential documents were on your computer and subsequently moved to a USB device and deleted (my hypothesis), I can conduct a forensic examination of your computer (my test). If that examination finds that a USB drive was connected to the computer and an undelete program recovers the deleted documents, I now have a fact.

The next step is to build a theory of the crime, based on multiple facts. A scientific theory is not a guess. It is a model that explains all of the available facts. Furthermore, if the theory/model is correct, one would expect future findings to be consistent with that model/theory. As an example, the fact that confidential documents were on your computer, while very interesting evidence, is not in and of itself enough to establish guild. There are numerous other possibilities. For example, someone else might have used your computer, or the confidential documents were transferred accidentally. This means we must find additional facts. For example, we would want to know if your username was the one logged in when the files were deleted. Once we recover the deleted files, we would want to know when they were last accessed and modified (this might tell us if you were using the files). We might also want to check your email to see if there is any communication with a third party that might have an interest in these documents.

In addition to hypotheses and theories, another principle in science is the issue of falsifiability. Falsifiability means that it is possible to falsify a question or to get a false answer. Put another way, it is possible to get a negative answer. This rules out questions of opinion or questions that cannot be refuted. Remember, you are functioning as a scientist. Science is a methodology for acquiring knowledge and testing that knowledge. Guesswork, biases, and similar thought processes have no role in science.

Writing a Digital Forensics Report

If you wish to pursue a career in digital forensics, you will have to detail your findings in a comprehensive digital forensics report. The way that the report is formulated has the potential to sway a judgment, making it one of the most crucial components of the computer forensics process. Digital forensics reports are used in a variety of ways: litigation support when in trial with the expert witness, settling disputes before going to court, and recovering data that may have been unintentionally or intentionally destroyed. The report should present the steps taken in sufficient detail that any competent forensic examiner can duplicate the steps and confirm or refute the findings. Screenshots can be quite helpful.

Important Criteria

It is important to keep in mind how the report you are writing will be evaluated. This will give a better sense of understanding on how to approach writing the report. Reports are evaluated by a variety of ways. For the purpose of simplification, we will split up the evaluation into four discrete criteria: the credentials of the analyst(s), the mechanism used to collect the evidence, the methods and tools used to analyze the data, and the conclusions that are drawn from the available evidence.

Strong credentials are preferred for writing a strong report. Forensic analysts should be qualified in the field of forensic analysis, in our case Windows forensics. Less seasoned examiners are more prone to superficial analysis (not knowing where to look for information) and making errors. They also may not have enough exposure to tools to know the limitations and alternatives available. For this reason, newer examiners should be trained and supervised by experienced examiners. While there is no set standard in determining which person is qualified, formal education, certifications, and real-word experience are often used by reviewers to identify whether an individual shows competency in Windows forensics. When detailing the credentials of all examiners that were involved in the report, be thorough in listing the past experiences and qualifications that are relevant. Have they used the software/method before? How many times have they used the software/tool? The credentials section should give insight to these questions as well of the overall experience of an examiner.

The mechanism of acquiring the data can affect its integrity, and therefore the way that the data was extracted from a computer could be a cause for scrutiny of a report. The preferred way of collecting data from a drive is by imaging the drive. This provides a bit-by-bit copy of the data. Recall that a forensic image includes the copy of all files, folders, and unallocated free and slack space. This provides better data integrity preservation; however, volatile data can be lost. Live acquisition, or the extracting of real-time system data prior to the system shutdown to preserve memory, process, and network information that would be otherwise lost by traditional acquisition method, is performed when volatile data is to be collected. Information gathered from volatile data could include browsing sessions, passwords, accessed files, etc. Windows memory management stores volatile memory in a variety of ways not limited to Pagefile.sys, Hiberfil.sys, and Swapfile.sys; it is important to make sure that volatile data found here is captured when live acquisition is performed. No matter which data extraction method is used, justifying your method of choice is essential when writing the report; the benefits and drawbacks should be addressed.

There are a variety of software available that aid in the forensic investigation. Some of the Windows forensic software we will cover later in the book include OSForensics, FTK Imager, and Autopsy. Deciding which tools and software to use requires keeping the purpose of use in mind. When writing the report, the software, version, and a description of its historical uses should be documented. The software should be considered reputable, generally accepted by the scientific community. Much of the digital forensics software allows for direct addition of the findings into the report. Using figures and screenshots from the software helps paint a full picture of the procedure performed. These steps taken should be detailed in a repeatable manner. Simultaneously recording the steps taken and findings discovered while gathering and analyzing data prevents missing steps or forgetting details.

Once the evidence has been presented in a detailed and cohesive manner in the digital report, conclusions may be made on the bases of the evidence. When forensics reports' conclusions come from detailed and properly documented sources, the report is better suited to withstand judicial scrutiny. It is essential that all conclusions are made directly on a strong basis of the recovered evidence and not deviate outside of the scope of the gathered evidence. Conclusions should also be reasonably reproducible from the procedure detailed in the report.

General Structure

Although the styling of the report may vary by the style of the analyst, there is a general breakdown of essential components that must be present. There are many templates that are available for writing a digital forensics report. The National Institute of Standards and Technology (NIST) provides a standardized template for a Digital Forensics Incident Report (DFIR). While this is the minimum, it provides a decent skeleton on which you can add with personal experience. The generic components involved in a digital forensics report include

1. **Cover Page**: Case number, case name, lead investigator name

2. **Table of Contents**: List of headers of the report

3. **Case Summary**: General overview of the case

4. **Tools Utilized**: Software's name, version, assumptions, and limitation(s)

5. **Evidence**

    a. **Summary of Evidence**: Serial number, make, model, overall description

    b. **Chain of Custody**: Documentation/validation

6. **Investigative Procedures**: Steps in forensic analysis procedure

7. **Relevant Findings**: Reiteration of important conclusions

8. **Recommendations**: Next steps

Often, a report will examine more than one piece of evidence at a time. If there are multiple Windows computers seized, then the Evidence and Investigative Procedures sections will be repeated. During the Investigative Procedures section, only include evidence that is relevant to the investigation. The report must be cohesively written for it to hold up in court.

Limit the use of technical jargon in the Case Summary, Relevant Findings, and Recommendations sections, where the audience are usually lawyers and judges. Appropriate phrasing can sway whether a report is used or thrown out of court. Many reports contain additional sections such as glossary, appendix, figures, etc. These are not necessary but are good practices to include. Depending on the case that is being investigated and the amount of relevant evidence available, it can be important to include a timeline of events, which is the order of what took place pertaining to an event. This may be helpful for drawing your conclusions.

Testifying As an Expert Witness

We mentioned earlier that the second way that evidence from a computer forensic investigation is presented is through the testimony of an expert witness. Testifying as an expert witness can be a challenging and rewarding experience. As an expert witness, you have the opportunity to share your knowledge and expertise with a judge or jury and help them understand complicated and technical information, especially when covering the Windows forensic process and findings. Expert witnesses provide their testimonies at depositions and/or in court during a trial. A deposition is a pretrial discovery process where attorneys ask questions of witnesses under oath and is held out of court and without a judge or jury. There are also no cross-examinations that occur during a deposition.

During a deposition, an expert witness's testimony can be crucial to establishing a party's or evidence's credibility. A strong expert witness's testimony could help persuade the opposing party to settle the case out of court. There are some core areas that are covered during a deposition of an expert witness. Opposing counsel often tries to discredit your credibility and/or undermine the report during the deposition. The first category of questions involves the expert witnesses' qualifications. Questions in this category aim to establish or discredit the expert witness's competency in the field. In order to establish their expertise, the expert witness should include a brief summary of their relevant education, certifications, and past experiences with the topic and Windows forensic knowledge. The next hot topic of questioning includes any biases that the expert witnesses may hold; financial compensations and conflicts of interest are generally questioned here. The main reason why expert witnesses are deposed is to provide their expert opinions on the case. They will be asked about the facts of the case, along with any conclusions and recommendations made during the investigation. This is where the Windows forensics report comes into play. As an expert witness, you need to know your report inside and out, as the opposing counsel is almost guaranteed to try to bring out any inconsistencies. The report is the foundation of the testimony, so it is important to absolutely nail that document.

The final main category that is questioned during the deposition is the methodologies that the expert witness applied to reach their opinions of the case. The opposing counsel frequently uses this questioning, intending to throw out the expert witness's testimony, by using the Daubert Standard. The Daubert Standard is a legal standard that is used to determine the admissibility of an expert witness's testimony, by deciding whether the methodologies they used are sound. Established in the 1993

Supreme Court Case *Daubert v. Merrell Dow Pharmaceuticals, Inc.*, an expert witness's testimony is reliable if the methodologies and techniques that they used (1) are testable and have been tested, (2) have been subjected to peer review and publication, (3) have potential or known error rate, (4) have maintained standards controlling its use, and (5) have widespread acceptance within the relevant scientific community. Once again, the importance of the digital forensics report is highlighted; expert witnesses should be able to provide clear and concise explanations of how their techniques meet the Daubert Standard.

Federal Rule 702 defines what an expert witness is, in federal courts. A witness who is qualified as an expert by knowledge, skill, experience, training, or education may testify in the form of an opinion or otherwise if

> **(a)** the expert's scientific, technical, or other specialized knowledge will help the trier of fact to understand the evidence or to determine a fact in issue;

> **(b)** the testimony is based on sufficient facts or data;

> **(c)** the testimony is the product of reliable principles and methods; and

> **(d)** the expert has reliably applied the principles and methods to the facts of the case

You might notice that these seem to overlap with the Daubert case. It is necessary that the expert witness have appropriate education, training, and experience, but that alone is not sufficient. Has the expert reliably applied appropriate scientific methodology? Is the expert's testimony based on sufficient data? These are important factors in expert testimony.

It is recommended that when writing your report, you provide references/citations to justify your use of tools as well as your methodology. These references should be well-regarded sources such as peer-reviewed journal articles, textbooks, government agency, or standards organization guidelines. For example, if you are using OSForensics to analyze a Windows system, you should have references that justify that this is a well-respected and accurate forensic tool.

Not all cases actually go to trial; many cases are resolved through settlement, mediation, or arbitration. Trials can be expensive and time-consuming, leading many parties to resolve conflict out of court. Even so, frequently trials that involve computer forensic investigations require the testimony of expert witnesses. When expert witnesses testify in court, the questioning of opposing counsel is similar to the questioning that occurs in depositions. This time, however, a judge and jury are present. When an expert witness provides a clear, authoritative, and concise explanation of the issues in a case, their deposition could help sway the judge or jury to rule in their party's favor.

Testifying as an expert witness in court can be intimidating. Their testimony has the potential to significantly affect their reputation as an expert witness. In order to ensure a solid testimony, the expert witness should know their report. This is the most important thing you can do. While the report is available for reference during the trial, the high-tension environment makes it difficult to find what you need if you are unfamiliar. When you do state your opinions, they should be relayed honestly, clearly, and concisely and in a respectful manner. Dishonest expert witness testimony can be subject to prosecution for perjury, and inappropriate responses or conduct can cause the expert witnesses to be held in contempt of court. Remember, you are not an advocate for either party. Your role is to provide scientifically sound evidence.

Your conduct can be improved on by practicing your testimony by yourself and with an attorney. The etiquette used in court is more formal than most interactions that we have. If not prepped properly, the language and mannerisms may seem foreign or even off-putting to a jury. It is vital to be able to put your best foot forward. Keeping your composure can be difficult during a cross-examination, especially without prior training. These difficult questions are regularly intended to rattle even prepared and skilled expert witnesses. Nevertheless, keeping calm and relying on your honest expert opinions is fundamental to your expert witness testimony.

Forensic Quality

Forensic quality is essentially how believable the information is. Is it easy to tamper with the information on the system? For example, on some operating systems, a file's access and modification timestamps can be arbitrarily set by its owner. The issue of forensic quality also applies to the quality of the forensic examination done by the examiner. Is it possible a mistake was made? Of course, it is. There are ways to counter that. The most obvious is to use two different tools to perform the same test. It is true that any tool could have an error, but the probability of two separate tools from two separate vendors making the exact same error is negligible at most.

There are other methods when working in a team of investigators. One could have peer review. That involves simply taking a sample of cases or a sample of individual tests and having another examiner verify the results. Supervisor review is a similar technique, but with a supervisor doing the review.

Conclusions

In this chapter, you have been exposed to forensics concepts. You were introduced to Windows forensics, why it is an important subset of digital forensics, and its scope. Comparisons were drawn between digital forensics, computer forensics, and Windows forensics. Relevant laws to Windows forensics were discussed along with their implications. The stages of the Windows forensics process – collection, analysis, and presentation – were explored. You learned about the components of a digital forensics report and how to approach going about writing one. We also reviewed situations that require an expert witness testimony and what one should keep in mind when testifying in a deposition or at the trial.

References

Arctic Wolf (2016). A Brief History of Cybercrime. Retrieved from `https://arcticwolf.com/resources/blog/decade-of-cybercrime/`

Computer Security Division, Barker, E., Smid, M., & Branstad, D., A. Profile for U.S. Federal Cryptographic Management Systems (2015). Department of Commerce. Retrieved July 5, 2023, from `https://nvlpubs.nist.gov/nistpubs/SpecialPublications/NIST.SP.800-152.pdf`

Computer Security Division, Jansen, W., & Ayers, R., Guideline on PDA Forensics (2004). Department of Homeland Security. Retrieved June 10, 2023, from `https://nvlpubs.nist.gov/nistpubs/Legacy/SP/nistspecialpublication800-72.pdf`

Constitution of the United States. U.S. Senate: Constitution of the United States (June 9, 2023). `www.senate.gov/about/origins-foundations/senate-and-constitution/constitution.htm#amdt_4_1791`

Desktop windows version market share worldwide. StatCounter Global Stats (June 2023). `https://gs.statcounter.com/os-version-market-share/windows/desktop/worldwide`

Hyper-connected web of profit emerges, as global cybercriminal revenues hit $1.5 trillion annually. HP Wolf Security (April 20, 2018). `www.bromium.com/press-release/hyper-connected-web-of-profit-emerges-as-global-cybercriminal-revenues-hit-1-5-trillion-annually/`

Joyce, R. E., Committee on National Security System (CNSS) Glossary (2022). Retrieved July 10, 2023, from `www.cnss.gov/CNSS/openDoc.cfm?a=17AOX6eNj5Q5ulZzVc8` `1%2FQ%3D%3D&b=32A59CB3F47BD34AFBA0541FD92FFAB4F8C2F5FB7851C4734C29ABC37CFA` `8D7C25DE0D772D79DAA9387E1EF172355DB4`

Taylor, P. (February 27, 2023). Desktop Operating System Market Share 2013-2023. Statista. `www.statista.com/statistics/218089/global-market-share-of-windows-7/`

Test Your Knowledge

A few questions are provided here to aid you in testing your knowledge before you proceed.

1. What term best describes the bit-by-bit direct copy of a physical storage device?

    a. Windows artifact

    b. Forensic image

    c. Computer forensics

    d. Digital evidence

2. Windows volatile memory can be stored in the following files except

    a. Swapfile.sys

    b. Hiberfil.sys

    c. Pagefile.sys

    d. Sextante.sys

3. Forensic steganography detection can be performed in the _____ stage of the Windows forensic process?

    a. Collection

    b. Analysis

    c. Presentation

    d. Documentation

4. The Daubert Standard includes all the following factors except

    a. Whether the theory/technique is testable

    b. Whether the theory/technique has a known or potential error rate

    c. Whether the theory/technique is widely accepted by the scientific community

    d. Whether the theory/technique is proven

5. Which of the following is a US Statutory Law that limits how law enforcement can intercept electronic communications and how the evidence can be used in court?

    a. Electronic Communications Privacy Act (ECPA)

    b. Riley vs. United States

    c. Computer Fraud and Abuse Act (CFAA)

    d. Daubert v. Merrell Dow Pharmaceuticals, Inc.

CHAPTER 3

Creating Forensic Images Using OSForensics, FTK Imager, and Autopsy

Jessica Phelan
Chuck Easttom, Ph.D., D.Sc.

In an era where technology permeates every aspect of our lives, the significance of digital footprints as evidence has become increasingly critical. As society becomes more reliant on digital devices, individuals leave behind a trail of electronic traces that can shed light on their activities and interactions. Simultaneously, the world of crime has evolved into a complex landscape, characterized by sophisticated techniques that are constantly changing at an incredibly rapid pace. In this context, forensic images play a crucial role as they provide investigators with a robust and thorough representation of the data landscape found on suspect storage devices, offering invaluable insights into the activities of the users of these devices. By harnessing the power of forensic images, investigators can delve deep into the digital realm, uncovering a wealth of information and unraveling intricate details that would otherwise remain concealed.

Forensic images play a pivotal role in modern investigations and legal proceedings, yielding immense power in the field of digital forensics. These images serve as exact replicas of digital storage devices (such as hard drives, USB drives, mobile devices, etc.), capturing every bit of information, metadata, and file structure within them. This comprehensive nature grants investigators unparalleled access to the entirety of a storage drive, enabling them to uncover vital evidence, identify hidden and deleted files, and track digital footprints. Furthermore, it enables secure and noninvasive examination of suspect devices, ensuring the preservation of the original evidence while facilitating a thorough analysis.

© Chuck Easttom, William Butler, Jessica Phelan, Ramya Sai Bhagavatula, Sean Steuber, Karely Rodriguez, Victoria Indy Balkissoon, Zehra Naseer 2024
C. Easttom et al., *Windows Forensics*, https://doi.org/10.1007/979-8-8688-0193-8_3

The creation of forensic images has emerged as a fundamental practice for acquiring and preserving digital evidence. Whether investigating a cybercrime, conducting corporate investigations, or performing incident response, the ability to capture accurate and complete replicas of storage devices is paramount. By leveraging the analysis of forensic images, investigators can achieve several significant advantages.

Firstly, forensic images enable the ability to recover evidence without altering the original drive. This includes the recovery of deleted or hidden data, shedding light on information that may have been intentionally or inadvertently deleted. This recovery process provides critical insights into the activities, intentions, and digital footprint of the user under investigation.

Secondly, forensic images serve as a preservation mechanism for volatile data. Digital evidence can be highly dynamic and prone to alteration or disappearance if not properly preserved. In addition to what is typically called "deadbox" imaging, one can also capture memory. Memory capture and memory forensics will be covered in Chapter 8. By capturing and analyzing volatile data (i.e., memory), such as running processes, network connections, and system states, investigators can maintain an accurate representation of the digital environment at the time of acquisition.

Most importantly, forensic images facilitate offline analysis, allowing investigators to perform thorough examinations without compromising the integrity of the original evidence. Working with forensic images rather than the original media ensures that the data remains unaltered and admissible in court, thereby preserving the evidentiary value.

Lastly, forensic images provide a foundation for advanced analysis techniques. These include file system analysis, keyword searches, timeline reconstruction, and carving, among others. By employing such techniques, investigators can uncover hidden information, establish connections, and reveal valuable insights that contribute to the overall investigation.

Using tools widely recognized by the scientific and academic communities is essential because the integrity and authenticity of an imaged drive significantly contribute to ensuring the admissibility of evidence in a court of law. In this chapter, our attention will be on the widely embraced forensic image acquisition tools, OSForensics and FTK Imager, which are trusted not only by the scientific and academic communities but also by government agencies. The aim of this chapter is to provide an in-depth exploration of these tools and elucidate their importance in the creation of forensic images. By examining their features and functionalities, this chapter seeks to explain the process and rationale behind creating forensic images, shedding light on both the "how" and "why" aspects of this essential practice.

In this chapter, we will cover the following:

- Key concepts

- Creating forensic images with OSForensics

- Creating forensic images with FTK Imager

- Forensic image mounting

- Understanding the contents of a forensic image through deeper analysis

- Recovering deleted files

- Uncovering recent activity

Key Concepts

Before delving into the process of creating forensic images, it is vital to establish a solid foundation in the fundamental principles and terminology essential to understanding the intricacies of forensic image acquisition. This section serves as a stepping stone, clarifying the distinctions between commonly encountered terms in forensic image acquisition, such as disk images and forensic images. By providing this clarity, we lay the groundwork for subsequent discussions, enabling a deeper comprehension of the subject matter.

Furthermore, we delve into the differentiation between the types of drives one may encounter when using image acquisition tools to create forensic images. Specifically, we explore the contrasting characteristics of logical and physical drives, as this will alter what may be captured through the image acquisition process.

Additionally, we delve into the significance of hashing algorithms, focusing on the renowned SHA-256 algorithms, as these are invaluable tools for generating digital fingerprints that ensure the integrity and authenticity of data. By understanding the role of these algorithms, investigators can enhance their ability to validate the accuracy and trustworthiness of forensic images.

Lastly, we address the best practices that should be followed when producing forensic images to ensure their admissibility in court. These practices encompass a range of considerations, including maintaining evidence integrity, meticulous documentation of the acquisition process, and adherence to industry standards.

Terminology: Distinguishing Between Disk Images and Forensic Images

Understanding the distinction between disk images and forensic images is crucial. To provide clarity and establish a solid foundation, let's explore the definitions and distinctions between these terms:

- **Disk Image**: A disk image refers to a bit-by-bit copy of an entire disk or a single partition from a disk. Its purpose is to preserve the exact state of the disk at a specific point in time. Disk images can capture all data, including the file system, metadata, and the actual content of files. They are valuable for data recovery, system restoration, and analysis.

- **Forensic Image**: A forensic image, on the other hand, is a verified and comprehensive bit-by-bit copy or exact replica of everything contained within a physical hard drive. This includes all data, metadata, deleted or hidden files, and unallocated space. Forensic images capture both the active and latent data present on the drive, providing investigators with a complete view of the storage media. Importantly, forensic images are created with a unique hash value to verify their authenticity and integrity in comparison to the original evidence.

Logical vs. Physical Drives

In the realm of forensic investigations, differentiating between logical and physical copies is essential. A logical copy involves extracting data at the file system level, focusing on the logical structure and organization of files and directories. This type of copy captures the information visible to the operating system and applications, providing a representation of how the user perceives the data. In contrast, a physical copy involves acquiring all latent and active data, capturing the entire contents of a storage device, including all data, deleted files, and unallocated space. Physical copies provide a more comprehensive view of the data, allowing for deeper analysis and recovery of hidden or fragmented information. Understanding the advantages and limitations of logical and physical copies is crucial for selecting the most appropriate approach based on the specific requirements and objectives of the investigation at hand.

To grasp the distinction between logical and physical copies, it can be helpful to think of a logical copy as reflecting what is readily visible within the file manager of a Windows device. In contrast, a physical copy captures the entirety of the device, encompassing both the visible and non-visible components. When utilizing FTK Imager for drive imaging, investigators must specify the appropriate source evidence type. Understanding this differentiation provides crucial context for making informed decisions during the image acquisition process. You can see this depicted in Figure 3-1.

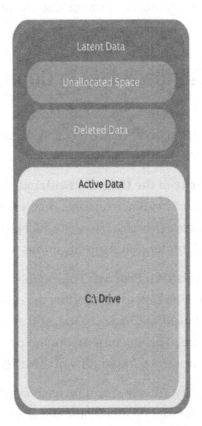

Figure 3-1. *Data and images*

Hashing Algorithms: SHA-256 As Digital Fingerprints

Hashing algorithms play a significant role in forensic image analysis, ensuring data integrity and authenticity. In the past, two commonly employed hashing algorithms are MD5 (Message Digest Algorithm 5) and SHA-1 (Secure Hash Algorithm 1). These algorithms generate unique hash values, often referred to as digital fingerprints, for forensic images and other digital data. However, these hashing algorithms have been shown to have flaws. It is recommended to use a newer hash, such as SHA-256. By calculating the hash values of the original media and the acquired forensic image, investigators can compare them to confirm the integrity and authenticity of the data. If any alterations or tampering have occurred, even the slightest change will result in a different hash value. Many forensic imaging tools allow one to calculate two hashes with two separate algorithms. If this is available in your tool, you should take advantage of that capability. This provides even more assurance that the image is a true and accurate copy of the original drive.

Best Practices for Admissibility in Court

Ensuring the admissibility of forensic images as evidence in court necessitates adherence to established best practices. To achieve this, there are several essential considerations to keep in mind:

- **Maintain the Integrity of the Original Evidence**: It is crucial to ensure that the original evidence remains unaltered during the acquisition and analysis process. Use write-blocking devices or software to prevent unintentional modifications to the evidence.

- **Document the Acquisition Process**: Thoroughly document the details of the acquisition process, including the dates of acquisition, acquisition method used, settings applied, and any observations or special considerations. This documentation helps establish the chain of custody and ensures the admissibility of the evidence in court.

- **Verify Image Integrity**: Always calculate hash values (such as MD5 or SHA-1) of the original media and the acquired image to ensure their integrity and authenticity. Compare the hash values to ensure they match, providing confidence in the accuracy of the forensic image.

- **Maintain Proper Storage and Backup**: Store forensic images securely to prevent unauthorized access or loss. Implement backup procedures to protect against data loss or corruption.

- **Use Validated and Reliable Tools**: Utilize trusted and validated forensic imaging and analysis tools such as OSForensics and FTK Imager. Stay updated with the latest versions and follow best practices recommended by the tool developers.

NIST Standards

Whatever tool you use, it is important that your forensic imaging process meet industry standards. The National Institute of Standards and Technology has a website dedicated to disk imaging specifications and evaluations (NIST, 2023). The document FS-TST 2.0: Forensic Software provides a report of testing of forensic tools. The document is quite detailed. The website also documents the specific test results for dozens of forensic imaging tools, including FTK Imager, Paraben E3, OSForensics, EnCase Forensic, Paladin, Image MASSter, X-Ways Forensics, and many others. Macintosh imaging tools such as MacQuisition were also tested. It should be noted that MacQuisition was purchased by Cellebrite, and this tool is now called the Cellebrite Digital Collector. It is important that you are certain the tools you are using are scientifically sound. Referring to NIST testing to validate your choice of tools is a good way to do that.

Creating Forensic Images with OSForensics

In this section, we will walk through the process of creating forensic images using OSForensics. We will delve into the reasons behind OSForensics' esteemed reputation as an effective tool for forensic image acquisition and analysis. Additionally, installation instructions for OSForensics will be provided, accompanied by a step-by-step outline of each step necessary to successfully image a drive. By the end of this section, you will possess a proficient understanding of OSForensics, will have acquired hands-on experience in imaging drives with OSForensics, and will appreciate the tool's widespread utilization in the field.

Why OSForensics?

OSForensics, developed by PassMark Software, is a comprehensive digital investigation tool that encompasses forensic imaging, analysis, and data recovery. It provides features for acquiring disk images, analyzing file systems, searching for files and artifacts, and performing advanced data recovery. OSForensics also supports memory imaging and analysis, as well as mobile device forensics. OSForensics has been widely embraced by the scientific and academic communities and by government agencies for its capabilities in reliably and effectively solving digital forensics problems. The US Department of Veterans Affairs and the Federal Law Enforcement Training Centers have used and endorsed this tool for its effectiveness.

OSForensics' cost-effectiveness also contributes significantly to its popularity. Despite being a commercial product, OSForensics offers a robust suite of features and functionalities available for free usage during the free trial period.

Installing OSForensics

To install OSForensics, you can find the link to download the most recent version at www. osforensics.com/download.html. For this demonstration, we will be using OSForensics 10.0, as it is the most recent version of OSForensics at the time this chapter is written. However, depending on when you are reading this, the version may differ. Download the most recent version.

Step-by-Step Guide to Image a Drive Using OSForensics

After installing OSForensics, launch the application. The main page will look something like what you see in Figure 3-2.

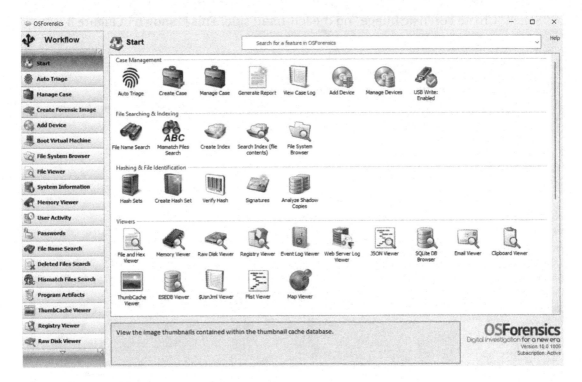

Figure 3-2. *OSForensics main screen*

Select "Create Forensic Image" on the left-hand side. This is shown in Figure 3-3.

Figure 3-3. *OSForensics imaging step 1*

Next, select "Add" and select a partition. Imaging an entire drive can take some time, so select the smallest partition you can find. In this example, we will be selecting "Partition 0." This is shown in Figure 3-4.

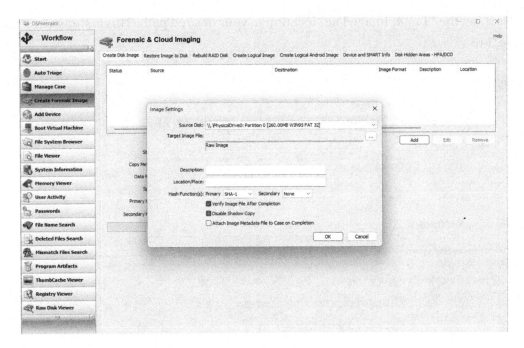

Figure 3-4. *OSForensics imaging step 2*

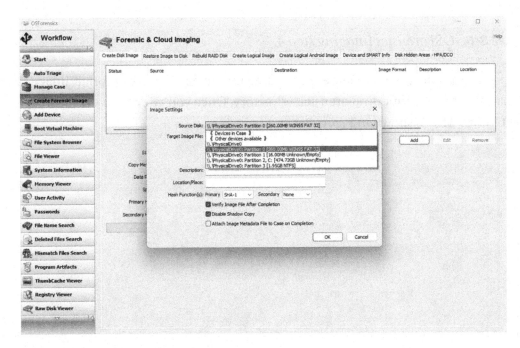

Figure 3-5. *OSForensics imaging step 3*

Next, set the "Target Image File" location to your desired path. This is shown in Figure 3-6.

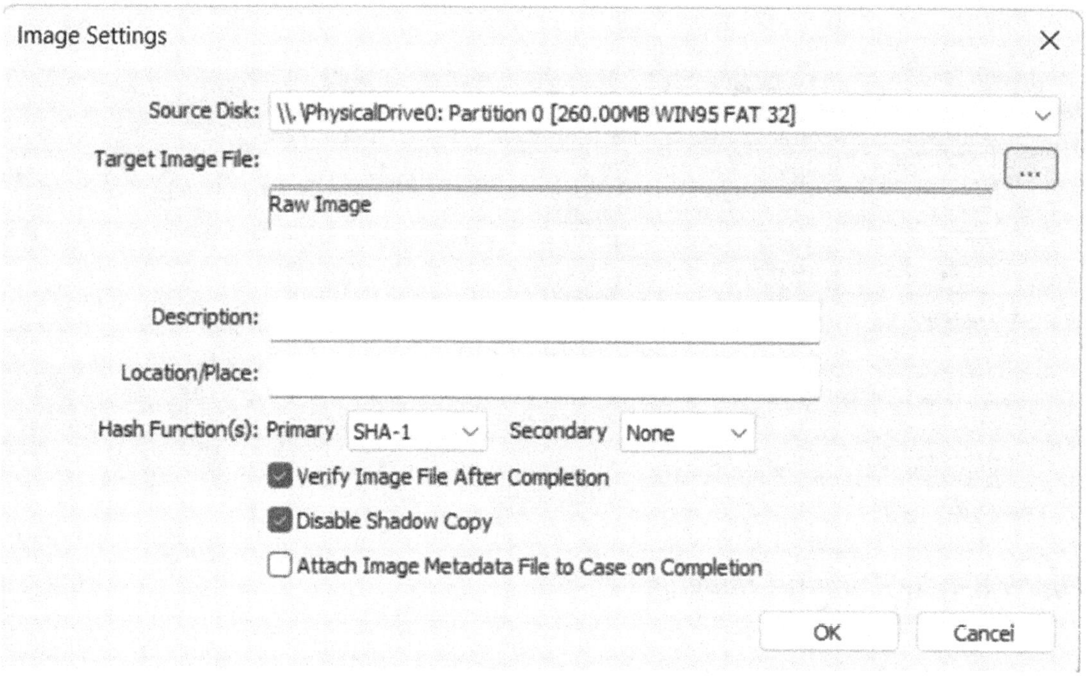

Figure 3-6. *OSForensics imaging step 4*

In this example, you can see we are creating the "imaging-drive-tutorial" image file and saving it to the "WindowsForensics" directory. Once you've created the file image, select "Save." This is shown in Figure 3-7.

Figure 3-7.   *OSForensics imaging step 5*

Before we select "OK," we want to ensure we have our desired hash function (as we discussed in the "Key Concepts" section). For this example, we will select SHA-256 for our primary hash function. You may select a secondary hash function such as SHA-1, or you can leave it blank. For this demonstration, we selected SHA-1. You can see this in Figure 3-8.

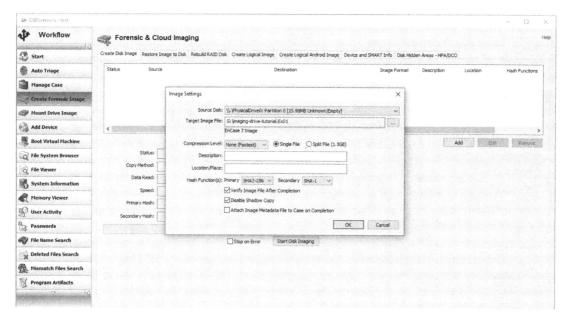

Figure 3-8. *OSForensics imaging step 6*

Select "OK." The file should now appear in the "Create Disk Image" window and show the status as pending. This can be seen in Figure 3-9.

Figure 3-9. *OSForensics imaging step 7*

Next, select "Create Image" as shown in Figure 3-10.

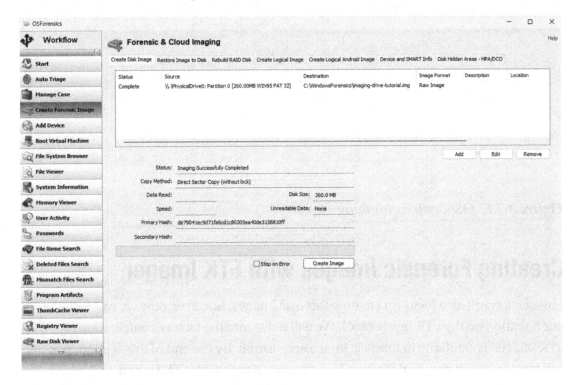

Figure 3-10. *OSForensics imaging step 8*

After we can see that the status has been updated to successfully completed, we can navigate to our directory in our file explorer and see that the image file appears as expected. This confirms that we have successfully created a forensic image with OSForensics and saved it in our desired path. You can see this in Figure 3-11.

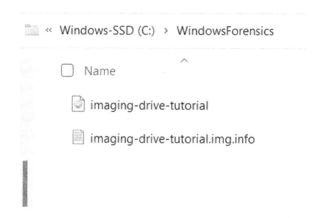

Figure 3-11. OSForensics imaging step 9

Creating Forensic Images with FTK Imager

This section will also focus on creating forensic images; however, now we will focus our attention on the FTK Imager tool. We will delve into the factors contributing to FTK Imager's popularity in forensic image acquisition. By the end of this section, you will have acquired practical forensic imaging experience with FTK Imager and have a greater understanding of its significance as a widely employed tool in the field of digital forensics.

Why FTK Imager?

FTK Imager, developed by AccessData (which has now been acquired by Exterro), is a powerful forensic imaging tool that allows investigators to create forensic images of various digital storage media. It offers features such as acquiring physical or logical images, mounting and exploring images, and verifying image integrity. Additionally, FTK Imager provides advanced capabilities for memory imaging, artifact extraction, and mobile device analysis. It has received endorsement from the US Department of Homeland Security as a reliable tool for forensic image acquisition, as well as being widely embraced by the scientific and academic communities. Notably, FTK Imager stands out as a cost-effective solution, providing an extensive range of features typically found in paid tools, making it an incredibly robust option available for free.

Installing FTK Imager

To install FTK Imager, you can find the link to download the most recent version at www. exterro.com/ftk-imager. It's important to note that many tutorials online will tell you to download directly from AccessData's website. These installation instructions are outdated as AccessData has since been acquired by Exterro.

Step-by-Step Guide to Imaging a Drive Using FTK Imager

Once FTK Imager has been installed, launch the application. Go to "File" in the menu bar, and select "Create Disk Image" as shown in Figure 3-12.

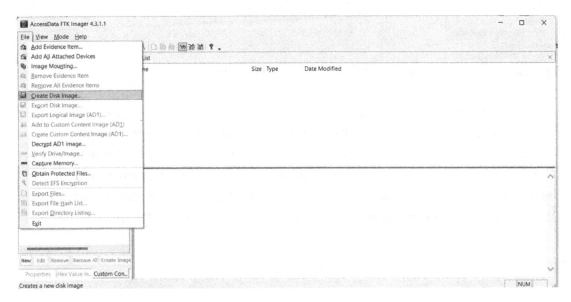

Figure 3-12. *FTK Imager step 1*

Next, it will prompt us to select the source evidence type. For this demonstration, we will select "Logical Drive" and select "Next," as shown in Figure 3-13.

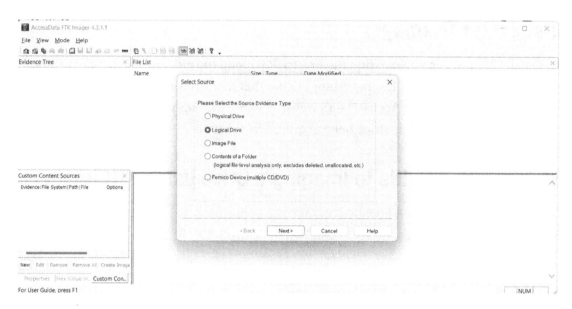

Figure 3-13. *FTK Imager step 2*

Now we will need to select from one of the available drives. In this demonstration, I will be using the "D:\ - [NTFS]" drive. If you do not have a D drive available, you may select another source evidence type. The quickest solution may be to select "Contents of a Folder" and follow along (although it may look slightly different from this demonstration). For now, follow along this demonstration where we will use the D drive. Once you've selected your source drive, select "Finish" as shown in Figure 3-14.

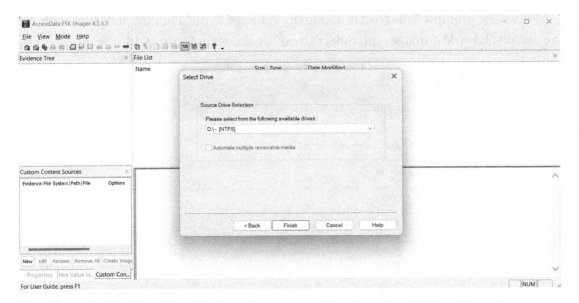

Figure 3-14. *FTK Imager step 3*

Next, select "Add" under "Image Destination(s)." This is depicted in Figure 3-15.

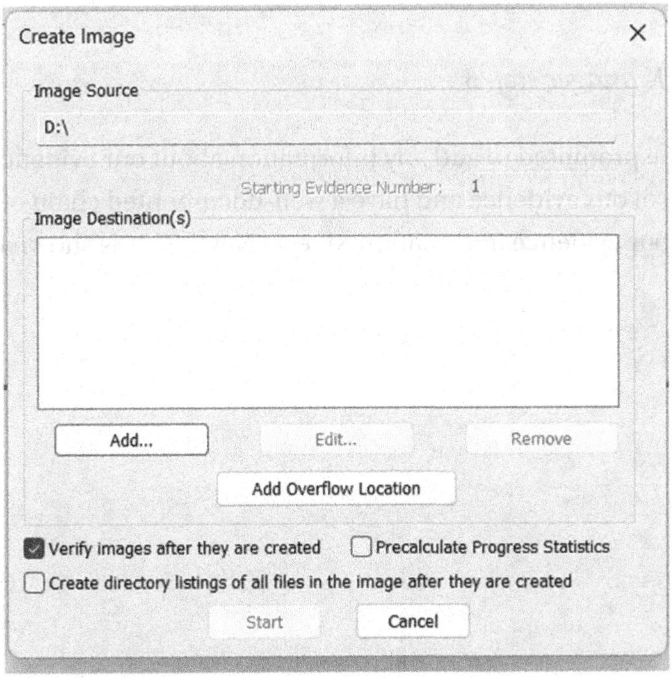

Figure 3-15. *FTK Imager step 4*

We will be prompted to select a "Destination Image Type." For now, let's stick with the default "Raw(dd)" image type. Select "Next" as shown in Figure 3-16.

Figure 3-16. *FTK Imager step 5*

Next, we will be prompted to add any information about our evidence. This will help us keep track of our evidence and have a well-documented chain of custody. Once you've added in your evidence information, select "Next." This is shown in Figure 3-17.

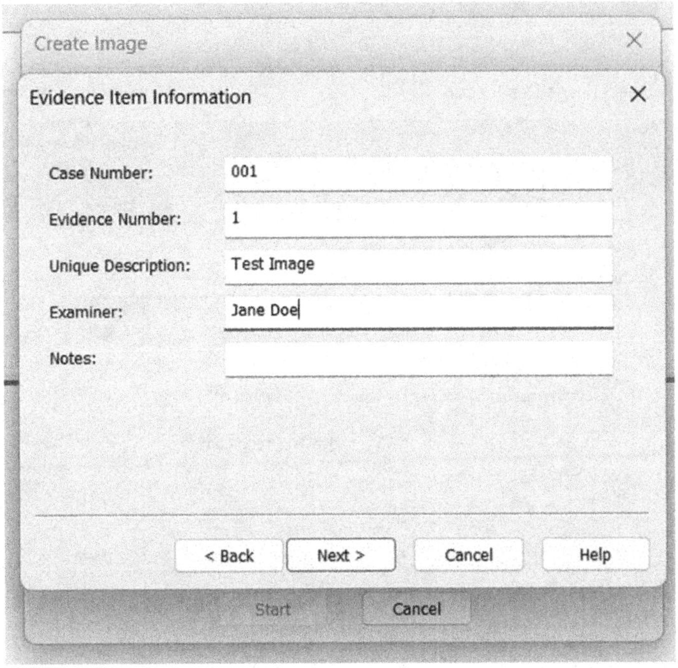

Figure 3-17. *FTK Imager step 6*

For the "Image Destination Folder," we will need to add our desired path. For the "Image Filename (excluding extension)," we will need to add our file name. Select "Finish" when you have added both your desired destination path and name of the image file. You can see this in Figure 3-18.

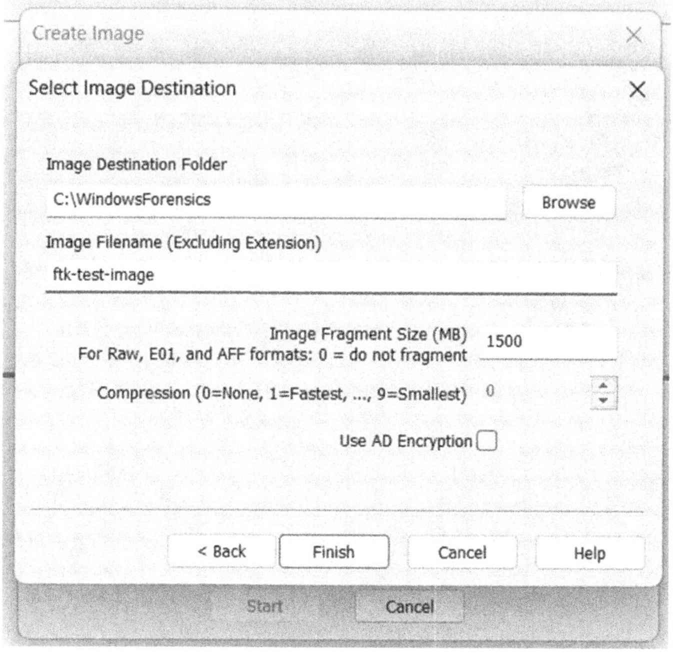

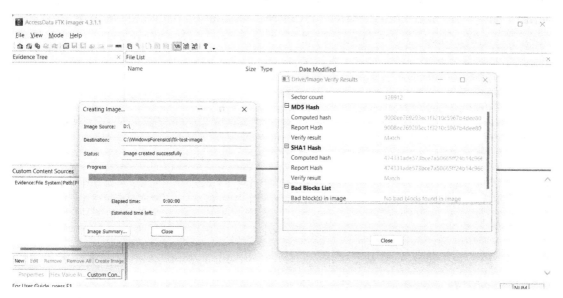

Figure 3-18. *FTK Imager step 7*

You will then see the new image appear in the image destination window. Select "Start" to create the image, as shown in Figure 3-19.

Figure 3-19. *FTK Imager step 8*

Once the image has been successfully created, you will see a "Drive/Image Verify Results" pop-up window that displays the MD5 and SHA-1 hash values. As we can see, it says "Match" next to each "Verify result," verifying that the image is an exact replica of the original evidence and there has been no tampering with the evidence. This is depicted in Figures 3-20 and 3-21.

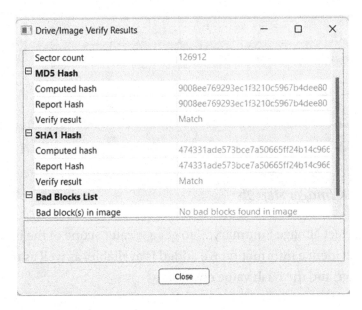

Figure 3-20. *FTK Imager step 9a*

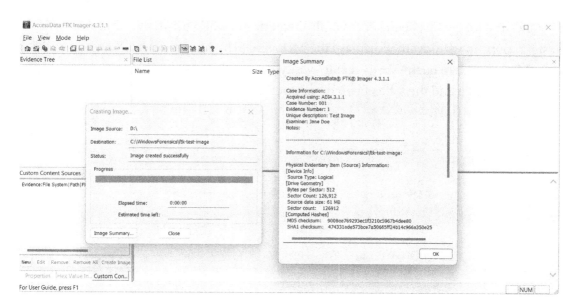

Figure 3-21. *FTK Imager step 9b*

We can also select "Image Summary…" to get a greater scope of the image. As you can see, the case evidence information we added is available, as well as the details regarding the image and the hash value checks.

Mounting a Drive

Now that we have a clearer understanding of how to image a drive, we need to understand how to mount a drive. We can do this by mounting our forensic copy (the images we created) so that we can analyze them in a read-only way. Mounting ensures that the user's computer can recognize the media's format, and it can become readily accessible for the user to access and go through its contents. Upon successful mounting of media, your computer seamlessly integrates the file system of the media with your local file system. This integration establishes a mount point, which acts as a local link enabling convenient access to the external device. In this section, we will be mounting a drive image using OSForensics.

Step-by-Step Guide to Mounting a Drive

Launch the OSForensics application and search for the "Mount Drive Image" in the search bar at the top of the home screen. As you can see in Figure 3-22, it will pop up as a suggestion.

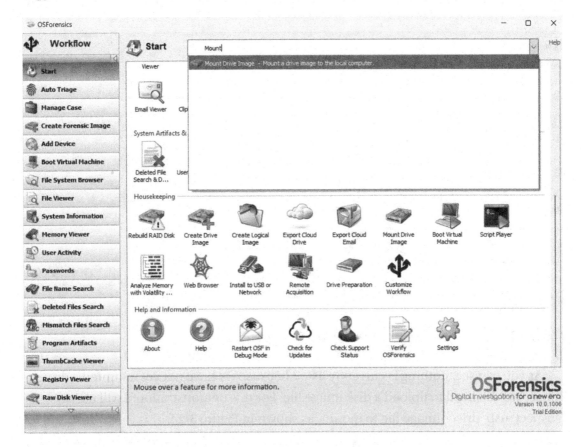

Figure 3-22. *OSForensics mounting an image step 1*

Once you select "Mount Drive Image," a pop-up window will appear where it will display the mounted virtual disks. This screen is depicted in Figure 3-23.

Figure 3-23. *OSForensics mounting an image step 2*

As you can see, nothing is currently listed because we have not yet mounted a drive image. We will need to upload a disk image file. For this demonstration, I will use a "suspect_usb_drive" image file to mount, as shown in Figure 3-24.

« Windows-SSD (C:) › WindowsForensics	Type	Size
Name		
suspect_usb_drive	Disc Image File	63,456 KB

Figure 3-24. *OSForensics mounting an image step 3*

Select "Mount new..." at the bottom of the pop-up window in OSForensics. The "Disk image file (.img, .dd, .vmdk, .E01, ...)" is the default type that is already selected. Select the disk image you would like to upload. You can see this in Figure 3-25.

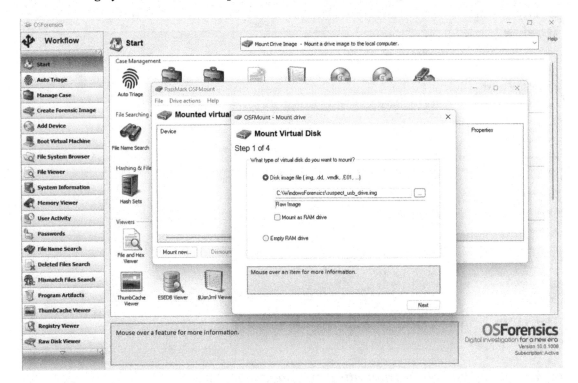

Figure 3-25. *OSForensics mounting an image step 4*

Next, it will prompt you to select which partition to mount. The default selection is "Mount entire image as virtual disk." Let's use that for now. Select "Next," as depicted in Figure 3-26.

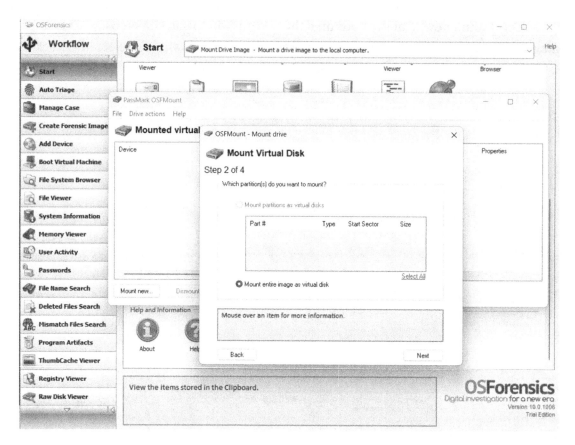

Figure 3-26. *OSForensics mounting an image step 5*

After hitting "Next" on Step 2 of 4, you may notice that it will immediately jump to
Step 4 of 4 (rather than providing Step 3). That is to be expected. Next, it will prompt us to
make any additional mount modifications. "Read-only drive" is checked as the default,
so let's stick with that. Next, we'll need to change the drive type and the drive letter. For
the drive type, select "HDD," and for the drive letter, select "D." Once these modifications
are made, select "Mount" at the bottom right, as shown in Figures 3-27 through 3-29.

Figure 3-27. *OSForensics mounting an image step 6*

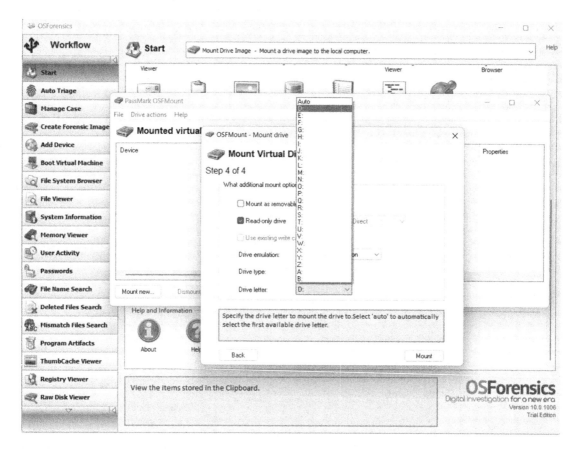

Figure 3-28. OSForensics mounting an image step 7

Figure 3-29. *OSForensics mounting an image step 8*

As you can see in Figure 3-30, the suspect_usb_drive is now appearing as a mounted virtual disk in the list.

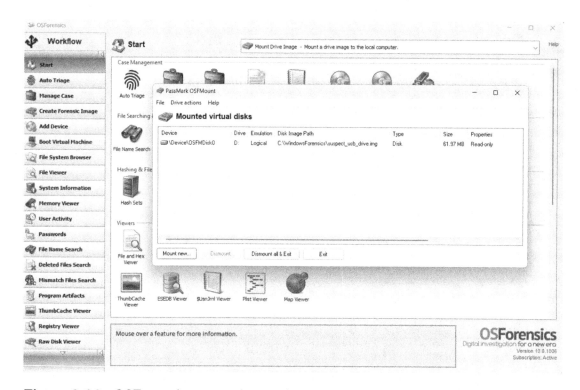

Figure 3-30. *OSForensics mounting an image step 9*

Once the image drive has been mounted, it can now be easily accessed for the user to go through its files in a format that the computer can recognize. From here, this will allow us to do deeper analysis in OSForensics. In the next section, we will explore how to take what we've learned so far a step further by beginning to make sense of the contents of our forensic images through deeper analysis.

Using Autopsy

Autopsy is an open source tool widely used in the digital forensic community. You can download a version of Autopsy for Windows, Linux, or OSX at www.autopsy. com/download/. Autopsy allows one to create a logical image. A logical image is still forensically valid, but may not capture all the information a physical image does. To create a logical image with Autopsy, you select *Tools* and *Logical Imager* as shown in Figure 3-31.

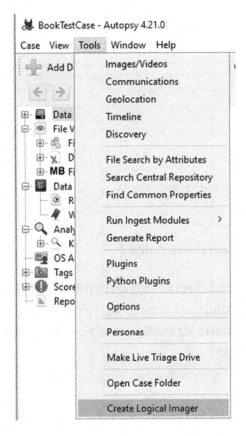

Figure 3-31. *Starting Autopsy logical imager*

This will start the imaging wizard. The first step of the wizard is shown in Figure 3-32.

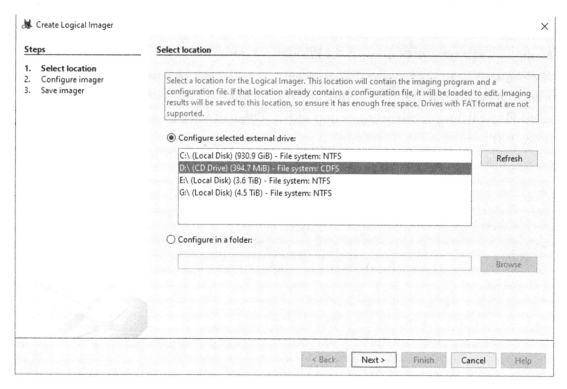

Figure 3-32. *Autopsy logical imager step 1*

Autopsy does have a few features not found in most tools. The first is that you can create a VHD (virtual disk) from the imaging. This would allow you to mount the VHD in a virtual machine, such as Oracle VirtualBox, and view the system as a user would see it. This is depicted in Figure 3-33.

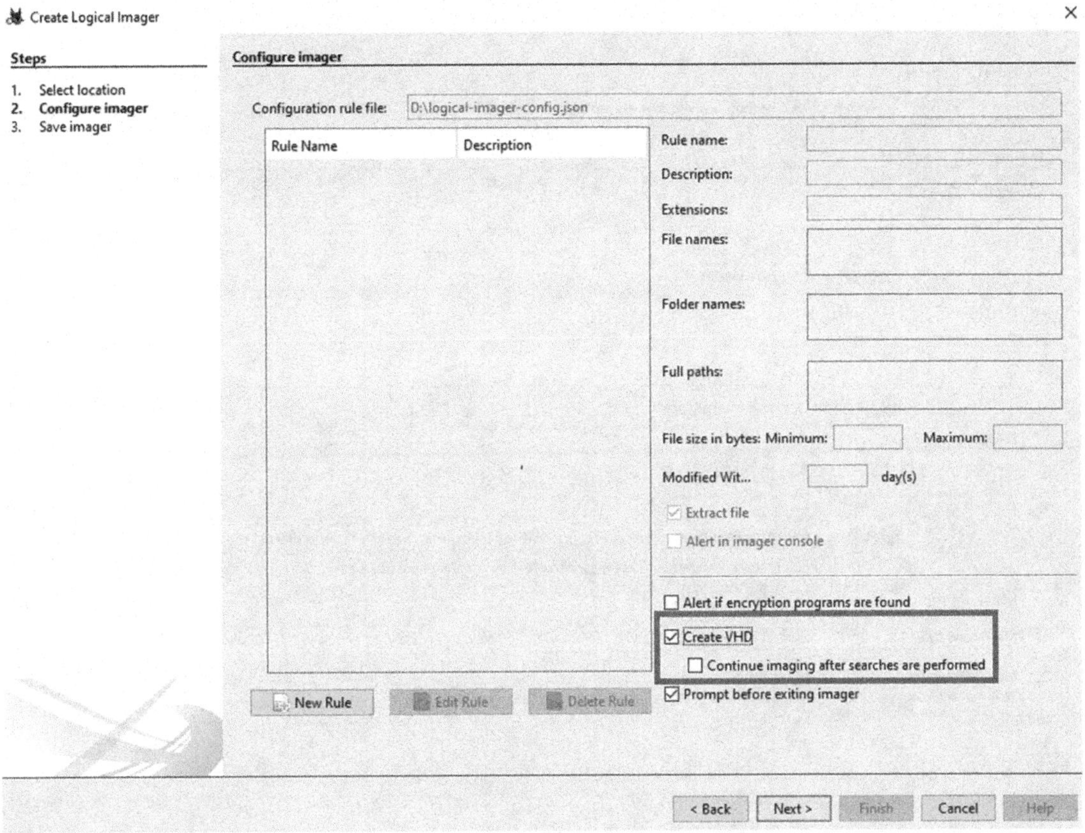

Figure 3-33. *Autopsy logical imager step 2a*

The second item that Autopsy provides is the ability to set rules. These rules are useful if you have a specific item you are searching for. You can choose to limit the files that are included in the image, as shown in Figure 3-34.

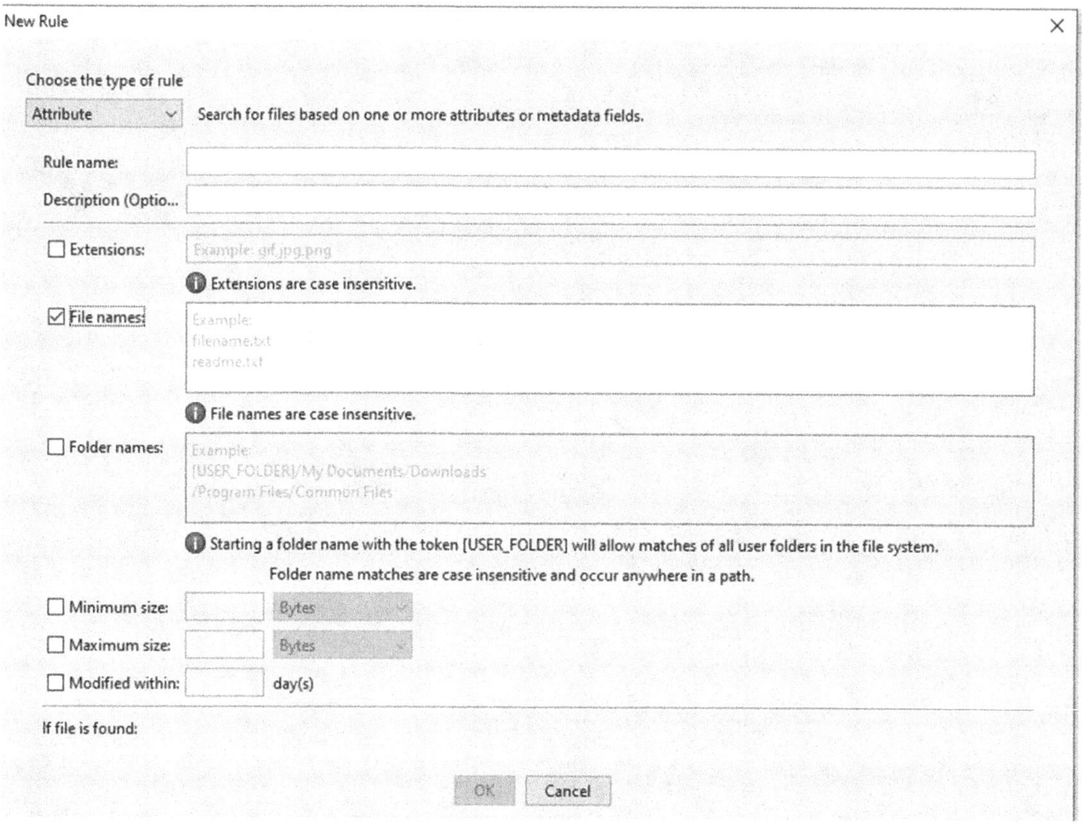

New Rule   ×

Choose the type of rule

Attribute   ∨   Search for files based on one or more attributes or metadata fields.

Rule name: [   ]

Description (Optio... [   ]

☐ Extensions: [Example: gif jpg png   ]

   ⓘ Extensions are case insensitive.

☑ File names: [Example:]
                   filename.txt
                   readme.txt

   ⓘ File names are case insensitive.

☐ Folder names: [Example:]
                   [USER_FOLDER]/My Documents/Downloads
                   /Program Files/Common Files

   ⓘ Starting a folder name with the token [USER_FOLDER] will allow matches of all user folders in the file system.
     Folder name matches are case insensitive and occur anywhere in a path.

☐ Minimum size: [   ] [Bytes   ∨]

☐ Maximum size: [   ] [Bytes   ∨]

☐ Modified within: [   ] day(s)

If file is found:

                              [OK] [Cancel]

Figure 3-34. *Autopsy logical imager step 2b*

Autopsy also allows you to mount an image. You simply select "Add Data Source" from the tool bar and follow the wizard, as shown in Figures 3-35 and 3-36.

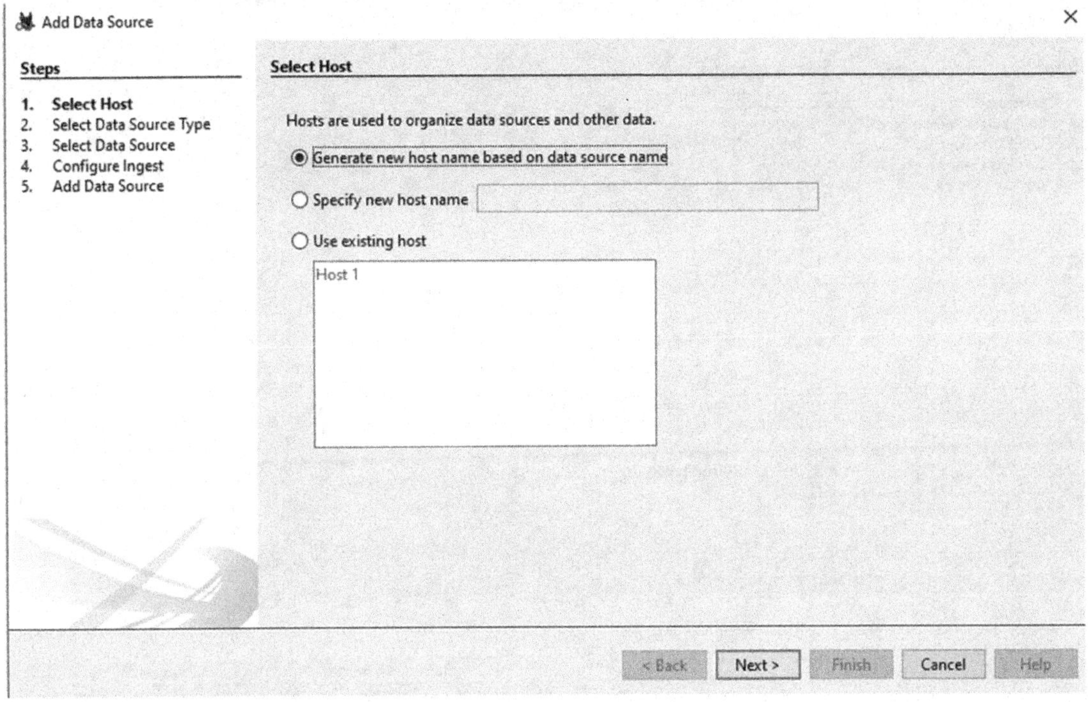

Figure 3-35. *Mount an image using Autopsy*

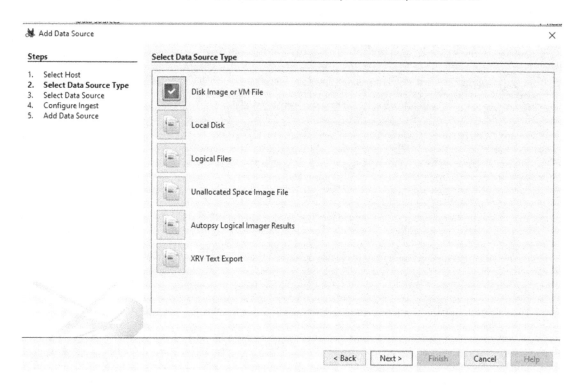

Figure 3-36. *Mount an image using Autopsy*

As can be seen, Autopsy offers many features that make it useful for digital forensics. At a minimum, Autopsy makes a very good backup tool used to verify results you obtain with other tools.

Understanding the Contents of a Forensic Image Through Deeper Analysis

In this section, we will delve into the exploration of forensic images and uncover the power behind their contents through two analysis techniques. Firstly, we will demonstrate the process of recovering deleted files, showcasing the valuable insights that can be gained from uncovering hidden information. Secondly, we will delve into the examination of recent activity, revealing the crucial role forensic images play in reconstructing digital footprints. As we transition from the "how" to the "why," this section aims to deepen our understanding of the immense value that forensic images bring to the field of digital forensics.

Recovering Deleted Files

On the left-hand side of OSForensics, select "Deleted File Search" and select the "Devices to Scan" drop-down menu. Select "Volume D: [NTFS]" to scan for deleted files. This is shown in Figure 3-37.

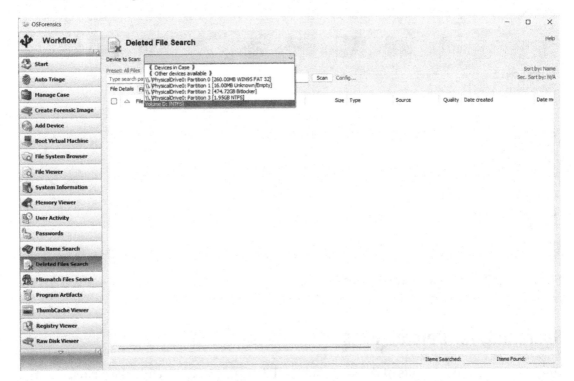

Figure 3-37. *Recover deleted files in OSForensics – step 1*

Next, select "Scan." You can see that process in Figure 3-38.

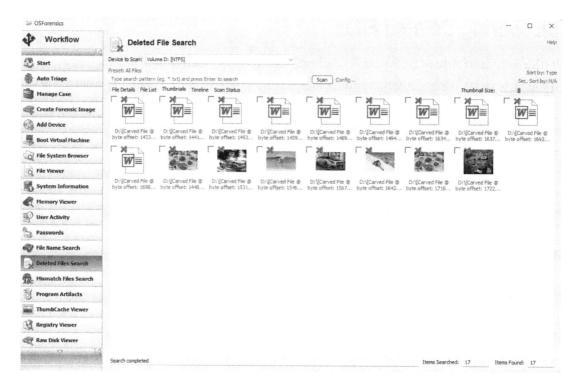

Figure 3-38. *Recover deleted files in OSForensics – step 2*

Searching for Deleted Files

Once we can see the results of the scan, select "File List." Here, we can take a closer
look at the quality and value of the files. Each deleted file will have a quality indicator
between 0 and 100. This gives investigators an idea of how intact the files are. A value
closer to 100 tells us that the deleted file is mainly intact, with only a few missing bits of
data. As you can see in the results of this particular scan, all of the files found were of
high quality/high value. This can be determined by the color and the quality indicator
on the thumbnail icon. All of the files had a quality indicator above 87, as shown in
Figure 3-39.

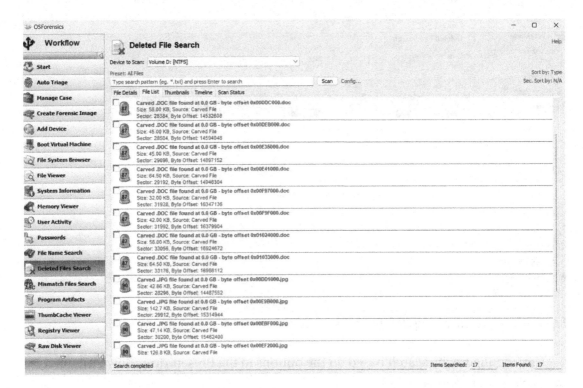

Figure 3-39. *Reviewing deleted files in OSForensics*

Next, configure the search according to string matching. To narrow down the results to only jpg images, use the string "*.jpg" in the Filter String field, as depicted in Figure 3-40.

Figure 3-40. *Searching deleted files in OSForensics*

Next, configure the search based on the options in the Presets drop-down menu. As you can see, the options include

- All Files

- Images

- Office Documents

- Compressed Files

- Email Files

This is shown in Figure 3-41.

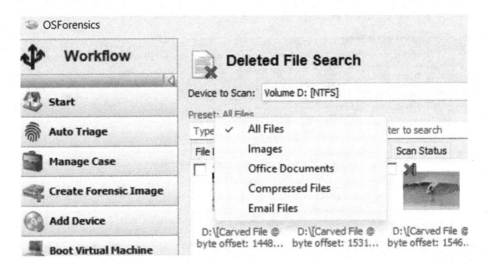

Figure 3-41. *Deleted file's preset file types*

Next, select "Office Documents" and run the scan again. The results are shown in Figure 3-42.

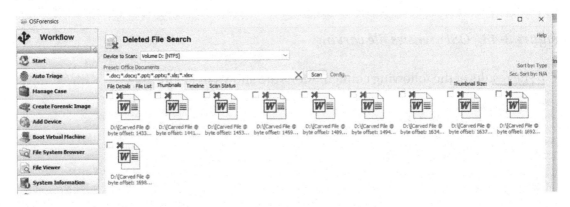

Figure 3-42. *Viewing deleted documents*

File Carving

Next, use the "Config..." window to make more modifications to the search. Leave all of the default options selected and select "Carve file index records" and "Include folders." This is shown in Figure 3-43.

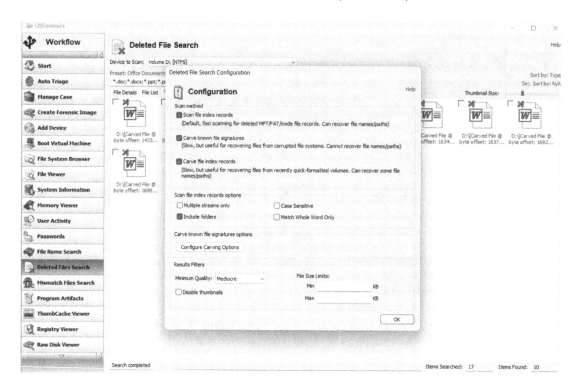

Figure 3-43. *OSForensics file carving*

The results of the following configurations are shown in Figure 3-44.

File Name	Location	Size	Type	Source	Quality	Date created
Carved .DOC file foun...	D:\[Carved File @ byte offset: 14331904-1439...	64.50 KB	[Deleted] Micro...	Carved File	87	
Carved .DOC file foun...	D:\[Carved File @ byte offset: 14413824-1447...	64.50 KB	[Deleted] Micro...	Carved File	87	
Carved .DOC file foun...	D:\[Carved File @ byte offset: 14532608-1459...	58.00 KB	[Deleted] Micro...	Carved File	87	
Carved .DOC file foun...	D:\[Carved File @ byte offset: 14594048-1464...	45.00 KB	[Deleted] Micro...	Carved File	87	
Carved .DOC file foun...	D:\[Carved File @ byte offset: 14897152-1494...	45.00 KB	[Deleted] Micro...	Carved File	87	
Carved .DOC file foun...	D:\[Carved File @ byte offset: 14946304-1501...	64.50 KB	[Deleted] Micro...	Carved File	87	
Carved .DOC file foun...	D:\[Carved File @ byte offset: 16347136-1637...	32.00 KB	[Deleted] Micro...	Carved File	87	
Carved .DOC file foun...	D:\[Carved File @ byte offset: 16379904-1642...	42.00 KB	[Deleted] Micro...	Carved File	87	
Carved .DOC file foun...	D:\[Carved File @ byte offset: 16924672-1698...	58.00 KB	[Deleted] Micro...	Carved File	87	
Carved .DOC file foun...	D:\[Carved File @ byte offset: 16986112-1705...	64.50 KB	[Deleted] Micro...	Carved File	87	
Carved .JPG file found...	D:\[Carved File @ byte offset: 14487552-1453...	42.66 KB	[Deleted] JPG File	Carved File	90	
Carved .JPG file found...	D:\[Carved File @ byte offset: 15314944-1546...	142.7 KB	[Deleted] JPG File	Carved File	90	
Carved .JPG file found...	D:\[Carved File @ byte offset: 15462400-1551...	47.14 KB	[Deleted] JPG File	Carved File	90	
Carved .JPG file found...	D:\[Carved File @ byte offset: 15671296-1580...	126.8 KB	[Deleted] JPG File	Carved File	90	
Carved .JPG file found...	D:\[Carved File @ byte offset: 16424960-1647...	48.62 KB	[Deleted] JPG File	Carved File	90	
Carved .JPG file found...	D:\[Carved File @ byte offset: 17182720-1722...	42.66 KB	[Deleted] JPG File	Carved File	90	
Carved .JPG file found...	D:\[Carved File @ byte offset: 17227776-1729...	62.25 KB	[Deleted] JPG File	Carved File	90	

Figure 3-44. *File carving results*

Viewing Contents of the Deleted Files

Next, right-click an individual deleted file and select "View with Internal Viewer." This is shown in Figure 3-45.

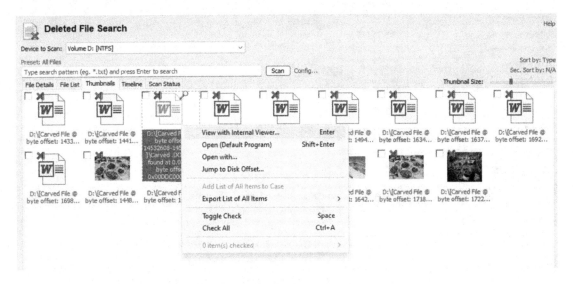

Figure 3-45. *View files with Internal Viewer part 1*

In Figures 3-46 to 3-48, we can see some of the contents of the deleted files using the Internal Viewer.

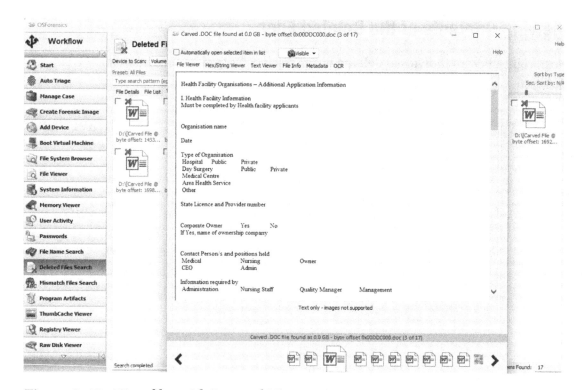

Figure 3-46. *View files with Internal Viewer part 2*

Figure 3-47. *View files with Internal Viewer part 3*

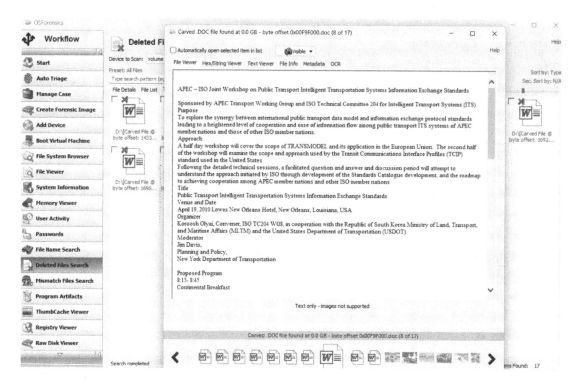

Figure 3-48. *View files with Internal Viewer part 4*

Next, let's open up a jpg image. Select "Analyze." You will notice a pop-up window appears showing an analysis of the results. As you can see, there are features such as AI facial detection and embedded thumbnail detection, among other results. This is shown in Figure 3-49.

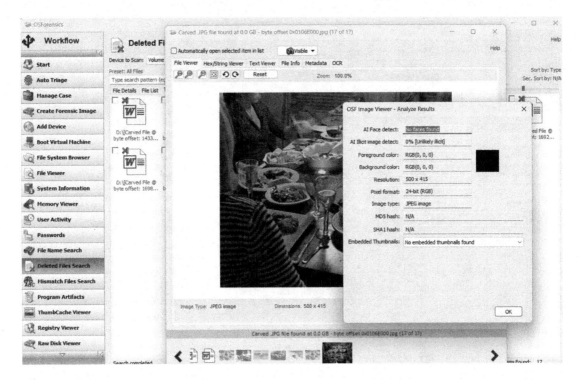

Figure 3-49. *Analyze files*

As you can see, this can be an incredibly powerful tool when trying to sort through the contents of a suspect USB device. Next, we will focus our attention on uncovering recent activity.

Autopsy and Deleted Files

The previously discussed Autopsy digital forensics tool also allows one to recover deleted files. One difference is that Autopsy automatically recovers deleted files, as shown in Figure 3-50.

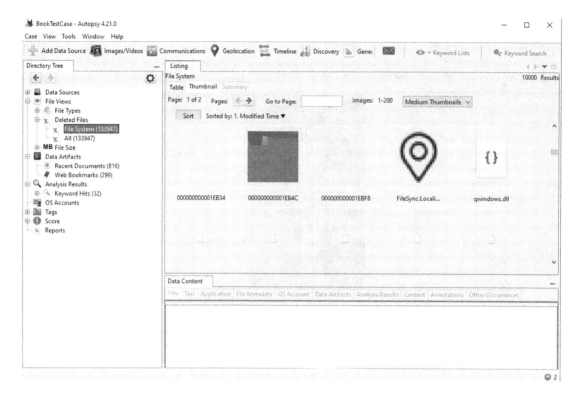

Figure 3-50. *Autopsy deleted files*

You can then right-click any deleted files and see multiple options, as shown in Figure 3-51.

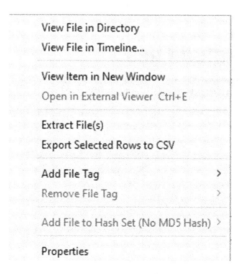

Figure 3-51. *Autopsy deleted file options*

Uncovering User Activity

Next, we will shift our attention to extracting all recent user activity from a Windows machine using OSForensics. By understanding how to access and interpret any Windows user's recent activity, it provides greater insight into the patterns and behaviors of an individual. Ultimately, all of which can be incredibly useful when building a case in a legal proceeding.

Scanning User Activity

On the left-hand side of OSForensics, select "User Activity." Select "Create Full Timeline." Here, you will be able to see a wide range of data on a user's activity, as is shown in Figure 3-52.

Figure 3-52. *OSForensics User Activity*

It is worth reviewing several of the different categories as it will provide a wide scope of information about the user. Some categories of interest for an investigator may be "Browser History," "USB," and "Mounted Volumes." All of this data is extremely useful when building a profile around someone's digital footprint, which is why it is such a powerful tool for investigators to use in legal proceedings.

Autopsy User Activity

This is an area where Autopsy is somewhat limited. On the left hand of Autopsy, you can select to view recent documents, web bookmarks, and OS accounts, as shown in Figure 3-53.

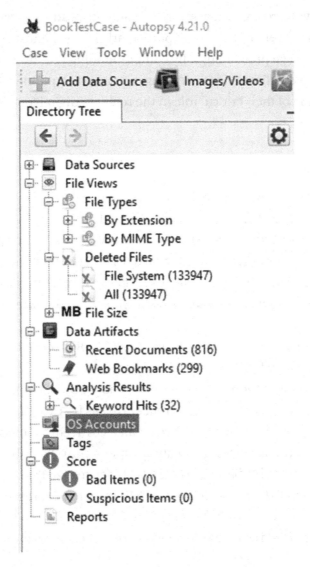

Figure 3-53. *Autopsy User Activity*

Conclusion

In conclusion, this chapter has endeavored to illustrate the significance of forensic image creation in digital forensics investigations, delving into both the practical aspects and the underlying rationale. Through the exploration of esteemed tools like OSForensics and FTK Imager, you have gained firsthand experience in the creation of forensic images, recognizing their pivotal role in uncovering the contents of suspect drives. The power of forensic images has been underscored, particularly in the context of constructing compelling cases for legal proceedings. By comprehending the "how" and appreciating the "why" behind the creation of forensic images, you have equipped yourself with a deeper understanding of their critical role in the realm of digital forensics.

References

Digital Data Acquisition Tool Test assertions and test plan (n.d.-a). www.nist.gov/system/files/documents/2017/05/09/da-atp-pc-01.pdf

Disk Imaging. NIST (April 17, 2023). www.nist.gov/itl/ssd/software-quality-group/computer-forensics-tool-testing-program-cftt/cftt-technical/disk

Drive imaging. OSForensics (n.d.). www.osforensics.com/drive-imaging.html

Easttom, C. (2022). *Digital Forensics, investigation, and response.* Jones & Bartlett Learning.

Editor, C. C. (n.d.). *Forensic copy - glossary: CSRC.* CSRC Content Editor. https://csrc.nist.gov/glossary/term/forensic_copy

Forensic clone. Forensic Clone – an overview | ScienceDirect Topics (n.d.). www.sciencedirect.com/topics/computer-science/forensic-clone#:~:text=A%20forensic%20image%20of%20a,the%20active%20and%20latent%20data

Global Information Assurance Certification Paper – GIAC (n.d.-b). www.giac.org/paper/gcfa/10182/forensic-images-viewing-pleasure/126976

Jansen, W., & Ayers, R. (June 24, 2021). *Guidelines on PDA Forensics, recommendations of the National Institute of Standards and Technology.* NIST. www.nist.gov/publications/guidelines-pda-forensics-recommendations-national-institute-standards-and-technology

Kam Woods University of North Carolina, Woods, K., Carolina, U. of N., Christopher A. Lee University of North Carolina, Lee, C. A., School, S. G. N. P., Garfinkel, S., School, N. P., University, C., Ucar/ncar, University, V., & Metrics, O. M. A. (June 1, 2011). *Extending digital repository architectures to support Disk Image Preservation and Access: Proceedings of the 11th Annual International ACM/IEEE Joint Conference on digital libraries.* ACM Conferences. https://dl.acm.org/doi/10.1145/1998076.1998088

Palavalli, V. (February 10, 2022). *Overview: The three types of forensic collections - physical vs. logical vs. targeted*. Percipient. `https://percipient.co/overview-the-three-types-of-forensic-collections-physical-vs-logical-vs-targeted/`

Person, Eddy, J., & Colloton, F. (November 2, 2022). *Disk Imaging as a backup tool for digital objects: 17: Conservation*. Taylor & Francis. `www.taylorfrancis.com/chapters/edit/10.4324/9781003034865-17/disk-imaging-backup-tool-digital-objects-eddy-colloton-jonathan-farbowitz-caroline-gil-rodr%C3%ADguez`

Test Your Knowledge

A few questions are provided here to aid you in testing your knowledge before you proceed.

1. What are the most common hash values to verify the authenticity of a forensic image?

   a. SHA-256 and RSA

   b. AES and SHA-1

   c. SHA-256 and SHA-1

   d. AES and RSA

2. What is a forensic image?

   a. Bit-by-bit copy or exact replica of everything contained within a physical hard drive

   b. Screenshot of everything on a C:\ drive

   c. A file containing only active data

   d. None of the above

3. What best practice makes a forensic image admissible in a court of law?

   a. Verified image integrity with hash values

   b. Well-documented acquisition process and chain of custody

   c. Using reliable image acquisition tools

   d. All of the above

CHAPTER 4

Windows File Artifacts

William H. Butler, D.Sc.
Chuck Easttom, Ph.D., D.Sc.

Windows file artifacts can provide an extensive amount of information regarding what has occurred on a Windows computer. These file artifacts range from the recycle bin for deleted files to log files used for forensic analysis. Windows uses specific file locations where these artifacts are stored. This chapter reviews where the Windows operating system stores those artifacts and their locations. These artifacts consist of file systems, registries, event logs, memory, and network artifacts. Analyzing these files requires specialized tools such as Autopsy and OSForensics, which we will use in this chapter. This chapter introduces you to these concepts, each artifact, its usefulness, and its location.

This chapter covers several Windows file artifacts and their usefulness to the average user and forensic analyst. These artifacts can be used to locate files on the computer, recover lost files, and examine event logs to discover certain activities on the computer. For example, by examining Windows artifacts, investigators can reconstruct events, identify potential security breaches, understand system behavior, and gather evidence in forensic investigations. Users can recover deleted files by locating them and then running the proper commands to recover the files. This chapter will focus on file system artifacts and log files.

In this chapter, we will cover the following Windows file artifacts:

- Deleted files

- .LNK files

- Log files

- Recycle bin

- $I30 file

© Chuck Easttom, William Butler, Jessica Phelan, Ramya Sai Bhagavatula, Sean Steuber, Karely Rodriguez, Victoria Indy Balkissoon, Zehra Naseer 2024
C. Easttom et al., *Windows Forensics*, https://doi.org/10.1007/979-8-8688-0193-8_4

There are many different forensics tools one could use to analyze Windows file artifacts. Autopsy Forensics is an open source tool that you may download for free from `www.autopsy.com/`. OSForensics is an easy-to-use tool that is both low priced and has a free 30-day trial. You can learn more about OSForensics at `www.osforensics.com/`.

Why Study Windows Artifacts?

One should study Windows artifacts for some very compelling reasons. First, as stated in the introduction, the better one knows their computer, the more useful the computer becomes to them. Knowing where to find temporary files and their locations can avert disaster when producing a time-sensitive document that was accidentally deleted. Every device produces log files that record the commands and their results. These log files can be useful to determine what actions a user took on a computer to reveal a breach of that system or an unintentional error by you. Some other useful file system artifacts include file metadata (timestamps, attributes), file access logs (NTFS, MFT), link files (LNK), prefetch files, and file system journal logs.

Several logs are very useful to the user, such as the System Event Log, Application Event Log, and Security Event Log. These logs record useful information that can be easily accessed for casual viewing or forensic investigations. As you can see, the logs are useful to both expert and novice computer users. Windows records various system events, errors, and user activities in event logs. For example, after a security breach is discovered, the incident handlers immediately examine the system logs for evidence to identify the intruder and to determine if data was compromised or exfiltrated.

What Are Windows Artifacts?

Artifacts are files or fragments of files that can provide information about the Windows system. These can be invaluable in a forensic investigation. Windows artifacts include the following deleted files, .LNK files, log files, recycle bin, $I30 files, and others:

- **Deleted files** refer to files that have been intentionally or unintentionally removed from a storage medium, such as a computer's hard drive or a removable storage device. When a file is deleted, it is typically moved to the recycle bin or trash folder, where it can be easily restored if needed. However, emptying the recycle bin or using specialized deletion methods can permanently remove the file from the system.

- **.LNK files** are file shortcuts in the Windows operating system. They are small files pointing to another file, folder, or application on your computer, allowing you to access the target item quickly without navigating through the entire file system.

- **Log files** record events, actions, or system activities on a computer system, software application, or network. They serve as a valuable source of information for troubleshooting, monitoring, security analysis, and auditing purposes. Various system components generate log files, including the operating system, applications, and network devices.

- **Recycle bin** is a special folder in the Windows operating system that serves as a temporary storage location for deleted files and folders. When you delete a file or folder in Windows, it is typically moved to the recycle bin rather than being immediately deleted from the system.

- **$I30** attribute in NTFS refers to the index allocation attribute of a directory. It stores the file names and associated metadata within a directory, allowing for efficient file name lookup and retrieval. The "I30" attribute is not a separate file but a component of the directory itself.

Deleted Files

Deleted files refer to files intentionally or unintentionally removed from a storage medium, such as a computer's hard drive, solid-state drive (SSD), or other storage devices. When a file is deleted from a storage medium, the file is moved to the recycle bin or trash folder, which will be discussed later in this chapter. The file can be restored to its original location if needed. However, emptying the recycle bin or using specialized deletion methods can permanently remove the file from the system, bypassing the recycle bin.

When a file is deleted from the file system, the actual content of the file may still exist on the storage medium until new data overwrite it. It is often possible to recover deleted files, at least partially, using specialized tools and techniques until new data overwrite them. Deleted files can be of various types, including documents, images, videos, audio files, program files, and more. The recovery of deleted files can be relevant in various scenarios, such as data recovery, forensic investigations, or restoring accidentally deleted files. It is important to note that the success of file recovery depends on several factors. These factors include the file system used, the time since the deletion, and whether any new data has overwritten the storage space previously occupied by the deleted file.

Solid-state drives (SSDs) are very common today, almost ubiquitous. SSDs implement garbage collection. Garbage collection basically copies data still in use to a new block and then deletes all data from the old one. A more detailed discussion of garbage collection requires at least some understanding of SSDs. Flash memory is divided into blocks which are further divided into pages. When data is saved, it is written on a page level. When data is deleted, it is erased on a block level. Before data can be erased, all the valid data from the original block must first be copied and written into the empty pages of a new block. To write to an already used block of data, an SSD controller would first copy all valid data and write it to empty pages of a different block, erase all the cells in the current block (both valid and invalid data), and then start writing new data to the newly erased block. This process can also affect the ability to recover deleted files.

OSForensics is one of many tools that can be used to recover deleted files. Once you have conducted a search for deleted files, you only have to click the file to be recovered. Figure 4-1 depicts the use of this utility to recover one's deleted files (Easttom, 2021; OSForensics, 2021).

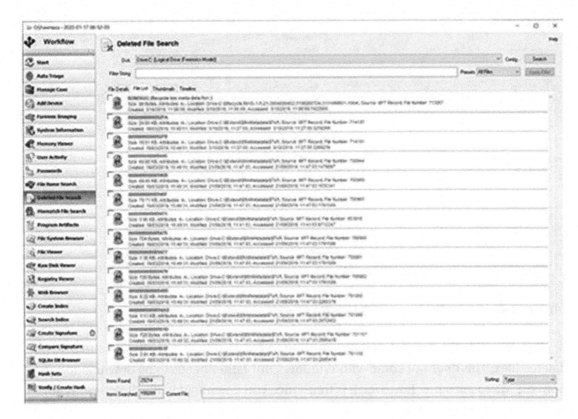

Figure 4-1. *OSForensics recover deleted files screen*

You can also view deleted files in Autopsy; this is shown in Figure 4-2.

Name	Location	▽ Modified Time	Change Time	Access Time	Created Time
x [parent folder]	/img_MattMcDaniel.E01/vol_vol6/$Extend/$Deleted/00370...	2022-05-23 17:40:38 CDT	2022-05-23 17:40:38 ...	2022-05-23 17:40:38 CDT	2019-11-29 03:07:35 CST
x [parent folder]	/img_MattMcDaniel.E01/vol_vol6/$Extend/$Deleted/00060...	2022-05-23 17:40:38 CDT	2022-05-23 17:40:38 ...	2022-05-23 17:40:38 CDT	2019-11-29 03:07:35 CST
x [parent folder]	/img_MattMcDaniel.E01/vol_vol6/$Extend/$Deleted/002E0...	2022-05-23 17:40:38 CDT	2022-05-23 17:40:38 ...	2022-05-23 17:40:38 CDT	2019-11-29 03:07:35 CST
x [parent folder]	/img_MattMcDaniel.E01/vol_vol6/$Extend/$Deleted/00520...	2022-05-23 17:40:38 CDT	2022-05-23 17:40:38 ...	2022-05-23 17:40:38 CDT	2019-11-29 03:07:35 CST
x [parent folder]	/img_MattMcDaniel.E01/vol_vol6/$Extend/$Deleted/00240...	2022-05-23 17:40:38 CDT	2022-05-23 17:40:38 ...	2022-05-23 17:40:38 CDT	2019-11-29 03:07:35 CST
x [parent folder]	/img_MattMcDaniel.E01/vol_vol6/$Extend/$Deleted/00650...	2022-05-23 17:40:38 CDT	2022-05-23 17:40:38 ...	2022-05-23 17:40:38 CDT	2019-11-29 03:07:35 CST
x [parent folder]	/img_MattMcDaniel.E01/vol_vol6/$Extend/$Deleted/00250...	2022-05-23 17:40:38 CDT	2022-05-23 17:40:38 ...	2022-05-23 17:40:38 CDT	2019-11-29 03:07:35 CST
x [parent folder]	/img_MattMcDaniel.E01/vol_vol6/$Extend/$Deleted/001D0...	2022-05-23 17:40:38 CDT	2022-05-23 17:40:38 ...	2022-05-23 17:40:38 CDT	2019-11-29 03:07:35 CST
x [parent folder]	/img_MattMcDaniel.E01/vol_vol6/$Extend/$Deleted/00190...	2022-05-23 17:40:38 CDT	2022-05-23 17:40:38 ...	2022-05-23 17:40:38 CDT	2019-11-29 03:07:35 CST
x [parent folder]	/img_MattMcDaniel.E01/vol_vol6/$Extend/$Deleted/006E0...	2022-05-23 17:40:38 CDT	2022-05-23 17:40:38 ...	2022-05-23 17:40:38 CDT	2019-11-29 03:07:35 CST
x [parent folder]	/img_MattMcDaniel.E01/vol_vol6/$Extend/$Deleted/003F0...	2022-05-23 17:40:38 CDT	2022-05-23 17:40:38 ...	2022-05-23 17:40:38 CDT	2019-11-29 03:07:35 CST
x [parent folder]	/img_MattMcDaniel.E01/vol_vol6/$Extend/$Deleted/000D0...	2022-05-23 17:40:38 CDT	2022-05-23 17:40:38 ...	2022-05-23 17:40:38 CDT	2019-11-29 03:07:35 CST
x [parent folder]	/img_MattMcDaniel.E01/vol_vol6/$Extend/$Deleted/000F0...	2022-05-23 17:40:38 CDT	2022-05-23 17:40:38 ...	2022-05-23 17:40:38 CDT	2019-11-29 03:07:35 CST
x [parent folder]	/img_MattMcDaniel.E01/vol_vol6/$Extend/$Deleted/00180...	2022-05-23 17:40:38 CDT	2022-05-23 17:40:38 ...	2022-05-23 17:40:38 CDT	2019-11-29 03:07:35 CST
x [parent folder]	/img_MattMcDaniel.E01/vol_vol6/$Extend/$Deleted/001B0...	2022-05-23 17:40:38 CDT	2022-05-23 17:40:38 ...	2022-05-23 17:40:38 CDT	2019-11-29 03:07:35 CST
x [parent folder]	/img_MattMcDaniel.E01/vol_vol6/$Extend/$Deleted/00280...	2022-05-23 17:40:38 CDT	2022-05-23 17:40:38 ...	2022-05-23 17:40:38 CDT	2019-11-29 03:07:35 CST
x [parent folder]	/img_MattMcDaniel.E01/vol_vol6/$Extend/$Deleted/00150...	2022-05-23 17:40:38 CDT	2022-05-23 17:40:38 ...	2022-05-23 17:40:38 CDT	2019-11-29 03:07:35 CST
x [parent folder]	/img_MattMcDaniel.E01/vol_vol6/$Extend/$Deleted/001C0...	2022-05-23 17:40:38 CDT	2022-05-23 17:40:38 ...	2022-05-23 17:40:38 CDT	2019-11-29 03:07:35 CST
x [parent folder]	/img_MattMcDaniel.E01/vol_vol6/$Extend/$Deleted/00210...	2022-05-23 17:40:38 CDT	2022-05-23 17:40:38 ...	2022-05-23 17:40:38 CDT	2019-11-29 03:07:35 CST
x [parent folder]	/img_MattMcDaniel.E01/vol_vol6/$Extend/$Deleted/01870...	2022-05-23 17:40:38 CDT	2022-05-23 17:40:38 ...	2022-05-23 17:40:38 CDT	2019-11-29 03:07:35 CST

Figure 4-2. *Autopsy view of deleted files*

Windows File Recovery is a command-line software utility from Microsoft to recover deleted files. This does not come with Windows, but rather needs to be downloaded from the Microsoft store; however, it is free. Once you download it, it will appear as an app as shown in Figure 4-3.

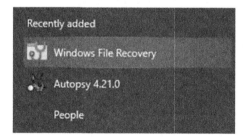

Figure 4-3. *Windows File Recovery app*

When you launch the Windows File Recovery app, a command prompt will be launched which conveniently gives you an overview of how to use the app. This is shown in Figure 4-4.

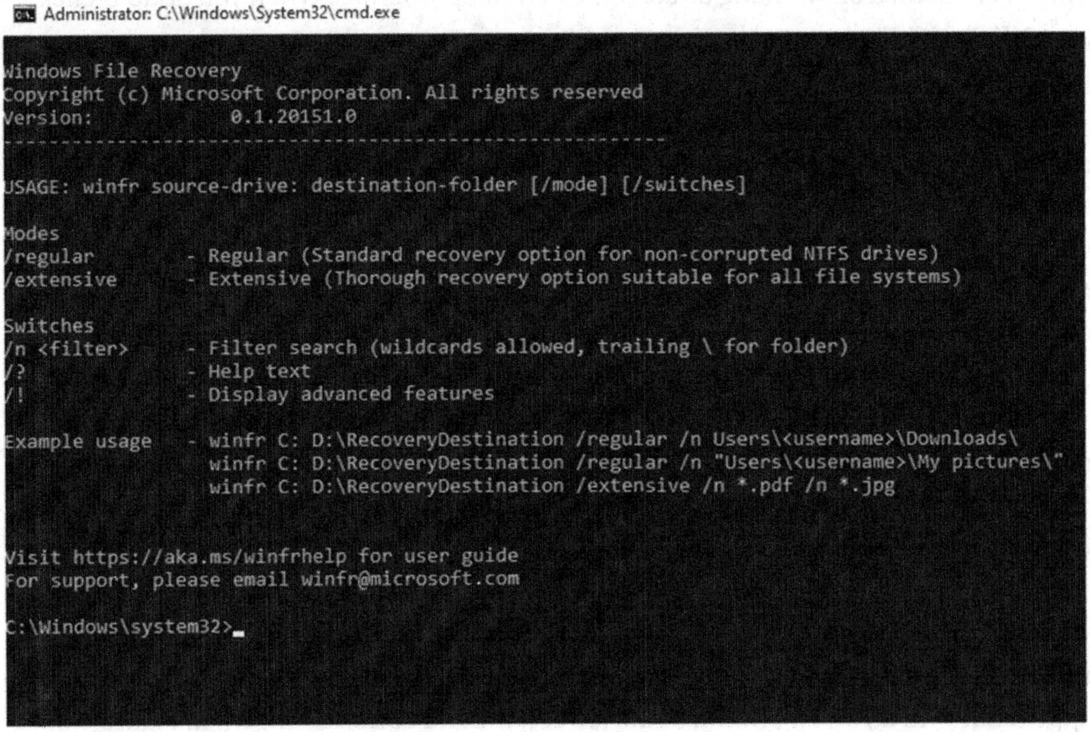

Figure 4-4. *Launch the Windows File Recovery app*

Individual Files

There are specific files in Windows that are artifacts. These files contain information that can be very informative. While most commercial forensics tools will recover these for you, it is important that you understand what the files are and what information they can provide.

.LNK Files

.LNK files serve as shortcuts or links to other files or folders. They provide an easy and convenient way to access frequently used items without needing to locate them manually. .LNK is the file extension associated with these shortcut files. For example, a shortcut to a Word document might have a file name like "Document Shortcut.lnk". .LNK files store information about the target file or folder they point to. This includes the target's path, icon, working directory, and other properties. When you double-click an .LNK file, it is interpreted by the operating system, which then opens the associated target item.

.LNK files are visually distinguished by a small arrow overlay icon, which indicates that they are shortcuts and not the actual target files themselves. One can create .LNK files in various ways. The most common method is by right-clicking a file, folder, or application and selecting "Create shortcut" from the context menu. This action creates a new .LNK file in the same location as the original item. .LNK files can be customized. One can change the shortcut's target, icon, and other properties by right-clicking the .LNK file and selecting "Properties."

.LNK files can be located anywhere on your computer, including the desktop, folders, or pinned to the taskbar or Start menu. It's important to note that .LNK files only serve as shortcuts and do not contain the actual content of the target file or folder. If the target is moved or deleted, the .LNK file will no longer function correctly and may display an error indicating the target is missing. To create a shortcut from the Windows desktop, simply place the cursor on the file or folder you wish to create a shortcut for, right-click, and select "Create shortcut." Once you click "Create shortcut," an identical icon will appear but with an arrow symbol in the lower left-hand corner as shown in Figure 4-5. Next, right-click the shortcut file, select properties, and you will see the image in Figure 4-6 (SANS, 2023; Easttom, 2021).

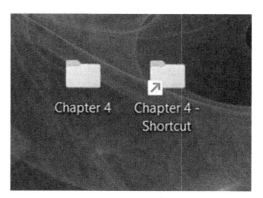

Figure 4-5. *File folder and shortcut folder*

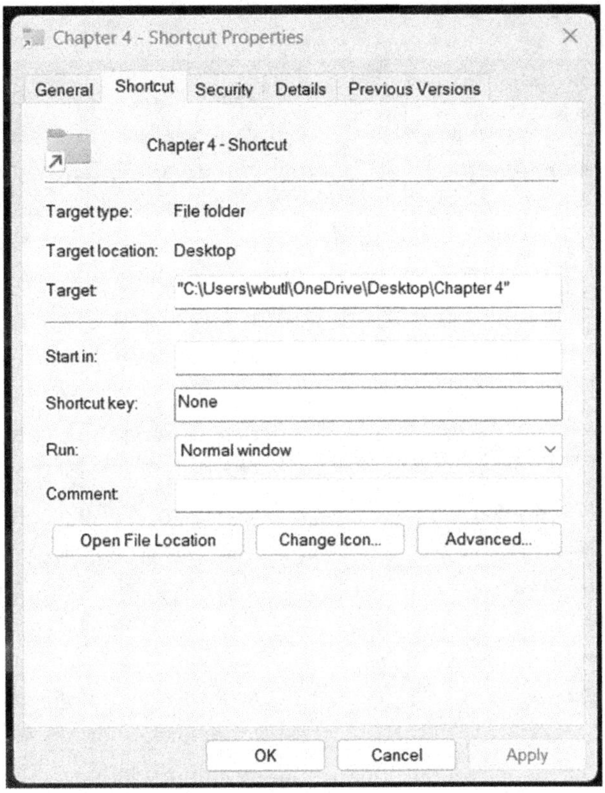

Figure 4-6. *Properties of the .LNK file*

The .LNK files as well as other types of file artifacts can also be viewed using Autopsy as shown in Figure 4-7.

Recent Documents

Table | Thumbnail

Source File	Path	Date/Time	D
All Tasks.lnk	No preferred path found	2020-05-19 22:26:09 CDT	M
ms-windows-store--switchwindows-.lnk	No preferred path found	2020-05-19 15:43:49 CDT	M
The Internet.lnk	No preferred path found	2020-05-19 15:43:49 CDT	M
Uninstall a program.lnk	No preferred path found	2020-05-19 22:26:09 CDT	M
March 28th Pipeline.LNK	No preferred path found	2022-03-28 12:25:19 CDT	M
April 12th Pipeline .LNK	No preferred path found	2022-04-11 18:09:27 CDT	M
April 13th Pipeline .LNK	No preferred path found	2022-04-12 17:33:02 CDT	M
April 18th Pipeline.LNK	No preferred path found	2022-04-18 10:02:22 CDT	M
April 4th Pipeline.LNK	No preferred path found	2022-04-04 12:51:40 CDT	M
Desktop.LNK	No preferred path found	2021-07-07 17:12:42 CDT	M
report - 2022-04-04T115857.226.LNK	No preferred path found	2022-04-04 12:00:02 CDT	M
report - 2022-04-11T180022.395.LNK	No preferred path found	2022-04-11 18:00:37 CDT	M
report - 2022-04-13T093622.286.LNK	No preferred path found	2022-04-13 09:36:57 CDT	M
report1648752291690.LNK	No preferred path found	2022-03-31 13:47:37 CDT	M
report1648752831099.LNK	No preferred path found	2022-03-31 13:54:03 CDT	M
REL Set Up Form (5)_JG (2).LNK	No preferred path found	2021-09-15 14:48:04 CDT	M
Signatures.LNK	No preferred path found	2022-03-07 10:49:49 CST	M
February 9th Pipeline.LNK	No preferred path found	2022-03-09 11:30:25 CST	M
report - 2022-03-09T112528.187.LNK	No preferred path found	2022-03-09 11:28:33 CST	M
CORE Accounts Pyramid.LNK	No preferred path found	2022-03-09 18:33:54 CST	M

Figure 4-7. *Viewing files (.LNK) in Autopsy*

Autopsy also provides the means to view different types of files; this is shown in Figure 4-8.

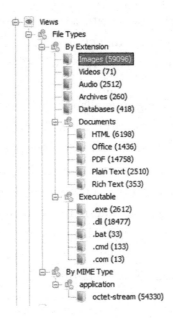

Figure 4-8. *Viewing all files in Autopsy*

Most forensics tools will provide some level of access to viewing multiple file types.

Log Files

The purpose of log files is to provide a detailed record of events, errors, warnings, and other activities that occur within a system. Log files help users diagnose issues, identify patterns, and monitor system health and performance. Log files typically contain information such as timestamps, event descriptions, error codes, user actions, system states, network activities, and other relevant details depending on the type of log file (SANS, 2020).

There are several types of log files, including system, application, security, network, and web server logs. System logs record events and activities related to the operating system, such as startup/shutdown events, hardware events, driver errors, and system crashes. Application logs capture events and actions specific to individual applications, such as error messages, warnings, user activities, and application-specific events. Security logs provide information about security-related events, including login attempts, access control violations, changes to system security settings, and audit trail records. Network logs record network activities, such as network connections, traffic statistics, firewall events, and intrusion detection system (IDS) alerts. Web server logs track web server activities, including HTTP requests, access attempts, errors, and visitor statistics.

Log files are often analyzed using specialized tools or scripts that help extract relevant information, identify patterns or anomalies, and gain insights into system behavior, performance, or security incidents. Log files are typically stored on the local system or centralized log servers. The retention period for log files may vary depending on the organization's policies, compliance requirements, or the importance of the information contained in the logs. Log rotation mechanisms are often implemented to manage log file sizes, prevent excessive disk usage, and improve performance. Log rotation involves archiving or purging older log files to make space for new entries. Log files are essential for system administrators, IT professionals, developers, and security analysts to monitor and maintain computer systems and networks' health, performance, and security. They are valuable sources of information for troubleshooting issues, investigating incidents, and ensuring system integrity (Crowdstrike, 2023).

OSForensics allows one to scan a drive or folder for loading a few Windows event logs from different systems. Also supported is the event viewer, advanced filtering capabilities, regular expressions, and export to formats such as CSV, TXT, or HTML. Figure 4-9 depicts the use of OSForensics to select and view a log.

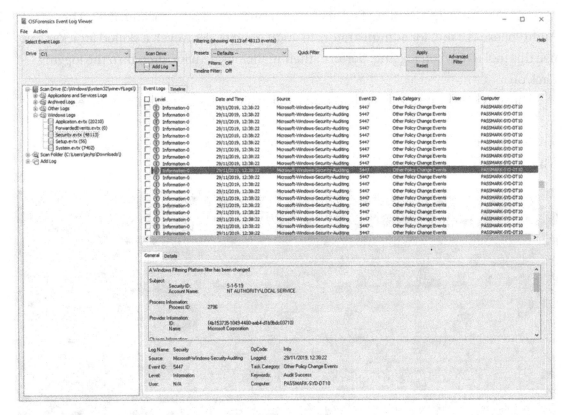

Figure 4-9. *OSForensics Event Log Viewer screen*

Windows event logs have number designations, or Event IDs. It is extremely unlikely that you would be able to memorize even a significant number of these, much less all. Fortunately, Microsoft lists them all online. You merely need to search for "Windows Event ID XXX." You can also find websites with many of the more common Event IDs (https://support.microsoft.com/en-us/kb/977519 is a good start). Here are a few that can be of interest:

4902: Changes to the Audit Policy such as using Auditpol.exe.

4741: A computer account was created.

4742: A computer account was changed.

4782: The password hash of an account was accessed.

4728: A member was added to a security-enabled global group.

4720: A user account was created.

4767: A user account was unlocked.

133

Any of these could be part of normal operations. However, consider 4902. The AuditPol.exe is a tool for administrators to audit policies. However, a skilled attacker can use this tool to turn off logging, perform their malicious activity, then turn the logging back on.

The SANS Institute also has produced a tool called EvtxECmd which is an explorer for Windows event logs (SANS, 2020). This tool was developed by Eric Zimmerman. You will need to download the tool, then launch it from the command line. You will first see what is shown in Figure 4-10.

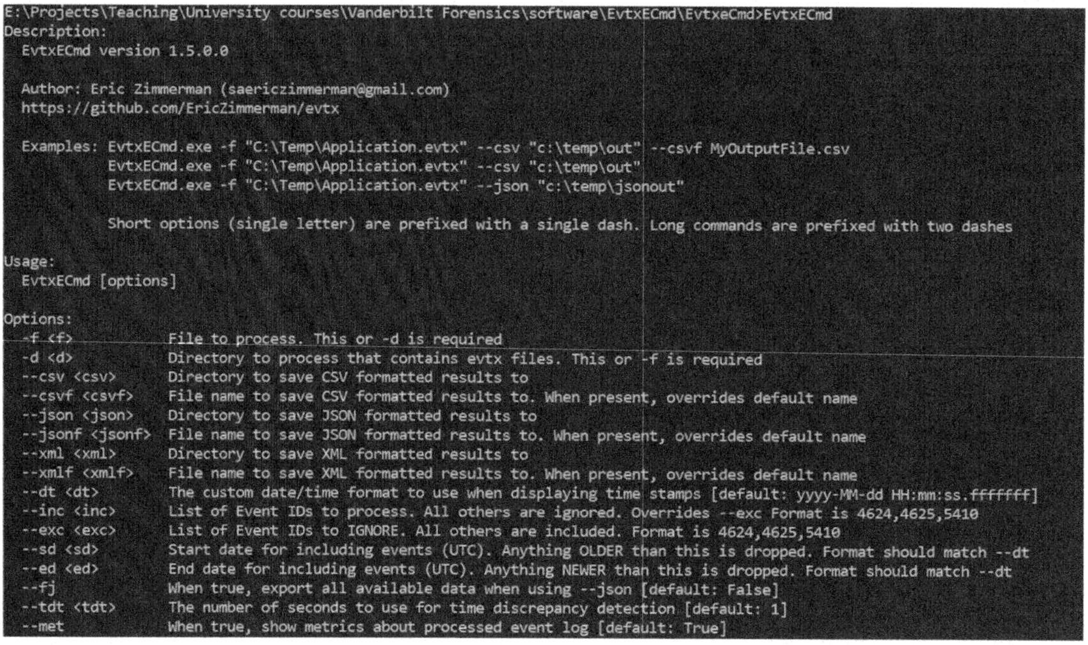

Figure 4-10. *EvtxECmd viewer*

There are, of course, other tools to view the Windows event logs. In fact, Windows itself has a built-in event viewer, shown in Figure 4-11.

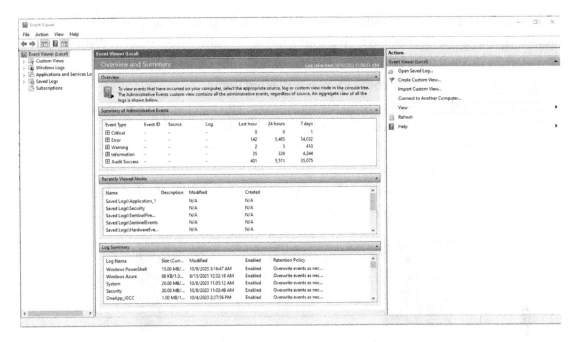

Figure 4-11. *Windows event viewer*

The existence of so many event log viewers should indicate how important these logs are. One will often find important evidence in the Windows event logs.

Recycle Bin

The main purpose of the recycle bin is to provide a safety net for deleted files. It allows users to recover accidentally deleted files or folders easily. The recycle bin is usually on the desktop, represented by an icon resembling a trash bin or recycling bin. You can also access it by opening Windows Explorer and navigating to the "Recycle Bin" folder. When you delete a file or folder, it is moved to the recycle bin rather than being permanently deleted from the system. You can access the recycle bin, select the items you want to restore, and then choose the "Restore" option to return them to their original location (this is shown in Figure 4-12).

In addition to restoring deleted items to their original location, you can also choose other options from the recycle bin context menu. These options include "Restore" (to return the items to their original location), "Cut" (to move the items to a different location), or "Delete" (to permanently remove the items from the recycle bin). The recycle bin has a storage limit, which determines the maximum amount of disk space allocated for deleted files. When the limit is reached, older files are automatically purged from the recycle bin to make room for newly deleted items.

To permanently delete files from the recycle bin, you can choose the "Empty Recycle Bin" option from the context menu. Once the recycle bin is emptied, the files are no longer recoverable using standard methods. It's important to note that the recycle bin is specific to the Windows operating system and behaves differently from directly deleting files using the "Shift+Delete" command, which bypasses the recycle bin and permanently deletes files immediately.

Figure 4-12. *The recycle bin and the properties screen*

OSForensics will allow you to view the recycle bin contents as shown in Figure 4-13.

User Activity

Device to Scan: ★ Live acquisition - Current machine ★   Quick Scan   Create Full Timeline

Activity Filters: Not active

Type keyword and press Enter to search   Config...

	Original File Name	Original File Path	File Size	Date Deleted	Username	Recycle Bin Name
All (67829)	walletdata.zip	C:\Users\User\Downloads\	1.25 GB	7/19/2023, 12:09:06	User	$RPCQG18.zip
Most Recently Used (3978)	What War Games Tell ...	C:\Users\User\Downloads\	21.21 KB	7/19/2023, 12:09:06	User	$RDY2U2V.docx
Installed Programs (2045)	RUSSIAN EXPANSION ...	C:\Users\User\Downloads\	23.48 KB	7/19/2023, 12:09:06	User	$RLW5IS4.docx
Autorun Commands (27)	Aspen-M-3_coherence...	C:\Users\User\Downloads\	1.21 KB	7/19/2023, 12:09:06	User	$RRLRKTQ.csv
Clipboard (1)	INTERPOL_DFI._Global...	C:\Users\User\Downloads\	1.54 MB	7/17/2023, 8:30:01	User	$RT67EW8.pdf
Event Logs (16545)	OneDrive_1_7-13-202...	C:\Users\User\Downloads\	2.28 GB	7/17/2023, 8:30:01	User	$RALINYH.zip
UserAssist (342)	Windows Memory For...	C:\Users\User\Downloads\	3.66 MB	7/17/2023, 8:30:01	User	$R8OC9VX.docx
Jump Lists (11770)	Cybersecurity and Qu...	C:\Users\User\Downloads\	44.41 KB	7/17/2023, 8:30:01	User	$RLDSMDZ.docx
Shellbags (4578)	Windows Memory For...	C:\Users\User\Downloads\	6.73 MB	7/17/2023, 8:30:01	User	$RKKZVG9.docx
Windows 10 Timeline (0)	QuantumComputingW...	E:\Projects\Teaching\Univ...	6.04 MB	7/16/2023, 17:37:46	User	$RGJKZWL.zip
Cortana History (0)	QuantumComputingW...	E:\Projects\Teaching\Univ...	17.78 MB	7/16/2023, 17:37:46	User	$RW6KHD7.pptx
Recycle Bin (45)	QuantumComputingBe...	E:\Projects\Teaching\Univ...	4.43 MB	7/16/2023, 17:37:46	User	$RN3KW5W.ppt
Shimcache (0)	QuantumNetworking.p...	E:\Projects\Teaching\Univ...	14.79 MB	7/16/2023, 17:37:46	User	$R0OHHD7.pptx
SRUM (0)	dosbmon1.png	C:\Users\User\Documents\	155.6 KB	7/6/2023, 10:59:04	User	$R4RKV4Z.png
Prefetch (0)	dosbmon2.png	C:\Users\User\Documents\	211.8 KB	7/6/2023, 10:59:04	User	$RKUSHL9.png
Windows Search (0)	dosattack.png	C:\Users\User\Documents\	63.63 KB	7/6/2023, 10:59:04	User	$RPER4T7.png
BAM/DAM (94)	dosattack2.png	C:\Users\User\Documents\	122.0 KB	7/6/2023, 10:59:04	User	$R4K4INT.png
Anti-Forensics Artifacts (10)	dosattackpart2.png	C:\Users\User\Documents\	65.65 KB	7/6/2023, 10:59:04	User	$RPXO9SP.png
Downloads (227)	dosattackpart2b.png	C:\Users\User\Documents\	132.6 KB	7/6/2023, 10:59:04	User	$RAEAIGB.png
Browser History (25571)	doshping1.png	C:\Users\User\Documents\	13.98 KB	7/6/2023, 10:59:04	User	$RRVPZFS.png
Search Terms (30)	doshping2.png	C:\Users\User\Documents\	98.78 KB	7/6/2023, 10:59:04	User	$RZ8JK9Y.png
Website Logins (386)	doscurlogin.png	C:\Users\User\Documents\	110.3 KB	7/6/2023, 10:59:04	User	$R7FGP7G.png
Form History (882)	DoSPHP.png	C:\Users\User\Documents\	86.49 KB	7/6/2023, 10:59:04	User	$RV37QPA.png
Bookmarks (502)	DoSPHP2.png	C:\Users\User\Documents\	313.1 KB	7/6/2023, 10:59:04	User	$RJ9STE1.png
Chat Logs (0)	DoSIRSSI.png	C:\Users\User\Documents\	73.43 KB	7/6/2023, 10:59:04	User	$RGA8YT6.png
Peer-to-Peer (0)	DoSIRSS2I.png	C:\Users\User\Documents\	265.8 KB	7/6/2023, 10:59:04	User	$RBMFBA0.png
WLAN (10)	DoSIRSS3I.png	C:\Users\User\Documents\	69.28 KB	7/6/2023, 10:59:04	User	$RP2A6J2.png
Cryptocurrency Wallet Apps (1)	DoSIRSS34.png	C:\Users\User\Documents\	31.26 KB	7/6/2023, 10:59:04	User	$RXO81QO.png
Cookies (0)	DoSIRSS35.png	C:\Users\User\Documents\	177.4 KB	7/6/2023, 10:59:04	User	$RU0YHUC.png
Browser Custom Dictionary (0)	DoSIRSS36.png	C:\Users\User\Documents\	125.7 KB	7/6/2023, 10:59:04	User	$R3GA0F9.png
USB (783)	DoSIRSS37.png	C:\Users\User\Documents\	459.3 KB	7/6/2023, 10:59:04	User	$R4DJUPQ.png
Mounted Volumes (2)	DoSIRSS38.png	C:\Users\User\Documents\	43.36 KB	7/6/2023, 10:59:04	User	$REDM5OU.png
Mobile Backups (0)	DoSIRSS39.png	C:\Users\User\Documents\	293.0 KB	7/6/2023, 10:59:04	User	$RHY4U8U.png
	DoSIRSS310.png	C:\Users\User\Documents\	99.14 KB	7/6/2023, 10:59:04	User	$RNAZ7CT.png
	doshomepate.png	C:\Users\User\Documents\	81.16 KB	7/6/2023, 10:59:04	User	$RVSMASJ.png
	doshomepate2.png	C:\Users\User\Documents\	205.5 KB	7/6/2023, 10:59:04	User	$RUMOTPB.png
	doshomepate3.png	C:\Users\User\Documents\	293.5 KB	7/6/2023, 10:59:04	User	$R052ADW.png

Figure 4-13. *Recycle bin in OSForensics*

When reviewing the recycle bin, it is important to note not only what has been deleted but when. A sudden increase in deletions in a short period of time may warrant further examination.

I30 File

When you access files and folders on a Windows system, you do not interact directly with the "I30" attribute. Instead, it is managed by the NTFS file system itself, working behind the scenes to facilitate file system operations and directory navigation. If you have encountered any specific reference to an "I30 file," it may be a misunderstanding or a reference to a particular file or concept in a specific context. Additional information about the specific context or source would help provide a more accurate response.

The NTFS $I30 (directory) can be scanned for evidence of deleted files. The NTFS file system maintains an index of all files/directories that belong to a directory called the $I30 attribute. Every directory in the file system contains an $I30 attribute that must be maintained whenever there are changes to the directory's contents. When files or folders are removed from the directory, the $I30 index records are rearranged accordingly. However, rearranging of the index records may leave remnants of the deleted file/folder entry within the slack space. This can be useful in forensics analysis for identifying files that may have existed on the drive.

OSForensics can display the index records stored in the $I30 attribute, including deleted records that were found in the slack space. The $I30 index records list can be viewed by opening an NTFS directory in the File System Browser with the internal viewer (PassMark Software, 2023).

Figure 4-14 depicts OSForensics displaying the index records stored in the $I30 attribute, including deleted records found in the slack space. The $I30 index records list can be viewed by opening an NTFS directory in the File System Browser with the internal viewer.

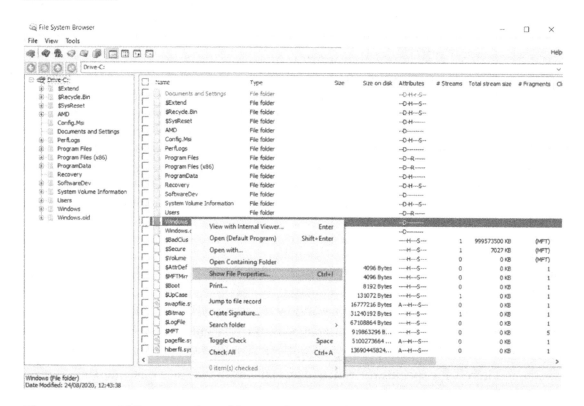

Figure 4-14. *OSForensics list of $I30 index records is displayed*

Switching to the "Metadata View" tab displays the list of $I30 index records. This is shown in Figure 4-15. Deleted records found in the slack space are highlighted in red. Note that the presence of a deleted file/folder record doesn't necessarily mean that it no longer exists in the directory; it may just be that the record was rearranged due to changes to the $I30 attribute and that the record found in the slack space is the previous, stale version.

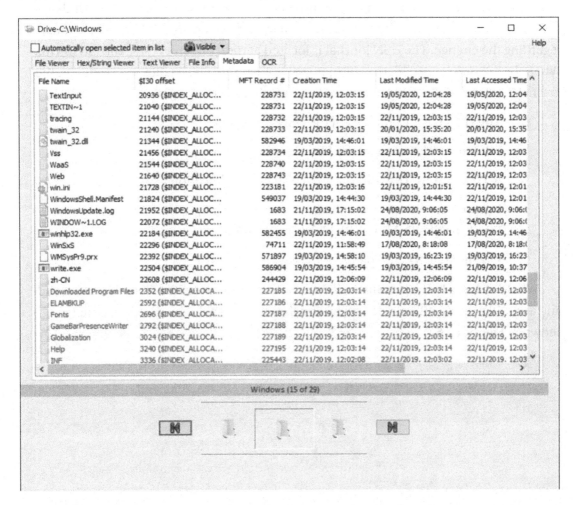

Figure 4-15. *OSForensics list of $I30 index records is displayed*

USN Journal

USN or Update Sequence Number is used by the system's File History to determine which files have changed since the last backup, thus enabling the backup of only changed files. However, this does also provide a record of all files that have been changed. Any time a change is made to a volume, a record is added to the USN journal (also sometimes called the change journal). Records are identified by a 64-bit Update Sequence Number. Each record contains the name of the file, the USN, and information regarding the change. The USN journal is located at root_directory\$Extend\$UsnJrnl. When the volume is created, the USN journal is an empty file. As files are modified, the journal is extended. Data contained in the journal includes

- **The USN ID**: A unique ID of the USN record

- **Filename**: The name of the file that is being affected

- **A Timestamp**: The timestamp for the file modification

- **Reason**: The specific modification, such as DATA_TRUNCATION, DATA_EXTEND, FILE_CREATE, FILE_DELETE, etc.

- **Parent MFT ID**: The parent record within the MFT

Windows has a built-in utility called fsutil that can be executed from the command line and will provide information regarding the USN journal. The use of this utility is shown in Figure 4-16.

```
E:\>fsutil USN
---- USN Commands Supported ----

createJournal            Create a USN journal
deleteJournal            Delete a USN journal
enableRangeTracking      Enable write range tracking for a volume
enumData                 Enumerate USN data
queryJournal             Query the USN data for a volume
readJournal              Reads the USN records in the USN journal
readData                 Read the USN data for a file

E:\>fsUTIL USN readJournal
Usage  : fsutil usn readJournal <volume pathname> [options]
Options : minVer=<number> - Minimum Major Version of USN_RECORD to return. Default=2.
        : maxVer=<number> - Maximum Major Version of USN_RECORD to return. Default=4.
        : startUsn=<USN number> - USN to start reading the USN journal from. Default=0.
        : csv - Print the USN records in CSV format.
        : wait - wait for more records to be added to the USN journal.
        : tail - starts reading at the end of the USN journal. If wait is not specified it will just return. Overrides a
ny startusn value.

    Eg : fsutil usn readJournal C:
       : fsutil usn readJournal C: minVer=2 maxVer=3 startUsn=88
       : fsutil usn readJournal C: startUsn=0xF00
       : fsutil usn readJournal C: wait
       : fsutil usn readJournal C: wait tail
       : fsutil usn readJournal C: csv

E:\>
```

Figure 4-16. *fsutil USN*

Major forensics tools such as OSForensics, AccessData FTK, and Guidance Software's EnCase all also provide tools for examining the USN journal.

$Standard_Information vs. $File_Name

Many Windows users and even many forensic analysts don't realize that in Windows, a file with a single name actually has 12 timestamps: 4 timestamps are derived from the $STANDARD_INFORMATION attribute in a file record, 4 timestamps are derived from the $FILE_NAME attribute in the same file record, and 4 timestamps are derived from the $FILE_NAME attribute in an index record ($I30) of a parent directory. The $STANDARD_INFORMATION attribute contains the file ownership information together with the file permissions and associated dates and times. The permission flags are shown in the following table:

Flag Value	Description
0x0001	Read only
0x0002	Hidden

(continued)

Flag Value	Description
0x0004	System
0x0020	Archive
0x0040	Device
0x0080	Normal
0x0100	Temporary
0x0200	Sparse file
0x0400	Reparse point
0x0800	Compressed
0x1000	Offline
0x2000	Content not indexed
0x4000	Encrypted

The fact that there are numerous timestamps, not all readily viewable by the user, can be quite helpful. There is an attack referred to as timestomping, which consists of modifying timestamps of a file to evade digital forensics investigations. However, it is quite difficult for someone to modify all the various timestamps. Many people are not even aware of the numerous timestamps.

Autorun Commands

It can be of interest to know what commands are set to run automatically on a Windows computer. It is quite common to find malware is loaded here. OSForensics provides an easy way to view this in the User Activity section. This is shown in Figure 4-17.

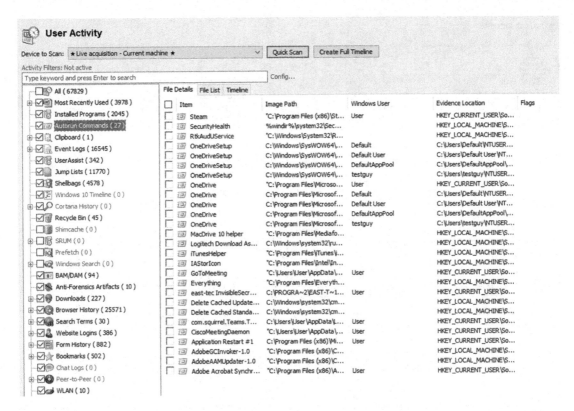

Figure 4-17. OSForensics autorun

Clearly, this is something that should be examined in any forensic investigation.

Browser Artifacts

The browser can be a source of both direct evidence and circumstantial or supporting evidence. Obviously, in cases of child pornography, the browser might contain direct evidence of the specific crime. You may also find direct evidence in the case of cyber stalking. However, if you suspect someone of creating a virus that infected a network, you will probably only find indirect evidence such as the person having searched virus creation/programming-related topics.

Even if the person erases their history, it is still possible to retrieve it. Windows stores a lot of information (such as web addresses, search queries, and recently opened files) in a file called index.dat. Most forensics tools can extract a wide range of evidence from a computer. OSForensics has multiple options for this. Among them is Recent Activity, shown in Figure 4-18.

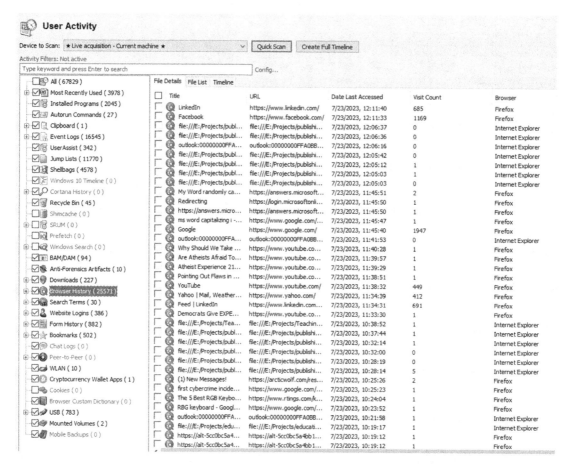

Figure 4-18. *Browser activity*

Autopsy also provides a view of browser activity; this is shown in Figure 4-19.

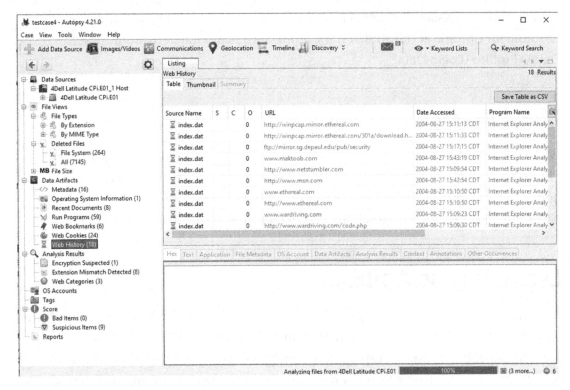

Figure 4-19. *Browser activity*

Stored Credentials

Anytime you save a password in Mozilla Firefox, it is stored. It is in fact in a .json file at %USERPROFILE%\AppData\Roaming\Mozilla\Firefox\Profiles\logins.js. Being a JSON file, it can be opened with any standard text editor. A typical entry looks like this:

```
[{"id":1,"hostname":"https://www.facebook.com","htt
pRealm":null,"formSubmitURL":"https://www.facebook.
com","usernameField":"email","passwordField":"pass","encryptedUsername":"
XXXXREDACTEDXXXXXXXX encryptedPassword":"XXXXREDACTEDXXXXXXXX","guid":
"{645a0929-6949-427d-b6df-212671af4d2f}","encType":1,"timeCreated":16315673
00978,"timeLastUsed":1639004618746,"timePasswordChanged":1631567300978,
"timesUsed":2},
```

For obvious reasons, the actual passwords have been redacted. Similar data can be found for Chrome at USERPROFILE%\AppData\Local\Google\Chrome\User Data\<Profile>\Login Data.

Cloud Storage

When a user is utilizing cloud storage, there are still artifacts on the local computer. The artifacts are in slightly different locations depending on the cloud service in question. OneDrive can be found at %USERPROFILE%\OneDrive. Box data is found at %USERPROFILE%\Box. Dropbox stores local data at %USERPROFILE%\Dropbox.

Less Common Artifacts

The artifacts discussed previously in this chapter are common and will likely be useful in almost any Windows forensic examination. In this section, we will briefly look at some artifacts that are only useful in specific, narrowly defined scenarios. It should also be noted that these artifacts are not always displayed by forensics software. You may need to manually examine them.

Windows Error Reporting (WER) Forensics

Windows reports errors with software. This will usually only be of interest in malware investigations. Malware is frequently not developed with extensive software engineering and testing methods, so errors are common. You can find these error reports at

> C:\ProgramData\Microsoft\Windows\WER\ReportArchive
>
> C:\ProgramData\Microsoft\Windows\WER\ReportQueue
>
> C:\Users\XXX\AppData\Local\Microsoft\Windows\WER\ReportArchive
>
> C:\Users\XXX\AppData\Local\Microsoft\Windows\WER\ReportQueu

The reports can be viewed with a standard text editor. Figure 4-20 shows an example of a Windows Error Report.

```
Report.wer - Notepad                                          –  □  :
File  Edit  Format  View  Help
Version=1
EventType=MoAppCrash
EventTime=133180982295400508
ReportType=2
Consent=1
UploadTime=133180982297250044
ReportStatus=268435456
ReportIdentifier=7438df83-00fe-4a4c-909e-
5b453128d73b
IntegratorReportIdentifier=9addd8fd-820f-465c-
81d5-b06b3cdcd1e5
Wow64Host=34404
Wow64Guest=332
NsAppName=praid:App
AppSessionGuid=00001bc0-0001-0038-bac4-
506a7625d901
```

Figure 4-20. *Windows Error Report*

This particular report is not from malware, but rather an Adobe Acrobat Crash. Furthermore, Figure 4-20 is only showing the beginning of the report. As one scrolls through it, many interesting items can be found. Most importantly for a malware investigation is a list of all DLLs that the software loaded.

RDP Cache Forensics

Remote Desktop Protocol is used to access a Windows computer from a different computer. Attackers can sometimes use this to access a target machine. You can locate and examine the RDP cache at C:\Users\XXX\AppData\Local\Microsoft\Terminal Server Client\Cache.

Windows Timeline

In addition to storing events in various artifacts and in the Windows Registry (which we will examine in Chapters 5 and 6), Windows maintains a database of timeline events. This can be found at C:\Users\<profile>\AppData\Local\ConnectedDevicesPlatform\<account-ID>\ActivitiesCache.db. This was first introduced in an update to Windows 10.

The .db format is an SQLite database. Fortunately, there are a number of free SQLite tools available for download on the Internet. SQLite stores the entire database (definitions, tables, indices, and the data itself) as a single cross-platform file on a host machine. It implements this simple design by locking the entire database file during writing. SQLite read operations can be multitasked, though writes can only be performed sequentially. D. Richard Hipp designed SQLite in the spring of 2000 while working for General Dynamics on contract with the US Navy.

- **DB Browser**: https://sqlitebrowser.org

- **SQLite Forensic Explorer**: www.sqliteviewer.org/database/

- **SQLite Viewer for Chrome**: There is an extension for Chrome that allows you to view SQLite databases. You can find it at https://chrome.google.com/webstore/detail/sqlite-viewer/golagekponhmgfoofmlepfobdmhpajia/related?hl=en

- **SQLite Viewer**: https://inloop.github.io/sqlite-viewer/

For demonstration purposes, DB Browser will be used. When first opening the database, you should see what is shown in Figure 4-21.

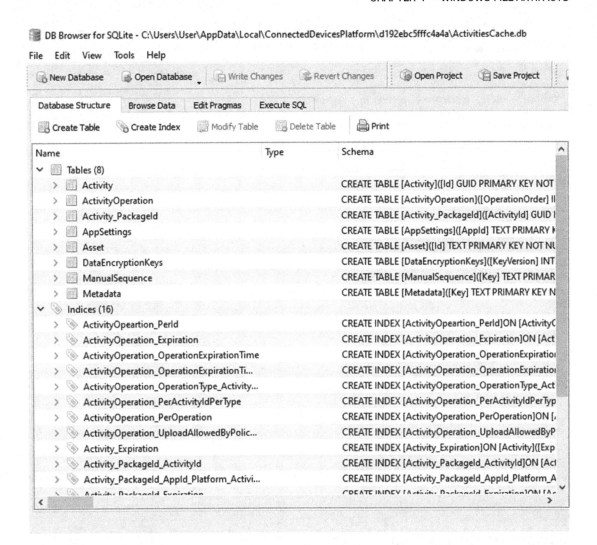

Figure 4-21. *DB Browser*

Next, you select the Browse Data tab and pick a specific table you wish to browse, as shown in Figure 4-22.

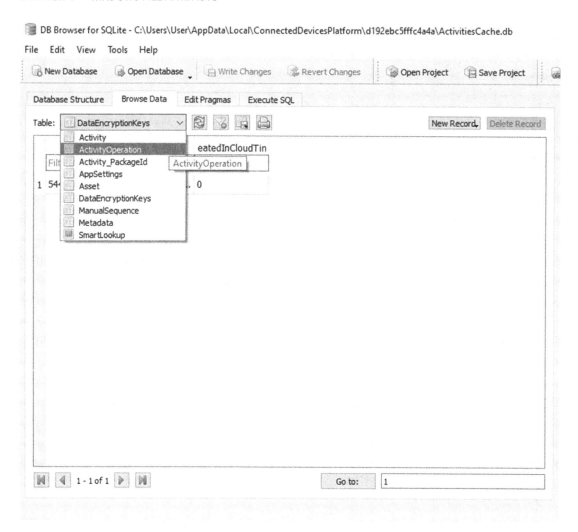

Figure 4-22. *Browsing Windows timeline*

ActivitiesCache.db contains the following tables: Activity, Activity_PackageId, ActivityAssetCache, ActivityOperation, AppSettings, ManualSequence, and Metadata. The ones that hold the most interest for investigators are Activity_PackageId and Activity. The Activity_PackageId table contains records for applications, including paths for executable files, names of executable files, and expiration times for these records. Values located in the Expiration Time column are stored in Epoch Time format. These records are only kept for 30 days but can contain information about files that are no longer on the drive.

The Activity table has the following fields: Id, AppId, PackageIdHash, AppActivityId, ActivityType, ActivityStatus, ParentActivityId, Tag, Group, MatchId, LastModifiedTime, ExpirationTime, Payload, Priority, IsLocalOnly, PlatformDeviceId, CreatedInCloud, StartTime, EndTime, LastModifiedOnClient, GroupAppActivityId, ClipboardPayload, EnterpriseId, OriginalLastModifiedOnClient, and ETag.

Browser Extensions

Browser extensions can be useful in web hacking/malware investigations. It is possible that malware on the victim machine was installed as a browser extension. You can find these extensions at the following locations:

Firefox 4-25

- %USERPROFILE%\AppData\Roaming\Mozilla\Firefox\ Profiles\<randomtext>.default\extensions.sqlite

- %USERPROFILE%\AppData\Roaming\Mozilla\Firefox\ Profiles\<randomtext>.default\addons.sqlite

Firefox 26+

- %USERPROFILE%\AppData\Roaming\Mozilla\Firefox\ Profiles\<randomtext>.default\addons.json

- %USERPROFILE%\AppData\Roaming\Mozilla\Firefox\ Profiles\<randomtext>.default\extensions.json

Chrome/Edge

- %USERPROFILE%\AppData\Local\Google\Chrome\User Data\<Profile>\Extensions\<GUID>\<version>

- %USERPROFILE%\AppData\Local\Microsoft\Edge\User Data\<Profile>\Extensions\<GUID>\<version>

These can be useful and, again, many forensic tools won't necessarily report these items. In addition to browser extensions, other interesting information can be found in the UserProfile\AppData\ directory, such as

Email attachments: %USERPROFILE%\AppData\Local\Microsoft\Outlook

Skype history: C:\%USERPROFILE%\AppData\Roaming\Skype\<skype-name>

Conclusions

This chapter discussed several Windows file artifacts and their usefulness to the average user and forensic analyst. This chapter briefly covered valuable Windows file artifacts such as Deleted files, .LNK files, log files, recycle bin, and I30 file. We discussed how these artifacts can be used to protect one's computer and investigate events on that computer. Valuable knowledge, such as locating and recovering deleted files on one's hard drive, is essential today. Knowledge of available tools such as OSForensics and Autopsy is also helpful to those seeking to expand their knowledge on this subject.

References

Autopsy (2023). Autopsy Digital Forensics. www.autopsy.com/

Crowdstrike (2023). Log Files Explained. www.crowdstrike.com/cybersecurity-101/observability/log-file/

Easttom, C. (2021). System Forensics, Investigation, and Response (4th edition). Jones & Bartlett Learning, LLC.

OSForensics (2023). OSForensics 10. www.osforensics.com/

PassMark Software (2023a). How to scan NTFS $I30 (directory) entries for evidence of deleted files. www.osforensics.com/faqs-and-tutorials/how-to-scan-ntfs-i30-entries-deleted-files.html

PassMark Software (2023b). Event Log Viewer. www.osforensics.com/event-log-viewer.html

SANS (2020). Introduction to EvtxEcmd. Retrieved from `https://isc.sans.edu/diary/Introduction+to+EvtxEcmd+Evtx+Explorer/25858`

SANS (2023). SANS Windows Forensic Analysis chart. `www.sans.org/posters/windows-forensic-analysis/`

Test Your Knowledge

1.   What is the file extension for Windows log files?

   a. .log

   b. .dat

   c. .evtx

   d. .info

2.   What directory should you look in to find cloud storage?

   %USERPROFILE%\

3.   What will you find at C:\Users\XXX\AppData\Local\Microsoft\Terminal Server Client\Cache?

   RDP cache

4.   What file extension are shortcuts?

   .LNK

5.   _____ in NTFS refers to the index allocation of a directory.

   a. $I30 attribute

   b. .LNK file

   c. .EVTX file

   d. INFO2 file

CHAPTER 5

Windows Registry Forensics Part 1

Chuck Easttom, Ph.D., D.Sc.

Introduction

The Windows Registry is an incredible repository of potential valuable forensics information. It is the heart of the Windows machine. There are a number of interesting pieces of data you can find here. It is beyond the scope of this chapter to make you an expert in the Windows Registry, but it is hoped that you will continue on and learn more. Microsoft describes the Registry as follows (Microsoft, 2023):

> A central hierarchical database used in the Microsoft Windows family of Operating Systems to store information necessary to configure the system for one or more users, applications and hardware devices.

> The registry contains information that Windows continually references during operation, such as profiles for each user, the applications installed on the computer and the types of documents that each can create, property sheet settings for folders and application icons, what hardware exists on the system and the ports that are being used.

Note that "Windows continually references...." This means that virtually every activity on a machine will be reflected in one or more registry keys. That is why Windows Registry analysis is critical to Windows forensics.

The Registry is used by the operating system and applications to store and retrieve configuration data. It can contain settings for the OS itself, installed software, hardware devices, user preferences, and system policies. The Registry can be viewed and edited

155

© Chuck Easttom, William Butler, Jessica Phelan, Ramya Sai Bhagavatula, Sean Steuber, Karely Rodriguez, Victoria Indy Balkissoon, Zehra Naseer 2024
C. Easttom et al., *Windows Forensics*, https://doi.org/10.1007/979-8-8688-0193-8_5

using the Registry Editor (`regedit.exe`), a tool included with Windows. It allows users to navigate the hierarchical structure and modify values. However, editing the Registry requires caution as incorrect changes can lead to system instability or malfunction.

The Registry is crucial for the operating system's performance and functionality. It's frequently accessed for information retrieval and updating settings. Over time, the Registry can become cluttered with outdated or unnecessary entries, which might impact system performance. The Registry can be a target for malware and viruses, as malicious changes here can deeply affect the system. Security software often monitors Registry changes to detect and prevent unauthorized modifications.

Registry Overview

The Registry is organized into five sections referred to as *hives*. Each of these sections contains specific information that can be useful to you. The five hives are described here:

- **HKEY_CLASSES_ROOT (HKCR):** This hive stores information about drag and drop rules, program shortcuts, the user interface, and related items.

- **HKEY_CURRENT_USER (HKCU):** This hive is very important to any forensic investigation. It stores information about the currently logged-on user, including desktop settings and user folders.

- **HKEY_LOCAL_MACHINE (HKLM):** This hive can also be important to a forensic investigation. It contains those settings common to the entire machine, regardless of the individual user.

- **HKEY_USERS (HKU):** This hive is very critical to forensics investigations. It has profiles for all the users, including their settings.

- **HKEY_CURRENT_CONFIG (HCU):** This hive contains the current system configuration. This might also prove useful in your forensic examinations.

You can see the Registry and these five hives in Figure 5-1.

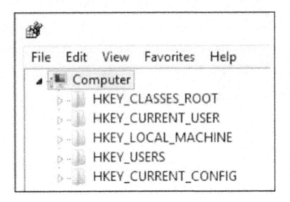

Figure 5-1. *Windows Registry*

These registry hives are located in separate locations:

HKEY_LOCAL_MACHINE\SYSTEM: \system32\config\system

HKEY_LOCAL_MACHINE\SAM: \system32\config\sam

HKEY_LOCAL_MACHINE\SECURITY: \system32\config\security

HKEY_LOCAL_MACHINE\SOFTWARE: \system32\config\
software

HKEY_USERS\UserProfile: \winnt\profiles\username

HKEY_USERS.DEFAULT : \system32\config\default

Each key has a name, and the key names are not case sensitive. Keys will often have subkeys. For example, under HKEY_LOCAL_MACHINE you will see subkeys HARDWARE, SAM, SECURITY, SOFTWARE, and SYSTEM. If you expand HARDWARE, you will see five subkeys, as shown in Figure 5-2.

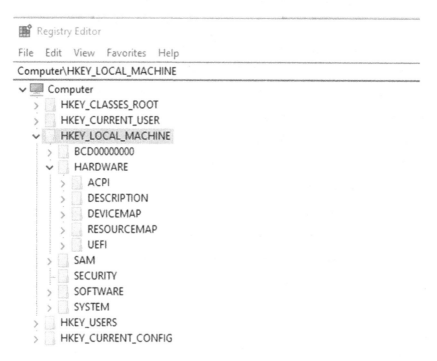

Figure 5-2. *Windows Registry HKEY_LOCAL_MACHINE*

You should note there may be some variation in this based on the Windows version you are using. However, looking at HKEY_LOCAL_MACHINE\HARDWARE is a good starting point for understanding the Registry. The first subkey we see here is ACPI. This is Advanced Configuration and Power Interface. You may not see this on system on a chip (SoC)–based platforms. ACPI is an open standard for configuring hardware and for power management. ACPI is a successor to several standards including Advanced Power Management (APM) and the Plug and Play BIOS (PnP) specification. If you look at the subkeys under ACPI, you will likely see variation based on your hardware and version of Windows. But some items you are likely to see are listed and briefly described here:

RSDT: Root System Description Table; includes pointers to other system description tables. Sometimes called XSDT

FADT: Fixed ACPI Description Table; includes information about fixed hardware features on the platform.

FACS: Firmware ACPI Control Structure

SSDx: Information about solid-state drives; SSD1, SSD2, etc.

Many of these are simply part of Windows and won't provide substantial forensic information. But just to aid you in gaining familiarity with the Windows Registry, let us examine one HKEY_LOCAL_MACHINE\HARDWARE\DEVICEMAP\VIDEO. You can see it in Figure 5-3.

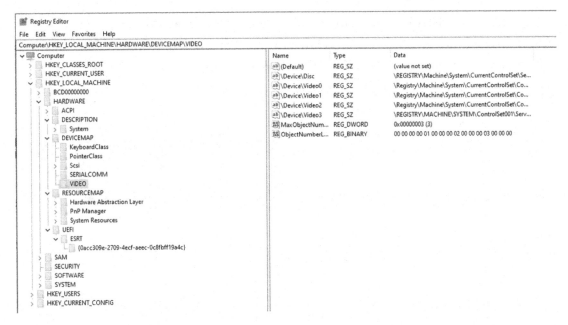

Figure 5-3. *HKEY_LOCAL_MACHINE\HARDWARE\DEVICEMAP\VIDEO*

But what does all of this actually mean? First, this key provides links to current video devices. As you look on the right side, you will notice \Device\Video0, \Device\Video1, etc. You will also note that these often have CurrentControlSet or ControlSet001 in the path name. A typical registry key could contain more than one control set:

- \ControlSet001

- \ControlSet002

- \CurrentControlSet

- \Clone

Each of these has a specific meaning:

- ControlSet001 may be the last control set you booted with.

- ControlSet002 could be what is known as the last known good control set or the control set that last successfully booted Windows.

- The CurrentControlSet subkey is just a pointer to one of the ControlSetXXX keys.

- Clone is a clone of CurrentControlSet and is created each time you boot your computer.

Many of the registry keys contain specific information about the system. For example, HKEY_LOCAL_MACHINE\HARDWARE\DESCRIPTION\System\BIOS has information about your system's BIOS/UEFI; this is shown in Figure 5-4.

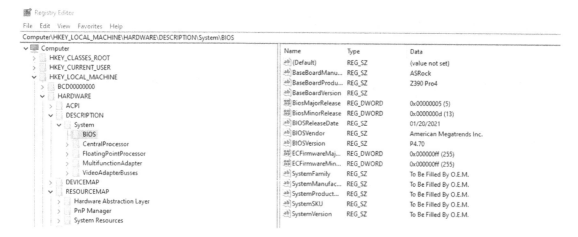

Figure 5-4. *BIOS information in the Registry*

Most people use the `regedit` tool to interact with the Registry. You can reach regedit either by using Start ➤ Run, and then typing in `regedit` or using the Windows+R key and typing in `regedit`. Most forensics tools provide a means for examining the Registry as well. The previous screenshots in this chapter were taken from Regedit. The SANS Institute offers a free Registry Explorer, which you can download from `www.sans.org/tools/registry-explorer/`. There are other such tools such as Registry Finder (`https://registry-finder.com/`). We will review some of these alternative tools later in this chapter.

As you explore the Registry, you will find a host of different keys. It would be impossible to cover them all in one chapter or even one book. As we move forward through this chapter, we will explore those registry keys most relevant to Windows forensics. Every registry key contains a value associated with it called LastWriteTime. This value indicates when this registry value was last changed. Rather than being a standard date/time, this value is stored as a FILETIME structure. A FILETIME structure represents the number of 100-nanosecond intervals since January 1, 1601. Clearly, this is important forensically.

It is also interesting to note that Microsoft rarely uses strong encryption to hide items in the Registry. If an item is encrypted, it is likely encrypted with some simple algorithm such as ROT 13. Most internal text strings are stored and processed as 16-bit Unicode characters. Unicode is an international character set standard that defines unique 2-byte values (maximum 65,536 characters) for most of the world's known character sets.

You can export a specific key from the command line with

```
reg export HKEY_LOCAL_MACHINE\System\ControlSet\Enum\UBSTOR
```

or within regedit, you can right-click a key and select Export.

Individual keys have specific data types. Table 5-1 summarizes these.

Table 5-1. *Registry Data Types*

Name	Data Type	Description
Binary Value	REG_BINARY	Raw binary data. Most hardware component information is stored as binary data and is displayed in Registry Editor in hexadecimal format.
DWORD Value	REG_DWORD	Data represented by a number that is 4 bytes long (a 32-bit integer). Many parameters for device drivers and services are this type.
Expandable String Value	REG_EXPAND_SZ	A variable-length data string. This data type includes variables that are resolved when a program or service uses the data.
Multi-String Value	REG_MULTI_SZ	A multiple string. Values that contain lists or multiple values in a form that people can read are generally this type. Entries are separated by spaces, commas, or other marks.
String Value	REG_SZ	A fixed-length text string.
Binary Value	REG_RESOURCE_LIST	A series of nested arrays that is designed to store a resource list that is used by a hardware device driver or one of the physical devices it controls.

(continued)

161

Table 5-1. (*continued*)

Name	Data Type	Description
Binary Value	REG_RESOURCE_REQUIREMENTS_LIST	A series of nested arrays that is designed to store a device driver's list of possible hardware resources the driver or one of the physical devices it controls can use.
Binary Value	REG_FULL_RESOURCE_DESCRIPTOR	A series of nested arrays that is designed to store a resource list that is used by a physical hardware device.
None	REG_NONE	Data without any particular type. This data is written to the Registry by the system or applications and is displayed in Registry Editor in hexadecimal format as a Binary Value
Link	REG_LINK	A Unicode string naming a symbolic link.
QWORD Value	REG_QWORD	Data represented by a number that is a 64-bit integer.

Editing registry keys requires specific permissions. If you have local administrator rights, then you should have access to all of these. The specific access rights for the Registry are numerous and are shown in Table 5-2.

Table 5-2. *Registry Permissions*

Value	Meaning
KEY_ALL_ACCESS (0xF003F)	Combines the STANDARD_RIGHTS_REQUIRED, KEY_QUERY_VALUE, KEY_SET_VALUE, KEY_CREATE_SUB_KEY, KEY_ENUMERATE_SUB_KEYS, KEY_NOTIFY, and KEY_CREATE_LINK access rights.
KEY_CREATE_LINK (0x0020)	Reserved for system use.
KEY_CREATE_SUB_KEY (0x0004)	Needed to create a subkey of a registry key.

(*continued*)

Table 5-2. (*continued*)

Value	Meaning
KEY_ENUMERATE_SUB_KEYS (0x0008)	Needed to enumerate the subkeys of a registry key.
KEY_EXECUTE (0x20019)	Equivalent to KEY_READ.
KEY_NOTIFY (0x0010)	Needed to request change notifications for a registry key or for subkeys of a registry key.
KEY_QUERY_VALUE (0x0001)	Needed to query the values of a registry key.
KEY_READ (0x20019)	Combines the STANDARD_RIGHTS_READ, KEY_QUERY_VALUE, KEY_ENUMERATE_SUB_KEYS, and KEY_NOTIFY values.
KEY_SET_VALUE (0x0002)	Needed to create, delete, or set a registry value.
KEY_WOW64_32KEY (0x0200)	Indicates that an application on 64-bit Windows should operate on the 32-bit registry view. This flag is ignored by 32-bit Windows.
KEY_WOW64_64KEY (0x0100)	Indicates that an application on 64-bit Windows should operate on the 64-bit registry view. This flag is ignored by 32-bit Windows.
KEY_WRITE (0x20006)	Combines the STANDARD_RIGHTS_WRITE, KEY_SET_VALUE, and KEY_CREATE_SUB_KEY access rights.

These permissions affect how you can interact with the Windows Registry. They also indicate what permission applications need to work with specific registry keys.

Specific Registry Keys

In the following subsections, we will be examining specific registry keys that are important to forensics. Some additional registry keys will be examined in Chapter 6.

General Information

General information about the Windows computer is, of course, stored in the Windows Registry. These are found in HKEY_LOCAL_MACHINE. Some keys that will provide basic information are summarized here:

Hostname System\ControlSet001\Control\ComputerName\ComputerName: Hostname. Normally, you should not need to consult the Registry to find out the computer's hostname.

Timezone System\ControlSet001\Control\TimeZoneInformation: TimeZone. There is actually more information than just time zone, as you can see in Figure 5-5.

Name	Type	Data
(Default)	REG_SZ	(value not set)
ActiveTimeBias	REG_DWORD	0x00000168 (360)
Bias	REG_DWORD	0x00000168 (360)
DaylightBias	REG_DWORD	0xffffffc4 (4294967236)
DaylightName	REG_SZ	@tzres.dll,-161
DaylightStart	REG_BINARY	00 00 03 00 02 00 02 00 00 00 00 00 00 00 00 00
DynamicDaylightTimeDisabled	REG_DWORD	0x00000000 (0)
StandardBias	REG_DWORD	0x00000000 (0)
StandardName	REG_SZ	@tzres.dll,-162
StandardStart	REG_BINARY	00 00 0b 00 01 00 02 00 00 00 00 00 00 00 00 00
TimeZoneKeyName	REG_SZ	Central Standard Time

Figure 5-5.   *Time information in the Registry*

Last Access Time System\ControlSet001\Control\Filesystem: Last time access (by default, it's disabled with NtfsDisableLastAccessUpdate=1; if 0, then, it's enabled). To enable it: fsutil behavior set disablelastaccess 0. This Registry section actually has more information than just last access time and is shown in Figure 5-6.

	Name	Type	Data
CoDeviceInstallers	(Default)	REG_SZ	(value not set)
COM Name Arbiter	DisableDeleteNotification	REG_DWORD	0x00000000 (0)
CommonGlobUserSettings	FilterSupportedFeaturesMode	REG_DWORD	0x00000000 (0)
Compatibility	LongPathsEnabled	REG_DWORD	0x00000001 (1)
ComputerName	NtfsAllowExtendedCharacter8dot3Rename	REG_DWORD	0x00000000 (0)
ContentIndex	NtfsBugcheckOnCorrupt	REG_DWORD	0x00000000 (0)
CrashControl	NtfsDisable8dot3NameCreation	REG_DWORD	0x00000002 (2)
Cryptography	NtfsDisableCompression	REG_DWORD	0x00000000 (0)
DeviceClasses	NtfsDisableEncryption	REG_DWORD	0x00000000 (0)
DeviceContainerPropertyUpdateEvents	NtfsDisableLastAccessUpdate	REG_DWORD	0x80000002 (2147483650)
DeviceContainers	NtfsDisableLfsDowngrade	REG_DWORD	0x00000000 (0)
DeviceGuard	NtfsDisableVolsnapHints	REG_DWORD	0x00000000 (0)
DeviceOverrides	NtfsEnableDirCaseSensitivity	REG_DWORD	0x00000001 (1)
DevicePanels	NtfsEncryptPagingFile	REG_DWORD	0x00000000 (0)
DevQuery	NtfsMemoryUsage	REG_DWORD	0x00000000 (0)
Diagnostics	NtfsMftZoneReservation	REG_DWORD	0x00000000 (0)
DmaSecurity	NtfsQuotaNotifyRate	REG_DWORD	0x00000e10 (3600)
EarlyLaunch	RefsDisableLastAccessUpdate	REG_DWORD	0x00000001 (1)
Els	ScrubMode	REG_DWORD	0x00000002 (2)
Errata	SuppressInheritanceSupport	REG_DWORD	0x00000001 (1)
FeatureManagement	SymlinkLocalToLocalEvaluation	REG_DWORD	0x00000001 (1)
FileSystem	SymlinkLocalToRemoteEvaluation	REG_DWORD	0x00000001 (1)
FileSystemUtilities	SymlinkRemoteToLocalEvaluation	REG_DWORD	0x00000000 (0)
GraphicsDrivers	SymlinkRemoteToRemoteEvaluation	REG_DWORD	0x00000000 (0)
GroupOrderList	UdfsCloseSessionOnEject	REG_DWORD	0x00000003 (3)
HAL	UdfsSoftwareDefectManagement	REG_DWORD	0x00000000 (0)
hivelist	Win31FileSystem	REG_DWORD	0x00000000 (0)
Hvsi	Win95TruncatedExtensions	REG_DWORD	0x00000001 (1)
Hypervisor			
IDConfigDB			
InitialMachineConfig			

Figure 5-6. *Filesystem information in the Registry*

Shutdown Time System\ControlSet001\Control\Windows: Shutdown time. This is shown in Figure 5-7.

	Name	Type	Data
Srp	(Default)	REG_SZ	(value not set)
SrpExtensionConfig	ComponentizedBuild	REG_DWORD	0x00000001 (1)
StillImage	CSDBuildNumber	REG_DWORD	0x00000df2 (3570)
Storage	CSDReleaseType	REG_DWORD	0x00000000 (0)
StorageManagement	CSDVersion	REG_DWORD	0x00000000 (0)
StorPort	Directory	REG_EXPAND_SZ	%SystemRoot%
StorVSP	ErrorMode	REG_DWORD	0x00000000 (0)
StSec	FullProcessInformationSID	REG_BINARY	01 06 00 00 00 00 00 05 50 00 00 00 5e f3 0f b1 81 64 ...
SystemInformation	NoInteractiveServices	REG_DWORD	0x00000001 (1)
SystemResources	ShellErrorMode	REG_DWORD	0x00000001 (1)
TabletPC	ShutdownTime	REG_BINARY	7d e7 d0 0c 9f 0c da 01
Terminal Server	SystemDirectory	REG_EXPAND_SZ	%SystemRoot%\system32
TimeZoneInformation			
Ubpm			
UnitedVideo			
USB			
usbflags			
usbstor			
VAN			
Version			
Video			
WalletService			
wcncsvc			
Wdf			
WDI			
Windows			

Figure 5-7. *Shutdown Time information in the Registry*

USB Information

One of the first things most forensic analysts learn about the Windows Registry is that they can find out what USB devices have been connected to the suspect machine. The registry key HKEY_LOCAL_MACHINE\System\ControlSet\Enum\USBSTOR lists USB devices that have been connected to the machine. Note that ControlSet will actually be ControlSet001 or CurrentControlSet. It is often the case that a criminal will move evidence to an external device and take it with them. This could indicate to you that there are devices you need to find and examine. This Registry setting will tell you about the external drives that have been connected to this system. You can see this in Figure 5-8.

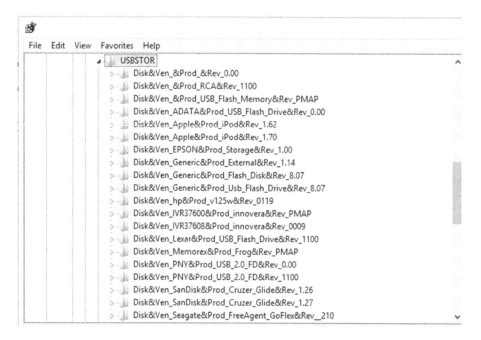

Figure 5-8. *Windows Registry USBSTOR*

However, this does not give the complete picture. Some related keys are quite useful. For example, SYSTEM\MountedDevices allows investigators to match the serial number to a given drive letter or volume that was mounted when the USB device was inserted. Incidentally, this particular registry key is not limited to USB devices. You can see this in Figure 5-9.

File   Edit   View   Favorites   Help

Name	Type	Data
\??\Volume{7b040cb9-984b-11e3-bec3-...	REG_BINARY	54 72 75 65 43 72 79 70 74 56 6f 6c 75 6d 65 4d
\??\Volume{89de9421-1c92-11e3-bea7-...	REG_BINARY	54 77 27 00 00 7e 00 00 00 00 00 00
\??\Volume{90e1d233-2632-11e4-bedb-...	REG_BINARY	5f 00 3f 00 3f 00 5f 00 55 00 53 00 42 00 53 00 54 00 4f 00 52 00 23 ...
\??\Volume{917d0351-815e-11e3-bebd-...	REG_BINARY	54 72 75 65 43 72 79 70 74 56 6f 6c 75 6d 65 4c
\??\Volume{956f0090-2f2d-11e4-bede-8...	REG_BINARY	5f 00 3f 00 3f 00 5f 00 55 00 53 00 42 00 53 00 54 00 4f 00 52 00 23 ...
\??\Volume{9938fae5-2dd0-11e4-bedd-...	REG_BINARY	5f 00 3f 00 3f 00 5f 00 55 00 53 00 42 00 53 00 54 00 4f 00 52 00 23 ...
\??\Volume{9ef154ab-6411-11e3-beb7-...	REG_BINARY	54 72 75 65 43 72 79 70 74 56 6f 6c 75 6d 65 4b
\??\Volume{a06251b3-9259-11e2-be8f-...	REG_BINARY	ff e1 13 00 00 7e 00 00 00 00 00 00
\??\Volume{ac3c132a-93c4-11e3-bec2-...	REG_BINARY	5f 00 3f 00 3f 00 5f 00 55 00 53 00 42 00 53 00 54 00 4f 00 52 00 23 ...
\??\Volume{ac3c1570-93c4-11e3-bec2-...	REG_BINARY	33 3c 28 00 00 7e 00 00 00 00 00 00 00
\??\Volume{b1a82a0f-b4f4-11e3-bec4-a...	REG_BINARY	5f 00 3f 00 3f 00 5f 00 55 00 53 00 42 00 53 00 54 00 4f 00 52 00 23 ...
\??\Volume{b36ca755-c6d7-11e2-bebd-...	REG_BINARY	54 72 75 65 43 72 79 70 74 56 6f 6c 75 6d 65 45
\??\Volume{b51d5121-fcf6-11e3-bed7-f...	REG_BINARY	5f 00 3f 00 3f 00 5f 00 55 00 53 00 42 00 53 00 54 00 4f 00 52 00 23 ...
\??\Volume{b579fa8c-5352-11e4-bee5-...	REG_BINARY	5a e0 ae b3 00 00 10 00 00 00 00 00
\??\Volume{b9b94601-a6ac-11e2-be9f-...	REG_BINARY	5f 00 3f 00 3f 00 5f 00 55 00 53 00 42 00 53 00 54 00 4f 00 52 00 23 ...
\??\Volume{bab6771b-550b-11e4-bee5-...	REG_BINARY	24 46 b7 5e 00 7e 00 00 00 00 00 00
\??\Volume{bab67b5a-550b-11e4-bee5-...	REG_BINARY	5f 00 3f 00 3f 00 5f 00 55 00 53 00 42 00 53 00 54 00 4f 00 52 00 23 ...
\??\Volume{d4cb75a4-970b-11e2-be90-...	REG_BINARY	5c 00 3f 00 3f 00 5c 00 53 00 43 00 53 00 49 00 23 00 43 00 64 00 52...
\??\Volume{d73983ce-3104-11e2-be69-...	REG_BINARY	5c 00 3f 00 3f 00 5c 00 53 00 43 00 53 00 49 00 23 00 43 00 64 00 52

Computer
  HKEY_CLASSES_ROOT
  HKEY_CURRENT_USER
  HKEY_LOCAL_MACHINE
    BCD00000000
    HARDWARE
    SAM
    SECURITY
    SOFTWARE
    SYSTEM
      ControlSet001
      CurrentControlSet
      DriverDatabase
      HardwareConfig
      MountedDevices
      RNG
      Select
      Setup
      WPA
  HKEY_USERS
  HKEY_CURRENT_CONFIG

Figure 5-9. *More USB information in the Registry*

The user who was using the USB device can be found here:

HKCU\Software\Microsoft\Windows\CurrentVersion\Explorer\MountPoints2.

Notice this is in HKCU, not HKLM.

The vendor and product ID can be found here:

SYSTEM\CurrentControlSet\Enum\USB

Another important key is

SYSTEM\ControlSet001\Enum\USBSTOR{VEN_PROD_VERSION}{USB serial}\

The values for this are

> **0064**: First connection

> **0066**: Last connection

All of these related USB registry keys should be examined in order to get a complete and accurate picture of what happened regarding specific USB devices.

MRU

The Most Recently Used list can show items that have been used recently.

HKCU\Software\Microsoft\Windows\CurrentVersion\Explorer\ComDlg32\
LastVisitedMRU

The data is in hex format, but you can see the text translation when using `regedit`, and you will probably be able to make out the site visited just by looking at `regedit`. Over time, this key's subkeys have changed. As of Windows 10, Figure 5-10 displays an image of the subkeys of HKCU\Software\Microsoft\Windows\CurrentVersion\Explorer\ComDlg32.

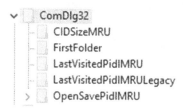

Figure 5-10. *Most Recently Used list*

The LastVisitedPidMRU shows the last folder location used by an application that saved or opened a file.

ShellBags

ShellBags were first introduced with Windows 7 and have been in every version of Windows since then. The intention of ShellBags is to keep information about a user's activity exploring Windows, but this also allows for a great deal of forensic evidence to be gathered from this registry entry. This entry can be found at HKCU\Software\Microsoft\Windows\Shell. ShellBag entries indicate a given folder was accessed, not a specific file. This portion of the Windows Registry is shown in Figure 5-11.

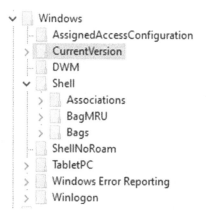

Figure 5-11. *ShellBags*

As you can see, there are subkeys. The two most interesting for forensics are Bags and BagMRU. BagMRU stores folder names and folder path similar to the tree structure. The root directory is represented by the first BagMRU key, that is, 0. BagMRU contains numbered values that compare to say subkey's nested subkeys. All of these subkeys contain numbered values aside from the last child in each branch. Bag stores view preference such as the size of the window, location, and view mode.

When a folder is deleted, the corresponding ShellBag registry keys and values are not deleted. The same is true when a ZIP file is deleted; its ShellBag information won't be deleted. If a folder or ZIP file is deleted and a new one is created with the same name, then the new one will inherit the old one's ShellBag information. ShellBags will be created when folders on removable devices are opened and closed. The fact that ShellBag entries are not deleted when the corresponding folder is deleted, and that there are ShellBag entries for removable devices, makes the ShellBag a very important area of the Registry for forensic analysis. Figure 5-12 shows the ShellBags as seen in OSForensics User Activity.

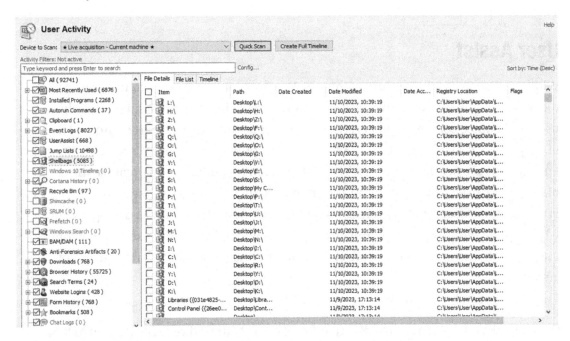

Figure 5-12. *ShellBags in OSForensics*

ShellBags are entries in the Windows Registry that retain user-specific settings about the size, view, icon, and position of folders when viewed through the Windows Explorer interface. They provide a record of how a user has interacted with the file system, including information about folders that may no longer exist or have been accessed on external or remote storage devices. These are useful in forensic analysis for

- **Activity Reconstruction**: ShellBags can be used to reconstruct a user's activities on a computer, especially in terms of file and directory access. They can show when a user accessed specific directories, even if those directories have been deleted.

- **Timeline Analysis**: By examining timestamp information within ShellBags, forensic analysts can establish a timeline of user actions.

- **External and Network Drive Accesses**: They also retain information about nonlocal directories, like those on external drives or network shares, visited by a user.

User Assist

Windows User Assist is a feature within the Windows operating system that tracks and records the frequency and time of application usage. This information is primarily used to enhance user experience, particularly in customizing the Start menu and list of frequently used programs. User Assist keeps a count of how many times specific applications are opened by a user. This data is used to populate and organize the list of frequently used programs in the Start menu. In digital forensics, User Assist data is valuable for reconstructing a user's activity on a computer. It provides insights into which applications were frequently used, potentially indicating the user's behavior or intent. It can also be used to corroborate other findings or to establish a timeline of user actions.

This key can be found at

```
HKEY_CURRENT_USER\Software\Microsoft\Windows\CurrentVersion\Explorer\
UserAssist
```

User Assist is a method used to populate a user's Start menu with frequently used applications. This is achieved by maintaining a count of application use in each user's NTUSER.DAT registry file. Thus, this registry entry will tell you how many times an application has been executed and the most recent time. This registry key is shown in Figure 5-13.

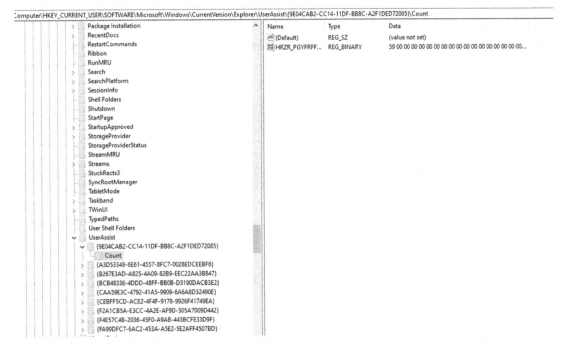

Figure 5-13. *User Assist in the Registry*

Prefetch

Windows Prefetch is a feature in Microsoft Windows operating systems designed to speed up the loading of software applications. Prefetch is designed to reduce the time it takes for applications to start. It achieves this by monitoring the files accessed by applications during startup and storing this information in specific Prefetch files. When an application is launched, Windows uses the data in the Prefetch file to anticipate and preload certain data and resources into memory, making the application start faster. Prefetch is often discussed alongside Superfetch, another optimization feature. While Prefetch focuses on speeding up application launch times, Superfetch aims to improve overall system performance by preloading frequently used applications into memory based on learned usage patterns. Prefetch files are valuable in forensic investigations.

They contain information about when an application was executed and how often, which can help in building timelines or understanding user behavior on a system.

This can be found at HKEY_LOCAL_MACHINE\SYSTEM\CurrentControlSet\ Control\Session Manager\Memory Management\PrefetchParameter.

Prefetch files contain the name of the executable, a Unicode list of DLLs used by that executable, a count of how many times the executable has been run, and a timestamp indicating the last time the program was run. In conjunction with User Assist, this registry key can give you a good picture of programs executed on the device. This registry key is shown in Figure 5-14.

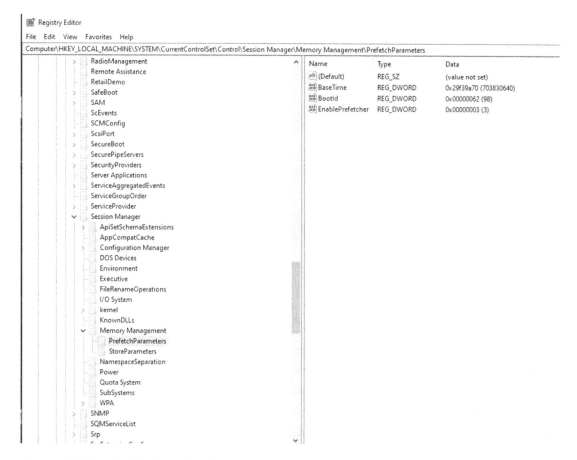

Figure 5-14. *Prefetch in the Registry*

Mounted Devices

Mounted devices can be found at HKEY_LOCAL_MACHINE\SYSTEM\MountedDevices. This information can be useful to a forensic examiner as it shows any connected storage device that has been recognized by the operating system. That key is shown in Figure 5-15.

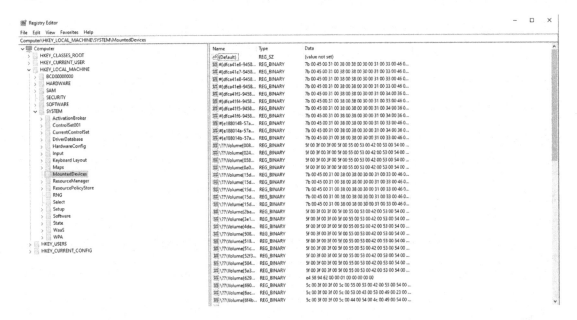

Figure 5-15. *Mounted devices in the Registry*

AutoStart Programs

It is common for malware, particularly spyware and ransomware, to start when the system boots up. This is accomplished by altering AutoStart registry locations. Those locations are

HKLM\Software\Microsoft\Windows\CurrentVersion\Run

HKLM \Software\Microsoft\Windows\CurrentVersion\RunOnce

HKLM \Software\Microsoft\Windows\CurrentVersion\Runonce

HKLM \Software\Microsoft\Windows\CurrentVersion\Policies\
Explorer\Run

HKLM \Software\Microsoft\Windows\CurrentVersion\Run

The key HKLM\Software\Microsoft\Windows\
CurrentVersion\Run

This is shown in Figure 5-16.

Name	Type	Data
(Default)	REG_SZ	(value not set)
AdobeAAMUpdater-1.0	REG_SZ	"C:\Program Files (x86)\Common Files\Adobe\OO...
AdobeGCInvoker-1.0	REG_SZ	"C:\Program Files (x86)\Common Files\Adobe\Ad...
Everything	REG_SZ	"C:\Program Files\Everything\Everything.exe" -sta...
IAStorIcon	REG_SZ	"C:\Program Files\Intel\Intel(R) Rapid Storage Tech...
iTunesHelper	REG_SZ	"C:\Program Files\iTunes\iTunesHelper.exe"
Logitech Download Assistant	REG_SZ	C:\Windows\system32\rundll32.exe C:\Windows\S...
MacDrive 10 helper	REG_SZ	"C:\Program Files\Mediafour\MacDrive 10\MDHel...
RtkAudUService	REG_SZ	"C:\Windows\System32\RtkAudUService64.exe" -b...
SecurityHealth	REG_EXPAND_SZ	%windir%\system32\SecurityHealthSystray.exe

Figure 5-16. *AutoStart information in the Registry*

In this case, we can readily see there are various programs that are set to run at startup, including Adobe Updater and iTunesHelper.

Tools

Most digital forensic tools will provide information from the Windows Registry. The tools won't always identify what registry key the evidence is coming from, but rather the information from the Registry that would be of interest.

OSForensics

OSForensics covers this information primarily under User Activity. That option in OSForensics will pull information from multiple registry keys and display them in a user-friendly format. Figure 5-17 shows the User Activity from OSForensics; you will likely recognize some of these as registry keys we have discussed in this chapter.

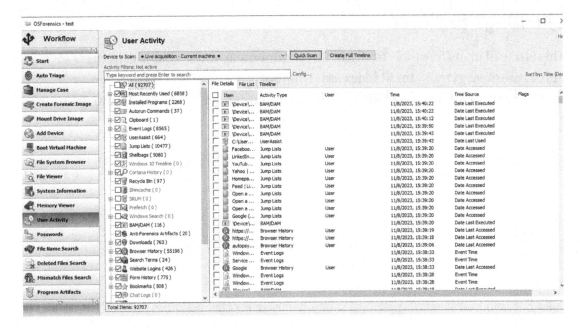

Figure 5-17. *OSForensics User Activity*

You can highlight specific items such as ShellBags, as shown in Figure 5-18.

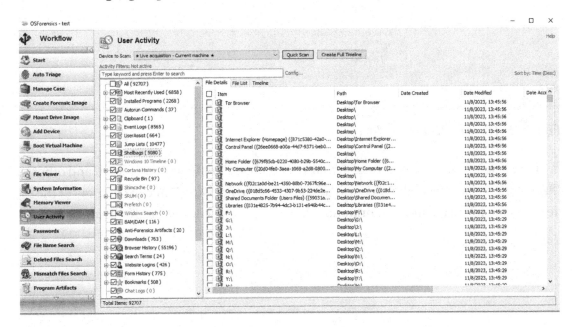

Figure 5-18. *OSForensics ShellBags*

ShellBags Explorer

This is one of many free tools from Mr. Eric Zimmerman and available at `https://ericzimmerman.github.io/#!index.md`. This tool is not a general registry viewer/analyzer, but rather focuses solely on ShellBags. You can see the tool in Figure 5-19.

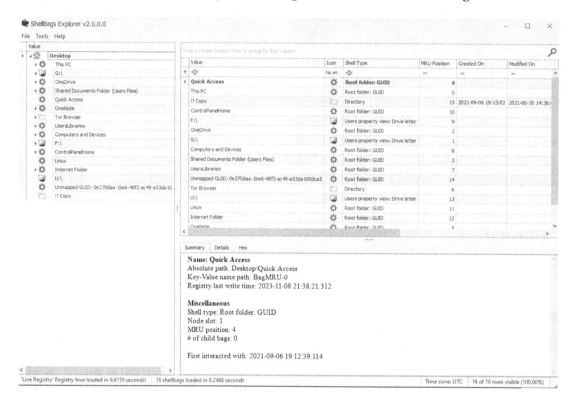

Figure 5-19. *ShellBags Explorer*

On the left, you can see several actual keys such as ShellBags, User Assist, and others. Other data is also shown that does not come from the Registry. You can click any of the items on the left to get more information. In Figure 5-20, I clicked the Tor Browser folder.

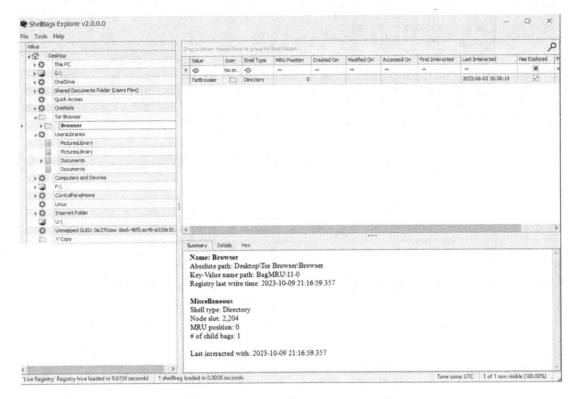

Figure 5-20. *Viewing a specific folder in ShellBags Explorer*

Notice that it is listing the last time any interaction occurred with this folder. When you highlight a given value, you will see the details in the summary window at the bottom. You can also click the Details tab and get even more information.

Registry Explorer

This is also a free tool available at `https://ericzimmerman.github.io/#!index.md`. Figure 5-21 shows loading the current live system hive.

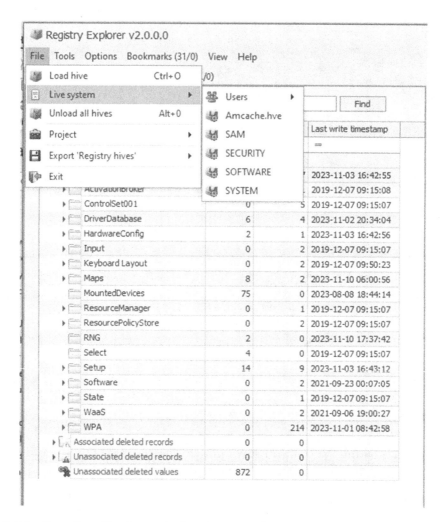

Figure 5-21. *Loading live hives in Registry Explorer*

You can now view the various subsections, often organized in a manner that is logical and easy to follow. For example, the MountedDevices key is shown in Figure 5-22.

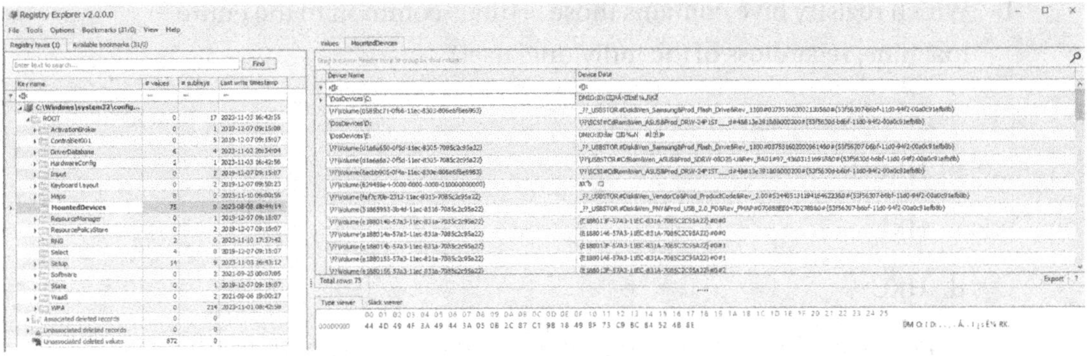

Figure 5-22. *MountedDevices in Registry Explorer*

Conclusions

The Windows Registry is critical to performing forensics on a Windows computer. Many tools will pull the information for you and will even display it in a user-friendly manner. However, to be effective in digital forensics, you need to understand the data. In this chapter, you have been introduced to basic facts about the Windows Registry, as well as being shown specific registry keys that are commonly used in Windows forensics. You have also been introduced to several tools that will aid you in performing Windows Registry forensics.

References

Microsoft (2023). Windows registry information for advanced users. Retrieved from `https://learn.microsoft.com/en-us/troubleshoot/windows-server/performance/windows-registry-advanced-users`

Test Your Knowledge

A few questions are provided here to aid you in testing your knowledge before you proceed.

1. Which registry hive contains those settings common to the entire machine, regardless of the individual user?

   a. HKLM

   b. HKCU

   c. HKU

   d. HKC

2. What registry location would be best to look for information regarding a count of how many times an executable has been run and a timestamp indicating the last time the program was run?

   a. ShellBags

   b. User Assist

   c. Executables

   d. Prefetch

3. What hive contains information about the user who was using the USB device?

   a. HKLM

   b. HKCU

   c. HKU

   d. HKC

4. When a folder is deleted, what happens to its ShellBag entry?

   a. It is moved to the recycle bin.

   b. It is marked as deleted.

   c. It is disabled.

   d. Nothing.

CHAPTER 6

Windows Registry Forensics Part 2

Chuck Easttom, Ph.D., D.Sc.

Introduction

In Chapter 5, you were provided a general introduction to the Windows Registry and to specific keys that are important to Windows forensics. You were also introduced to several tools for performing Windows forensics. In this chapter, we will expand on that knowledge.

Let us begin by introducing you to RegEdt32. Regedit and RegEdt32 are both Registry editors for Microsoft Windows operating systems, but they have different characteristics and were more distinct in older versions of Windows. Regedit was introduced with Windows 95 and is used to make broad changes to the Registry. RegEdt32 was part of Windows NT and before Windows XP. In its original form, it provided more advanced features, such as setting permissions and other security settings on registry keys, which Regedit did not offer in earlier versions of Windows. In Windows XP and later versions, Microsoft combined the functionalities of RegEdt32 and Regedit into a single program (Regedit). The modern Regedit thus encompasses the capabilities of both original programs. This is important because some sources recommend using RegEdt32 rather than Regedit, not knowing that both have the same features today.

Specific Keys

In this section, additional keys in the Registry will be discussed. This is essentially an extension of the discussion of the keys from Chapter 5.

© Chuck Easttom, William Butler, Jessica Phelan, Ramya Sai Bhagavatula, Sean Steuber, Karely Rodriguez, Victoria Indy Balkissoon, Zehra Naseer 2024
C. Easttom et al., *Windows Forensics*, https://doi.org/10.1007/979-8-8688-0193-8_6

ComDlg32

The ComDlg32 key in the Windows Registry is associated with the common dialog boxes used in the Windows operating system. These dialog boxes are part of the Windows API and provide standard interfaces for common tasks like opening files, saving files, choosing colors, and printing documents. The common dialog boxes in Windows are designed to provide a consistent user experience across different applications. When an application needs to perform tasks like opening a file, it can use these common dialog boxes instead of creating its own, ensuring that the look and feel remain consistent with the rest of the operating system. The ComDlg32 key in the Windows Registry stores configuration settings and other information related to these common dialog boxes. This can include things like the last directory accessed, user preferences for viewing files (such as list view or detail view), and other state information that Windows uses to provide a consistent experience across different uses of the dialog boxes. The ComDlg32 key is usually located under the HKEY_CURRENT_USER branch of the Windows Registry, reflecting its role in storing user-specific settings. The exact path can vary based on the version of Windows, but it typically looks something like HKEY_CURRENT_USER\Software\ Microsoft\Windows\CurrentVersion\Explorer\ComDlg32.

MUICache

Each time that you start using a new application, the Windows operating system automatically extracts the application name from the version resource of the exe file and stores it for using it later in a registry key known as the "MUICache." MUI is a technology in Windows that allows for the interface of an application to be displayed in multiple languages. This is particularly important in environments where computers are used by speakers of different languages. It enables users to switch the language of the operating system and applications without having to reinstall them. The MUICache registry key stores data related to the MUI of various applications. Specifically, it keeps track of the names and locations of application files and their corresponding MUI files (if available). This cache helps Windows quickly retrieve and display the correct language resources for an application, improving performance and user experience. Forensically, this means that you can also track how many times a program is launched. You can find this key at HKEY_CURRENT_USER\SOFTWARE\Classes\Local Settings\MuiCache, and it is shown in Figure 6-1.

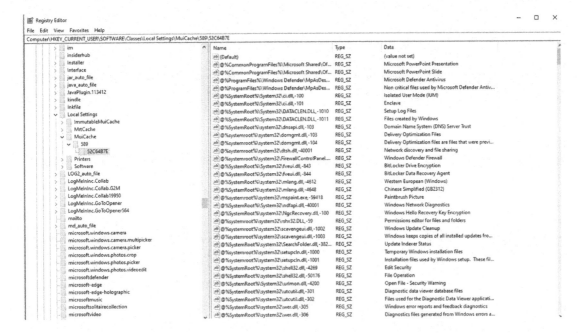

Figure 6-1. *MUICache*

You will notice that there is a great deal of information about software that has been executed on this computer.

Wireless Networks

Wireless networks can be of interest in a forensic examination. It may be of interest to know what wireless networks a computer has connected to – particularly, if it is suspected that a computer (often a laptop) has been connecting to a specific wireless network:

HKEY_LOCAL_MACHINE\SOFTWARE\Microsoft\Windows NT\ CurrentVersion\ NetworkList\Nla\Wireless

This is shown in Figure 6-2.

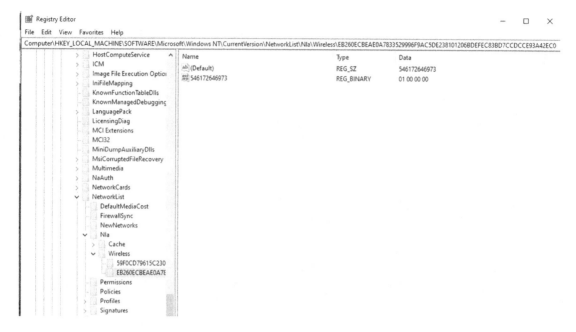

Figure 6-2. *Wireless networks*

Another key that is of interest can provide information regarding the specific network cards, HKEY_LOCAL_MACHINE\SOFTWARE\Microsoft\Windows NT\CurrentVersion\ NetworkCards\, as shown in Figure 6-3.

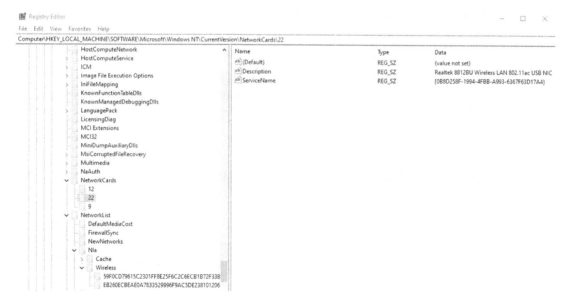

Figure 6-3. *Network cards*

184

Specific registry keys can also provide you with information about the settings such as DHCP information, as shown in Figure 6-4:

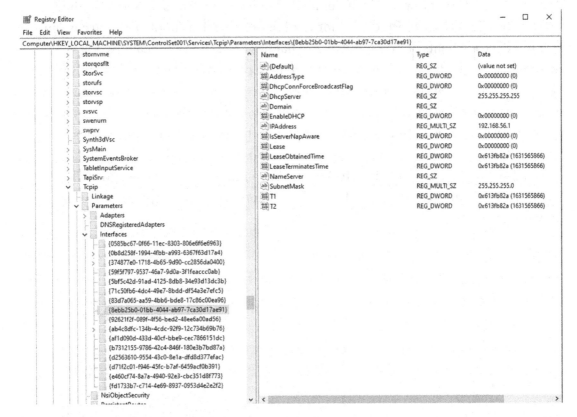

Figure 6-4. *TCP/IP information*

HKLM\SYSTEM\CurrentControlSet\Services\Tcpip\Parameters\Interfaces\{GUID}

The information in these keys can provide a fairly complete picture of the network connections on a given Windows computer.

Malware Analysis

Automatic running was discussed in the previous chapter. It is mentioned again here, but additional relevant registry keys are also discussed.

Run keys: HKEY_CURRENT_USER\Software\Microsoft\Windows\ CurrentVersion\Run.

AppInit_DLLs was added to Windows 7 in order to allow a list of DLLs to be loaded into each user mode process in the system. It is used to specify a list of DLLs (Dynamic

Link Libraries) to be loaded by every process that calls the User32.dll. Essentially, this key allows specific DLLs to be loaded automatically with any application that uses the standard User32 library, which includes most Windows applications. Some legitimate software programs use AppInit_DLLs for valid reasons, such as implementing custom user interface elements or extending functionalities of existing applications. For example, some graphics drivers and accessibility tools make use of this mechanism. Malware often exploits the AppInit_DLLs mechanism to achieve persistence and stealth. By registering a malicious DLL with this key, the malware ensures that its code is executed every time a User32 application starts, effectively infecting numerous processes. This makes it a common target for various types of malware, including spyware, keyloggers, and rootkits. The key can be found at HKEY_LOCAL_MACHINE\SOFTWARE\Microsoft\Windows NT\CurrentVersion\Windows\AppInit_DLLs. This is shown in Figure 6-5.

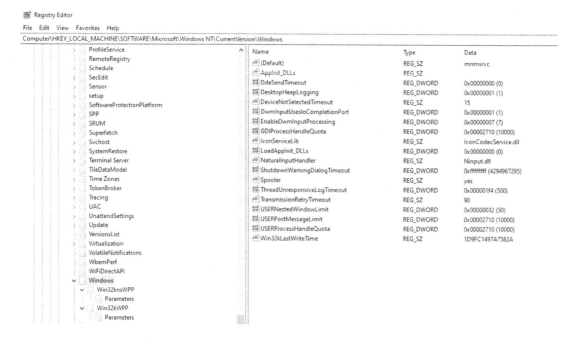

Figure 6-5. *AppInit_DLLs*

In digital forensic investigations, examining the AppInit_DLLs key can reveal whether any unusual or unauthorized DLLs are configured to load with system processes. This can be a critical indicator of a system compromise or infection. You should look for the following:

- Unrecognized or suspicious DLL names

- DLLs that don't correspond to installed software

- Any changes in the key that correlate with the timing of a suspected security incident

Recently Used

We saw this discussed briefly in Chapter 5. However, there are many such most recently used lists. A few are listed in Table 6-1.

Table 6-1. *Most Recently Used (MRU)*

Data	Key
Pictures, music, and videos	Software\Microsoft\Search Assistant\ACMru\5604
Regedit – Last accessed key	Software\Microsoft\Windows\CurrentVersion\Applets\Regedit
Mapped network drives	Software\Microsoft\Windows\CurrentVersion\Explorer\Map Network Drive MR
Word – Recent files	Software\Microsoft\Office\10.0\Excel\Recent Files

These keys are just a few of the registry keys that will provide information about the recently used applications.

Registered Applications

This key provides a list of all applications registered on the computer. The key is found at HKEY_LOCAL_MACHINE\SOFTWARE\RegisteredApplications. You can see it in Figure 6-6.

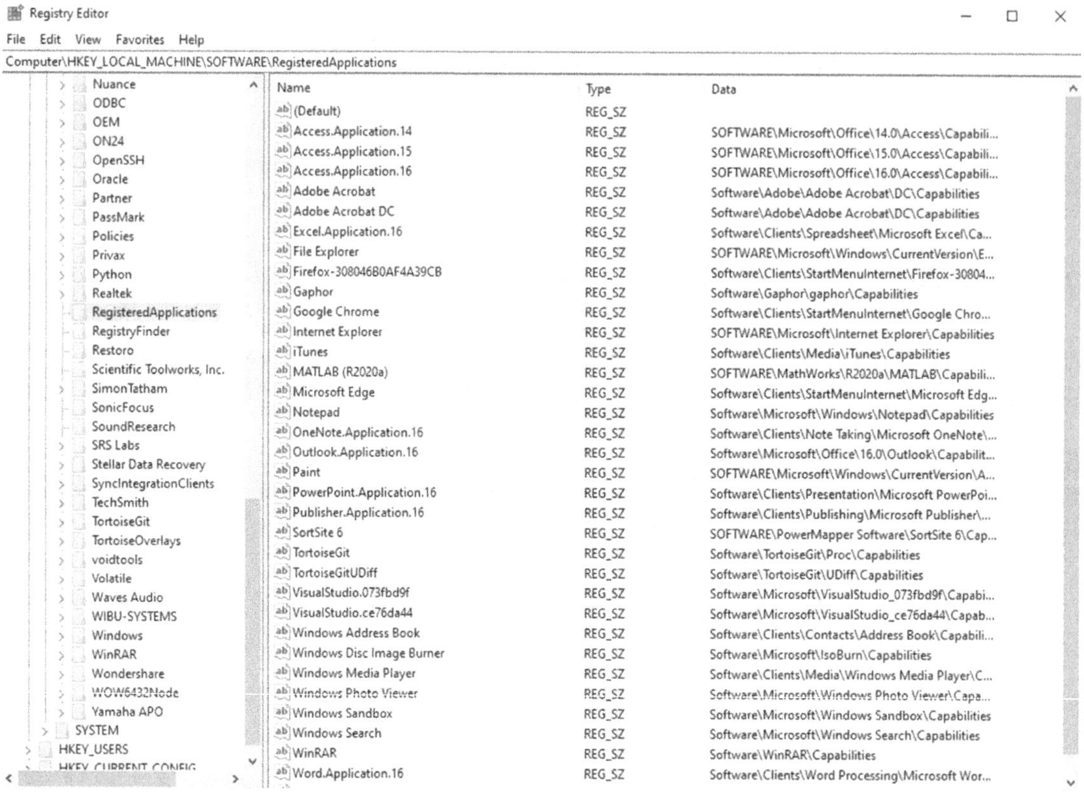

Figure 6-6. *Registered Applications*

This registry key provides a single location to find out about all applications on that computer. That makes forensically enumerating applications much easier.

Other Software

This section is related to the previous *Registered Applications*. There are many different applications one could find on a Windows computer. Of particular interest in many forensic investigations are peer-to-peer (P2P) applications. There are many peer-to-peer communication apps. It would not be possible to discuss all of them. Two commonly discussed in forensics books are as follows:

- Kazaa has data in the key HKCU\Software\Kazaa.

- Morpheus stores data at HKCU\Software\Morpheus\GUI\ SearchRecent.

Note that both are in HIVEKEY_CURRENT_USER\Software. When in doubt as to where to look for any software information, this is a good starting point. How much information you will find will vary based on the software. A few are discussed here.

WinRAR is a popular tool for compressing files. By looking in \HKEY_CURRENT_USER\SOFTWARE\WinRAR\ArcHistory, you will find the files that have been zipped. This is shown in Figure 6-7. This figure is from my own computer, and one file had to be redacted for confidentiality reasons.

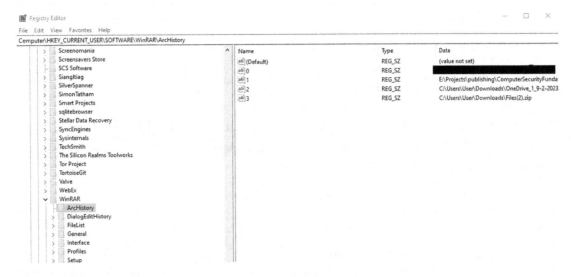

Figure 6-7. *ArcHistory*

Intuit TurboTax can also be found in the Registry. This could be of interest in financial investigations. You will find this key at \HKEY_CURRENT_USER\SOFTWARE\Intuit.

Forensics tools such as AccessData FTK and Registry Viewer are also found in the registry at \HKEY_CURRENT_USER\SOFTWARE\AccessData. This can be seen in Figure 6-8.

Figure 6-8. *AccessData in the Registry*

Adobe applications store a great deal of information in the Windows Registry at \
HKEY_CURRENT_USER\SOFTWARE\Adobe\Adobe Acrobat\DC\AdobeViewer. This
can be seen in Figure 6-9.

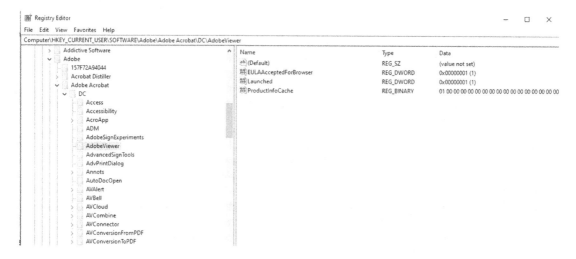

Figure 6-9. *Adobe in the Registry*

Cryptocurrency wallets will often have information in the Registry, for example,
Bitcoin information can be found at \HKEY_CURRENT_USER\SOFTWARE\Bitcoin\, as
shown in Figure 6-10.

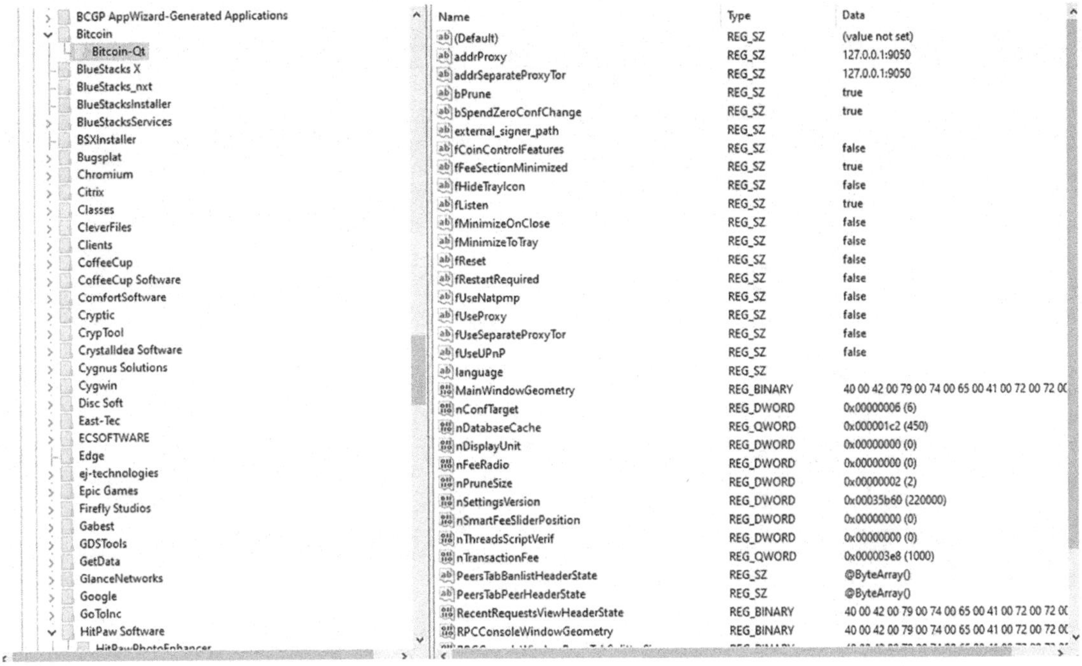

Figure 6-10. *Bitcoin in the Registry*

Obviously, these are not all the keys related to software. These keys will vary based on what software is installed on the computer. However, the information in this section should provide enough information for you to explore software installed on a computer.

Installed Applications

You have already seen places in the Windows Registry to look for registered software and other software. There is also a registry location for installed software. It can be useful to know what has been installed on the computer. There are several registry keys that can help with this analysis. One is found at \HKEY_CURRENT_USER\SOFTWARE\ Microsoft\Installer\Products. This key is shown in Figure 6-11 and a related key in 6-12.

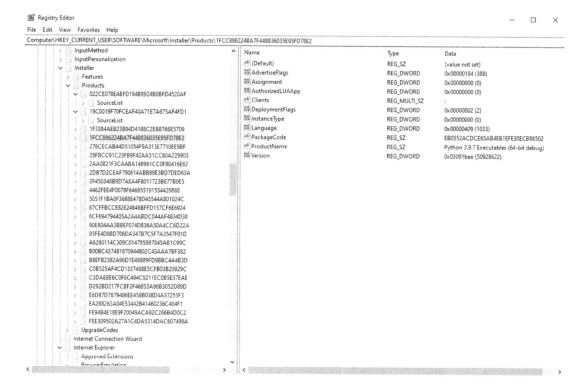

Figure 6-11. *Installed applications*

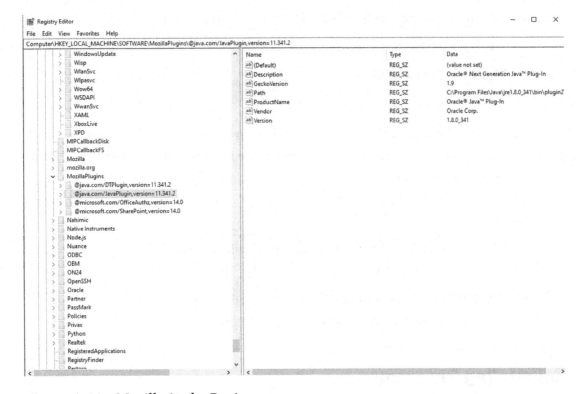

Figure 6-12. *Mozilla in the Registry*

Mozilla

Mozilla Firefox is a common browser, and you can find information about it in the Windows Registry at Computer\HKEY_LOCAL_MACHINE\SOFTWARE\MozillaPlugins

There are other places to find evidence regarding Mozilla outside the Registry. File located in

> C:\Documents and Settings\user\Application Data\Mozilla\
> Firefox\Profiles\<random text>\history.dat

> C:\Documents and Settings\user\Application Data\Mozilla\
> Profiles\<profile name>\<random text>\history.dat

There are three types of files in this directory:

A cache map file

Three cache block files

Separate cache data files

Along with the information in the Windows Registry, this can provide a good understanding of what that user has been doing in the Mozilla browser. Browser extensions can be useful in web hacking/malware investigations. It is possible that malware on the victim machine was installed as a browser extension. You can find these extensions at the following locations:

- %USERPROFILE%\AppData\Roaming\Mozilla\Firefox\ Profiles\<randomtext>.default\addons.json

- %USERPROFILE%\AppData\Roaming\Mozilla\Firefox\ Profiles\<randomtext>.default\extensions.json

Uninstalled Programs

Programs that have been removed via uninstall will still be listed in the Windows Registry. The key to search is

HKLM\Software\Wow6432Node\Microsoft\Windows\CurrentVersion\Uninstall\

This registry key will have numerous subkeys. Often, if a new version of software is installed, the old version is uninstalled. In Figure 6-13, you can see the Camtasia 9.0 key.

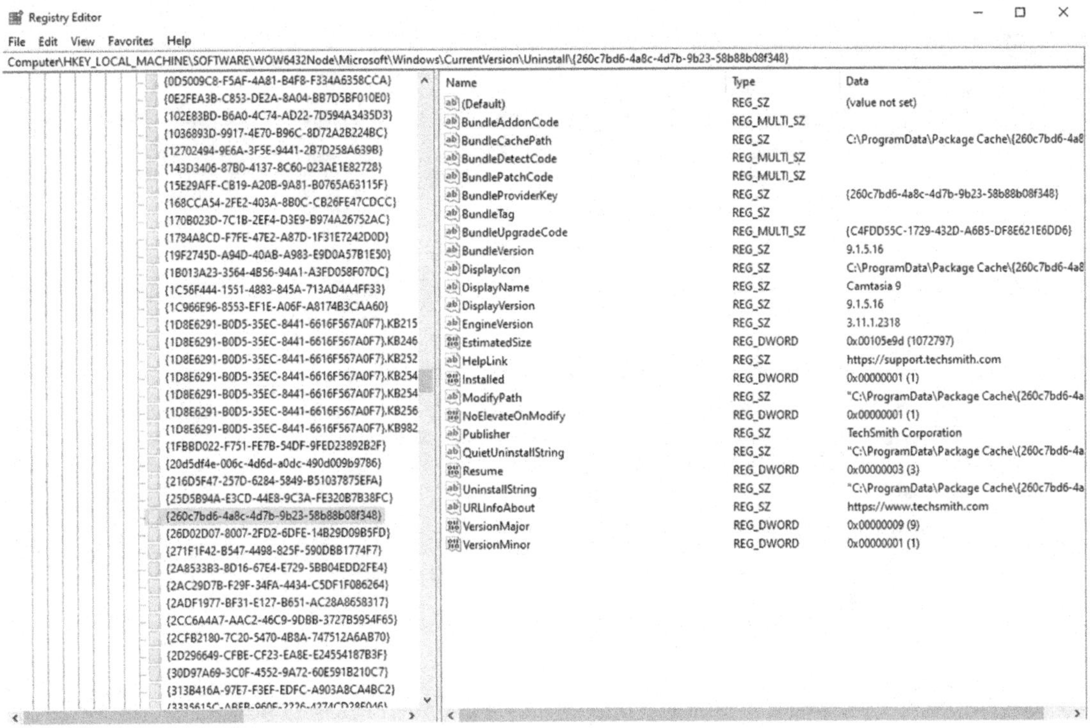

Figure 6-13. *Uninstalled programs*

This is a key that one can read without having to translate from hexadecimal. As can be seen, this was Camtasia 9.1.15.16. You can even see the website for the vendor of the software. If someone has used a password cracker, steganography tool, or something else they wish to deny using, they might believe that uninstalling will remove the evidence. This is incorrect.

Page File Management

This is a very interesting key. Normally, the Windows Page File is not cleared when a computer shuts down. Many people, even those quite proficient, are not aware of this fact. This allows a skilled forensic investigator to find evidence in that Page File. However, by using this registry key, one can change that, HKLM\SYSTEM\CurrentControlSet\ Control\Session Manager\Memory Management, as shown in Figure 6-14.

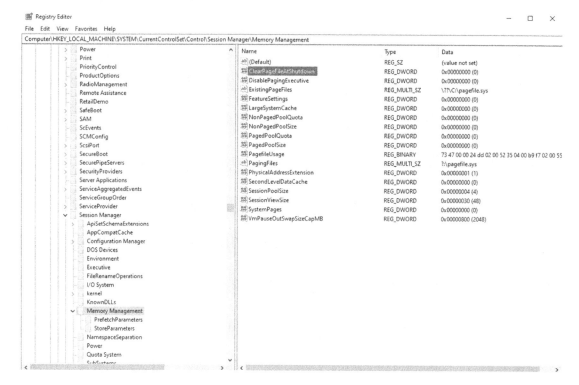

Figure 6-14. *Windows memory management*

This key maintains Windows virtual memory (paging file) configuration. Changing the data value of the ClearPageFileAtShutdown value in the preceding registry key to a value of 1 ensures that the pagefile.sys will be cleared upon system shutdown. Since this key can only be set by manually entering the Registry, if you find it is set, that indicates technical sophistication on the part of the computer owner.

BAM/DAM

The Background Activity Moderator (BAM) and Desktop Activity Moderator (DAM) are features in modern Windows operating systems designed to manage and optimize system resources, particularly focusing on the activity of background and foreground applications. BAM is designed to manage the activity of background applications, especially when the system is running on battery power. Its primary goal is to conserve energy and extend battery life by controlling how and when background apps can run.

DAM's role is more focused on managing the activities of applications when they are in the foreground, that is, actively being used by the user. It ensures that foreground applications have the necessary resources for smooth operation.

From a forensic perspective, the BAM registry keys (located under HKEY_LOCAL_ MACHINE\SYSTEM\CurrentControlSet\Services\bam\state\UserSettings\) can provide valuable information about the execution of applications, especially in a post-system shutdown scenario. They can indicate which applications were running before the system was shut down, aiding in reconstructing user activities; this is shown in Figure 6-15.

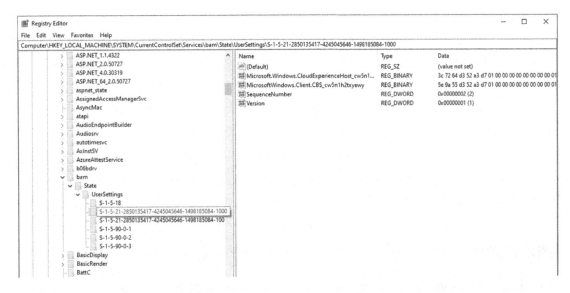

Figure 6-15. *BAM in the Registry*

DAM keys are found in the same general area, just down a bit lower, as shown in Figure 6-16.

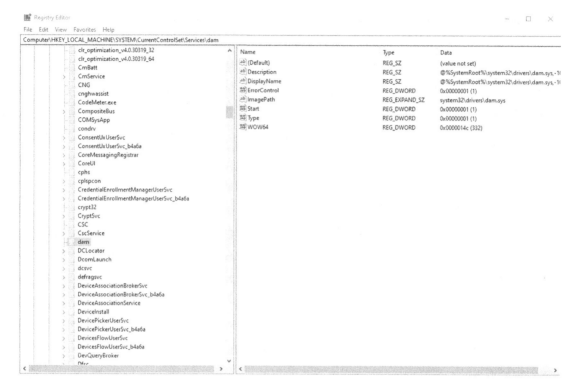

Figure 6-16. *DAM in the Registry*

AmCache

AmCache is an important artifact in forensic investigations of Windows systems. It's part of the Windows Registry and plays a crucial role in tracking and storing information about installed applications and executed programs. It was first introduced in Windows 8. One of the most valuable aspects of AmCache in forensics is its record of program execution. This includes timestamps indicating when a specific executable was first and last run on the system, which can be crucial in building a timeline of events. It also keeps track of installed software, including details about the installation such as the installer's file path, install date, and publisher information. Information about connected devices (e.g., USB devices) may also be recorded, providing insights into peripheral device usage. It can help identify if and when a particular piece of software, including malware, was executed. The AmCache.hve file is located at C:\Windows\appcompat\Programs\ Amcache.hve.

To view this hive, I will use Registry Explorer, described in the last chapter. For demonstration purposes, I am showing a game, *Civilization V*; this is shown in Figure 6-17.

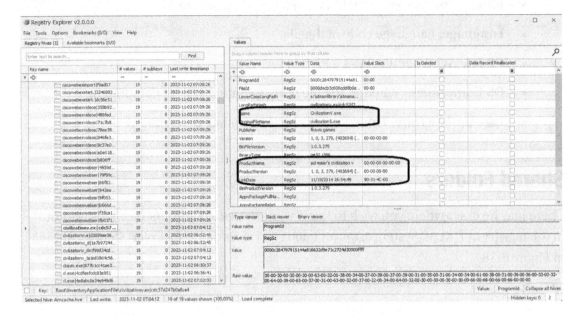

Figure 6-17. *AmCache*

Data you can find related to an application includes the following:

- **Application ID**: Application unique identifier

- **Application Name**: Name of the application

- **File Path**: The path of the application file

- **Size**: The size of the application file

- **SHA-1 Hash**: Application file signature

- **Long Path Hash**: Hash of the long path associated with the file

- **Publisher**: Name of published application

- **Application Version**: Application version

- **Link Date/Time**: Link date and time of the file

- **Binary File Version**: Binary file version of the application

- **Binary Type**: Binary type of the application

199

- **Product Name**: Name of the product

- **Product Version**: Product version of the application

- **Binary Product Version**: Binary version of the product

- **Language**: Language code of the file

- **PE File**: Whether the file is a PE header

- **OS Component**: Whether the file is an operating system component

- **Last Update Date/Time**: Registry key last update date/time

Shared Folders

There may be cases where you wish to know what shares a computer has. This is found in the registry at HKLM\System\ControlSet001\Services\lanmanserver\Shares\, shown in Figure 6-18.

Figure 6-18. *Shared folders*

This information, like much of what is found in the Registry, is in hexadecimal. You will need to convert from hexadecimal to text in order to read the values.

Typed Path

Windows Registry keeps information regarding when a user types in a path in Windows Explorer. That is found at \HKEY_CURRENT_USER\SOFTWARE\Microsoft\Windows\ CurrentVersion\Explorer\TypedPaths. Figure 6-19 shows the typed path registry keys. Some were redacted due to confidentiality issues.

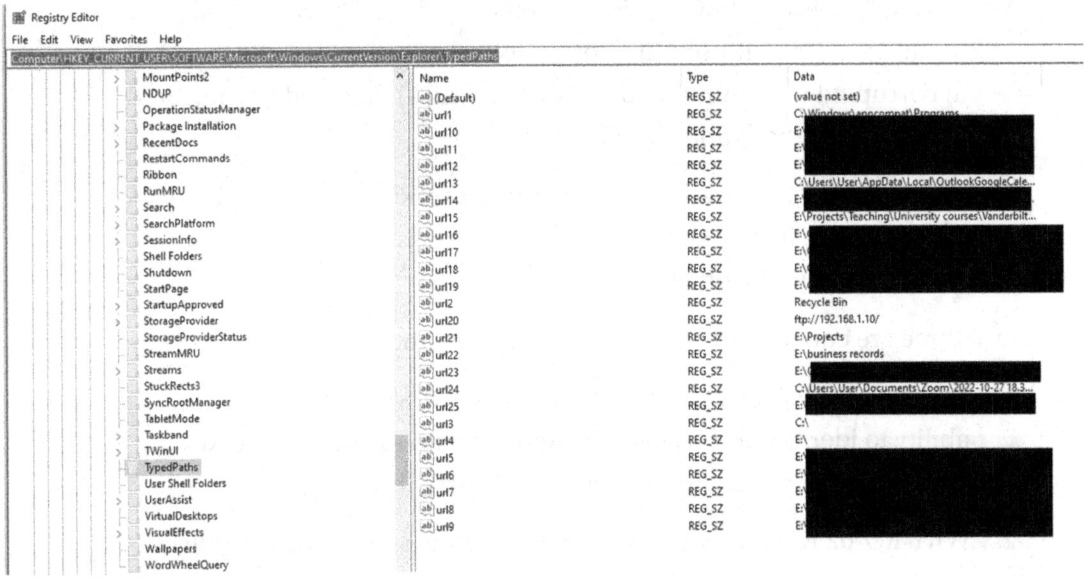

Figure 6-19. *Typed path*

This is another key that one can read without having to convert from hexadecimal. This is useful when someone is denying that they are even aware that certain data is on the computer. The fact that the user typed in the path and went directly to that data belies any such claim. Also, note this is under the HKEY_CURRENT_USER, so it is also tied directly to a specific user.

Using the Correct Tools

As you learned in Chapter 2, the correct forensic tools are important. The tool must be scientifically sound. Regarding Registry-specific tools, the National Institute of Standards and Technology (NIST) published recommendations on tools in 2018 (`www.nist.gov/system/files/documents/2018/06/28/wrt-spec-v1.0-public-draft-2.pdf`).

Rather than identify specific tools, NIST identified criteria a tool must meet:

- WRT-CR-01 A Windows Registry forensic tool shall support at least one of possible input data types, which include an independent hive file, a set of hive files, and a disk image containing Windows system partitions.

- WRT-CR-02 A Windows Registry forensic tool shall have the ability to notify the user of abnormal information (that can usually be found in corrupted or manipulated registry hive files) detected during data processing without application crash.

- WRT-CR-03 A Windows Registry forensic tool shall have the ability to perform an interpretation of supported registry objects without modification to the objects.

Those three are core features; optional features include

1. WRT-RO-01 A Windows Registry forensic tool shall have the ability to identify and recover deleted registry objects such as keys, values, and their data from supported registry hive files.

2. WRT-RO-02 A Windows Registry forensic tool shall have the ability to extract registry forensic artifacts.

These guidelines should help you to evaluate registry forensics tools and choose those that are forensically sound.

More Details on the Registry

It is certainly possible to perform effective Windows Registry forensics with the knowledge you have obtained so far in this and the preceding chapter. However, in digital forensics more knowledge is always better. You may have to manually search for data that tools don't locate, or you may need to simply understand what it is the tool is telling you. In this section, we will cover details of the Windows Registry that are often overlooked in many forensics books and courses.

As you learned in Chapter 5, the Registry isn't simply one large file but rather a set of separate files called *hives*. Each hive contains a Registry tree, which has a key that serves as the starting point or root for that tree. The values beneath that root are subkeys, and their values reside beneath the root. It might surprise you to learn that none of the root keys directly correlate to hives. Table 6-2 lists registry hives and their on-disk file names. The Windows Configuration Manager creates the root keys and then links the hives together to build the Registry structure you have been reviewing in this chapter and the previous chapter.

Table 6-2. *Registry Hives and Their On-Disk File Names*

Hive Registry Path	Hive File Path
HKEY_LOCAL_MACHINE \SYSTEM	\winnt\system32\config\system
HKEY_LOCAL_MACHINE \SAM	\winnt\system32\config\sam
HKEY_LOCAL_MACHINE \SECURITY	\winnt\system32\config\security
HKEY_LOCAL_MACHINE \SOFTWARE	\winnt\system32\config\software
HKEY_LOCAL_MACHINE \HARDWARE	Volatile hive
HKEY_LOCAL_MACHINE \SYSTEM \Clone	Volatile hive
HKEY_USERS \UserProfile	Profile; usually under \winnt\profiles\user
HKEY_USERS.DEFAULT	\winnt\system32\config\default

The Configuration Manager logically divides a hive into allocation units that are called *blocks* which are 4096 bytes (4KB). The first block of a hive is the *base block*. If additional data requires the hive to expand, it does so in blocks, not parts of blocks. That means in 4096-byte increments. The base block includes global information about the hive, including the following:

A signature that identifies the file as a hive

The hive format version number

The hive file's full name (e.g., SystemRoot\CONFIG\SAM)

A timestamp that shows the last time a write operation was initiated on that hive

Windows organizes the Registry data that a hive contains into *cells*. A cell can hold a key, a value, a security descriptor, a list of subkeys, or a list of key values. The cell's header is a field that specifies the size of the cell. When a cell joins a hive, the hive must grow to hold the cell. Windows creates an allocation unit called a *bin*. Bins also have headers that contain a signature and a field that records the offset into the hive file of the bin and the bin's size. Table 6-3 describes each cell data type in detail.

Table 6-3. *Cell Data Types*

Cell	Data Type
Key cell	A key cell contains a Registry key (sometimes called a key node). A key cell contains • A signature • The timestamp of the most recent update to the key • The cell index of the key's parent key cell • The cell index of the subkey-list cell that identifies the key's subkeys • The cell index for the key's security descriptor cell • The cell index for a string key that specifies the class name of the key • The name of the key
Value cell	A value cell contains information about a key's value. This cell includes • A signature • The value's name • The value's type (REG_BINARY, REG_LINK, REG_QWORD, etc.)
Subkey-list cell	A subkey-list cell is simply a list of cell indexes for key cells that are subkeys of a common parent key.
Value-list cell	A value-list cell is simply a list of cell indexes for value cells that are values of a common parent key.
Security-descriptor cell	A security-descriptor cell, as the name suggests, contains a security descriptor.

Windows uses bins, instead of cells, to track active parts of the Registry, in order to optimize maintenance. The links that create the structure of a hive are referred to as *cell indexes*. A cell index is simply the offset into the hive file of a cell. You can think of a cell index as a pointer from one cell to another cell.

Windows Configuration Manager doesn't access a hive's image on disk every time a Registry access occurs. Rather, Windows keeps a version of every hive in the kernel's address space. When a hive initializes, the Configuration Manager determines the size of the hive file, allocates sufficient memory from the kernel's paged pool to store the hive file, then reads the hive file into memory. Early in the Windows boot sequence, this process is what Ntldr does with the SYSTEM hive. Ntldr reads the SYSTEM hive into memory as a read-only hive and adds the cell indexes to the base of the in-memory hive image to locate cells.

Conclusions

This chapter built on what you learned in Chapter 5. By combining the knowledge of these two chapters, you should have a solid working knowledge of the Windows Registry, as well as its importance in forensics. As you work in forensics you may discover that not all registry keys are examined or reported by all forensics tools. Some, such as the USB keys described in chapter 5 are described by almost all forensics tools. Other, such as MuiCache are frequently not reported. One reason to gain a deep understanding of the Windows Registry is so that you can manually examine registry keys should the need arise. You have also seen in this chapter, and the previous chapter, that some evidence is actually stored in several locations. For example, we explored four different Registry areas to look for evidence of software on a computer. This redundancy makes it difficult for a suspect to remove all evidence. Even a technically proficient suspect is unlikely to find and eliminate all evidence from a Windows computer, short of completely wiping the machine.

Test Your Knowledge

1. On Windows 10 or 11, what is the primary difference between RegEdt32 and Regedit?

    a. RegEdt32 is read only.

    b. Regedit is read only.

    c. None.

    d. RegEdt32 has advanced search features.

2. _____ is a technology in Windows that allows for the interface of an application to be displayed in multiple languages.

    a. AmCache

    b. MUICache

    c. BAM

    d. DAM

3. What size are registry blocks?

    a. 256 bits

    b. 256 bytes

    c. 4096 bytes

    d. Variable

4. Windows organizes the Registry data that a hive contains into ___.

    a. Blocks

    b. Subkeys

    c. Hives

    d. Cells

5. The ____ registry keys can indicate which applications were running before the system was shut down, aiding in reconstructing user activities.

    a. AmCache

    b. MUICache

    c. ComDlg

    d. BAM

CHAPTER 7

Windows Shadow Copy

Chuck Easttom, Ph.D., D.Sc.

Introduction

Having backups of key data, data that has changed, is important. Since Windows 7, Microsoft has included a feature called Volume Shadow Copy, often abbreviated VSS, to accomplish this goal. With VSS, data is backed up once per day. Windows Shadow Copy was first introduced in Windows Server 2003 and has been available in all Windows versions since Windows 7, although the features vary slightly from one version to another. Windows Volume Shadow Copy state changes in blocks of data are compared daily and changed blocks copied to volume shadow. VSS service runs once per day. VSS backs up 16kb blocks of data. In differential copies of VSS, only the changes are backed up, on a cluster-by-cluster basis. For a full copy or clone, entire files are backed up.

How It Works

The Windows Shadow Copy feature automatically makes a copy of files that have changed and been saved. This feature allows a user to open an earlier version of a file using the Previous Versions feature. It should be turned on automatically, but if for some reason it is not, then it is easy to activate it. You first type in *create a restore point* in the Windows search bar. This is shown in Figure 7-1.

© Chuck Easttom, William Butler, Jessica Phelan, Ramya Sai Bhagavatula, Sean Steuber, Karely Rodriguez, Victoria Indy Balkissoon, Zehra Naseer 2024
C. Easttom et al., *Windows Forensics*, https://doi.org/10.1007/979-8-8688-0193-8_7

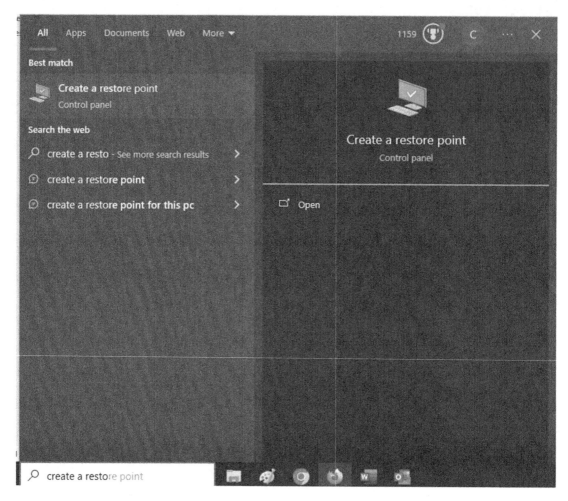

Figure 7-1. *Create a restore point*

The next step is to select a drive and click *configure*. This is shown in Figure 7-2.

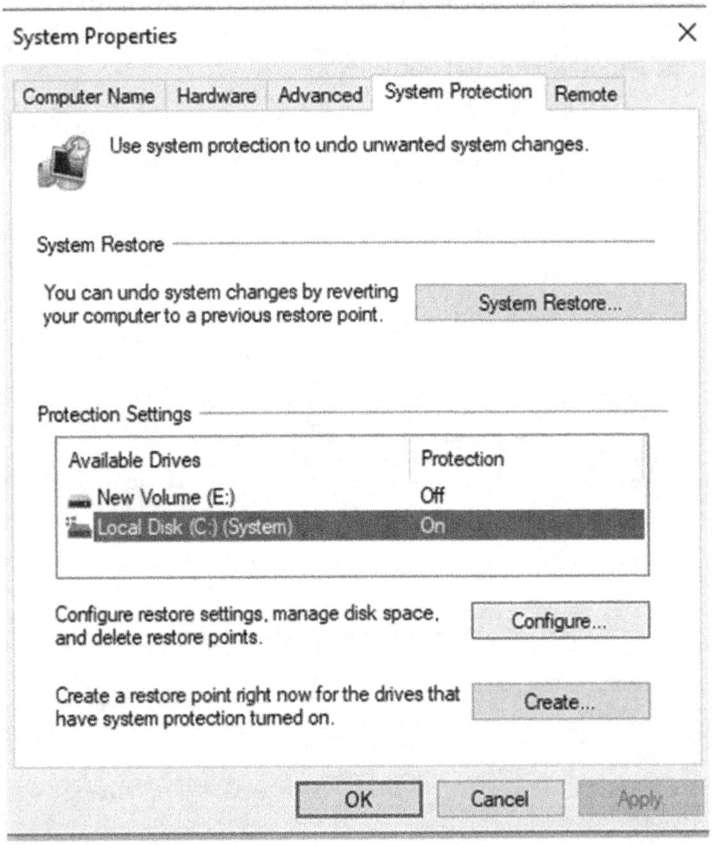

Figure 7-2. *Configuration step 1*

You will then be presented with a screen that allows you to turn on system protection and set disk space to be used for this feature. This is shown in Figure 7-3.

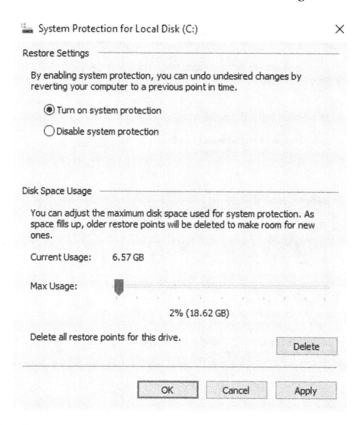

Figure 7-3. *Configuration step 2*

To schedule Volume Shadow Copy, or any other process, you type Task Scheduler in the Windows search bar to launch the scheduler. This is shown in Figure 7-4.

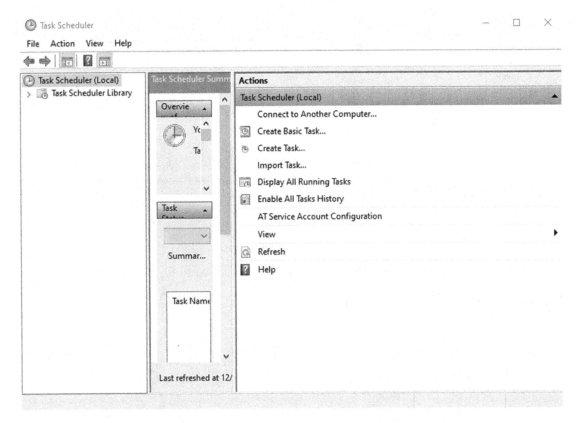

Figure 7-4. *Task Scheduler*

Then you can schedule the task as shown in Figures 7-5 to 7-10.

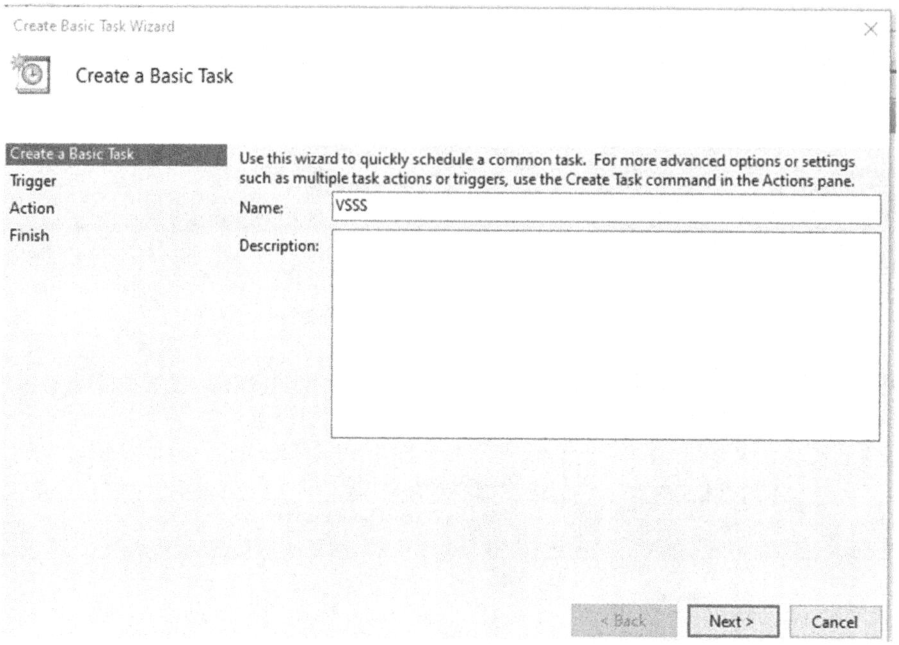

Figure 7-5. *Schedule a task step 1*

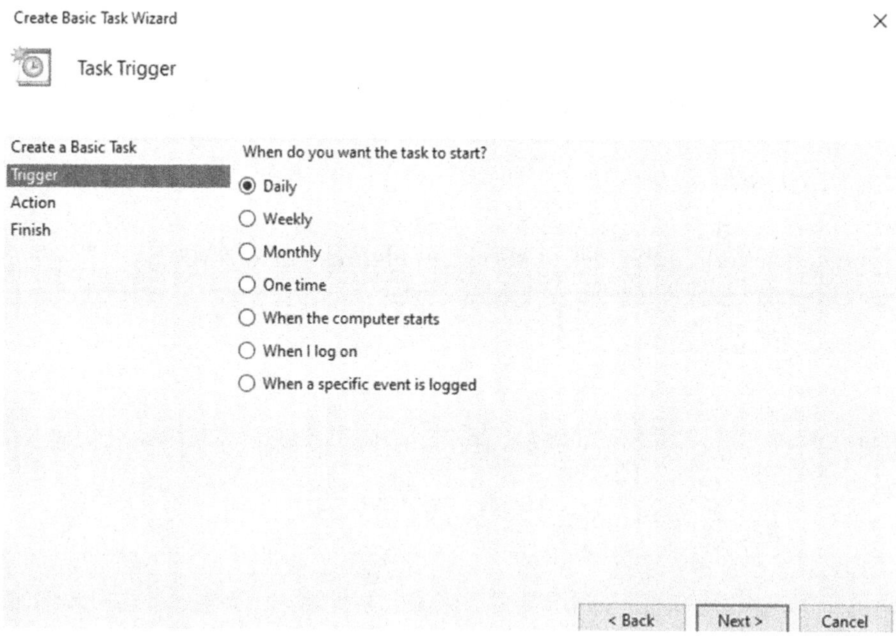

Figure 7-6. *Schedule a task step 2*

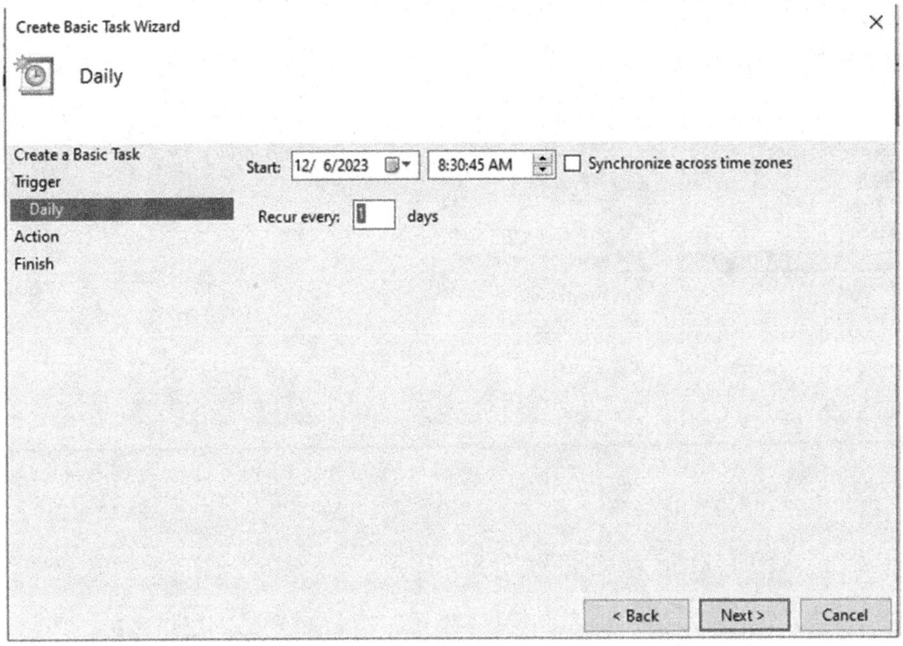

Figure 7-7. *Schedule a task step 3*

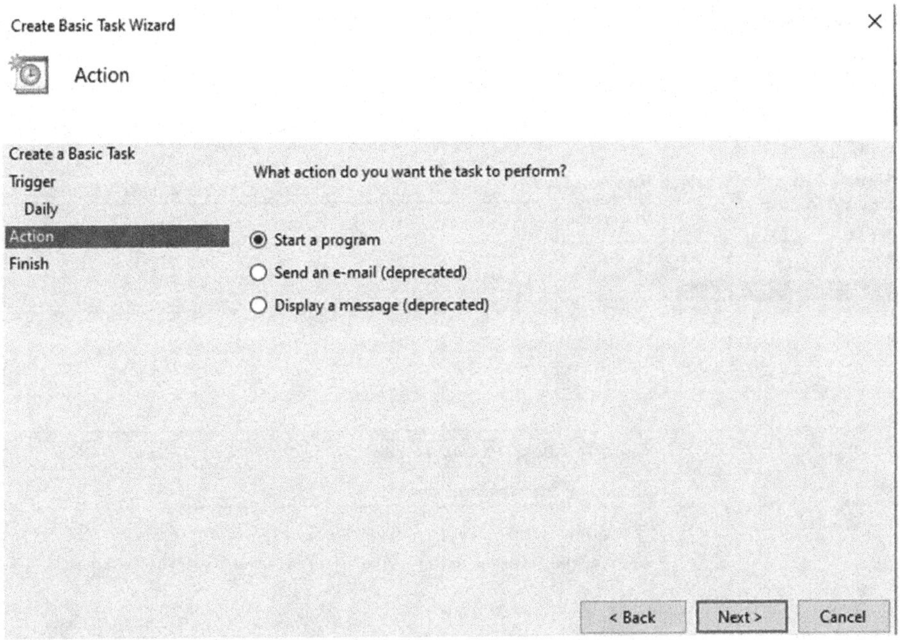

Figure 7-8. *Schedule a task step 4*

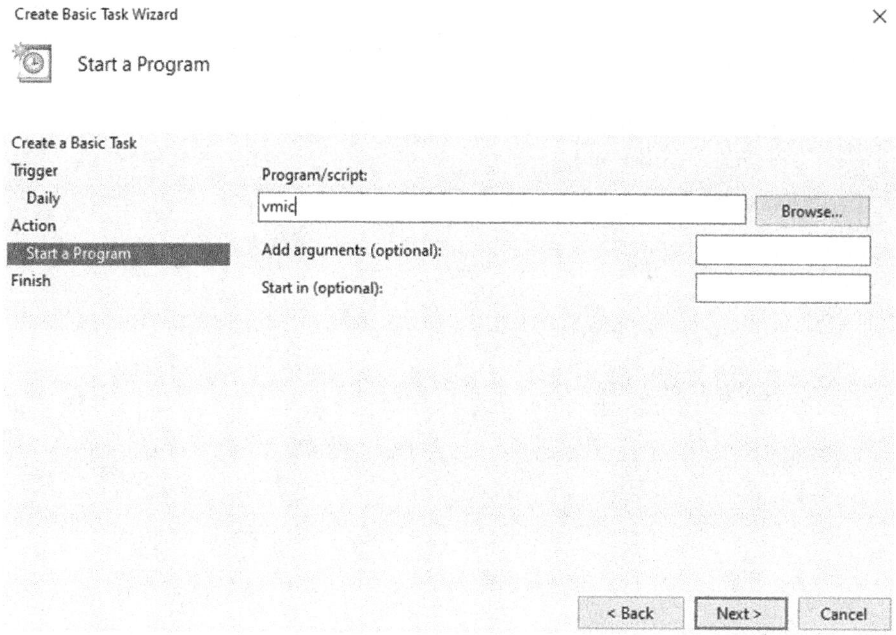

Figure 7-9. Schedule a task step 5

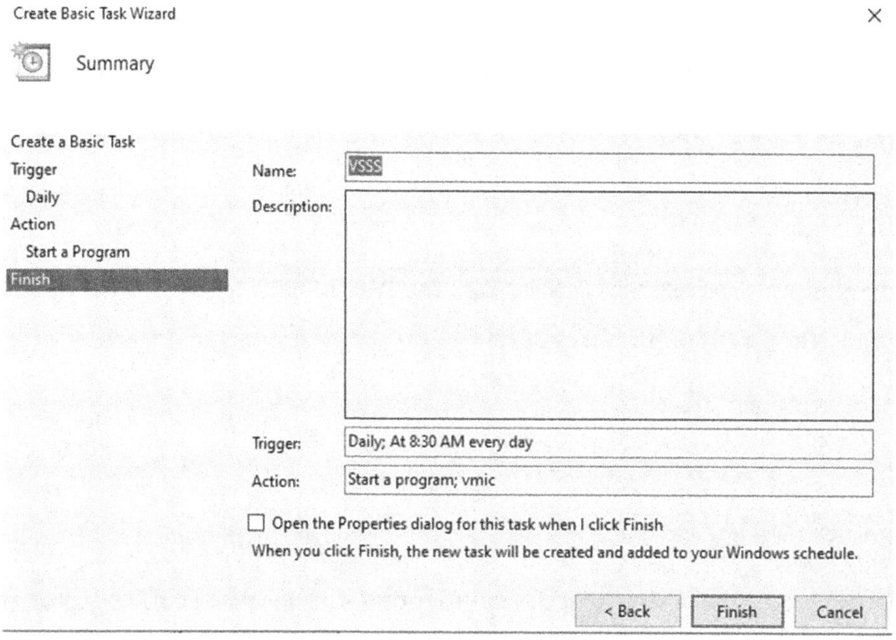

Figure 7-10. Schedule a task step 6

To view past copies of a given file or folder, right-click the current version of that file and select Properties from the shortcut menu. Next, select the Previous Versions tab to view available version of the file. Select the desired file and then click Restore. This is shown in Figure 7-11.

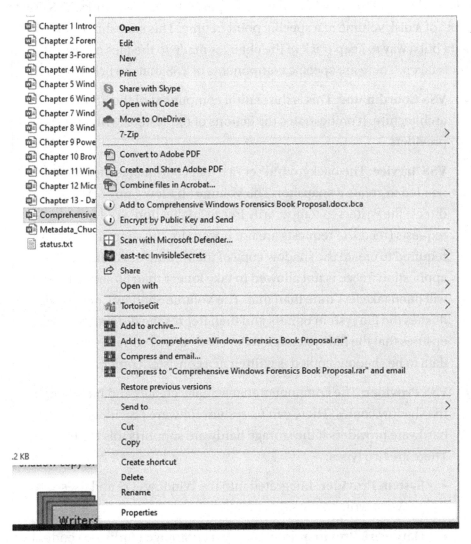

Figure 7-11. *Restore previous version*

Working with VSS is rather simple via the Windows interface. Given it has backups of data, the forensic importance of VSS should be rather clear. Forensically analyzing VSS will be described later in this chapter.

VSS Details

While various forensics tools will provide you information from VSS, this book is focused on you understanding the how and why behind the Windows technologies you analyze. Therefore, in this section, we will dive a bit deeper into how VSS works. VSS creates a "snapshot" of a disk volume at a specific point in time. This snapshot is not a full copy of the data but a way to keep track of the changes made to the files or disk after the snapshot is taken. There are specific components of VSS that are briefly described here:

- **VSS Coordinator**: This is the central component of the VSS architecture. It orchestrates the actions of requesters, writers, and providers.

- **VSS Service**: The background service that coordinates the actions needed to create a snapshot. The Volume Shadow Copy Service directs the writers to temporarily freeze application write I/O requests (read I/O requests are not frozen) for the short time that is required to create the shadow copy of the volume or volumes. The application freeze is not allowed to take longer than 60 seconds and will often take less time than that. The Volume Shadow Copy Service flushes the file system buffers and then freezes the file system, which ensures that the file system metadata is recorded correctly and the data to be shadow-copied is written in a consistent order.

- **VSS Provider**: The component that actually creates and maintains the shadow copies. There can be system software providers or hardware providers if the storage hardware supports this feature. There are two types:

  - **System Provider**: Integrated into the Windows OS and uses copy-on-write to manage changes.

  - **Hardware Provider**: Implemented by storage hardware vendors and can leverage the capabilities of the storage array (like creating hardware-based snapshots.

- **VSS Requesters**: These are backup applications or other software that request the creation of shadow copies. They communicate with the VSS coordinator to initiate the process. Essentially, requesters request the Volume Shadow Copy Service to enumerate the writers, gather the writer metadata, and prepare for shadow copy creation.

- **VSS Writers**: Each VSS Writer is specific to an application and ensures that the application's data is in a consistent state for a shadow copy. For example, a database system might need to flush transactions to disk or pause writes momentarily. Writers create an XML description of the components and data stores that are to be backed up and provide that XML description to the Volume Shadow Copy Service. The writer also defines a restore method. The Volume Shadow Copy Service provides the writer's description to the requester, which selects the components that will be backed up.

It is also important to understand how and why VSS is used. Clearly, VSS is used for backups, but there are specific backups it is used for. The most common uses are listed here:

- **Backups**: The most common use of VSS is to create backups. By taking a snapshot, backup software can copy files without worrying about them being changed during the copy process.

- **System Restore**: Windows uses VSS to create restore points, which can be used to roll back the system to a previous state.

- **Volume Cloning**: In some scenarios, VSS can be used to clone volumes or migrate data.

When a snapshot is taken, VSS temporarily redirects writes to the volume to a different area (called a diff area or delta area). This way, the snapshot represents the volume's state at a specific point in time. Read operations on the snapshot are redirected to the original data or to the diff area as appropriate, making it appear as if the snapshot is a full read-only copy of the volume.

While generally efficient, VSS can impact system performance, especially if many snapshots are maintained or if the diff area becomes large. Snapshots require additional storage space, which can grow with the number of changes made to the original volume. The diff area can grow over time as changes are made to the original volume. Managing the size and location of the diff area is important for performance and storage efficiency.

VSS should not be relied upon as the sole backup mechanism since it does not protect against hardware failures, and snapshots can be corrupted if the original volume is damaged. Administrators can manage VSS through various tools provided by Windows, like the Disk Management snap-in and the VSSAdmin command-line tool, which we will examine a little later in this chapter. One can also manage VSS with PowerShell cmdlets. PowerShell will be discussed in detail in Chapter 9.

The process of creating a shadow copy is relatively straightforward and is summarized in the following steps:

1. **Initialization**: A VSS requester initiates the shadow copy process.

2. **Preparation**: The VSS coordinator communicates with VSS writers to ensure that the data is in a consistent state. Writers prepare their data, often by completing transactions or flushing buffers.

3. **Freeze**: After preparation, the writers are instructed to freeze their write activity. This freeze window is typically very short (a few seconds) to minimize disruption.

4. **Snapshot Creation**: The VSS provider then creates a shadow copy of the volume. If using the system provider, it implements a copy-on-write mechanism. When data on the volume is modified, the original data is copied to a different location (the diff area) before the modification, preserving the state of the data at the time of the snapshot. VSS can manage multiple snapshots of the same volume. Each snapshot has its own diff area.

5. **Thaw**: Once the snapshot is taken, the writers are instructed to resume their normal activities.

6. **Post-Processing**: Any final steps are completed, such as logging.

Data changes are managed in a few different ways, depending on the specific change:

Copy-on-Write: When a write operation occurs to a block on the original volume, the system first copies the original block to the diff area (if this is the first write to this block since the snapshot was taken). The write operation then proceeds on the original volume.

Reading from Snapshot: When reading data from a shadow copy, the system reads from the original volume unless the block was modified after the snapshot, in which case it reads from the diff area.

The primary registry keys related to Volume Shadow Copy are

HKEY_LOCAL_MACHINE\SYSTEM\CurrentControlSet\Services\VSS

and

HKEY_LOCAL_MACHINE\SYSTEM\CurrentControlSet\Control\BackupRestore

The first key provides general settings on VSS. It is the second key that has the most interesting information and is shown in Figure 7-12.

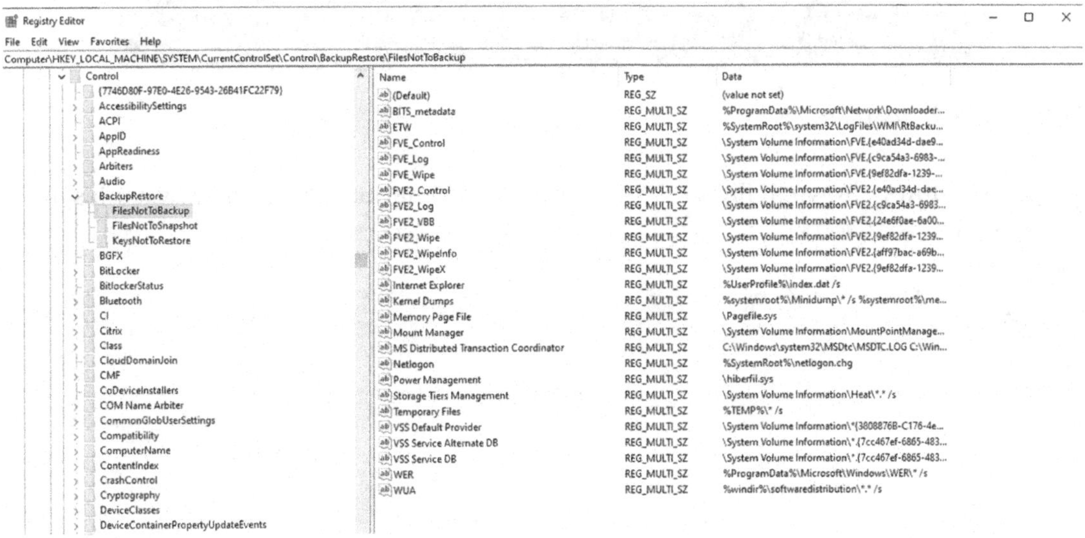

Figure 7-12. *VSS registry keys*

As you can see in Figure 7-12, this has specific files and keys that are not to be backed up or restored. You don't need to edit the Registry directly in order to configure VSS, but it is important to know as much about VSS as you can, including the relevant registry keys.

Windows has a built-in utility named VSSAdmin. You will need to execute it from a command-line window with administrator privileges. By typing in vssadmin, you will see the options, as shown in Figure 7-13.

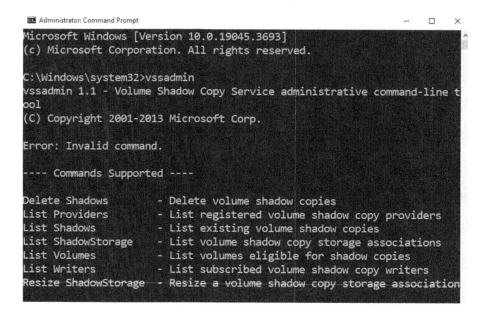

Figure 7-13. *vssadmin*

List Shadows, shown in Figure 7-14, provides information on the shadow copies on this system.

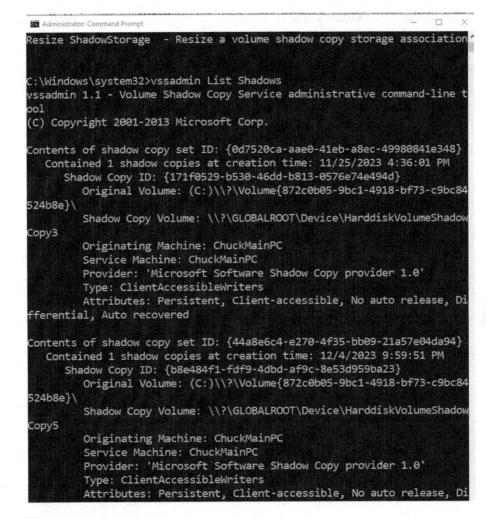

Figure 7-14. *List Shadows*

The vssadmin utility is the primary method that administrators use to interact with Volume Shadow Copy. There are a number of commands you may find useful:

- Add a volume shadow copy storage association:

    - VSSADMIN add shadowstorage /for=ForVolumeSpec / on=OnVolumeSpec [/maxsize=MaxSizeSpec]

- Create a new volume shadow copy:

    - VSSADMIN create shadow /for=ForVolumeSpec [/ autoretry=MaxRetryMinutes]

- Delete volume shadow copies:

  - VSSADMIN delete shadows /for=ForVolumeSpec [/oldest | /all | /shadow=ShadowID] [/quiet]

- Delete volume shadow copy storage associations:

  - VSSADMIN delete shadowstorage /for=ForVolumeSpec [/on=OnVolumeSpec] [/quiet]

- List registered volume shadow copy providers:

  - VSSADMIN list providers

- List existing volume shadow copies:

  - VSSADMIN list shadows [/for=ForVolumeSpec] [/shadow=ShadowID]

- List all shadow copy storage associations on the system:

  - VSSADMIN list shadowstorage {/for=ForVolumeSpec | /on=OnVolumeSpec}

- List volumes that are eligible for shadow copies:

  - VSSADMIN list volumes

- List all subscribed volume shadow copy writers on the system:

  - VSSADMIN list writers

VSS Forensics

Volume Shadow Copy can provide forensically relevant information. One area that Volume Shadow Copy can help with is deleted files. Files that have been deleted from the current file system may still exist in a shadow copy. Because shadow copies clone on a block level rather than a file level, changes to individual files may not be enough to cause Windows to make the changes in a corresponding shadow copy. Shadow copies also help with timeline analysis. By examining multiple shadow copies, investigators can build a timeline of file changes.

There are a number of tools that will help you view the contents of the Volume Shadow Copy. *Shadow Copy View* from NirSoft[1] is freeware. You can see *Shadow Copy View* in Figure 7-15.

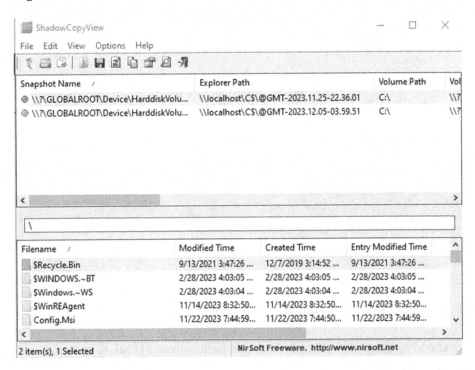

Figure 7-15. *Shadow Copy View*

You can right-click any file or folder and see the properties, as shown in Figure 7-16.

---

[1]www.nirsoft.net/utils/shadow_copy_view.html

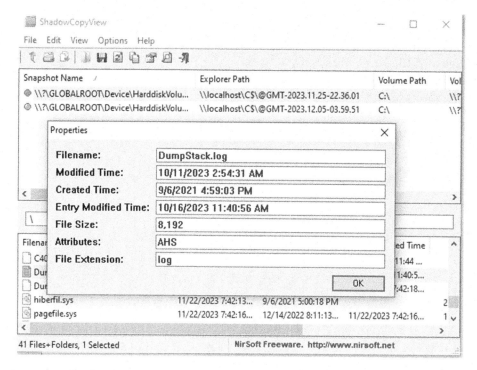

Figure 7-16. *Shadow Copy View file properties*

Under the View drop-down menu, you can generate an HTML report of the files. This is shown in Figure 7-17.

Files List In Shadow Copy

Created by using ShadowCopyView

Filename	Modified Time	Created Time	Entry Modified Time	File Size	Attributes	File Extension
$Recycle.Bin	9/13/2021 3:47:26 PM	12/7/2019 3:14:52 AM	9/13/2021 3:47:26 PM		HSD	Bin
$WINDOWS.~BT	2/28/2023 4:03:05 PM	2/28/2023 4:03:05 PM	2/28/2023 4:03:05 PM		D	~BT
$Windows.~WS	2/28/2023 4:03:04 PM	2/28/2023 4:03:04 PM	2/28/2023 4:03:04 PM		HDI	~WS
$WinREAgent	11/14/2023 8:32:50 PM	11/14/2023 8:32:50 PM	11/14/2023 8:32:50 PM		HD	
Config.Msi	11/22/2023 7:44:59 PM	11/22/2023 7:44:50 PM	11/22/2023 7:44:59 PM		HSD	Msi
Documents and Settings	9/6/2021 5:00:27 PM	9/6/2021 5:00:27 PM	3/15/2023 2:38:54 PM		HSDI	
EvtxECmd	10/8/2023 11:02:16 AM	10/8/2023 11:02:16 AM	10/8/2023 11:02:18 AM		D	
inetpub	3/7/2023 11:07:20 AM	3/7/2023 11:07:20 AM	3/7/2023 11:07:20 AM		D	
Intel	11/22/2023 7:42:20 PM	9/6/2021 2:04:36 PM	11/22/2023 7:42:20 PM		D	
jmp	9/30/2022 3:04:52 PM	9/30/2022 3:03:06 PM	9/30/2022 3:04:52 PM		D	
MSOCache	10/31/2023 12:06:08 PM	10/31/2023 12:06:08 PM	10/31/2023 12:10:33 PM		RHDI	
N-Stalker	2/17/2023 7:28:06 PM	1/27/2023 12:04:39 PM	2/17/2023 7:28:06 PM		D	
NRC	11/12/2021 8:36:35 AM	11/12/2021 8:36:35 AM	11/12/2021 8:36:35 AM		D	
OneDriveTemp	9/13/2021 3:58:39 PM	9/13/2021 3:58:39 PM	9/13/2021 3:58:39 PM		HD	
PerfLogs	12/7/2019 3:14:52 AM	12/7/2019 3:14:52 AM	9/6/2021 5:58:27 PM		D	
platform-tools	8/20/2022 3:40:50 PM	8/20/2022 3:40:47 PM	8/20/2022 3:40:54 PM		D	

Figure 7-17. *Shadow Copy View HTML report*

This tool is rather easy to use. The file attributes might be confusing to you at first:

> D is a directory.

> I indicates content is not indexed.

> H indicates a hidden file.

> R indicates an associated reparse point.

OSForensics has a tool to analyze shadow copies. It can be found in the OSForensics workflow shown in Figure 7-18.

Figure 7-18. *OSForensics Analyze Shadow Copies*

The window for Analyze Shadow Copies is shown in Figure 7-19.

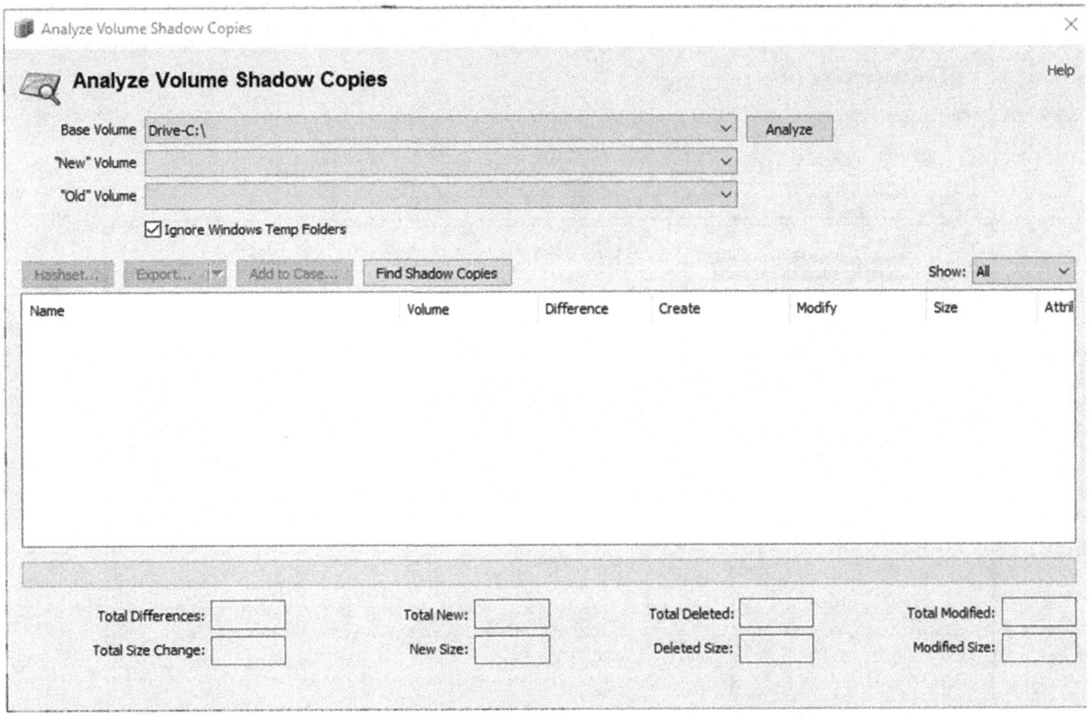

Figure 7-19. *Analyze Shadow Copies part 1*

You first select Find Shadow Copies, then click Analyze. It will take a few minutes to run, but when done you will see the window shown in Figure 7-20.

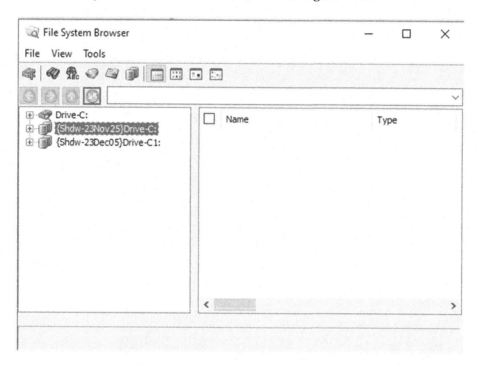

Figure 7-20. *Analyze Shadow Copies part 2*

You can expand the shadow copies shown and explore. This is a relatively easy tool that allows you to navigate through a shadow copy.

Conclusions

Volume Shadow Copy can be useful in digital forensics in establishing a timeline and in recovering files that have been deleted. Many users are not even aware of Volume Shadow Copy, making it less likely to have been deleted by someone attempting to hide evidence. In any Windows forensics investigation, you should at least examine the VSS. As you have seen in this chapter, there are many tools for accomplishing this task.

References

Microsoft Volume Shadow Copy Service, `https://learn.microsoft.com/en-us/windows-server/storage/file-server/volume-shadow-copy-service`

Stanford, `www2.slac.stanford.edu/comp/winnt/system-administration/ou_admin_meeting_minutes/volume_shadow_copy.htm`

Test Your Knowledge

1. What component of VSS actually creates the shadow copies?

    a. VSS service

    b. VSS provider

    c. VSS requester

    d. VSS cloner

2. Once a snapshot is taken, what is the next step?

    a. Freeze

    b. Thaw

    c. Restore

    d. Cloning

3. The _____ orchestrates the actions of requesters, writers, and providers.

    a. VSS service

    b. VSS system provider

    c. VSS coordinator

    d. VSS hardware provider

4. At what level does VSS clone?

   a. Bit level

   b. Byte level

   c. File level

   d. Block level

5. What version of Windows first introduced VSS?

   a. Server 2003

   b. Windows 2000

   c. Windows 7

   d. Server 2008

CHAPTER 8

Windows Memory Forensics

Ramya Sai Bhagavatula
Chuck Easttom, Ph.D., D.Sc.

Introduction

In the field of digital forensics and cybersecurity, the analysis of volatile memory has emerged as an extremely important technique for uncovering valuable artifacts and investigating cyber incidents. By analyzing the contents of computer memory, one can obtain critical information such as active processes, network connections, user interactions, and even encrypted data. This chapter focuses on Windows memory forensics, an area of study dedicated to extracting and interpreting digital evidence residing in the volatile memory of Windows operating systems. This chapter will delve more into various memory acquisition techniques, exploring both live and offline approaches and discussing their advantages, limitations, and potential forensic implications. You will also learn the advanced analysis techniques employed to identify and extract specific artifacts from memory dumps. Through comprehensive knowledge and the implementation of these techniques, individuals can enhance their personal cybersecurity and effectively protect themselves against ever-present cyber threats.

As of 2020 the number of smartphone users in the world is 6.92 billion, which translates to 86.11% of the world's population owning a smartphone (BankMyCell, 2023) and over 67% using laptops or computers to access the Internet. As technology keeps advancing day by day, our dependence on these digital systems also increases significantly. Cybercriminals continuously adapt their strategies, executing complex attacks that can jeopardize personal and organizational information, disrupt critical infrastructure, and inflict substantial financial and reputational harm. In 2022, it was

© Chuck Easttom, William Butler, Jessica Phelan, Ramya Sai Bhagavatula, Sean Steuber, Karely Rodriguez, Victoria Indy Balkissoon, Zehra Naseer 2024
C. Easttom et al., *Windows Forensics*, https://doi.org/10.1007/979-8-8688-0193-8_8

stated that over 2.8 billion malware attacks were launched in just the first half of 2022 alone, with an estimated 2200 cyberattacks per day (Packetlabs, 2023). As of 2023, there are an estimated 800,000 cyberattacks per year, with those numbers only increasing in the upcoming years. With that said, the importance of efficient digital forensics practices for both individuals and organizations becomes crucial.

During investigations involving malware attacks, it may be necessary for the computer's memory to be examined. This is where memory forensics plays a key role in completely understanding the malware attack and its nature. Memory forensics is the process of capturing the running memory of a device and later analyzing the captured output for evidence of malicious software. In this section, we'll delve deeply into memory forensics, specifically as it pertains to computers running the Windows operating system. We'll explore the methods used to scrutinize evidence found in memory and conduct analyses using tools like Volatility Workbench CMD and PassMark OSForensics Volatility Workbench.

What Is Computer Memory?

It is first important to have a working understanding of memory in order to proceed with memory forensics. Computer memory stores information, such as data and programs, for immediate use on the computer. Memory is first categorized as volatile or nonvolatile. Examples of nonvolatile memories include all types of flash, EPROM, and EEPROM. Most modern embedded systems use some type of flash memory for nonvolatile storage. Volatile memories only hold their contents while power is applied to the memory device. Examples of volatile memories include static RAM (SRAM), synchronous static RAM (SSRAM), synchronous dynamic RAM (SDRAM), and FPGA on-chip memory. It is the volatile memory that we are interested in when conducting memory forensics.

There is a "distinct hierarchy" that is followed when the CPU requests this data, as there are various memory options available. When a computer receives input from sources like a keyboard, microphone, mouse, or data from permanent storage devices such as a hard drive or removable media, the data is initially stored in the Random Access Memory (RAM). Data is rapidly transferred between the CPU and RAM. When an application is closed, it and its files are usually deleted from RAM to make way for new data. If modified files are not saved to permanent storage before this deletion, they will be lost. Windows operating systems also employ virtual memory, a technique that allows processes to use more memory than is physically available. This technique helps with efficient memory allocation and utilization.

Frequently accessed data may also be stored in cache memory to improve performance. Additionally, certain special instructions or data are stored in registers, which are small, high-speed memory locations within the processor. These registers hold data that the processor needs to access quickly during its operations. Registers and caches are crucial components of a computer's memory. In Windows memory forensics, analyzing registers reveals processor states during incidents, while cache analysis uncovers vital artifacts such as user activities and recent file accesses, process execution states, memory addresses, cryptographic keys, passwords, and traces of user activities. These artifacts can provide insights into the behavior of malicious software, user interactions, data manipulation, and the overall state of the system during the occurrence of security incidents. Understanding both is vital for reconstructing events, identifying malware, and gathering evidence.

How Does Computer Memory Work?

RAM is made up of millions or billions of individual memory cells, each capable of storing a certain amount of data. The memory cell is an electronic circuit that holds a bit of binary information and is the fundamental block of memory. Each memory cell has a unique address, allowing the CPU to access and manipulate specific data in RAM. A 4-bit RAM has 4 memory cells per address; a 32-bit system can handle up to 4,294,967,295 bytes, or 4 gigabytes of RAM. Most modern computers have 64-bit addressing, which can handle 18,446,744,073,709,551,616 bytes of data, which is technically millions and millions of bytes of data used for processing information. 32-bit programs can also be installed on 64-bit systems, making it flexible to install either application.

Apart from memory cells, there is a controller that is used to store and fetch data from memory addresses. A memory address register (MAR or CPU register) is used to hold these addresses in memory, and a memory data register (MDR) is used to store data that is being transferred to and from the memory. To put all this terminology into an example, suppose you have opened an application that is stored on your SSD. It is first temporarily loaded into memory. The address of the cell is stored in the MAR, and its data is stored in the MDR. This is how the whole process works in memory on a Windows computer.

Another topic we must understand is memory allocation. Memory allocation is the process of reserving a partial or complete portion of computer memory for the execution of programs and processes. A forensic examiner should be aware that there are two types of memory, that is, stack and heap.

Stack memory is a LIFO-based region for storing local variables and function call information. The compiler automatically manages it, ensuring effective allocation and deallocation. With a fixed size and fast access, stack memory is ideal for small variables with short lifespans.

Heap memory, on the other hand, enables the dynamic allocation of data structures like arrays and objects at runtime. It offers flexibility but requires manual allocation and deallocation. Programming languages such as C use functions like malloc() and free() to manage heap memory.

Windows Memory Management

As this book is focused on Windows forensics, this section will address how Windows manages memory. It should first be noted that Windows, as well as all operating systems, use what is called virtual address space. Essentially, the physical RAM has addresses, and data is loaded into those addresses. However, the data might not be in contiguous address spaces. So, Windows uses virtual addresses so that programs will see what appears to be contiguous address spaces. When some process reads or writes to virtual address spaces, that address is translated (also called mapping) to a physical address space. This process is facilitated by a translation lookaside buffer (TLB). This is basically a cache that is searched first for an item in memory. If not found in the TLB, the page table is searched.

The virtual memory is divided into *pages* that are contiguous blocks of virtual memory. A page is the smallest unit of data for memory management in virtual memory. A page frame is the smallest contiguous block of physical memory that virtual memory pages are mapped to. Pages are organized into page tables. This means the smaller the page size, the more pages are needed; thus, the page table grows larger.

Pages in a process virtual address space are *free, reserved, committed*, or *shareable*. Shareable and committed pages ultimately translate to valid pages in physical memory. Committed pages cannot be shared with other processes and are thus often called *private* pages. Private memory pages are allocated using the Windows *VirtualAlloc*, *VirtualAllocEx*, and *VirtualAllocExNuma* functions. Pages that are free are available for allocation, whereas reserved pages are not available for allocation.

The Windows memory manager is part of the Windows executive and resides in the Ntoskrnl.exe. Windows memory manager handles the virtual memory including the page table and the TLB. The memory manager also provides a core set of services that other Windows subsystems can use. These services include files that are mapped to memory, called *section objects*. The memory manager also includes a fault trap for hardware-detected memory exceptions.

The memory manager creates specific memory pools that the Windows operating system uses to allocate memory. These pools are the nonpaged pool and the paged pool. The paged pool consists of the virtual memory pages previously discussed. The nonpaged pool consists of virtual memory addresses that are guaranteed to reside in physical memory. The total number of pools is based on the processor. Single processor systems have three paged pools, whereas multiprocessor systems have five.

What Is Memory Forensics?

Memory forensics refers to the process of analyzing volatile data from a snapshot of the system's memory, a.k.a. the computer's memory dump. Security experts utilize this technique to investigate and uncover attacks, malicious activities, or malware that may not leave obvious traces in traditional hard drive data. A forensic investigator can extract this file for offsite analysis because it contains the current state of the system's memory. By examining the contents of the memory, hidden insights can be revealed, enabling the identification and analysis of elusive or malware threats. One may ask, how is it different from hard drive forensics? Essentially, memory forensics focuses on the current snapshot of memory while the target machine is in use, whereas hard drive forensics is more used toward data recovery usually made from an image of the hard drive postmortem of events that have already passed. In fact, hard drive forensics is often referred to as "dead-box forensics."

Understanding Malware

According to Cisco, malware is defined as *"intrusive software developed by cybercriminals (often called hackers) to steal data and damage or destroy computers and computer systems"* (Cisco, n.d.). It should be pointed out that the term hackers does not refer exclusively to cybercriminals. There is an entire hacking community that never commits any crimes. These people are simply interested in understanding systems better.

Malware can typically be divided into several categories, such as viruses, worms, spyware, logic bombs, Trojan horses, and ransomware. The list goes on, as new categories are created every single day. There are various ways in which we can get malware on our devices. It can come from malicious websites or harmful emails, and it can be hidden in document files and even the most unexpected areas, such as .exe files. It can infect our PC without our knowledge and cause severe damage, such as encrypting our files and making them unreadable. So how do we determine if we are victims of malware? Some indicators would be if your browser redirects you to websites you didn't intend to visit, slow computer performance, frequent pop-up ads, and problems restarting your PC.

A virus usually spreads primarily in one of just a few ways. The first is to simply email itself out to everyone in your email address book. Another method is to scan your computer for connections to a network and then copy itself to other machines on the network to which your computer has access. Viruses can also reside on portable media such as USB devices or optical media. It is also possible to mask a virus with a legitimate file; in this case, it is called a Trojan horse. Sometimes, a website is infected with a virus, and when someone visits the website, that person's computer becomes infected.

Since its beginnings, malware – a contraction of "malicious software" – has undergone substantial evolution. Its inception dates back to the 1970s, when the Creeper worm was created – more of an experiment than a malicious deed – in the early days of computing. The first real viruses, such as the Vienna and Brain viruses, appeared in the 1980s as personal computers became more common. The Brain virus spread by infecting floppy disks, which would then contain a copy of the virus in the boot section. The virus was meant to track pirated copies of certain disks. The malware's affected victim could get in touch with the developers to get the virus removed. Similar to numerous early computer viruses, the Brain was intended to be little more than an annoyance and was largely benign.

Soon after the Internet was made available to the general public, the first computer viruses that could propagate online appeared. The Morris Worm is among the most well-known early examples of computer viruses. The Morris Worm was not purposefully made to harm infected computers. Rather, it was intended to highlight flaws in the networks of the day. This led to the formation of the antivirus industry, where antivirus pioneers such as McAfee and Avast emerged. Worms like ILOVEYOU and Slammer became more prevalent in the 1990s and 2000s, taking advantage of network weaknesses to disrupt systems all across the world. Trojans, spyware, and ransomware also emerged during this time; ransomware has grown significantly in importance in recent years due to assaults like WannaCry and Mindware. Malware is always evolving along with technology, which puts our cybersecurity defenses to the test. According to the IBM Security X-Force Threat Intelligence Index 2023 (IBM, 2023), ransomware accounted for 21% of all malware infections that the business remedied in 2022, making it the most prevalent sort of attack. About one-third of those attacks were linked to a particular ransomware strain called "Sodinokibi" or "REvil." A ransomware variant known as "Ryuk" ranked second on IBM's index and accounted for almost 20% of attacks on its own.

In today's malware landscape, phishing and social engineering have emerged as the main vehicles for delivery malware. Preying on people's weaknesses, these techniques trick people into disclosing private information or unintentionally running harmful software. Particularly with regard to phishing, victims are frequently tricked into compromising their data or systems by appearing authentic in emails, chats, or web pages. These strategies' growing popularity highlights an important fact: although strong digital defenses are essential, people are still a major area of conflict. Our defenses against these sneaky dangers must be strengthened by teaching users about the telltale signs of dubious communications and encouraging a culture of skepticism. With so many different types of malware being introduced every day, it would be helpful to have a brief understanding of the types of malware.

Types of Malware

Different resources will likely have some differentiation in how malware is categorized. The following categories are widely used, but you might find some variation.

Viruses

Viruses are any software that self-replicates (Easttom, 2022). Some sources define a virus as malware that attaches itself to a specific file. That second definition is simply not always true anymore. There are indeed many types of viruses. A list of common virus categories is given here:

- **Macro**: Macro viruses infect the macros in office documents. Many office products, including Microsoft Office, allow users to write mini-programs called macros. These macros can also be written as a virus. A macro virus is written into a macro in some business application. For example, Microsoft Office allows users to write macros to automate some tasks. Microsoft Outlook is designed so that a programmer can write scripts using a subset of the Visual Basic programming language, called Visual Basic for Applications (VBA). This scripting language is, in fact, built into all Microsoft Office products. Programmers can also use the closely related VBScript language. Both languages are quite easy to learn. If such a script is attached to an email and the recipient is using Outlook, then the script can execute. That execution can do any number of things, including scan the address book, look for addresses, send out email, delete email, and more.

- **Boot Sector**: As the name suggests, this type of virus infects the boot sector of the drive. Such viruses can be difficult for antivirus software to find because most antivirus software runs within the operating system, not in the boot sector.

- **Multipartite**: Multipartite viruses attack the computer in multiple ways, for example, infecting the boot sector of the hard disk and one or more files.

- **Memory Resident**: A memory-resident virus installs itself and then remains in RAM from the time the computer is booted up to when it is shut down.

- **Armored**: An armored virus uses techniques that make it hard to analyze. Code confusion is one such method. The code is written such that if the virus is disassembled, the code won't be easily followed. Compressed code is another method for armoring a virus.

- **Sparse Infector**: A sparse infector virus attempts to elude detection by performing its malicious activities only sporadically. With a sparse infector virus, the user will see symptoms for a short period, then no symptoms for a time. In some cases, the sparse infector targets a specific program, but the virus executes only every 10th time or 20th time that target program executes. Or a sparse infector may have a burst of activity and then lie dormant for a period of time. There are a number of variations on the theme, but the basic principle is the same: to reduce the frequency of attack and thus reduce the chances for detection.

- **Polymorphic**: A polymorphic virus literally changes its form from time to time to avoid detection by antivirus software.

- **Metamorphic**: A metamorphic virus is a special case of the polymorphic virus that completely rewrites itself periodically. Such viruses are very rare.

- **Memory Resident**: A memory resident virus loads into memory. If this virus was launched by a host application, then even after the host application has unloaded and stopped executing, the memory resident virus will stay active in memory.

Worms

Worms are self-replicating programs that spread across networks without human intervention. It is also known as a more virulent virus. They exploit security vulnerabilities to infect systems and can cause network congestion or perform malicious actions.

Trojan Horse

Trojans can either be malware attached to a legitimate file or malware that disguises itself as legitimate software, tricking users into installing them. A Trojan horse is often a doorway for other activities. It might do any of the following:

- Download harmful software from a website

- Install a key logger or other spyware on your machine

- Delete files

- Open a backdoor for a hacker to use

Ransomware

Ransomware encrypts user files, rendering them inaccessible until a ransom is paid. It is a growing threat that can lead to data loss, financial losses, and significant disruptions for businesses and individuals. It often spreads like a virus and is therefore frequently categorized as a virus. It is quite common for modern ransomware to also deliver additional malware such as spyware. This is one reason that memory forensics is so important. You cannot simply remove the ransomware and assume your system is safe. Rather, you must ascertain the full extent of what happened.

Spyware

Spyware is designed to spy on users' activities, collecting sensitive information without their knowledge or consent. It can capture keystrokes, monitor browsing habits, and steal personal data. However, placing such monitoring software on a machine you do not own without the consent of the owner is a criminal act.

Logic Bomb

Logic bombs are malicious activities executed when a logical condition is met. It can be either at a specific time or a logic in software that causes the software to fail.

While numerous other malware variants exist, this provides an initial foundation for deeper exploration. With this background in place, you are now well positioned to delve into advanced subjects like volatile data analysis and the intricacies of live acquisition.

Malware Hiding Techniques

Attackers utilize various methods to conceal malware on the victim's computer. The following are some of the Windows system utilities that attackers can exploit to utilize and conceal malware:

1. **Windows Registry**: Malicious software frequently utilizes strategies to conceal its presence within the Windows Registry, a vital system component responsible for storing configuration settings and important information. Having the malware using the Registry also allows it to be persistent and to survive a reboot. These techniques involve altering registry keys, values, or permissions to camouflage alongside genuine entries or avoid detection. The following is a good source on Poweliks – a Registry-based malware technique cited from OTX – `https://otx.alienvault.com/pulse/61af50344614e8bca2539017`. OTX is a platform designed for the sharing of threat data, enabling security researchers and threat data producers to collaborate in research and analysis of emerging threats.

2. **Process Injection**: It involves secretly executing code into a running process. It avoids detection by disguising itself by using known processes such as "svchost.exe" or "explorer.exe". Malware authors utilize Windows APIs, such as setting debug mode, to inject themselves into trusted processes. By setting a process as debug, it gains privileged access to debug API calls, enabling it to attach to other processes and allocate additional memory. This allocation of extra memory provides an opportunity for the malicious technique to inject any desired code into the target process. One of the most famously used process injections is Poison Ivy. The following is a good OTX source of the same: `https://otx.alienvault.com/browse/pulses/?q=poison%20ivy`.

3. **DLL Injection**: DLL, also known as dynamic link library, involves injecting a harmful DLL file into a targeted process, where it is loaded and executed. This allows the malware to exploit the process's functionality or gain control over system resources.

DLL injection is commonly employed to intercept system calls, hook functions, and carry out activities like keylogging, screen capturing, or network monitoring. User32.dll is a module that contains Windows API functions related to the Windows user interface. Now every DLL that is listed in the registry HKEY_LOCAL_MACHINE\SOFTWARE\MICROSOFT\WINDOWS NT\CurrentVersion\Windows\AppInit_DLLs will be loaded into a process that calls the User32.dll. So, if the attacker can get their DLL listed in the Registry, they can get access to many programs. Printkey is the most commonly used command for examining DLL injection.

4. **Process Hallowing**: Process hallowing, a.k.a. process replacement, is a technique in which malware is disguised as a good system process, and when it is about to execute, the good code is scooped out and the bad code is placed in the available cleared-out space. We can look for calls such as *CreateRemoteThread()* and *-VirtualAllocEx()* in the memory dumps to see if this process exists. Dridex is a good example from the malware family that checks for this technique. Here is a good OTX source for the same: `https://otx.alienvault.com/puls e/6409cb72f47082331f3d4508`.

Memory Analysis

According to the National Institute of Standards and Technology (NIST), "data on a live system that is lost after a computer is powered down" is defined as volatile data (NIST, 2023). Volatile data is extremely delicate and, once rebooted, is lost. Due to the volatility of memory, it must be captured as soon as possible. If you shut down the computer, or even wait a period of time, you will likely lose evidence.

Memory forensics begins with obtaining a memory dump from the computer. A **memory dump** is a file that contains the entirety of the data stored in RAM. If you believe you might need to perform memory forensics, it is best to perform a memory dump. If you find later that it was not needed, you will simply not use it. But if you decide later you do need to do memory forensics, and you did not perform a memory dump, you have simply lost evidence.

There are numerous software applications available on the Web to collect volatile memory dumps. These programs are to run on live systems and collect memory data. The only challenge forensic analysts may face is maintaining data consistency, as in live system forensics, data is not acquired at a unified moment and thus may be inconsistent. While we understand that dumping of memory is essential, we should also understand that there are two types of memory, that is, stack and heap. In the next section, let us learn more about their memory allocation types and how they are actually helpful in memory forensics.

Memory Artifacts

Once you have acquired a memory dump and begin analyzing it, what you are examining are *memory artifacts*. Examples of memory artifacts include

- **Active Processes**: Information about currently running programs, including their names, IDs, command-line details, and associated network connections

- **RAM Artifacts**: Remnants of data in RAM, such as unencrypted passwords, decrypted data, traces of deleted files, and fragments of user activities

- **Network Connections**: Details about active network connections, such as IP addresses, ports, protocols, and communication endpoints

- **System and User Configuration**: Configuration settings, environment variables, and system-specific information that contribute to reconstructing the system's state and user actions

- **Clipboard Contents**: Text or data that has been copied to the system clipboard and might contain sensitive or relevant information

- **Open Files and Handles**: Details about the files that currently running processes are accessing or holding open, including file names, access modes, and timestamps

- **Loaded Modules and Libraries**: Information about dynamic link libraries (DLLs) and other modules currently loaded in the memory space of running processes earlier

To analyze volatility artifacts, experts rely on specialized techniques and tools like memory forensics frameworks such as Volatility, Belkasoft, or Rekall. As stated earlier, there are a lot of tools available on the Web, both paid and free, that we can use to perform a live analysis of our laptop. In the next section, let's get some hands-on experience analyzing our own system.

Capturing Memory

The first step in memory analysis is to capture a memory dump. There are a number of tools that one can use for this purpose. A few common tools are discussed briefly in this section. Be aware that while capturing memory, you are actually using the systems memory. It is best to have only the memory capture tool running and don't initiate any other applications nor perform other actions on the computer.

FTK Imager

FTK Imager is a forensic tool used to create disk images and capture memory. It is a trusted resource in the cybersecurity industry. You can download it from `www.exterro.com/ftk-imager`. The primary screen for FTK image is shown in Figure 8-1.

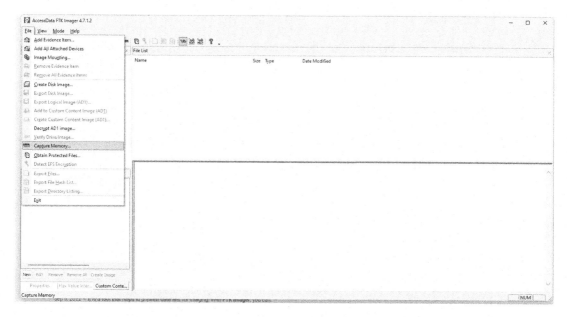

Figure 8-1. *How to capture RAM on FTK Imager*

Figure 8-1 shows us how to capture memory using an FTK Imager, and Figure 8-2 shows us that after we click "Capture Memory," we can select the destination path for where we want to store the file. The generated file would have the following extension: .mem.

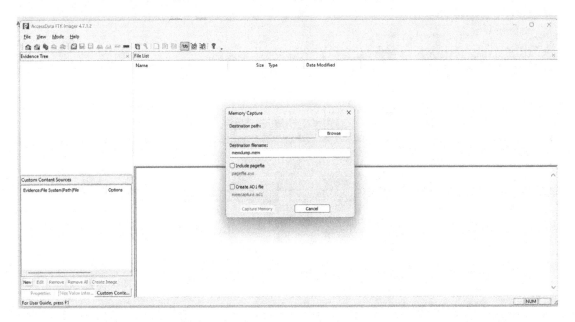

Figure 8-2. *How to save your memory file*

As you can see, using FTK Imager to capture memory is a simple process.

OSForensics Memory Viewer

OSForensics is a tool from PassMark Software that allows you to do a complete forensic examination. OSForensics, offered by PassMark Software, has a free 30-day trial version you can use to avail yourself of amazing features such as capturing and analyzing memory, imaging disks, analyzing user activity, etc. It can be downloaded at www.osforensics.com/download.html. You can find the memory forensics portion of OSForensics as shown in Figure 8-3.

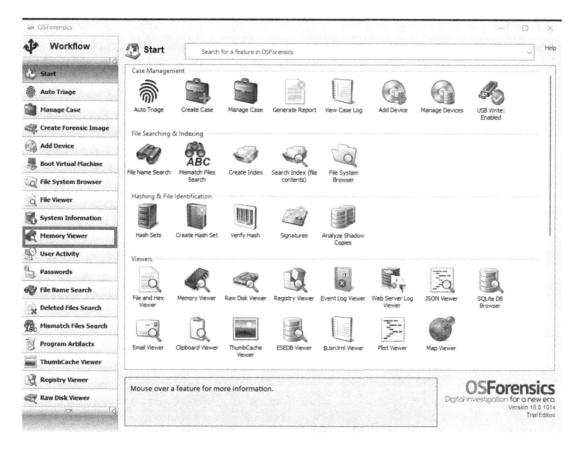

Figure 8-3. *Memory Viewer used to capture memory*

Figure 8-3 is the main page as soon as the software starts. Of all the options available, select Memory Viewer to capture memory. This is shown in Figure 8-4.

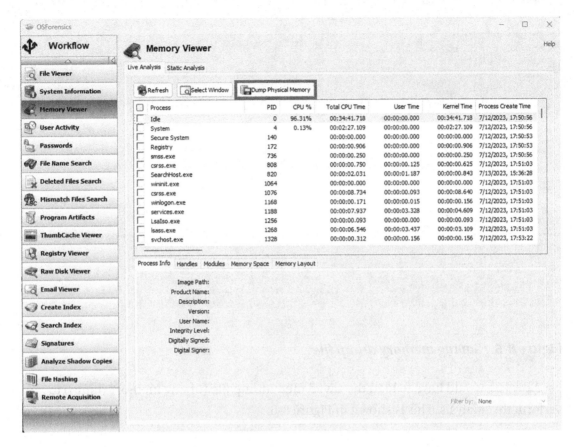

Figure 8-4. *Dump physical memory*

Figure 8-4 is the first view as you open the Memory Viewer on OSForensics. As you can see, you have two ways to perform a memory capture. You can perform a live acquisition on the physical memory, or you can perform a static analysis. When you click Dump physical memory, you have to first save the memory dump of the physical memory somewhere as shown in Figure 8-5.

Figure 8-5. *Saving memory dump file*

Now you would have to load the saved mem dump file (or any memory dump) to perform the analysis. This is shown in Figure 8-6.

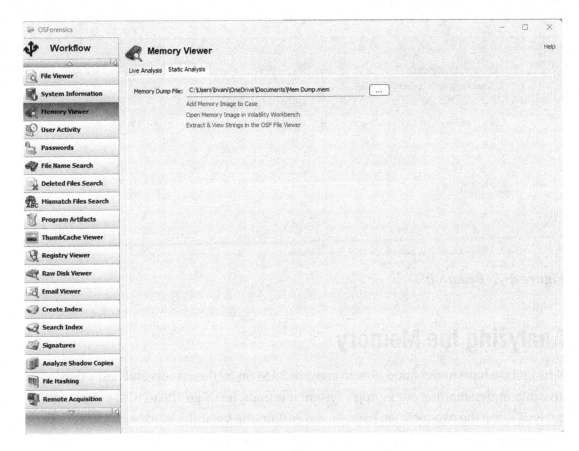

Figure 8-6. *Loading the memory dump file*

You would load the file in the static analysis tab and click Open memory image in the Volatility Workbench to get started. You can also download Volatility Workbench as a separate and free tool from www.osforensics.com/memory-viewer.html. The screens look the same as what has been discussed in this section, except you don't start from the main OSForensics screen; rather, you are directly in the Volatility Workbench.

Belkasoft Live RAM Capturer

Another free tool you can use to capture memory is the Belkasoft Live RAM Capturer. You can download it at https://belkasoft.com/get. After you download the software, you can open the application and just click Capture, and the memory capture will begin as shown in Figure 8-7.

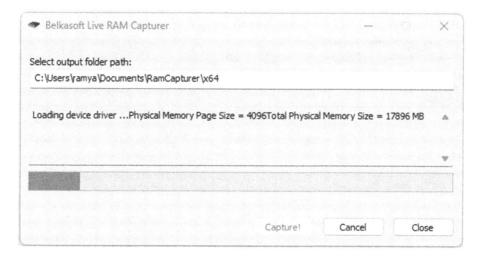

Figure 8-7. *Belkasoft*

Analyzing the Memory

Now that we have understood how to capture RAM on all these tools and had a deep dive into understanding our laptop's system internals, let us go ahead with a thorough analysis using the two tools we have shown earlier: the Volatility Workbench CMD line version and the Volatility Workbench through OSForensics.

Volatility

Volatility is the premier tool used to perform memory analysis. It is the first go-to tool for many when performing volatile analysis. The tool can be, luckily, downloaded for free from the website Volatility (`www.volatilityfoundation.org/releases`). The most updated version of Volatility is 3.1. That version is provided as a series of Python scripts. As not all readers will be proficient in Python, the 2.6 stand-alone version. Volatility is a powerful command-line tool used in these examples, including running processes, network connections, and processes with injected code. It also allows the dumping of DLLs and processes for deeper analysis. Specific plugins will be examined in this section, and you can get a complete list of all Volatility commands with a brief explanation at `https://github.com/volatilityfoundation/volatility/wiki/Command-Reference`.

First, let us get the essential information to make sure the application is working correctly.

The command used to get the information would be ***volatility_2.6_win64_standalone.exe --info***. If this provides you a list of profiles you can use for memory analysis, then all is working well. This is shown in Figure 8-8.

```
C:\Users\bvani\Downloads\volatility_2.6_win64_standalone (2)\volatility_2.6_win64_standalone>volatility_2.6_win64_standalone.exe --info
Volatility Foundation Volatility Framework 2.6


Profiles
--------
VistaSP0x64           - A Profile for Windows Vista SP0 x64
VistaSP0x86           - A Profile for Windows Vista SP0 x86
VistaSP1x64           - A Profile for Windows Vista SP1 x64
VistaSP1x86           - A Profile for Windows Vista SP1 x86
VistaSP2x64           - A Profile for Windows Vista SP2 x64
VistaSP2x86           - A Profile for Windows Vista SP2 x86
Win10x64             - A Profile for Windows 10 x64
Win10x64_10586       - A Profile for Windows 10 x64 (10.0.10586.306 / 2016-04-23)
Win10x64_14393       - A Profile for Windows 10 x64 (10.0.14393.0 / 2016-07-16)
Win10x86             - A Profile for Windows 10 x86
Win10x86_10586       - A Profile for Windows 10 x86 (10.0.10586.420 / 2016-05-28)
Win10x86_14393       - A Profile for Windows 10 x86 (10.0.14393.0 / 2016-07-16)
Win2003SP0x86        - A Profile for Windows 2003 SP0 x86
Win2003SP1x64        - A Profile for Windows 2003 SP1 x64
Win2003SP1x86        - A Profile for Windows 2003 SP1 x86
Win2003SP2x64        - A Profile for Windows 2003 SP2 x64
Win2003SP2x86        - A Profile for Windows 2003 SP2 x86
Win2008R2SP0x64      - A Profile for Windows 2008 R2 SP0 x64
Win2008R2SP1x64      - A Profile for Windows 2008 R2 SP1 x64
Win2008R2SP1x64_23418 - A Profile for Windows 2008 R2 SP1 x64 (6.1.7601.23418 / 2016-04-09)
Win2008SP1x64        - A Profile for Windows 2008 SP1 x64
Win2008SP1x86        - A Profile for Windows 2008 SP1 x86
Win2008SP2x64        - A Profile for Windows 2008 SP2 x64
```

Figure 8-8. *--info on Volatility*

If you don't see something similar to what is shown in Figure 8-8, then something went wrong in the installation. For performing analysis using Volatility, we need to first set a profile to tell Volatility what operating system the dump came from, such as Windows 10, 11, Linux distribution, etc. The structure of all Volatility commands includes a profile.

The basic format for running a Volatility command is

> ***volatility-version.exe commandname -f filepath -profile***
> ***=profilename***

Note that commandname is often referred to as a *plugin*. Due to path names sometimes being unwieldy, you may find it useful to put the memory dump file in the same folder as the volatility executable. Then you can type in just the executable name and ignore path names. This is how the examples in this chapter will be done. Also, if you don't know what profile to use, the following command will try to determine this: volatility_2.6_win64_standalone.exe imageinfo -f newmemory.mem.

Volatility offers a number of commands or plugins that can be used to scan the memory dump for specific data. The file path is the path to access the memory dump file. Common extensions of memory dump files are .mem, .bin, .dump, and .raw. When the command is run, it may take several minutes before providing the output, as the whole dump is searched and there are thousands of processes being run. Common issues you will find are getting an error due to using the wrong profile name. That will usually give you the error message *no suitable address space mapping found*. If you type the command in incorrectly, you will get an error often stating *you must specify something to do (try -h)*. This is often due to misspelling the command.

The pslist Command

This is a common command and lists all the processes running as well as process ID (PID), the parent process ID (PPID), number of threads (Thds), number of handles (hnds), sessions (sess), when it was started, and if it has exited. The command is executed as follows:

> volatility_2.6_win64_standalone.exe pslist -f memdump.mem
> --profile=Win8SP0x64

Obviously, you will use the appropriate file name for your memory number and the proper profile. The command output is shown in Figure 8-9.

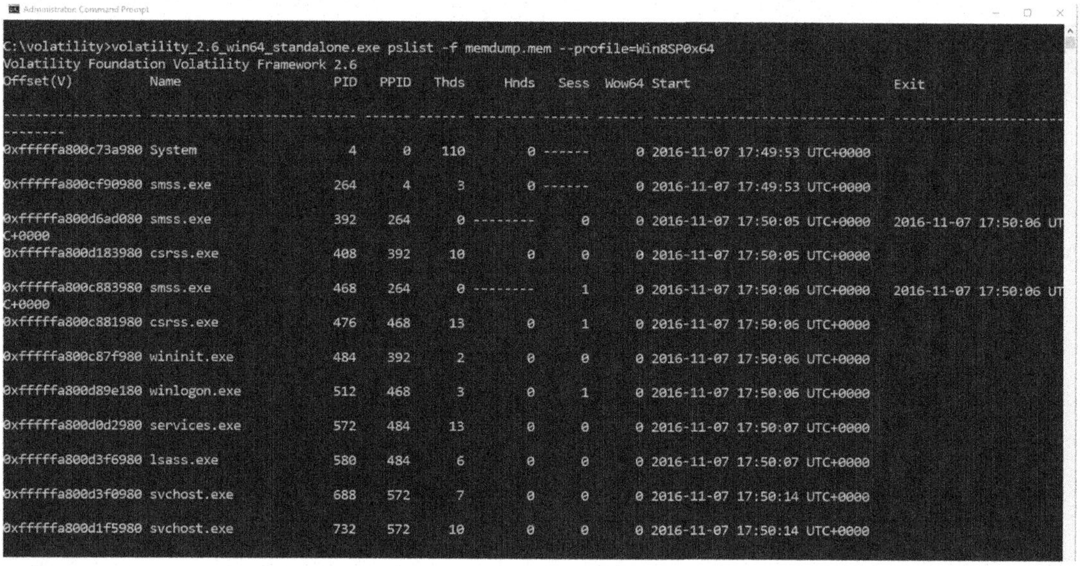

Figure 8-9. *Plist command on Volatility*

When looking at processes, it is helpful to know the order that processes start in Windows and what the major system processes do. Session Manager Subsystem (SMSS) first marks itself and its main thread as critical objects. (Note you will see more than one SMSS.)

SMSS starts both Wininit and the CSRSS (Client/Server Runtime Subsystem). Then Wininit starts services.exe. Services.exe starts all the other services. Expect to see many svchost.exe. Svchost.exe is a process on your computer that hosts, or contains, other individual services that Windows uses to perform various functions. For example, Windows Defender uses a service that is hosted by a svchost.exe process.

DLLList

This command lists DLLs and the executable they are associated with. This can be quite useful in malware forensics. There are techniques such as DLL injection and process hollowing the attackers can use. The command is volatility_2.6_win64_standalone.exe dlllist -f memdump.mem --profile=Win8SP0x64. You can see the command executed in Figure 8-10.

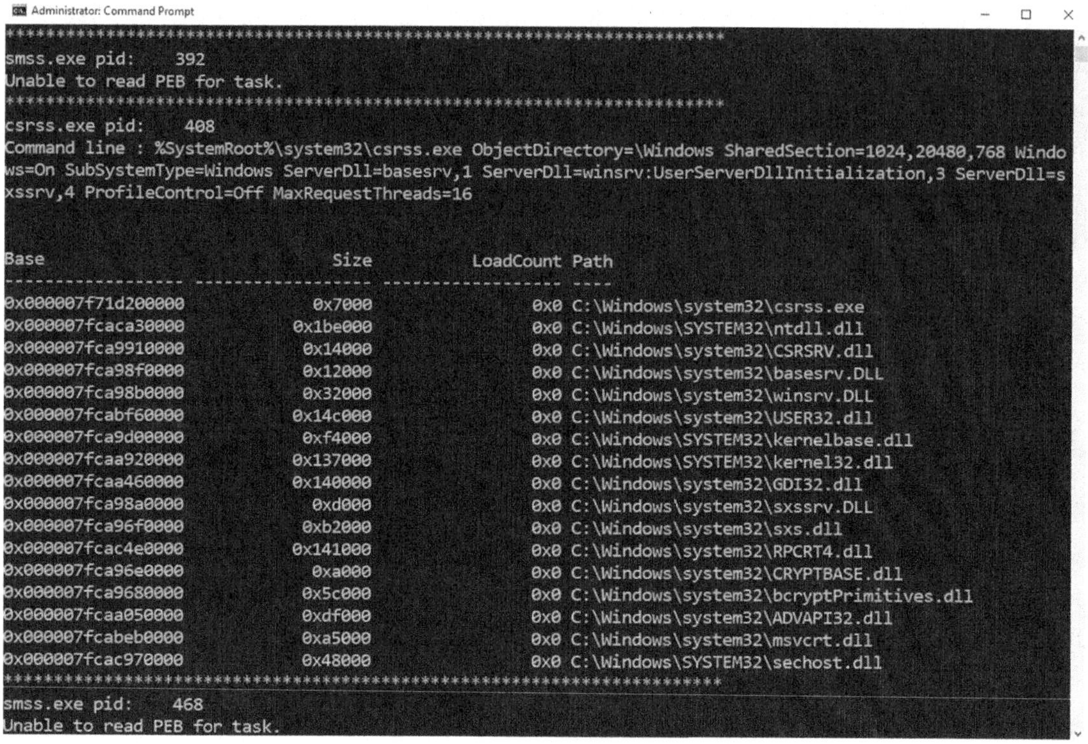

Figure 8-10. *dlllist command on Volatility*

Notice you also get the PID for the executable. This allows you to match information found with this command to information you retrieve using pslist command.

SVSCAN

The service can provide details on all the services running. The command is phrased as volatility_2.6_win64_standalone.exe svcscan -f memdump.mem --profile=Win8SP0x64. You can see this command executed in Figure 8-11.

```
C:\volatility>volatility_2.6_win64_standalone.exe svcscan -f memdump.mem --profile=Win8SP0x64
Volatility Foundation Volatility Framework 2.6
Offset: 0xb47f757e60
Order: 400
Start: SERVICE_AUTO_START
Process ID: 1372
Service Name: W3SVC
Display Name: World Wide Web Publishing Service
Service Type: SERVICE_WIN32_SHARE_PROCESS
Service State: SERVICE_RUNNING
Binary Path: C:\Windows\system32\svchost.exe -k iissvcs

Offset: 0xb47f759180
Order: 399
Start: SERVICE_DEMAND_START
Process ID: -
Service Name: W32Time
Display Name: Windows Time
Service Type: SERVICE_WIN32_SHARE_PROCESS
Service State: SERVICE_STOPPED
Binary Path: -
```

Figure 8-11. *svcscan command on Volatility*

The services can have quite a bit of information. Items like the start and process ID are self-explanatory. However, others need some explanation. The service type tells you what kind of service this is. Service types are summarized here:

- **SERVICE_WIN32_SHARE_PROCESS**: A service type flag that indicates a Win32 service that shares a process with other services

- **SERVICE_WIN32_OWN_PROCESS**: A Win32 service that runs in its own process

- **SERVICE_KERNEL_DRIVER**: A Windows NT device driver

- **SERVICE_FILE_SYSTEM_DRIVER**: A Windows NT file system driver

- **SERVICE_ADAPTER**: An interface for a Windows Service

- **SERVICE_INTERACTIVE_PROCESS**: Service that can interact with the desktop

Modscan

This plugin searches for drivers, including unlinked drivers. The modscan command finds LDR_DATA_TABLE_ENTRY structures by scanning physical memory for pool tags. The LDR_DATA_TABLE_ENTRY contains information about the loaded modules for the process.[1] This can pick up previously unloaded drivers and drivers that have been hidden/unlinked by rootkits. Unlike modules, the order of results has no relationship with the order in which the drivers loaded. The syntax is volatility_2.6_win64_standalone.exe modscan -f memdump.mem --profile=Win8SP0x64. The output can be seen in Figure 8-12.

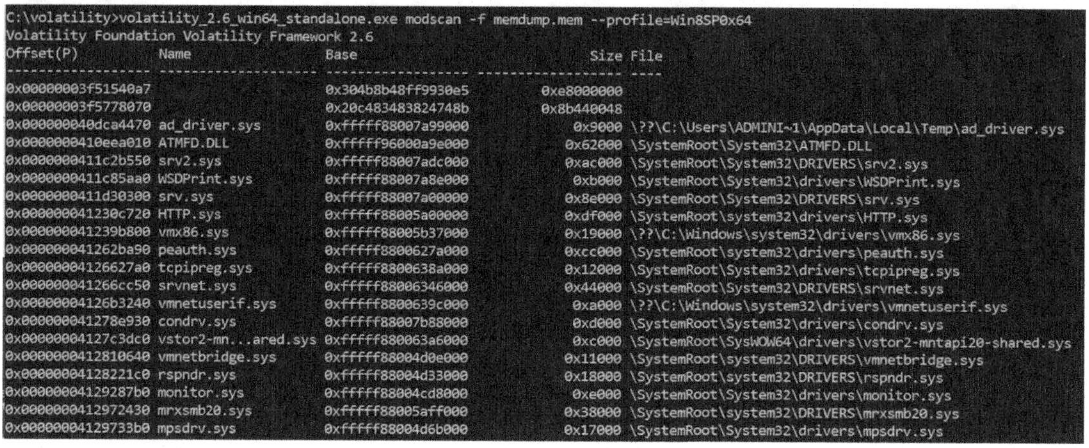

```
C:\volatility>volatility_2.6_win64_standalone.exe modscan -f memdump.mem --profile=Win8SP0x64
Volatility Foundation Volatility Framework 2.6
Offset(P)          Name                 Base                             Size File
------------------ -------------------- ------------------ ------------------ ----
0x000000003f51540a7                     0x304b8b48ff9930e5         0xe8000000
0x000000003f5778070                     0x20c483483824748b         0x8b440048
0x00000000040dca4470 ad_driver.sys      0xfffff88007a99000             0x9000 \??\C:\Users\ADMINI~1\AppData\Local\Temp\ad_driver.sys
0x0000000410eea010 ATMFD.DLL            0xfffff96000a9e000            0x62000 \SystemRoot\System32\ATMFD.DLL
0x0000000411c2b550 srv2.sys             0xfffff88007adc000            0xac000 \SystemRoot\System32\DRIVERS\srv2.sys
0x0000000411c85aa0 WSDPrint.sys         0xfffff88007a8e000             0xb000 \SystemRoot\System32\drivers\WSDPrint.sys
0x0000000411d30300 srv.sys              0xfffff88007a00000            0x8e000 \SystemRoot\System32\DRIVERS\srv.sys
0x00000041230c720 HTTP.sys              0xfffff88005a00000            0xdf000 \SystemRoot\system32\drivers\HTTP.sys
0x00000041239b800 vmx86.sys             0xfffff88005b37000            0x19000 \??\C:\Windows\system32\drivers\vmx86.sys
0x00000041262ba90 peauth.sys            0xfffff8800627a000            0xcc000 \SystemRoot\system32\drivers\peauth.sys
0x000000004126627a0 tcpipreg.sys        0xfffff8800638a000            0x12000 \SystemRoot\System32\drivers\tcpipreg.sys
0x00000041266cc50 srvnet.sys            0xfffff88006346000            0x44000 \SystemRoot\System32\DRIVERS\srvnet.sys
0x000000004126b3240 vmnetuserif.sys     0xfffff8800639c000             0xa000 \??\C:\Windows\system32\drivers\vmnetuserif.sys
0x00000041278e930 condrv.sys            0xfffff88007b88000             0xd000 \SystemRoot\System32\drivers\condrv.sys
0x000000004127c3dc0 vstor2-mn...ared.sys 0xfffff880063a6000            0xc000 \SystemRoot\SysWOW64\drivers\vstor2-mntapi20-shared.sys
0x0000000412810640 vmnetbridge.sys      0xfffff88004d0e000            0x11000 \SystemRoot\system32\DRIVERS\vmnetbridge.sys
0x00000004128221c0 rspndr.sys           0xfffff88004d33000            0x18000 \SystemRoot\system32\DRIVERS\rspndr.sys
0x00000004129287b0 monitor.sys          0xfffff88004cd8000             0xe000 \SystemRoot\System32\drivers\monitor.sys
0x0000000412972430 mrxsmb20.sys         0xfffff88005aff000            0x38000 \SystemRoot\system32\DRIVERS\mrxsmb20.sys
0x00000004129733b0 mpsdrv.sys           0xfffff88004d6b000            0x17000 \SystemRoot\System32\drivers\mpsdrv.sys
```

Figure 8-12. *modscan command on Volatility*

Netscan

This plugin finds TCP endpoints, TCP listeners, UDP endpoints, and UDP listeners. It distinguishes between IPv4 and IPv6, prints the local and remote IP, the local and remote port, the time when the socket was bound or when the connection was established, and the current state. You can see the output in Figure 8-13.

[1] https://learn.microsoft.com/en-us/windows/win32/api/winternl/ns-winternl-peb_ldr_data

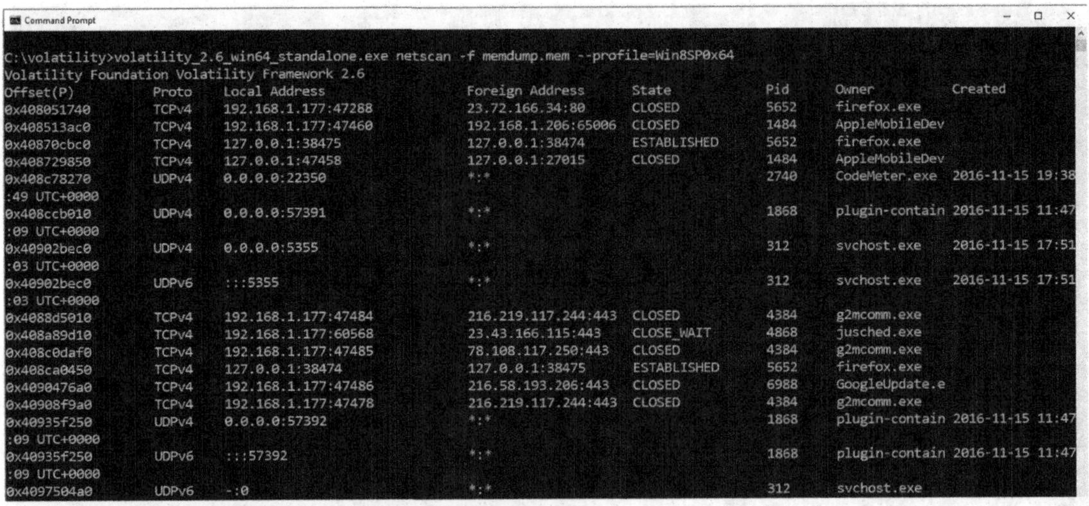

Figure 8-13. netscan command on Volatility

This command is particularly useful if you suspect malware was communicating outside the infected computer. This occurs with botnets communicating with a command and control server as well as spyware exfiltrating data.

Getsids

SIDS, or security identifiers, identify users and their privilege level in Windows. The Volatility plugin getsids will provide information for each process and the SID of who launched it. The command syntax is volatility_2.6_win64_standalone.exe getsids -f memdump.mem --profile=Win8SP0x64. You can see the command in Figure 8-14.

```
C:\volatility>volatility_2.6_win64_standalone.exe getsids -f memdump.mem --profile=Win8SP0x64
Volatility Foundation Volatility Framework 2.6
System (4): S-1-5-18 (Local System)
System (4): S-1-5-32-544 (Administrators)
System (4): S-1-1-0 (Everyone)
System (4): S-1-5-11 (Authenticated Users)
System (4): S-1-16-16384 (System Mandatory Level)
smss.exe (264): S-1-5-18 (Local System)
smss.exe (264): S-1-5-32-544 (Administrators)
smss.exe (264): S-1-1-0 (Everyone)
smss.exe (264): S-1-5-11 (Authenticated Users)
smss.exe (264): S-1-16-16384 (System Mandatory Level)
smss.exe (392): S-1-5-18 (Local System)
smss.exe (392): S-1-5-32-544 (Administrators)
smss.exe (392): S-1-1-0 (Everyone)
smss.exe (392): S-1-5-11 (Authenticated Users)
smss.exe (392): S-1-16-16384 (System Mandatory Level)
csrss.exe (408): S-1-5-18 (Local System)
csrss.exe (408): S-1-5-32-544 (Administrators)
csrss.exe (408): S-1-1-0 (Everyone)
csrss.exe (408): S-1-5-11 (Authenticated Users)
csrss.exe (408): S-1-16-16384 (System Mandatory Level)
smss.exe (468): S-1-5-18 (Local System)
smss.exe (468): S-1-5-32-544 (Administrators)
smss.exe (468): S-1-1-0 (Everyone)
smss.exe (468): S-1-5-11 (Authenticated Users)
smss.exe (468): S-1-16-16384 (System Mandatory Level)
csrss.exe (476): S-1-5-18 (Local System)
csrss.exe (476): S-1-5-32-544 (Administrators)
```

Figure 8-14. *getsids command on Volatility*

Psscan

This command helps to find processes that were previously terminated (inactive processes) and processes that are hidden or unlinked. It is an important command used during malware investigations.

Command to run the psscan command on volatility:

> ***volatility_2.6_win64_standalone.exe psscan -f C:path\ tovolatility\dump.bin --profile=Win8SP0x64***

You can see the command in Figure 8-15.

```
C:\volatility>volatility_2.6_win64_standalone.exe psscan -f memdump.mem --profile=Win8SP0x64
Volatility Foundation Volatility Framework 2.6
Offset(P)            Name             PID   PPID  PDB                  Time created                    Time exited
--------------       ------           ----  ----  ---                  -----------------               -----------------
0x0000000408033780   calc.exe         4648  2872  0x000000017ac23000   2016-11-15 16:50:21 UTC+0000
0x0000000408682600   POWERPNT.EXE     5520  2872  0x0000000000d90000   2016-11-15 19:32:33 UTC+0000
0x0000000408904980   cosh.dll         5916  5560  0x00000003db358000   2016-11-11 02:50:53 UTC+0000    2016-11-11 02:50:53 UTC+0000
0x0000000408a6c080   cosh.dll         3344  3396  0x00000003b78b2000   2016-11-10 03:08:00 UTC+0000    2016-11-10 03:08:00 UTC+0000
0x0000000408c55480   cosh.dll         916   3412  0x00000003882bb000   2016-11-14 03:08:43 UTC+0000    2016-11-14 03:08:44 UTC+0000
0x0000000408c80080   taskeng.exe      7860  856   0x000000002c245000   2016-11-15 19:39:00 UTC+0000
0x0000000408ce4080   GameOverlayUI.   7892  4512  0x00000003b6066000   2016-11-13 02:18:51 UTC+0000    2016-11-13 02:32:05 UTC+0000
0x0000000408d1b400   FTK Imager.exe   5208  2872  0x0000000285ff8000   2016-11-15 19:37:51 UTC+0000
0x0000000408da5180   cosh.dll         6884  3556  0x000000004b71c000   2016-11-15 00:43:38 UTC+0000    2016-11-15 00:43:38 UTC+0000
0x0000000408e51200   GameOverlayUI.   6752  4512  0x00000002b1b03000   2016-11-14 03:08:32 UTC+0000    2016-11-14 03:26:12 UTC+0000
0x0000000408e7f080   cosh.dll         44    32    0x00000003994c8000   2016-11-13 23:41:49 UTC+0000    2016-11-13 23:41:49 UTC+0000
0x0000000408e8f080   notepad.exe      9184  2872  0x0000000041287000   2016-11-15 19:14:35 UTC+0000
0x0000000408f65680   firefox.exe      2592  2872  0x000000038561f000   2016-11-12 16:34:20 UTC+0000    2016-11-12 17:50:27 UTC+0000
0x00000004092291c0   GameOverlayUI.   5292  4512  0x000000023d7a1000   2016-11-13 03:41:40 UTC+0000    2016-11-13 23:55:26 UTC+0000
0x0000000409286980   OUTLOOK.EXE      1396  2872  0x0000000036406a000  2016-11-10 21:20:22 UTC+0000
0x00000004093f6980   GameOverlayUI.   8124  4512  0x0000000595e4000    2016-11-15 00:43:31 UTC+0000    2016-11-15 01:05:59 UTC+0000
0x0000000409463540   splwow64.exe     5720  680   0x0000000397cfa000   2016-11-12 17:07:31 UTC+0000
0x000000040961a980   mspaint.exe      7612  2872  0x00000003e1ea0000   2016-11-15 19:13:18 UTC+0000
0x0000000409657980   WINWORD.EXE      7328  2872  0x000000022403fd000  2016-11-14 15:46:17 UTC+0000
0x0000000409667980   plugin-contain   1284  1264  0x00000002f0606000   2016-11-10 01:56:42 UTC+0000    2016-11-10 02:09:38 UTC+0000
```

Figure 8-15.   psscan command on Volatility

The psscan works using pool tag scanning. A pool tag is a 4-byte character that is associated with a dynamically allocated chunk of pool memory. The tag is specified by a driver when it allocates the memory. The routine ExAllocatePoolWithTag is called to allocate pool memory. A memory pool is a pre-allocated memory space with a fixed size. If there is a need to allocate new data, then the requested amount of the memory is allocated from the pool instead of requesting a new memory from the system.

Pstree

The pstree plugin also shows processes, but it shows them as a tree, so you can easily see what process started the process you are interested in. The basic command is *volatility_2.6_win64_standalone.exe pstree -f C:\path\tovolatility\dump.bin --profile=Win8SP0x64*. This can be seen in Figure 8-16.

```
C:\volatility>volatility_2.6_win64_standalone.exe pstree -f memdump.mem --profile=Win8SP0x64
Volatility Foundation Volatility Framework 2.6
Name                                      Pid    PPid   Thds   Hnds Time
-------------------------------------- ------ ------ ------ ------ ----
 0xfffffa800c73a980:System                  4      0    110      0 2016-11-07 17:49:53 UTC+0000
. 0xfffffa800cf90980:smss.exe              264      4      3      0 2016-11-07 17:49:53 UTC+0000
.. 0xfffffa800d6ad080:smss.exe             392    264      0 ------ 2016-11-07 17:50:05 UTC+0000
... 0xfffffa800c87f980:wininit.exe         484    392      2      0 2016-11-07 17:50:06 UTC+0000
.... 0xfffffa800d0d2980:services.exe       572    484     13      0 2016-11-07 17:50:07 UTC+0000
..... 0xfffffa800e3b8980:sqlservr.exe     1796    572     63      0 2016-11-07 17:50:34 UTC+0000
..... 0xfffffa800d3f0980:svchost.exe       688    572      7      0 2016-11-07 17:50:14 UTC+0000
...... 0xfffffa800e56c980:WmiPrvSE.exe    3900    688      7      0 2016-11-07 17:51:18 UTC+0000
...... 0xfffffa800e751980:WmiPrvSE.exe    4236    688      5      0 2016-11-07 17:51:24 UTC+0000
...... 0xfffffa800eea8080:WISPTIS.EXE     1012    688      6      0 2016-11-07 17:53:27 UTC+0000
..... 0xfffffa800db98980:vmware-authd.e   3116    572      7      0 2016-11-07 17:50:59 UTC+0000
..... 0xfffffa800d8c5980:mDNSResponder.   1588    572      4      0 2016-11-07 17:50:30 UTC+0000
..... 0xfffffa800d8c3980:OfficeClickToR   1608    572     18      0 2016-11-07 17:50:30 UTC+0000
..... 0xfffffa800e561980:svchost.exe      3516    572      4      0 2016-11-07 17:51:20 UTC+0000
..... 0xfffffa800d8db980:svchost.exe      1140    572     16      0 2016-11-07 17:50:20 UTC+0000
...... 0xfffffa800d8bc980:dasHost.exe     1712   1140     10      0 2016-11-07 17:50:33 UTC+0000
..... 0xfffffa800d8c1980:dirmngr.exe      1680    572      4      0 2016-11-07 17:50:32 UTC+0000
..... 0xfffffa800e3e2980:vmnat.exe        1812    572      5      0 2016-11-07 17:50:43 UTC+0000
..... 0xfffffa800eef2980:CodeMeter.exe    2740    572     12      0 2016-11-07 17:53:38 UTC+0000
..... 0xfffffa800e3ea980:sqlwriter.exe    1216    572      3      0 2016-11-07 17:50:42 UTC+0000
```

Figure 8-16. *pstree command on Volatility*

Malfind

This Volatility plugin provides information about injected code or DLLs that might be in memory. It does this based on properties such as VAD tag. VAD is an acronym for virtual address descriptor. VAD provides information about the address space of a specific process. The basic command is ***volatility_2.6_win64_standalone.exe malfind -f C:path\tovolatility\dump.bin --profile=Win8SP0x64***. You can see this command in Figure 8-17.

```
E:\volatility>volatility_2.6_win64_standalone.exe  malfind  -f  memdump.mem  --profile=Win8SP0x64
Volatility Foundation Volatility Framework 2.6
Process: svchost.exe Pid: 1140 Address: 0x5d00000000
Vad Tag: VadS Protection: PAGE_EXECUTE_READWRITE
Flags: PrivateMemory: 1, Protection: 6

0x5d00000000  00 00 00 00 00 00 00 00 00 00 00 00 00 00 00 00   ................
0x5d00000010  00 00 00 00 00 00 00 00 00 00 00 00 00 00 00 00   ................
0x5d00000020  00 00 00 00 5d 00 00 00 00 00 00 00 00 00 00 00   ....]...........
0x5d00000030  00 00 00 00 00 00 00 00 00 00 00 00 00 00 00 00   ................

0x00000000 0000                ADD [EAX], AL
0x00000002 0000                ADD [EAX], AL
0x00000004 0000                ADD [EAX], AL
0x00000006 0000                ADD [EAX], AL
0x00000008 0000                ADD [EAX], AL
0x0000000a 0000                ADD [EAX], AL
0x0000000c 0000                ADD [EAX], AL
0x0000000e 0000                ADD [EAX], AL
0x00000010 0000                ADD [EAX], AL
0x00000012 0000                ADD [EAX], AL
0x00000014 0000                ADD [EAX], AL
```

Figure 8-17. *malfind command on Volatility*

What is shown in Figure 8-18 are commands being executed at specific memory addresses.

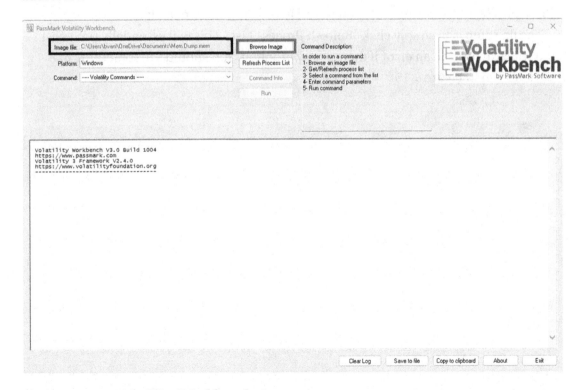

Figure 8-18. *Volatility Workbench start page*

PassMark OSForensics Volatility Workbench

The second technique we will use to analyze the memory is the Volatility Workbench offered by PassMark Software. As we've seen before, OSForensics offers this tool as the Memory Viewer option. It is also available as a stand-alone version as part of Free Tools. Hence, don't feel bad if your OSForensics trial expires. The only catch would be that you need to have your memory dump file available, so maybe you can pick a tool from what we've discussed in the "Capturing Memory" section and get your dump file. Volatility is a widely recognized set of utilities utilized for extracting digital evidence from volatile memory (RAM). The memory dump acquired through OSForensics is compatible with Volatility. PassMark Software has introduced the Volatility Workbench as a supportive tool to enhance the utilization of Volatility in conjunction with OSForensics. It is a GUI application for Volatility that also allows us to select the Volatility command we want to execute from the list present. It works pretty similar to the Volatility command-line version we worked on earlier. The only difference would be that the output would be generated within the software.

The first step is to browse to the memory dump file. You will note you don't have to select a profile as you do from the command line. This is shown in Figure 8-18.

The first step is to simply click "Refresh Process List." This will essentially run pslist, but it will also provide an error if there is any problem. You should see something like what is shown in Figure 8-19.

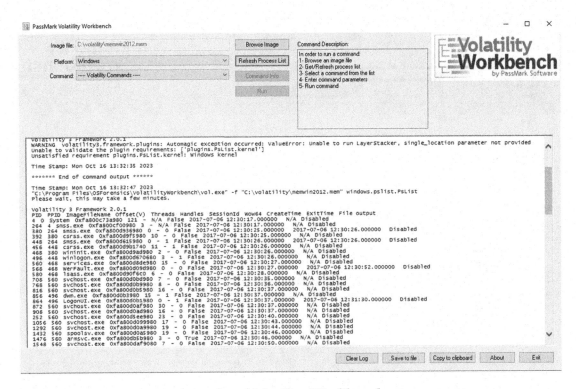

Figure 8-19. *pstree command on Volatility Workbench*

You can now perform any command you would normally do from the Volatility command line. You simply select the command from the drop-down box and click run. For example, you can run the dlllist command that you saw earlier in this chapter. The output generated from the "dlllist" command in Volatility Workbench provides information about the loaded DLLs in a memory dump. This includes details like base addresses, entry points, sizes, and file paths of the DLLs. The output aids in identifying active dynamic libraries and understanding their significance in the system, helping to analyze potential malicious activity or dependencies. This command is shown in Figure 8-20.

Figure 8-20. *Output by running the dlllist command*

If you would like to save the output generated from the run, you can click the Save to File option, as shown in Figure 8-21. You can select your file name and destination to store your file.

Figure 8-21. *Save the process output*

If you are using the full OSForensics and not just the Volatility Workbench, you can add these results to a case as part of the Manage Case module so that you can have all your analysis related to a target machine in one specific place. First, you have to create a new case with your details. Now, you can add the file to the case by using the Add Attachment option to store the file, as shown in Figure 8-22.

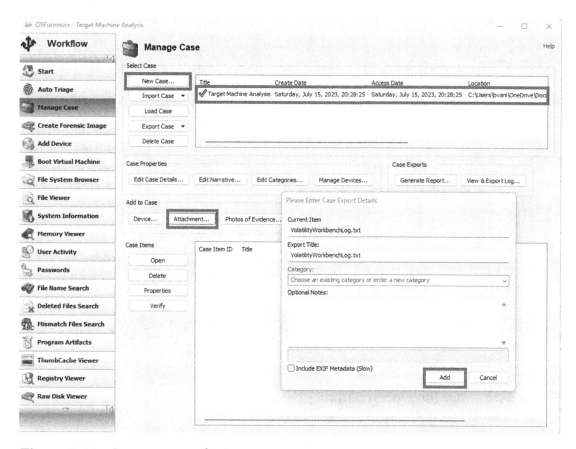

Figure 8-22. *Save your results in a case*

Now that we have learned how to perform memory analysis on our system using two popularly used software programs to analyze memory, let us understand the whole process of analyzing a target machine when you receive it.

Process of Analyzing a Computer's Memory Dump

Clearly, there is a wide array of plugins to use with Volatility, whether you use the command line or OSForensics Volatility Workbench. As you gain more experience in memory forensics, you may have your own process, but the following steps can be considered a starter guide:

1. The ***pslist*** command can be used to view all the processes and thread statistics of a system. Note any unexplained processes or processes that do not have a parent process ID listed.

2. Next, you can check for any open files associated with a process. This method is extremely useful because it reveals which files a suspicious process on the target system is accessing. By analyzing the location of these files, it becomes possible to identify malware. Furthermore, if these files contain logs of user keyboard inputs, it could indicate the inadvertent exposure of passwords to the malware authors. Such findings greatly enhance the strength of the investigator's case.

3. Now we can use the **connections** (Volatility command) or **netstat** command to check both the incoming and outgoing network connections. Look for any "pokerhands." This is where the attackers have set ports that have all the same numbers, such as "4444," or increments, such as "1234." See any suspicious processes coming through? [36]

4. Malware can manipulate system file timestamps to hide its presence, hindering investigators from identifying the initial infection. By comparing process timestamps from the memory dump with system file timestamps, investigators can determine the exact moment of compromise. This enables further analysis of records like emails and browser history to identify correlations between process timestamps and application activities, which can help uncover the infection's cause.

5. You can also check **sockets** for any suspicious process IDs that have a socket connection.

6. You could also use the **malfind** plugin to identify any hits on malware.

7. If you find any memory sections marked as **Page_Execute_ReadWrite,** this can be a sign of code injection on the device. The utility allows a piece of code to run and write itself.

8. Another plugin **handles** identifies any handles on the device.

9. One can also use the **-t Mutant** option, which will show any mutants or mutexes that are used to control access to any shared resources and can identify malware.

10. You can also utilize the system log files to determine user involvement and detect unauthorized access. This aids in assessing the extent of compromise with the organization's network protocols.

The preceding process will give you a good starting point to begin and understand analyzing memory dumps with the Volatility Workbench, and it will also help us understand if any additional techniques should be applied to the target machine.

Conclusion

Windows memory forensics is a vital discipline within the field of digital forensics, offering powerful techniques and tools to investigate and analyze volatile memory in Windows systems. By examining the data stored in memory, investigators can uncover valuable evidence, identify malware, reconstruct user activities, and detect security incidents that may have been hidden through traditional disk-based forensics.

In this chapter, we were introduced to an understanding of the Windows memory forensics. We explored the essentials of computer memory and how it works. Later, we dived into the fundamentals of memory forensics and its usage in the field of forensics. You also saw how to analyze memory with tools such as Volatility and their role in extracting and interpreting memory data. We also explored the basics of malware and various malware hiding techniques. Memory forensics is an extremely valuable area in the field of incident response.

References

BankMyCell (2023). How many phones are in the world. Retrieved from www.bankmycell.com/blog/how-many-phones-are-in-the-world

Cisco (n.d.). What is malware? Retrieved from www.cisco.com/site/us/en/products/security/what-is-malware.html

Easttom, C. (2022). Digital Forensics, Investigation, and Response (4th ed.). Jones and Bartlett Learning LLC

The History of Computer Viruses & Malware (2022). Retrieved from www.esecurityplanet.com/threats/computer-viruses-and-malware-history/

IBM (2023). IBM Security X-Force Threat Intelligence Index 2023. Retrieved from www.ibm.com/reports/threat-intelligence

Microsoft (n.d.). FAT, HPFS, and NTFS file systems. Retrieved from https://learn.microsoft.com/en-us/troubleshoot/windows-client/backup-and-storage/fat-hpfs-and-ntfs-file-systems

NIST (2023). Glossary: Volatile data. Retrieved from https://csrc.nist.gov/glossary/term/volatile_data

Nyholm, H., Monteith, K., Lyles, S., Gallegos, M., DeSantis, M., Donaldson, J., & Taylor, C. (2022). The Evolution of Volatile Memory Forensics. Journal of Cybersecurity and Privacy, 2(3), 556-572. https://doi.org/10.3390/jcp2030028

Packetlabs (2023). 239 cybersecurity statistics 2023. Retrieved from www.packetlabs.net/posts/239-cybersecurity-statistics-2023/

UFS Explorer (n.d.). File systems basics. Retrieved from www.ufsexplorer.com/articles/file-systems-basics/

US District Courts for the Southern Districts of Texas (n.d.). Self-authentication of electronic evidence: New rules. Retrieved from www.txs.uscourts.gov/sites/txs/files/Self-Authentication%20of%20Electronic%20Evidence%20-%20New%20Rules%20-%20G.Joseph.pdf

Test Your Knowledge

A few questions are provided here to aid you in testing your knowledge before you proceed.

1. Which type of memory is analyzed in Windows memory forensics?

   a. Secondary storage

   b. Virtual memory

   c. Volatile memory (RAM)

   d. Cache memory

2. What is the primary purpose of Windows memory forensics?.

   a. Analyzing network traffic

   b. Identifying malware and malicious activities

   c. Monitoring system performance

   d. All of the above

3. Which of the following artifacts can be recovered from memory to aid in Windows memory forensics?

   a. Registry keys and values

   b. User login credentials

   c. File system metadata

   d. Network packet captures

4. What is the purpose of the "pslist" command in Volatility for Windows memory forensics?

   a. Retrieve network connection details

   b. List all loaded DLLs in memory

   c. Extract file handles and open files in memory

   d. Display information about running processes

5. What maps virtual addresses to physical addresses?

   a. MDR

   b. Page

   c. MAR

   d. Heap

CHAPTER 9

PowerShell Forensics

Sean Steuber
Chuck Easttom, Ph.D., D.Sc.

Introduction

PowerShell can be a very powerful forensics tool. Once ubiquitous with Windows, PowerShell is no longer beholden to one brand of operating system but almost all brands thanks to the release of PowerShell Core. The ability to install and run PowerShell on any given major operating system makes learning PowerShell all the more beneficial. Additionally, in respect to digital forensics, where more often than not tools are separated out by OS brands, anyone seeking to pursue a career in digital forensics is forced to juggle multiple toolboxes depending on the operating system under investigation. With PowerShell (more specifically, PowerShell Core or PowerShell version 6+), a digital investigator can forge their hammer as it were and always have a go-to tool for forensics. In this chapter, the focus will be on PowerShell for Windows, using both PowerShell 5 and 6+, but understand that PowerShell is one of those "old" technologies that many modern-day digital forensics specialists might look past when choosing their tools for a job. Having been created in the early 2000s and first released with Windows XP, Windows Server 2003, and Windows Vista, PowerShell has been around for a good while relative to the world of computing. Commonly, the technology is seen as antiquated, but this is not fair nor accurate. As the most cutting-edge software frameworks for Windows are developed, .NET and .NET Core, so too is PowerShell kept at the front lines. Though not as flashy, PowerShell is continuously more capable as time goes on since its underlying framework is under constant improvement. With the creation of PowerShell Core or PowerShell 6+ built on top of the .NET Core framework,

© Chuck Easttom, William Butler, Jessica Phelan, Ramya Sai Bhagavatula, Sean Steuber, Karely Rodriguez, Victoria Indy Balkissoon, Zehra Naseer 2024
C. Easttom et al., *Windows Forensics*, https://doi.org/10.1007/979-8-8688-0193-8_9

PowerShell was made able to run on more operating systems than just Windows. Though for the time being, certain functionality has not been fully ported from PowerShell 5+ to PowerShell Core. As we will see though, Microsoft is pushing forward with PowerShell Core as the main focus of their PowerShell development, so even though PowerShell for Windows may be a better choice for PowerShell forensics on a Windows machine than PowerShell Core, I would not bet that would be for long.

In this chapter, we will cover the following:

- PowerShell background

- Different frameworks PowerShell is built on

- Open sourced nature of PowerShell

- PowerShell basics

- PowerShell Gallery

- Digital forensics with PowerShell

What Is PowerShell?

PowerShell should be thought of as an "Execution Engine" rather than a shell or a scripting language as really it is both and more. Microsoft, which maintains PowerShell, says the following about it:

PowerShell is a cross-platform task automation solution made up of a command-line shell, a scripting language, and a configuration management framework. PowerShell runs on Windows, Linux, and macOS.

As a shell, it is important to note that while most shells deal primarily with string values returned, PowerShell almost exclusively works with objects (either COM or .NET). Thinking of all the interactions of PowerShell commands as strings is likely one of the most common incorrect assumptions made around PowerShell. If the PowerShell user were to ask PowerShell what version of PowerShell was running, the tool would return a String object describing the version. If the user asked for a list of all active processes without specifying any details of how they wanted the output to be, PowerShell will return a list of Process objects full of attributes, handles, and supported methods. For instance, the Get-Process native command or cmdlet (pronounced "command let") returns a list of Process objects, but what is outputted to the shell is effectively the Process object's ToString() method that pulls various attributes from the objects to display on the screen as a string much like any common object-oriented language would handle printing out an object class. The understanding of this "objects vs. strings" topic is critical when talking about larger PowerShell scripts or chaining PowerShell commands together with pipe (|) characters. The user is piping objects between commands and not strings.

The PowerShell shell allows the user to run all native PowerShell commands (cmdlets) and any commands available to the user on the machine running PowerShell. For instance, in the situation where PowerShell is running on a Windows machine, Figure 9-1 shows a Venn diagram of available operations out of the box within a PowerShell shell.

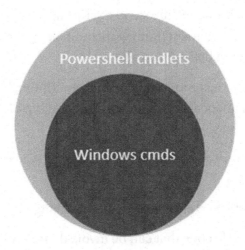

Figure 9-1. *Venn diagram of out-of-the–box available operations in PowerShell on a Windows machine*

With that said, any familiar Windows commands, such as dir, move, tree, openfiles, tasklist, taskkill, etc., will work in PowerShell running on Windows. Something to note really quick: When running non-cmdlet commands in PowerShell such as the Windows dir or the Linux ls, the return values for these commands will be simple string objects and not complex class objects. If piping is necessary, some parsing might be needed when chaining non-cmdlet commands with cmdlets. However, return types aside, when considering PowerShell for digital forensics operations, out of the box the user will be able to leverage industry standard Windows or Linux commands, depending on the underlying OS, and at the very least be able to alias more complex, chained operations than if the user only used, say, the cmd shell.

As a scripting language, PowerShell is built on the .NET Framework, giving it the ability to do almost any programming you might require. If you can do an operation with C/C#/C++ code, then you can do the same operation with a PowerShell script. On top of this, you can extend PowerShell by adding C# libraries for the tool to import and leverage. Since a PowerShell script comes out of the box on all Windows machines, is quick to get running, and is more than capable of almost all operations for which a digital forensics specialist could hope, PowerShell is a wonderful option for digital forensics.

There will be a lot of technical vocabulary thrown around the chapter, so please use the following list as a reference as you study PowerShell for digital forensics in this chapter:

- **PowerShell**: A command-line shell, a scripting language, and a configuration management framework built on top of the .NET Framework, PowerShell version ~5

- **PowerShell Core**: A command-line shell, a scripting language, and a configuration management framework built on top of the .NET Core Framework, PowerShell version 6+

- **PowerShell Shell**: The command-line interface (CLI) to PowerShell, denoted with a PS

- **PowerShell Code/Script**: The programming language of PowerShell

- **Cmdlet**: Executable code that can be invoked directly from the PowerShell prompt or from within PowerShell scripts

- **Verb-Noun Pair**: The naming convention used for cmdlets, where the verb represents the action, and the noun represents the target

- **Parameter**: An input provided to a cmdlet to modify its behavior or specify additional information

- **.NET Framework**: A software framework developed by Microsoft that supports building and running applications on Windows

- **.NET Core Framework**: The open sourced .NET Framework built to run on a myriad of operating systems

- **Pipeline**: A mechanism in PowerShell that allows the output of one cmdlet to be used as input for another, creating a powerful way to chain commands together

- **Execution Policy**: A security feature in PowerShell that determines which scripts are allowed to run on a system

- **Windows Management Instrumentation (WMI)**: A set of tools and interfaces for accessing system management information in Windows

- **Script Block**: A collection of PowerShell commands enclosed in curly braces, used to create reusable code

- **PowerShell Integrated Scripting Environment (PowerShell ISE)**: A graphical user interface for PowerShell scripting and testing

- **Module**: A self-contained package of cmdlets, functions, and other resources that extend PowerShell's capabilities

- **PowerShell Gallery**: An online repository for discovering and sharing PowerShell modules

- **Piping**: The process of passing output from one cmdlet as input to another using the pipeline operator |

- **Visual Studio Code**: A lightweight interactive development environment made by Microsoft

Frameworks

There are two main frameworks that PowerShell is built on top of: Windows Management Framework (WMF) and presently the .NET (or .NET Core for PowerShell Core) framework. Consider the distinction between the two by name as Desktop/Windows PowerShell and PowerShell Core, respectively. For the most part, syntax and the basics are the same between the PowerShells, but various features may only be in PowerShell Desktop and vice versa for PowerShell Core. These differences are important to understand when considering which PowerShell to leverage in a forensics case.

PowerShell Desktop

PowerShell Desktop or Windows PowerShell is the traditional PowerShell most users use when they pull up PowerShell on a Windows machine. PowerShell Desktop was built on WMF, but more recently, PowerShell Desktop is built on top of the .NET Framework (important to note that this is simply .NET and not .NET Core). This version of PowerShell Desktop is simply PowerShell version 5.*, where PowerShell Core ends up being PowerShell version 6+. The Windows or Desktop version of PowerShell is the powerhouse version for working on a Windows machine if the user intends to use PowerShell out of the box without installing additional modules. Certain cmdlets really only make sense on a Windows machine and thus are not included in PowerShell Core out of the box but are included with Windows PowerShell. PowerShell Desktop comes installed on any machine running the Windows operating system.

PowerShell Core

As mentioned previously, PowerShell Core, which is PowerShell version 6+, is built on top of the .NET Core Framework. The biggest pro here with PowerShell Core being built with the .NET Core Framework and not simply .NET is that while .NET needs to be on a Windows operating system to function properly, .NET Core is a package framework capable of running on nearly any operating system. Therefore, products built with .NET Core (assuming no other dependencies require a specific operating system) can run on almost all operating systems themselves. This makes it possible for PowerShell Core to be installed and operate on, say, a Mac operating system as well as a Windows operating system. PowerShell Core does not include as many modules and cmdlets out of the box as PowerShell Desktop does. This can be observed by installing PowerShell Core via its GitHub page `https://github.com/PowerShell/PowerShell` and running the following PowerShell command: "Get-Module -ListAvailable | Measure" and "Get-Command * | Measure" which return 75 and 3003, respectively (PowerShell 7.3.4). Those very same commands on an out-of-the-box preinstalled PowerShell Desktop on a Windows 10 machine return the following: 84 and 3044, respectively (PowerShell 5.1.19). Not to fear though, if the user would like to use any PowerShell module/cmdlets that were not included with the out-of-the-box version of PowerShell Core, the user can simply leverage the Install-Module cmdlet and add the module to their PowerShell. Though at the moment, some modules or features have not been fully ported from PowerShell to PowerShell Core.

Open Source

Much like the .NET Framework, whenever PowerShell 6.0 was built on .NET Core and released, the code for PowerShell 6+ was made open sourced on GitHub. This means anyone is capable of diving into the PowerShell code to find out exactly how it works, follow updates as the Microsoft team and open source community correct issues and add features, and so on. For instance, anyone can go and see how the Get-Process command is implemented by starting at line 440 of the Process.cs file located here: `https://github.com/PowerShell/PowerShell/blob/master/src/Microsoft.PowerShell.Commands.Management/commands/management/Process.cs`. This may or may not be helpful, but having that transparency of the codebase can be insightful at the very least. You can even pull down the PowerShell Core repository and compile/build it yourself to experience the newest features/fixes that might yet be built in a specific PowerShell Core version. All you would need to do is anytime you want the latest work, you would do a git pull to the local repository and build it. Then features/fixes such as those in Figure 9-2 would automatically be available to them.

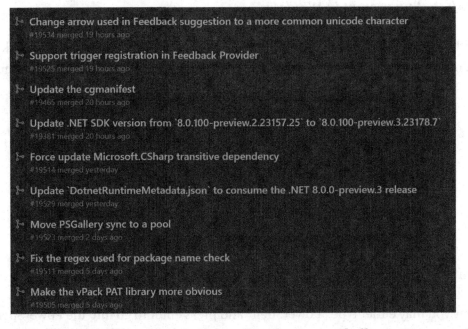

Figure 9-2. *Recent pull requests completed on the PowerShell repository as of April 19, 2023 14:20 CST*

Getting Started with PowerShell

To begin using PowerShell on a Windows machine, you have a few options. First, you may wish to simply use the Windows Command Prompt. To do so, you will want to locate the command prompt either by the Windows search ability or the shortcut of Windows key + R which will open up the "Run" dialog box, as shown in Figure 9-3.

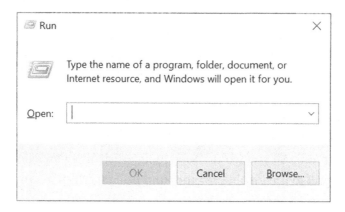

Figure 9-3. *Run prompt in Windows*

With the run dialog box open, type "cmd" in the text input field and either click OK or press enter. Doing so will open the Windows Command prompt, as shown in Figure 9-4.

Figure 9-4. *The Windows Command Prompt*

Now you may either type "PowerShell" and press enter to go into the PowerShell shell within the command prompt, or you can run PowerShell commands by using the word "PowerShell" before any command to run the cmdlet but not necessarily hop into a PowerShell shell. To demo this, say you want to know what version of PowerShell is running on your Windows machine. You can do this by tapping into the $PSVersionTable global PowerShell variable that stores this information. If you are in a PowerShell shell, then you can simply type "$PSVersionTable" and enter; however, if you are not in the shell and attempt to look into that variable without the word "PowerShell" before it, then an error will occur, as shown in Figure 9-5.

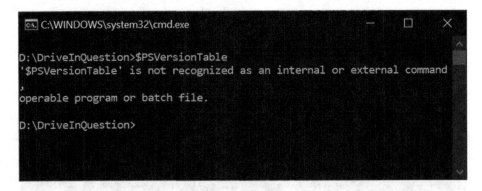

Figure 9-5. *Attempting to access PowerShell variables directly without being in a PowerShell shell*

Now let's see what happens if we try the same command but with "PowerShell" before it, as shown in Figure 9-6.

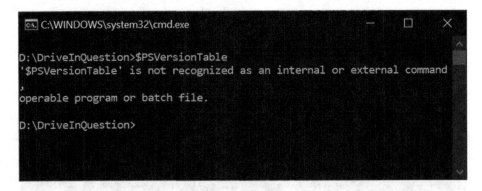

Figure 9-6. *The $PSVersionTable contents*

As described previously, you may instead wish to enter a PowerShell shell inside of the command prompt. This can be achieved by typing and running the following command in the console: "PowerShell". When you do this, you will notice a "PS" before your directory location in the console, such as in the snapshot shown in Figure 9-7, helping you to know that you are currently in the PowerShell shell and not simply the Windows command-line prompt.

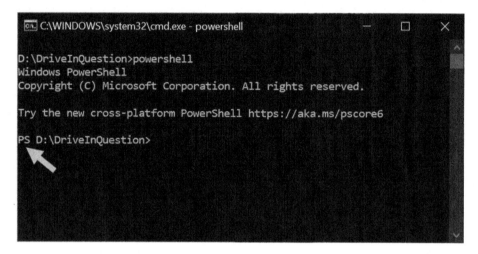

Figure 9-7. *Inside the PowerShell shell from within the command-line prompt*

While in the PowerShell shell, you can look at PowerShell variables by just typing and entering their name. Therefore, to see what version of PowerShell you are running while in a PowerShell shell, you can simply run "$PSVersionTable", as shown in Figure 9-8.

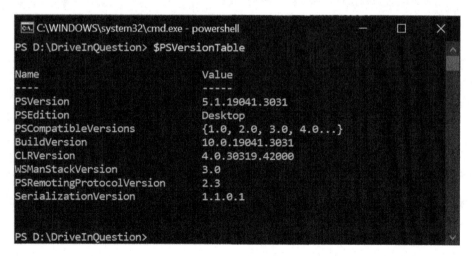

Figure 9-8. *The $PSVersionTable contents while in the PowerShell shell*

Another method to use PowerShell on a Windows machine is by running the

PowerShell Integrated Scripting Environment (ISE) that ships with the Windows operating system. However, according to the Windows article for PowerShell ISE, PowerShell ISE is no longer receiving feature updates. The article has a cautionary note that reads as follows:

The PowerShell ISE is no longer in active feature development. As a shipping component of Windows, it continues to be officially supported for security and high-priority servicing fixes. We currently have no plans to remove the ISE from Windows.

The article continues by directing readers from PowerShell ISE to install Visual Studio Code and the Visual Studio Code PowerShell extension, which is in active development and supports PowerShell v6 and beyond. With that in mind, modern PowerShell users and future digital forensics investigators hoping to leverage the tool should move to using Visual Studio Code and the PowerShell extension if they wish to use the latest PowerShell features and environment. You should do just that and get Visual Studio Code and the corresponding PowerShell extension installed on their machine to use for some of the future examples in this chapter.

To begin, it is important to note what Visual Studio Code is exactly. To lay it out rapidly, Visual Studio Code or VS Code is a lightweight interactive development environment (IDE) capable of running on Windows, macOS, and Linux. On the official VS Code "Why did we build Visual Studio Code?" page, they state the following:

[VS Code] is an editor that gets out of your way. The delightfully frictionless edit-build-debug cycle means less time fiddling with your environment, and more time executing on your ideas.

Those with software development experience in the Windows stack, including C/C++/C#/, .NET Framework, and more, are very familiar with VS Code's older sibling "Visual Studio." On the official Visual Studio site, the following is used to describe Visual Studio:

The Visual Studio IDE is a creative launching pad that you can use to edit, debug, and build code, and then publish an app. Over and above the standard editor and debugger that most IDEs provide, Visual Studio includes compilers, code completion tools, graphical designers, and many more features to enhance the software development process.

The best way to think about the difference between Visual Studio and Visual Studio Code is to think of Visual Studio Code as a development tool that starts incredibly lightweight, and with the addition of various extensions you choose such as the PowerShell extension, VS Code can be tailored to fit the exact needs of the user without all the fluff (unless they want the fluff, in which case they should simply install the

various extensions). Visual Studio on the other hand comes jam-packed with tools for
.NET development, being tailored out of the box for C type languages and the .NET or
.NET Core Framework. Using VS Code instead of Visual Studio for PowerShell scripting
then makes a bit more sense, in the context of wanting to be a bit more lightweight
and custom tailored to PowerShell development. VS Code however does not ship with
Windows OS, but the tool is free to download and install off the following web page:
`https://code.visualstudio.com/docs/?dv=win`.

Once you have followed through the installation package for VS Code and run the
application, you will see that in Figure 9-9.

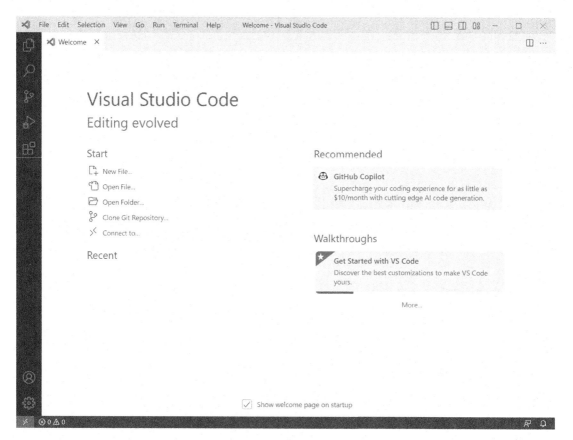

Figure 9-9. *Visual Studio Code home screen*

From here, you will want to navigate to the left-side menu and click the extension
icon as seen in Figure 9-10.

Figure 9-10. *Visual Studio Code access the plugins menu*

This will open the plugins menu where you can then type in "PowerShell" into the "Search Extensions in Marketplace" input text field. At this point, a myriad of plugins will return as possible extensions for the user to install, as shown in Figure 9-11.

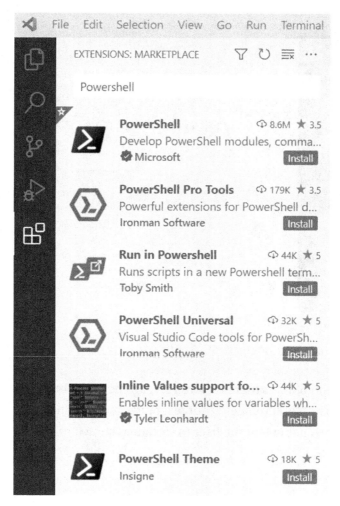

Figure 9-11. *Visual Studio Code search for plugins*

Something to note is that anyone can create a plugin and submit it to the Windows VS Code Plugins marketplace for download. You must take caution when searching and installing plugins just as they should with installing any kind of software onto their machines. The way to be safest, generally, is to only install plugins by verified authors. Verified authors will have the blue checkmark icon beside their name such as seen for the "PowerShell" and "Inline Values support..." plugins with Microsoft and Tyler Leonhardt, respectively. By clicking any of the plugins, you will navigate to that plugin's extension page where you can read about the plugin and install the plugin (of course, you can just click the install button without checking out the extension page, but that is ill advised). By clicking the blue install button for the "PowerShell" plugin authored by

Microsoft, the installation will begin and finish rather quickly. An alternative method to install the plugin would be to simply run the following command in the command prompt given the user selected to add "code" to the PATH commands which will enable "code" to call upon the VS Code CLI:

```
code --install-extension PowerShell-<version>.vsix
```

Once the PowerShell extension is successfully installed, a new PowerShell icon will be visible on the left-hand side of VS Code. When this icon is clicked, they will open up what is effectively PowerShell ISE but within VS Code with the list of available commands and that the terminal has PS before the current directory location, indicating the terminal is booted up into a PowerShell shell, as shown in Figure 9-12.

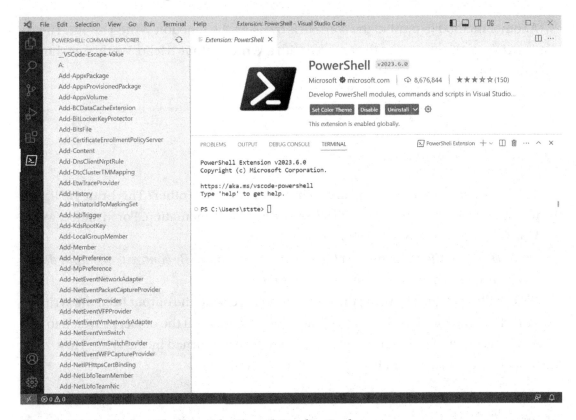

Figure 9-12. *PowerShell inside Visual Studio Code*

Your First PowerShell Command!

As is the tradition of learning any new programming language, novice users of PowerShell will want to start off with the quintessential "Hello, World!" With PowerShell, you may use the Write-Host function, among other cmdlets. The cmdlet takes a myriad of parameters, among which is the Object parameter. Remember that PowerShell treats almost everything as objects, so the Write-Host -Object "Hello, World!" will print "Hello, World!" to the user's console by invoking the ToString() method from the object provided. In this case, the object parameter is set to a String object with the contents of "Hello, World!" with a method ToString() that returns that as a string. To simplify the command, a simple Write-Host "Hello, World" as shown in Figure 9-13.

```
PS D:\DriveInQuestion> Write-Host 'Hello, World!'
Hello, World!
```

Figure 9-13.   *Write-Host hello world*

Another method to print to the console is by using the function Write-Output. The iconic string can be printed to the console with a Write-Output "Hello, World!", as shown in Figure 9-14.

```
PS D:\DriveInQuestion> Write-Output 'Hello, World!'
Hello, World!
```

Figure 9-14.   *Write-Output hello world*

With that said then, why would users choose one over the other? This brings to light the importance of referring to the official PowerShell documentation. For instance, we read the following description for Write-Host:

Write-Host uses the ToString() method to write the output. By contrast, to output data to the pipeline, use Write-Output or implicit output.

We can illustrate this by using the pipe symbol, |, to send the output from the Write-Host function into the Get–Member function, which will detail the object provided to the console, presumably to see details of the data object returned by the Write-Host function. However, as seen in Figure 9-15, that is not the case.

```
PS D:\DriveInQuestion> Write-Host 'Hello, World!' | Get-Member
Hello, World!
Get-Member: You must specify an object for the Get-Member cmdlet.
```

Figure 9-15.   *Write-Host does not provide objects for the pipeline error.*

But if we use Write-Output instead, what is printed to the console is shown in Figure 9-16.

```
PS D:\DriveInQuestion> Write-Output 'Hello, World!' | Get-Member

   TypeName: System.String

Name                   MemberType            Definition
----                   ----------            ----------
Clone                  Method                System.Object Clone(), System.Object ICloneable.Cl(
CompareTo              Method                int CompareTo(System.Object value), int CompareTo(:
Contains               Method                bool Contains(string value), bool Contains(string \
CopyTo                 Method                void CopyTo(int sourceIndex, char[] destination, ii
EndsWith               Method                bool EndsWith(string value), bool EndsWith(string \
EnumerateRunes         Method                System.Text.StringRuneEnumerator EnumerateRunes()
Equals                 Method                bool Equals(System.Object obj), bool Equals(string
GetEnumerator          Method                System.CharEnumerator GetEnumerator(), System.Coll(
GetHashCode            Method                int GetHashCode(), int GetHashCode(System.StringCor
GetPinnableReference   Method                System.Char&, System.Private.CoreLib, Version=7.0.(
GetType                Method                type GetType()
GetTypeCode            Method                System.TypeCode GetTypeCode(), System.TypeCode ICor
IndexOf                Method                int IndexOf(char value), int IndexOf(char value, ii
IndexOfAny             Method                int IndexOfAny(char[] anyOf), int IndexOfAny(char[]
Insert                 Method                string Insert(int startIndex, string value)
IsNormalized           Method                bool IsNormalized(), bool IsNormalized(System.Text.
LastIndexOf            Method                int LastIndexOf(char value), int LastIndexOf(char \
LastIndexOfAny         Method                int LastIndexOfAny(char[] anyOf), int LastIndexOfAr
Normalize              Method                string Normalize(), string Normalize(System.Text.Nc
PadLeft                Method                string PadLeft(int totalWidth), string PadLeft(int
PadRight               Method                string PadRight(int totalWidth), string PadRight(ii
Remove                 Method                string Remove(int startIndex, int count), string R(
Replace                Method                string Replace(string oldValue, string newValue, bc
ReplaceLineEndings     Method                string ReplaceLineEndings(), string ReplaceLineEnd:
Split                  Method                string[] Split(char separator, System.StringSplitOp
StartsWith             Method                bool StartsWith(string value), bool StartsWith(str:
Substring              Method                string Substring(int startIndex), string Substring(
ToBoolean              Method                bool IConvertible.ToBoolean(System.IFormatProvider
ToByte                 Method                byte IConvertible.ToByte(System.IFormatProvider pr(
ToChar                 Method                char IConvertible.ToChar(System.IFormatProvider pr(
ToCharArray            Method                char[] ToCharArray(), char[] ToCharArray(int start:
ToDateTime             Method                datetime IConvertible.ToDateTime(System.IFormatProv
ToDecimal              Method                decimal IConvertible.ToDecimal(System.IFormatProvic
ToDouble               Method                double IConvertible.ToDouble(System.IFormatProvidei
ToInt16                Method                short IConvertible.ToInt16(System.IFormatProvider [
ToInt32                Method                int IConvertible.ToInt32(System.IFormatProvider pr(
ToInt64                Method                long IConvertible.ToInt64(System.IFormatProvider pi
ToLower                Method                string ToLower(), string ToLower(cultureinfo cultui
ToLowerInvariant       Method                string ToLowerInvariant()
ToSByte                Method                sbyte IConvertible.ToSByte(System.IFormatProvider [
ToSingle               Method                float IConvertible.ToSingle(System.IFormatProvider
ToString               Method                string ToString(), string ToString(System.IFormatPi
ToType                 Method                System.Object IConvertible.ToType(type conversionT)
ToUInt16               Method                ushort IConvertible.ToUInt16(System.IFormatProvidei
ToUInt32               Method                uint IConvertible.ToUInt32(System.IFormatProvider [
ToUInt64               Method                ulong IConvertible.ToUInt64(System.IFormatProvider
ToUpper                Method                string ToUpper(), string ToUpper(cultureinfo cultui
ToUpperInvariant       Method                string ToUpperInvariant()
Trim                   Method                string Trim(), string Trim(char trimChar), string 1
TrimEnd                Method                string TrimEnd(), string TrimEnd(char trimChar), s1
TrimStart              Method                string TrimStart(), string TrimStart(char trimChar]
TryCopyTo              Method                bool TryCopyTo(System.Span[char] destination)
Chars                  ParameterizedProperty char Chars(int index) {get;}
Length                 Property              int Length {get;}
```

Figure 9-16. *Write-Output does provide objects for the pipeline*

Note that while the Write-Host method failed on the Get-Member function call, we can see "Hello, World!" printed to the console; however, though Write-Output does not fail on the Get-Member call, "Hello, World!" is never printed out to the screen. Why would that be? Well, remember that the PowerShell documentation for Write-Host mentioned "implicit output," but did not detail what that meant. Basically, implicit output would be whenever a function call is not set to a variable or piped into another function, the ToString() method is invoked on that object, displaying to the console, whereas Write-Host would be explicit output since the function invokes the ToString() method directly. The following PowerShell executions achieve the same operation of printing "Hello, World!", but the first leverages implicit output and the second leverages explicit output, as shown in Figure 9-17.

```
PS D:\DriveInQuestion> 'Hello, World!'
Hello, World!
PS D:\DriveInQuestion> 'Hello, World!'.ToString()
Hello, World!
```

Figure 9-17. *Implicit vs. explicit output*

In the case of "Write-Host 'Hello, World!' | Get-Member," the first function call "Write-Host 'Hello, World!'" explicitly fires off the ToString() method printing "Hello, World" to the console, but whenever explicit output occurs, there is no object to pipe into the following function Get-Member. That causes Get-Member to fail, but Write-Host did its job.

PowerShell Basic Concepts

All PowerShell commands begin with the command name such as Get-Help. In general, most cmdlet names are of the following form: Verb-Noun such as Get-Processes, Remove-Item, Resolve-Path, etc. After the command name, you may set 0 to many parameters depending on the specifications of that command. Parameters will be of the form -[Parameter Name] [Parameter Value/s] after the command name such as the following: New-Alias -Name utd -Value Update-TypeData. Additionally, though, the user may skip typing out the parameter names like this: New-Alias utd Update-TypeData, which forces PowerShell to go off of the parameter and value positions to determine what parameter to bind the values to. For example, the statements shown in Figure 9-18 all complete the same goal of creating a new alias.

```
PowerShell

New-Alias -Name utd -Value Update-TypeData
New-Alias -Name utd Update-TypeData
New-Alias utd -Value Update-TypeData
New-Alias utd Update-TypeData
```

Figure 9-18. *Passing parameters to commands*

Chaining Commands

By using the pipe | character, the PowerShell user is able to send the results from one command to another. The results will be .NET or COM objects. Here is an example of chaining commands with Get-Process, Where-Object, and Format-Table cmdlets: Get-Process | Where-Object {$_.mainWindowTitle} | Format-Table Id, Name, mainWindowtitle -AutoSize. This statement will take the list of all active processes as Process objects from the Get-Process cmdlet and send those to the Where-Object cmdlet as its input. Where-Object will then filter that list down to Process objects that have a main window title. The filtered list of Process objects will then be piped into the Format-Table cmdlet which will pretty print Id, Name, and mainWindowTitle from every Process object that arrived with an autosize parameter to keep the table display nice and orderly. Those results can be seen in Figure 9-19.

```
PS D:\DriveInQuestion> Get-Process | Where-Object {$_.mainWindowTitle} | Format-Table Id, Name, mainWindowtitle -AutoSize

   Id Name                                                          MainWindowTitle
   -- ----                                                          ---------------
 9408 ApplicationFrameHost                                          Calculator
15320 CalculatorApp                                                 Calculator
14224 chrome                                                        Steuber_2023_PowerShellForensics.docx - Google Docs - Google Chrome
  668 Code                                                          CyberDetective.ps1 - DriveInQuestion - Visual Studio Code
 5600 CodeSetup-stable-74f6148eb9ea00507ec113ec51c489d6ffb4b771.tmp Setup
10988 SnagitEditor                                                  Snagit Editor - [2023-07-25_19-24-43.snagx]
 2724 Spotify                                                       Wolfgang Amadeus Mozart - Sonata No. 16 in C Major for Piano, K. 545
13772 TextInputHost                                                 Microsoft Text Input Application
```

Figure 9-19. *Current processes with a main window title in a table format*

Important Commands

Here are a couple of quick but immensely helpful commands to have memorized to accelerate work in PowerShell. First, the cmdlet Get-Help -Full Command-Name is about equivalent to man in Linux. This can be incredibly helpful for poking around and determining all of the little details about a command. Another helpful command would be Get-Member, which gets and displays all of the members, the properties, and methods of an object. Get-Process | Get-Member will display all public information for the Process object, such as seen in Figure 9-20.

```
PS D:\DriveInQuestion> Get-Process | Get-Member


    TypeName: System.Diagnostics.Process

Name                   MemberType      Definition
----                   ----------      ----------
Handles                AliasProperty   Handles = Handlecount
Name                   AliasProperty   Name = ProcessName
NPM                    AliasProperty   NPM = NonpagedSystemMemorySize64
PM                     AliasProperty   PM = PagedMemorySize64
SI                     AliasProperty   SI = SessionId
VM                     AliasProperty   VM = VirtualMemorySize64
WS                     AliasProperty   WS = WorkingSet64
Parent                 CodeProperty    System.Object Parent{get=GetParentP
Disposed               Event           System.EventHandler Disposed(System
ErrorDataReceived      Event           System.Diagnostics.DataReceivedEven
Exited                 Event           System.EventHandler Exited(System.Ol
OutputDataReceived     Event           System.Diagnostics.DataReceivedEven
BeginErrorReadLine     Method          void BeginErrorReadLine()
BeginOutputReadLine    Method          void BeginOutputReadLine()
CancelErrorRead        Method          void CancelErrorRead()
CancelOutputRead       Method          void CancelOutputRead()
Close                  Method          void Close()
```

Figure 9-20. *Showing all of the members of the Get-Process cmdlet*

Additionally, PowerShell users can use the function Get-Command to return a list of all available PowerShell functions to the user. To take it a step further, we can chain Get-Command with Where-Object and Select-Object to return all of commands that contain "Write" in the name, as shown in Figure 9-21.

```
PS D:\DriveInQuestion> Get-Command | Where-Object { $_.Name -like '*Write*' } | Select-Object -ExpandProperty Name
Write-FileSystemCache
Write-DtcTransactionsTraceSession
Write-PrinterNfcTag
Write-VolumeCache
Write-Debug
Write-Error
Write-Host
Write-Information
Write-Output
Write-Progress
Write-Verbose
Write-VSCodeHtmlContentView
Write-Warning
```

Figure 9-21. *Cmdlets that contain "Write" in their name*

Get-Command pipes all of the commands as an object list to Where-Object that will filter the list down to only commands that contain "Write" in their name which pipes those objects into the Select-Object command which will allow the user to focus the output from all of the details of the commands to just displaying their names.

Note $_ is referred to as the "current object" or "pipeline variable" in the case of the previous command; Where-Object will receive a list of CommandInfo objects which contain an attribute Name. Therefore, whenever $_.Name is used, PowerShell is saying "get me the Name attribute of the current piped variable."

Now let's use Get-Help -Full Write-Host to determine all of the details on Write-Host. When running the command, all of the details of the command will be output via implicit output to the console, including the following: Name, Syntax, Parameters, Inputs, Outputs, Aliases, and Remarks. From this, we can determine that Write-Host has multiple parameters including BackgroundColor and ForegroundColor, so to liven our Hello World print, you can see this in Figure 9-22.

```
PS D:\DriveInQuestion> Write-Host 'Hello, World!' -ForegroundColor red
Hello, World!
PS D:\DriveInQuestion> Write-Host 'Hello, World!' -ForegroundColor blue
Hello, World!
```

Figure 9-22. *Passing color parameters to Write-Host*

Logical Computing

To start with some more complicated logic operations with PowerShell, we will move from writing commands directly to a PowerShell console to writing script in a .ps1 file and executing it. To start, create a new file called MyLogicScripts.ps1 in a folder that is easily accessible to you. These script files can be executed together line by line, instead of running each command manually with the enter key as is the case with typing commands to the shell directly. In the MyLogicScripts.ps1 file, add the following line of PowerShell:

Write-Host 'Hello, World!' -ForegroundColor cyan

Save the file. Then run the command "PowerShell ./MyLogicScripts.ps1", assuming you are in the directory of the script file (alternatively, in the PowerShell shell, just running ./MyLogicScripts.ps1 would also work), shown in Figure 9-23.

```
PS D:\DriveInQuestion> Powershell ./MyLogicScripts.ps1
Hello, World!
```

Figure 9-23. *Running a .ps1 script file*

Putting that Write-Host command in MyLogicScripts.ps1 was simply to demonstrate quickly how we can execute the .ps1 scripts and get familiar results. Remove the Write-Host command and replace it with what is shown in Figure 9-24.

```
>_ MyLogicScripts.ps1 > ...
1    # Set Variable $i to a value of 0
2    $i = 0
3
4    # While $i is not equal to 3, loop
5    while($i -ne 3)
6    {
7        $i++
8        Write-Host $i
9    }
```

Figure 9-24. *A simple PowerShell while loop*

Note   The pound symbol, #, is used at the start of a line in a PowerShell script to tell PowerShell and the .NET/COM runner that the following line is a comment and should be ignored during runtime. Comments are useful for explaining pieces of a script for readability.

In this script, we initialize a new variable $i with line 2 setting it to a value of 0. Then on lines 5–9 the script will loop as long as $i is not equal to 3, but every time the loop iterates, the value of $i is incremented by 1 as seen on line 7. This means the loop would be expected to run three times, as shown in Figure 9-25.

```
PS D:\DriveInQuestion> Powershell ./MyLogicScripts.ps1
1
2
3
```

Figure 9-25. *A simple PowerShell while loop output*

Alternative to -ne for not equal, the following can be used as comparison operators:

Equals: -eq, -ieq, -ceq

Not equals: -ne, -ine, -cne

Greater than: -gt, -igt, -cgt.

Greater than or equal: -ge, -ige, -cge

Less than: -lt, -ilt, -clt

Less than or equal: -le, -ile, -cle

These same comparison operators can be used with if blocks such as shown in Figure 9-26.

```
1    $count = 11
2    if ($count -gt 10){
3        Write-Host -Object $count
4    }
5    else {
6        Write-Host -Object 'Less than 11'
7    }
```

Figure 9-26. *A simple PowerShell if else block*

When iterating over a list or array object, it is better to use the Foreach loop for simplicity, shown in Figure 9-27.

>_ MyLogicScripts.ps1 ●

>_ MyLogicScripts.ps1 > ...

```
1    # Set Variable $i to an array of Integer objects
2    $i = 0,1,2
3
4    # For each object in $i, loop
5    Foreach($num in $i)
6    {
7        Write-Host $num
8    }
```

Figure 9-27. *A simple PowerShell Foreach loop*

In this script, we initialize a new variable $i with line 2 setting it to an array of Integer objects 0, 1, and 2. Then on lines 5–8, the for each loop will iterate over each object in the array $i. This means the loop would be expected to run three times since there are three Integer objects in the array, as shown in Figure 9-28.

```
● PS D:\DriveInQuestion> Powershell ./MyLogicScripts.ps1
  0
  1
  2
```

Figure 9-28. *A simple PowerShell Foreach loop output*

Let's put together something a bit more interesting with this newfound PowerShell logic and looping abilities. By using [enum]::GetValues([System.ConsoleColor]), we can get an enumerable array of colors, which can be showcased by just executing that line of code, as shown in Figure 9-29.

```
● PS D:\DriveInQuestion> [enum]::GetValues([System.ConsoleColor])
  Black
  DarkBlue
  DarkGreen
  DarkCyan
  DarkRed
  DarkMagenta
  DarkYellow
  Gray
  DarkGray
  Blue
  Green
  Cyan
  Red
  Magenta
  Yellow
  White
```

Figure 9-29. *Colors available for System.ConsoleColor*

These are all of the available ConsoleColor values. We can store these in a variable $colors with $colors = [enum]::GetValues([System.ConsoleColor]). Then using Foreach, we can iterate over each color printing the color name, but also using the color to set the ForegroundColor parameter of Write-Host. Modify your MyLogicScripts.ps1 to match what is shown in Figure 9-30.

>_ MyLogicScripts.ps1 ✕

>_ MyLogicScripts.ps1 > ...

```
1     # Set Variable $colors to an array of all available colors
2     $colors = [enum]::GetValues([System.ConsoleColor])
3
4     # For each color in $colors, loop
5     Foreach($color in $colors)
6     {
7         Write-Host $color -ForegroundColor $color
8     }
```

Figure 9-30. *Looping over all of the colors as foregrounds for Write-Host*

This gives the output shown in Figure 9-31.

```
● PS D:\DriveInQuestion> Powershell ./MyLogicScripts.ps1
  Black
  DarkBlue
  DarkGreen
  DarkCyan
  DarkRed
  DarkMagenta
  DarkYellow
  Gray
  DarkGray
  Blue
  Green
  Cyan
  Red
  Magenta
  Yellow
  White
```

Figure 9-31. *Looping over all of the colors as foregrounds for Write-Host output*

We can take this a step further by nesting another Foreach loop within the main loop, giving us a matrix of all [color, color] combinations. If we say that the outer loop is $bgcolor and the inner loop is $fgcolor for BackgroundColor and ForegroundColor, respectively, then we can tweak our script to as shown in Figure 9-32.

```
>_ MyLogicScripts.ps1  ×

>_ MyLogicScripts.ps1 > ...
   1    # Set Variable $colors to an array of all available colors
   2    $colors = [enum]::GetValues([System.ConsoleColor])
   3
   4    # For each color in $colors, loop
   5    Foreach ($bgcolor in $colors){
   6        Foreach ($fgcolor in $colors) {
   7            Write-Host "$fgcolor|" -ForegroundColor $fgcolor -BackgroundColor $bgcolor -NoNewLine
   8        }
   9        Write-Host " on $bgcolor"
  10    }
```

Figure 9-32. *Code to create the background foreground color matrix (https://stackoverflow.com/questions/20541456/list-of-all-colors-available-for-PowerShell)*

We get the output shown in Figure 9-33.

Figure 9-33. *Background foreground color matrix output*

Functions

With PowerShell, users may create custom functions which are lists of PowerShell statements given a name by the user that when invoked via that name and parameters passed will execute the statements in the list as though they were being typed and executed directly in the command prompt/shell. Like other programming languages, functions can be incredibly useful for commonly used operations within one's scope. For instance, take our background/foreground matrix for the Write-Host function nested loop. We can easily wrap this code up in a nice executable component as a function called Write-ColorPalette with some simple syntax, shown in Figure 9-34.

```
>_ MyLogicScripts.ps1 > ...
     1 reference
  1    function Write-ColorPalette {
  2        # Set Variable $colors to an array of all available colors
  3        $colors = [enum]::GetValues([System.ConsoleColor])
  4
  5        # For each color in $colors, loop
  6        Foreach ($bgcolor in $colors){
  7            Foreach ($fgcolor in $colors) {
  8                Write-Host "$fgcolor|"  -ForegroundColor $fgcolor -BackgroundColor $bgcolor -NoNewLine
  9            }
 10            Write-Host " on $bgcolor"
 11        }
 12    }
```

Figure 9-34. *Write-ColorPalette custom function*

That simple syntax being added to lines 1 and 12 where line 1 states that everything in the curly braces is a new function with a name Write-Palette. This function may now be called and executed in the MyLogicScripts.ps1 script file by using the function name:

`Write-ColorPalette`

A large benefit of functions in any scripting language would be the ability to limit redundant code and rely on functions to have the code for a particular operation in one place. Another large benefit that is important to understand before we continue is the idea of parameterization. In "Write-Host -Object 'Hello, World!'" the 'Hello, World!' is a String object that is being passed into the Write-Host function, parameterizing what Write-Host writes to the console. Alternatively, a non-parameterized Hello World function could be created, called Write-HelloWorld, as shown in Figure 9-35.

```
1 reference
function Write-HelloWorld {
    Write-Host -Object 'Hello, World!'
}
```

Figure 9-35. *Non-parameterized Hello World function*

Notice how limited this would be. Sure, we can now call Write-HelloWorld to say "Hello, World!", but the parameterized Write-Host function can be used to write "Hello, World!" or anything the user wishes. We want to keep that in mind when we write investigative type functions, parameterizing the functions for multiuse. Create functions for some core functionality, and parameterize them to be leveraged in a myriad of situations calling for that type of core functionality. Let's add another function to our MyLogicScripts.ps1 called Write-Rainbow that can be passed a required string Text parameter and an optional integer AltColorsEvery parameter that defaults to 1. The Object parameter will be printed to the screen such that every AltColorsEvery many characters have randomized background and foreground colors. First, create the function shell "shell" as shown in Figure 9-36.

```
                    0 references
18      function Write-Rainbow {
19
20      }
```

Figure 9-36. *Function shell for Write-Rainbow*

Then to add parameters, PowerShell gives the following syntax:

```
param ([type]$parameter1 [,[type]$parameter2])
```

In our case with the Write-Rainbow function, we then require param ([string] $Text, [int] $AltColorsEvery), which is shown in Figure 9-37.

```
            0 references
18      function Write-Rainbow {
19          param ([string] $Text, [int] $AltColorsEvery)
20
21          # function body
22      }
```

Figure 9-37. *Basic parameters for Write-Rainbow*

Now we want to make $Text required and $AltColorsEvery optional with a default value of 1. We can do this with Parameter attribute tags of the following form:

```
[attribute1] [attribute2].... [attributeN][type] $parameter
```

These are some of the available parameter attribute tags: [Parameter()], [Alias()], and [ValidatePattern()]. With Parameter(), we can pass in a parameter of Mandatory=$true to make the parameter with this tag required. Additionally, you can set the position of the parameter for implicit parameter binding based on order. When you add this attribute tag to the parameters, you see what is shown in Figure 9-38.

```
      0 references
18    function Write-Rainbow {
19        param (
20            [Parameter(Mandatory=$true, Position=1)][string] $Text, [Parameter(Position=2)][int] $AltColorsEvery)
21
22        # function body
23    }
```

Figure 9-38. *Basic parameters extended for Write-Rainbow*

Note   With a long list of parameters and parameter tags, the width of the parameter line can become a bit overwhelming and difficult to maintain. It is generally better to extend the parameters vertically with their attribute tags as shown in Figure 9-39.

```
      0 references
18    function Write-Rainbow {
19        param (
20            [Parameter(Mandatory=$true, Position=1)]
21            [string] $Text,
22            [Parameter(Position=2)]
23            [int] $AltColorsEvery)
24
25        # function body
26    }
```

Figure 9-39. *Basic parameters extended for Write-Rainbow formatted vertically*

Lastly, to set a default value for $AltColorsEvery, we can say $AltColorsEvery = 1 in the param:

```
[int] $AltColorsEvery=1
```

From here, we can use the Get-Random function and some of the looping code from our Write-ColorPalette custom function to write the function body leveraging these parameters, as shown in Figure 9-40.

```
      1 reference
 18   function Write-Rainbow {
 19       param (
 20           [Parameter(Mandatory=$true, Position=1)]
 21           [string] $Text,
 22           [Parameter(Position=2)]
 23           [int] $AltColorsEvery=1)
 24
 25       # Set Variable $colors to an array of all available colors
 26       $colors = [enum]::GetValues([System.ConsoleColor])
 27       $fgcolor = $bgcolor = $colors[0] # Set initial
 28
 29       # Set $i to track iteration count for $AltColorsEvery ability
 30       $i = 0
 31
 32       # For each color in $colors, loop
 33       Foreach ($character in $Text.ToCharArray()){
 34           $i++ # increment iteration count
 35           if ($i % $AltColorsEvery -eq 0){ # if divisible by AltColorsEvery, alternate colors
 36               # Get random integers in range of colors array
 37               $randomIndex1 = Get-Random -Minimum 0 -Maximum $colors.Length
 38               $randomIndex2 = Get-Random -Minimum 0 -Maximum $colors.Length
 39
 40               # Set random colors
 41               $fgcolor = $colors[$randomIndex1]
 42               $bgcolor = $colors[$randomIndex2]
 43           }
 44
 45           # Write single character
 46           Write-Host -Object $character -NoNewLine -ForegroundColor $fgcolor -BackgroundColor $bgcolor
 47       }
 48
 49       # Write a new line character
 50       Write-Host ''
 51   }
```

Figure 9-40. *Full Write-Rainbow function code*

Now in our MyLogicScripts.ps1, let's call this new Write-Rainbow a couple different ways as shown in Figure 9-41.

```
Write-Rainbow -Text 'Hello, World!'
Write-Rainbow 'Hello, World!'
Write-Rainbow 'Hello, World!' -AltColorsEvery 2
Write-Rainbow 'Hello, World!' 3
```

Figure 9-41. *Write-Rainbow function calls inside MyLogicScripts.ps1*

This results in what is shown in Figure 9-42.

Figure 9-42. *Four different Write-Rainbow outputs*

Script Modules

PowerShell users may save PowerShell scripts as module (.psm1) files that can be imported, giving the user the ability to add their custom or other's custom functions to their PowerShell. First, we can run the following command to see what all modules are currently loaded in our PowerShell shell: Get-Module or Get-Module | Select-Object -ExpandProperty Name to clean up the results a bit. The latter returns the following list:

- Microsoft.PowerShell.Management

- Microsoft.PowerShell.Security

- Microsoft.PowerShell.Utility

- Microsoft.WSMan.Management

- PowerShellEditorServices.Commands

- PowerShellEditorServices.VSCode

- PSReadLine

Let's modify our MyLogicScripts file. First, modify the contents such that we only have function declarations and no called functions. Next, change the file name and extension from MyLogicScripts.ps1 to Custom.RainbowServices.psm1. Finally, run the import module command to import the new module into our PowerShell shell: Import-Module -Name ./Custom.RainbowServices.psm1 -Verbose. This is shown in Figure 9-43.

```
● PS D:\DriveInQuestion> Import-Module -Name ./Custom.RainbowServices.psm1 -Verbose
  VERBOSE: Loading module from path 'D:\DriveInQuestion\Custom.RainbowServices.psm1'.
  VERBOSE: Exporting function 'Write-ColorPalette'.
  VERBOSE: Exporting function 'Write-Rainbow'.
  VERBOSE: Importing function 'Write-ColorPalette'.
  VERBOSE: Importing function 'Write-Rainbow'.
```

Figure 9-43. *Importing the Custom.RainbowServices module*

Rerun the Get-Module | Select-Object -ExpandProperty Name command, and we should see our custom module loaded, as shown in Figure 9-44.

```
● PS D:\DriveInQuestion> Get-Module | Select-Object -ExpandProperty Name
  Custom.RainbowServices
  Microsoft.PowerShell.Management
  Microsoft.PowerShell.Security
  Microsoft.PowerShell.Utility
  Microsoft.WSMan.Management
  PowerShellEditorServices.Commands
  PowerShellEditorServices.VSCode
  PSReadLine
```

Figure 9-44. *Custom.RainbowServices module seen in loaded modules*

Now we can run any functions that were included in the Custom.RainbowServices module anywhere from within the shell as though the functions were built in, as shown in Figure 9-45.

```
● PS D:\DriveInQuestion> Write-Rainbow 'Hello, World!'
  Hello, World!
```

Figure 9-45. *Using the Write-Rainbow custom function directly now that the module is imported*

Note   If you were to exit or otherwise restart the PowerShell shell, this custom module would become unloaded and would need to be re-imported. To make it where a module is loaded every time the PowerShell shell starts up, you will need to modify the system variable PSModulePath and append the folder address to the list of folder addresses in PSModulePath.

PowerShell Gallery

As mentioned previously, with both PowerShell Desktop and PowerShell Core, the user may run the Install-Module command to add PowerShell modules to their disposal. By default, the site www.PowerShellgallery.com is the repository of modules to install provided to the Install-Module cmdlet. This can be seen by running the Get-PSRepository cmdlet on both PowerShell Desktop and PowerShell Core, shown in Figure 9-46.

```
PS C:\Users\stste> Get-PSRepository

Name              InstallationPolicy   SourceLocation
----              ------------------   --------------
PSGallery         Untrusted            https://www.powershellgallery.com/api/v2
```

Figure 9-46. *Get-PSRepository on PowerShell Desktop*

In PowerShell Core, it appears as shown in Figure 9-47.

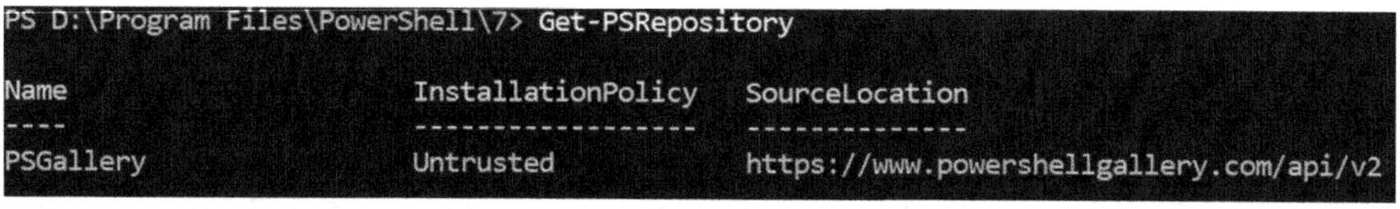

```
PS D:\Program Files\PowerShell\7> Get-PSRepository

Name              InstallationPolicy   SourceLocation
----              ------------------   --------------
PSGallery         Untrusted            https://www.powershellgallery.com/api/v2
```

Figure 9-47. *Get-PSRepository on PowerShell Core*

Of course, it is the API endpoint that is tied to PowerShell, but anyone can use a browser and open www.PowerShellgallery.com to find modules for almost any kind of operation possible with PowerShell. For instance, if a PowerShell user went to the gallery and searched for "forensics," they would see the results shown in Figure 9-48.

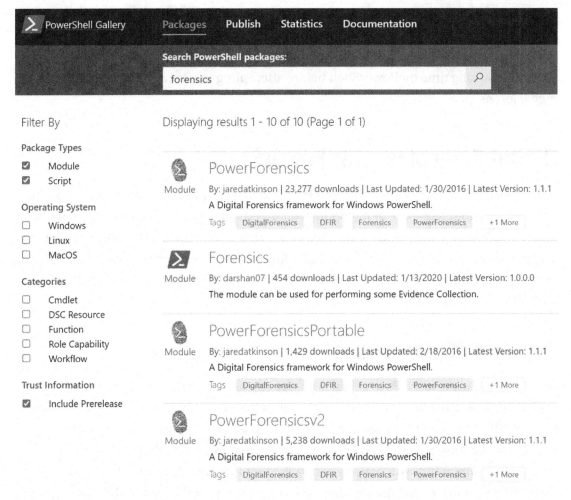

Figure 9-48.   PowerShell Gallery "forensics" search results

With everything stated up to this point, you should have a better grasp of all things PowerShell. Of course, if you would like to expand your general understanding of the PowerShell shell or scripting language, please check out any of the following websites:

```
https://learn.microsoft.com/en-us/training/modules/
introduction-to-PowerShell/
```

```
www.udemy.com/course/master-PowerShell-from-basic-to-
professional-level/
```

```
www.codecademy.com/learn/learn-PowerShell
```

This chapter will now focus on some digital forensics operations possible with PowerShell. If you are still unsure about some of the basics and high-level topics of PowerShell that have been discussed, it is advised that you spend some additional personal learning time on PowerShell before attempting to leverage PowerShell for digital forensics.

Digital Forensics with PowerShell

When looking into digital forensics with PowerShell, the options are nearly endless. This chapter will showcase some of the options an investigator may take advantage of with both PowerShell Desktop and PowerShell Core. This will not be a full list of operations available or even modules helpful for digital forensics with PowerShell but hopefully will get the gears running for the reader to know just how powerful PowerShell can be for digital investigation.

Standard OS Commands

As mentioned previously, PowerShell is able to run any command available to the underlying operating system. Though remember that if running a non-cmdlet command in PowerShell, the result will be a string and not an object, so some parsing will be necessary if chaining cmdlets and non-cmdlets is required. With that said, most standard OS commands will have a near equivalent PowerShell cmdlet that would benefit the user more than the standard command in PowerShell – mainly avoiding the need for additional parsing, but also when using the cmdlet version, the objects returned will likely come with more information and actual methods that can be invoked on the objects specifically. For instance, instead of using the ps command on a Windows operating system, use Get-Process. Get-Process will return a list of Process objects of currently running processes instead of ps which will return a System.String result of the command. The ps string result could be parsed into Process objects by parsing the ps output as a csv with a space for the delimiter like the following: ps | ConvertFrom-Csv -Delimiter ' ' -Header 'Name','PID','CPU','Memory','Command'. This extra step is unnecessary though if the user simply uses Get-Process. With that said, as you migrate from standard OS commands for digital forensics to PowerShell forensics, you should look up PowerShell equivalent commands for any standard OS command that you may have used in the past and wish to use in PowerShell. Chances are that a

PowerShell cmdlet exists or at the very least a module in PowerShell Gallery exists that performs nearly or exactly the same action while also returning nice PowerShell objects. Figure 9-49 shows a short list of a few Windows commands helpful for forensics and their equivalent cmdlets in PowerShell.

Windows	PowerShell cmdlet	Description
ps	Get-Process	Get a snapshot of currently running processes.
netstat	Get-NetTCPConnection	Get active network connections.
net	Get-NetAdapter	Get information about network interfaces.
fc	Compare-Object	Compare the contents of files/objects.

Figure 9-49. *PowerShell commands*

Powerful Built-In Functions

We will now do a brief pass over some of the most common built-in functions in PowerShell that are helpful for digital forensic investigations.

Note   Get-CimInstance is only on PowerShell for Windows or PowerShell 5.

Local Users and Groups
Get-LocalUser

Gets the local user accounts on the machine, including some information about them.

Get-LocalGroup

Gets the local user groups on the machine, including their descriptions.

Get-LocalGroupMember

By passing a -Group parameter, this will get all users that are in a specified group. For instance, the following grabs all users that are admins:

    Get-LocalGroupMember -Group "Administrators"

Machine Information

Get-CimInstance Win32_OperatingSystem
Returns information about the Windows operating system on the machine.

Get-CimInstance Win32_Processor

Returns information about the processor on the machine.

Get-CimInstance Win32_BIOS

Returns information about the BIOS on the machine.

Get-CimInstance Win32_LogicalDisk

Gets a list of all the logical disks on the machine. This will also return their size and amount of free space, among other information.

Get-CimInstance Win32_ComputerSystem

Returns information about the machine such as the name, owner name, domain, total physical memory, model, and manufacturer.

Services and Processes

Get-CimInstance Win32_Service

This will return all active and stopped services. At this point, it is helpful to know that the cmdlet get-CimInstance has a very helpful -Query parameter that can be used to help sift through the numerous results. The syntax of the parameter by default is that of SQL or WQL, more specifically. Instead of Get-CimInstance Win32_Service, we can use the following:

```
Get-CimInstance -Query "SELECT * from Win32_Process WHERE name LIKE 'T%'"
```

This is shown in Figure 9-50.

ProcessId	Name	HandleCount	WorkingSetSize	VirtualSize
8664	taskhostw.exe	297	12382208	2203592036352
13772	TextInputHost.exe	1862	15212544	2203789897728
10376	taskhostw.exe	269	19873792	2203471912960
2716	taskhostw.exe	380	21180416	2203479994368

Figure 9-50. *CimInstance Win32_Process results filtered with WQL*

Alternatively, the following command using the -Filter parameter achieves the same results:

```
Get-CimInstance Win32_Process -Filter "Name like 'T%'"
```

Get-CimInstance Win32_Process

This will return all active processes on the machine. Again, be sure to use either -Filter or -Query to help sift through the results.

Get-Process

Just like Get-CimInstance Win32_Process, the Get-Process cmdlet will return a list of active processes; however, Get-Process returns more of a high-level, user-friendly view of the active processes.

Get-Service

Similar to the distinction between Get-Process and Get-CimInstance Win32_Process, Get-Service like Get-CimInstance Win32_Service will return a list of running and stopped services on the machine but in a more user-friendly manner.

Networking

Get-CimInstance Win32_NetworkAdapter

Returns information about the network adapters installed on the local machine.

Get-NetIPAddress

Returns the configurations for IP address interfaces and families. Will return all configurations without any parameters provided.

Get-DnsClientCache

Retrieves the contents of the local DNS client cache.

Get-NetNeighbor

This will get neighbor cache entries including information about IP addresses and link-layer addresses.

Get-NetRoute

Gets the IP routing information from the IP routing table.

Scheduled Tasks and Startup Commands

Get-CimInstance Win32_StartupCommand

This cmdlet will return a list of all the configured startup executions on the machine.

Get-CimInstance Wind3_ScheduledJob

This cmdlet will return a list of all scheduled jobs on the machine, if any.

Files and Folders

Get-ChildItem

This cmdlet will return a list of all files and directories in the current location. By using the -Recurse parameter, Get-Child will recursively navigate through all subdirectories starting with the current location. If you add the -Force parameter, Get-Child will even return hidden folders. Here is a command that will recursively grab all .txt files hidden or not in the current directory and any subdirectories:

```
Get-ChildItem -Path *.txt -Recurse -Force
```

   -Depth can also be set to limit how deep the Get-ChildItem cmdlet will seek:

```
Get-ChildItem -Path *.txt -Recurse -Force -Depth 3
```

Of course, Get-ChildItem can be used then to browse registry keys as long as the hive is passed in the -Path parameter. For instance, the following will get child items under the HKEY_LOCAL_MACHINE\HARDWARE registry hive on a Windows machine:

```
Get-ChildItem -Path HKLM:\HARDWARE
```

Event Log

Get-WinEvent

This cmdlet gets events from event logs and tracing log files from either the local machine or remote ones. By using the following command, we can see a list of all event logs:

```
Get-WinEvent -ListLog *
```

This can be seen in Figure 9-51.

```
PS D:\DriveInQuestion> Get-WinEvent -ListLog *

LogMode    MaximumSizeInBytes RecordCount LogName
-------    ------------------ ----------- -------
Circular             15728640       10620 Windows PowerShell
Circular             20971520       23491 System
Circular             20971520       31144 Security
Circular              1052672        2869 OAlerts
Circular             20971520           0 Key Management Service
Circular              1052672           0 Internet Explorer
Circular             20971520           0 HardwareEvents
Circular             20971520       36211 Application
Circular              1052672             Windows Networking Vpn Plugin Platform/OperationalVerbose
Circular              1052672             Windows Networking Vpn Plugin Platform/Operational
Circular              1052672           0 SMSApi
Circular              1052672         206 Setup
Circular             15728640         339 PowerShellCore/Operational
Circular              1052672           0 OpenSSH/Operational
Circular              1052672           0 OpenSSH/Admin
Circular              1052672             Network Isolation Operational
Circular              1052672           0 Microsoft-WindowsPhone-Connectivity-WiFiConnSvc-Channel
Circular              1052672           0 Microsoft-Windows-WWAN-SVC-Events/Operational
Circular              1052672          51 Microsoft-Windows-WPD-MTPClassDriver/Operational
Circular              1052672           0 Microsoft-Windows-WPD-CompositeClassDriver/Operational
Circular              1052672           3 Microsoft-Windows-WPD-ClassInstaller/Operational
Circular              1052672           0 Microsoft-Windows-Workplace Join/Admin
Circular              1052672           0 Microsoft-Windows-WorkFolders/WHC
Circular              1052672           0 Microsoft-Windows-WorkFolders/Operational
Circular              1052672             Microsoft-Windows-Wordpad/Admin
Circular              1052672           0 Microsoft-Windows-WMPNSS-Service/Operational
Circular              1052672        1514 Microsoft-Windows-WMI-Activity/Operational
```

Figure 9-51. List of all the event logs found on local machine

Then by leveraging either the -FilterHashtable, -FilterXml, or -FilterXPath parameters, we can filter through the logs to see just what we wish among the millions and millions of entries. For instance, using the -FilterHashtable parameter, let's get all events from the "Windows PowerShell" event log that are more severe than information and occurred in the last 24 hours:

```
Get-WinEvent -FilterHashtable @{LogName='Windows PowerShell';
Level=2,3,4,5; StartTime=(Get-Date).AddHours(-24); EndTime=Get-Date}
```

PowerForensics Module

The most installed module specifically for digital forensics with PowerShell is called "PowerForensics" and can be found in the PowerShell Gallery site at www.PowerShellgallery.com/packages/PowerForensics/1.1.1. This module is not created by Microsoft and does not come standard with PowerShell Desktop or PowerShell Core. And right now, it is not ported over to PowerShell Core quite yet. If a PowerShell user would like to take advantage of this module, they must first run the following command: Install-Module -Name PowerForensics, shown in Figure 9-52.

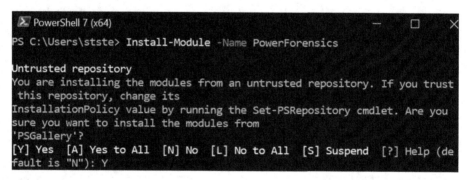

***Figure 9-52.** Install PowerForensics*

Once installed, run the following cmdlet to ensure that installation was successful and the PowerForensics module cmdlets are available for use: Get-Command -Module Powerforensics. Something interesting to note is that though PowerForensics is the most downloaded forensics module for PowerShell, the module in PowerShell Gallery has not been updated since January 30, 2016, whereas PowerShell 6 or PowerShell Core did not come out until January 10, 2018. Therefore, if you tried to run the install command for PowerForensics in VS Code, the command would have "run," but when you ran the Get-Command cmdlet, there would be no results, shown in Figure 9-53.

```
● PS D:\DriveInQuestion> Install-Module -Name PowerForensics
● PS D:\DriveInQuestion> Get-Command -Module Powerforensics
```

Figure 9-53. *PowerForensics module did not successfully install as Get-Command had no results*

This is because VS Code is built upon the .NET Core Framework; thus, the default PowerShell shell is PowerShell version 6+. With that said, this forensics module has not been ported to be used by PowerShell Core yet, so from here on when talking about using PowerForensics, assume we are running a version of PowerShell 5 or PowerShell Desktop. As mentioned earlier in this chapter, you can run PowerShell 5 with the Windows Command Prompt as that version of PowerShell is the standard version shipped with the Windows operating system.

If installation of the PowerForensics is successful, then "Get-Command -Module Powerforensics" should return a list of commands like what is shown in Figure 9-54.

CommandType	Name	Version	Source
Cmdlet	ConvertFrom-BinaryData	1.1.1	PowerForensics
Cmdlet	ConvertTo-ForensicTimeline	1.1.1	PowerForensics
Cmdlet	Copy-ForensicFile	1.1.1	PowerForensics
Cmdlet	Get-ForensicAlternateDataStream	1.1.1	PowerForensics
Cmdlet	Get-ForensicAmcache	1.1.1	PowerForensics
Cmdlet	Get-ForensicAttrDef	1.1.1	PowerForensics
Cmdlet	Get-ForensicBitmap	1.1.1	PowerForensics
Cmdlet	Get-ForensicBootSector	1.1.1	PowerForensics
Cmdlet	Get-ForensicChildItem	1.1.1	PowerForensics
Cmdlet	Get-ForensicContent	1.1.1	PowerForensics
Cmdlet	Get-ForensicEventLog	1.1.1	PowerForensics
Cmdlet	Get-ForensicExplorerTypedPath	1.1.1	PowerForensics
Cmdlet	Get-ForensicFileRecord	1.1.1	PowerForensics
Cmdlet	Get-ForensicFileRecordIndex	1.1.1	PowerForensics
Cmdlet	Get-ForensicFileSlack	1.1.1	PowerForensics
Cmdlet	Get-ForensicGuidPartitionTable	1.1.1	PowerForensics
Cmdlet	Get-ForensicMasterBootRecord	1.1.1	PowerForensics
Cmdlet	Get-ForensicMftSlack	1.1.1	PowerForensics
Cmdlet	Get-ForensicNetworkList	1.1.1	PowerForensics
Cmdlet	Get-ForensicOfficeFileMru	1.1.1	PowerForensics
Cmdlet	Get-ForensicOfficeOutlookCatalog	1.1.1	PowerForensics
Cmdlet	Get-ForensicOfficePlaceMru	1.1.1	PowerForensics
Cmdlet	Get-ForensicOfficeTrustRecord	1.1.1	PowerForensics
Cmdlet	Get-ForensicPartitionTable	1.1.1	PowerForensics
Cmdlet	Get-ForensicPrefetch	1.1.1	PowerForensics
Cmdlet	Get-ForensicRecentFileCache	1.1.1	PowerForensics
Cmdlet	Get-ForensicRegistryKey	1.1.1	PowerForensics
Cmdlet	Get-ForensicRegistryValue	1.1.1	PowerForensics
Cmdlet	Get-ForensicRunKey	1.1.1	PowerForensics
Cmdlet	Get-ForensicRunMru	1.1.1	PowerForensics
Cmdlet	Get-ForensicScheduledJob	1.1.1	PowerForensics
Cmdlet	Get-ForensicShellLink	1.1.1	PowerForensics
Cmdlet	Get-ForensicShimcache	1.1.1	PowerForensics
Cmdlet	Get-ForensicSid	1.1.1	PowerForensics
Cmdlet	Get-ForensicTimeline	1.1.1	PowerForensics
Cmdlet	Get-ForensicTimezone	1.1.1	PowerForensics
Cmdlet	Get-ForensicTypedUrl	1.1.1	PowerForensics
Cmdlet	Get-ForensicUnallocatedSpace	1.1.1	PowerForensics
Cmdlet	Get-ForensicUserAssist	1.1.1	PowerForensics
Cmdlet	Get-ForensicUsnJrnl	1.1.1	PowerForensics
Cmdlet	Get-ForensicUsnJrnlInformation	1.1.1	PowerForensics
Cmdlet	Get-ForensicVolumeBootRecord	1.1.1	PowerForensics
Cmdlet	Get-ForensicVolumeInformation	1.1.1	PowerForensics

Figure 9-54. *PowerForensics commands*

The documentations for any of these PowerForensics commands can be found with Get-Help in PowerShell but are also located at this site: `https://powerforensics.readthedocs.io/en/latest/#overview`. For this module, we will go over the following helpful commands:

1.   Invoke-ForensicDD

2.   Get-ForensicNetworkList

3.   Get-ForensicTimeline

Note   This is obviously not an exhaustive list of cmdlets provided with the PowerForensics library. We will only dip our toes into these few to demonstrate the possibilities of digital forensics with PowerShell with a custom module.

Invoke-ForensicDD

Invoke-ForensicDD will get a byte-for-byte copy of a file, disk, or partition. This cmdlet can be used much like the Linux dd command to get an exact copy of a file, disk, or partition to save away for analysis ensuring the data is backed up. As you might guess, this is an incredibly powerful command for doing digital forensics on a Windows machine. Going off the documentation provided for the cmdlet, we see this example:

```
Invoke-ForensicDD -InFile \\.\PHYSICALDRIVE0 -Offset 0 -Count 1
```

which will copy the first sector of the Master Boot Record of the \\.\PHYSICALDRIVE0 disk to the console, via implicit output. The command can be used to image entire drives such as the following that images the entire D: drive and saves it to ./dImage.img:

```
Invoke-ForensicDD -InFile "\\.\D:" -OutFile "./dImage.img"
```

We can limit the output of the Invoke-ForensicDD cmdlet to just 512 bytes (1 block) by adding -Count 1 to the command. Let's grab the first block and print it to the console by dropping the outfile parameter and adding the count parameter:

```
Invoke-ForensicDD -InFile "\\.\D:" -Count 1
```

Figure 9-55 shows the results of the command are hexadecimal numbers, with each row representing 16 bytes of data.

```
PS C:\WINDOWS\system32> Invoke-ForensicDD -InFile "\\.\D:" -Count 1
235
82
144
78
84
70
83
32
32
32
32
0
2
8
0
0
```

Figure 9-55. *Invoke-ForensicDD output without formatting*

We can pipe the results of this command into another PowerShell cmdlet called "Format-Hex" that will give us a much better view of the byte, as shown in Figure 9-56.

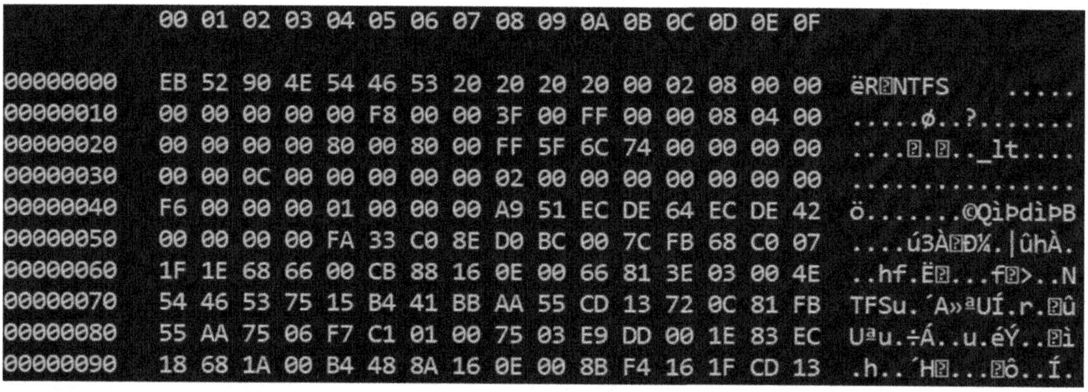

```
          00 01 02 03 04 05 06 07 08 09 0A 0B 0C 0D 0E 0F

00000000  EB 52 90 4E 54 46 53 20 20 20 20 00 02 08 00 00   ëR?NTFS     .....
00000010  00 00 00 00 00 F8 00 00 3F 00 FF 00 00 08 04 00   .....ø..?.......
00000020  00 00 00 00 80 00 80 00 FF 5F 6C 74 00 00 00 00   ....?.?.._lt....
00000030  00 00 0C 00 00 00 00 00 02 00 00 00 00 00 00 00   ................
00000040  F6 00 00 00 01 00 00 00 A9 51 EC DE 64 EC DE 42   ö.......©QiÞdìÞB
00000050  00 00 00 00 FA 33 C0 8E D0 BC 00 7C FB 68 C0 07   ....ú3À?Ð¼.|ûhÀ.
00000060  1F 1E 68 66 00 CB 88 16 0E 00 66 81 3E 03 00 4E   ..hf.Ë?...f?>..N
00000070  54 46 53 75 15 B4 41 BB AA 55 CD 13 72 0C 81 FB   TFSu.´A»ªUÍ.r.?û
00000080  55 AA 75 06 F7 C1 01 00 75 03 E9 DD 00 1E 83 EC   Uªu.÷Á..u.éÝ..?ì
00000090  18 68 1A 00 B4 48 8A 16 0E 00 8B F4 16 1F CD 13   .h..´H?...?ô..Í.
```

Figure 9-56. *Invoke-ForensicDD output with Hex formatting*

We can then provide an offset parameter with a value of 512 to get the next block or page of 512 bytes:

```
Invoke-ForensicDD -InFile "\\.\D:" -Count 1 -Offset 512 | Format-Hex
```

Note   -Offset bytes must be divisible by the block size, which is 512 bytes.

This is shown in Figure 9-57.

```
PS C:\WINDOWS\system32> Invoke-ForensicDD -InFile "\\.\D:" -Count 1 -Offset 512 | Format-Hex


          00 01 02 03 04 05 06 07 08 09 0A 0B 0C 0D 0E 0F

00000000  07 00 42 00 4F 00 4F 00 54 00 4D 00 47 00 52 00  ..B.O.O.T.M.G.R.
00000010  04 00 24 00 49 00 33 00 30 00 00 D4 00 00 00 24  ..$.I.3.0..Ô...$
00000020  00 00 00 00 00 00 00 00 00 00 00 00 00 00 00 00  ................
00000030  00 00 00 00 00 00 00 00 00 00 00 00 00 00 00 00  ................
00000040  00 00 00 00 00 00 00 00 00 00 00 00 00 00 00 00  ................
00000050  00 00 00 00 00 00 E9 C0 00 90 05 00 4E 00 54 00  ......éÀ.▯..N.T.
00000060  4C 00 44 00 52 00 07 00 42 00 4F 00 4F 00 54 00  L.D.R...B.O.O.T.
00000070  54 00 47 00 54 00 07 00 42 00 4F 00 4F 00 54 00  T.G.T...B.O.O.T.
00000080  4E 00 58 00 54 00 00 00 00 00 00 00 00 00 00 00  N.X.T...........
00000090  00 00 00 00 00 00 00 00 00 00 0D 0A 41 6E 20 6F  ............An o
000000A0  70 65 72 61 74 69 6E 67 20 73 79 73 74 65 6D 20  perating system
000000B0  77 61 73 6E 27 74 20 66 6F 75 6E 64 2E 20 54 72  wasn't found. Tr
000000C0  79 20 64 69 73 63 6F 6E 6E 65 63 74 69 6E 67 20  y disconnecting
000000D0  61 6E 79 20 64 72 69 76 65 73 20 74 68 61 74 20  any drives that
000000E0  64 6F 6E 27 74 0D 0A 63 6F 6E 74 61 69 6E 20 61  don't..contain a
000000F0  6E 20 6F 70 65 72 61 74 69 6E 67 20 73 79 73 74  n operating syst
00000100  65 6D 2E 00 00 00 00 00 00 00 00 00 00 00 00 00  em..............
00000110  00 00 00 00 00 00 00 9A 02 66 0F B7 06 0B 00 66  .......▯.f.·...f
00000120  0F B6 1E 0D 00 66 F7 E3 66 A3 52 02 66 8B 0E 40  .¶...f÷ãf£R.f▯.@
00000130  00 80 F9 00 0F 8F 0E 00 F6 D9 66 B8 01 00 00 00  .▯ù..▯..öÙf.....
00000140  66 D3 E0 EB 08 90 66 A1 52 02 66 F7 E1 66 A3 86  fÓàë.▯f¡R.f÷áf£▯
```

Figure 9-57. *Invoke-ForensicDD output with Hex formatting for the second block on drive D:*

The gears should be turning as you think of possible ways to use looping with this to iterate block by block over a drive looking for an ASCII word or array of ASCII words. This would be able to find instances of ASCII in files they may have been "deleted" but not yet overwritten.

From the perspective of digital forensics, we would want to save the image of the drive using

```
Invoke-ForensicDD -InFile "\\.\D:" -OutFile "./dImage.img"
```

Then we want to make that image read only so as not to be contaminated accidentally during investigation:

```
Set-ItemProperty -Path "./dImage.img" -Name IsReadOnly -Value $true.
```

Get-ForensicNetworkList

Get-ForensicNetworkList will get the networks that were connected to the system. This cmdlet can be used to determine what networks the user of the system was accessing directly or indirectly. We can pipe the results of the cmdlet into a table for easy readability:

```
Get-ForensicNetworkList | Format-Table -AutoSize
```

This is shown in Figure 9-58.

```
PS C:\WINDOWS\system32> Get-ForensicNetworkList | Format-Table -AutoSize

WriteTimeUtc          ProfileGuid                              Description Source DnsSuffix FirstNetwork DefaultGatewayMac
------------          -----------                              ----------- ------ --------- ------------ -----------------
3/20/2023 04:52:41 AM {A9800EA7-88CD-4DAF-8624-7BC3C0B29E97} Network           8 <none>    Network      {22, 171, 135, 67...}
12/31/2021 08:22:16 AM {E62A18E1-3FE3-48D2-9DD9-0FF99A3DA915} RollTide         8 lan       RollTide     {40, 189, 137, 109...}
2/25/2022 02:49:19 AM {EE47453E-E7E3-4E33-82D2-BE59368E7D8E} Network           8 <none>    Network      {78, 0, 82, 245...}
9/8/2022 11:24:39 PM  {DEBE5E02-8F01-4746-8A85-169254E84B5D} Network           8 <none>    Network      {122, 121, 25, 0...}
```

Figure 9-58. *Formatted output of Get-ForensicNetworkList*

Note   These are the results running on a desktop computer that has rarely moved and thus rarely connected to different networks.

This can be used to quickly see when the machine connected to new networks.

Get-ForensicTimeline

Get-ForensicTimeline creates a forensic timeline. This cmdlet can be used to determine an order of events of executions, updates, event logs, etc. A limitation of this cmdlet would be that we are not able to pass in a date range for the command to check against. We can save and then pipe the results into various Where-Object functions, but this will always require an initial pull of all the various events on the volume that make up the forensic timeline. The following could be used to get all events that occurred on the timeline within the last hour:

```
Get-ForensicTimeline | Where-Object { $_.Date -ge (Get-Date).AddHours(-1) }
| Format-Table -AutoSize
```

However, you would want to set the results of Get-ForensicTimeline to a variable like $forensicTimelineC and then pipe that variable to the Where-Object any way you want to investigate.

```
$forensicTimelineC = Get-ForensicTimeline
$forensicTimelineC | Where-Object { $_.Date -ge (Get-Date).AddHours(-1) } |
Format-Table -AutoSize
```

Conclusions

PowerShell is more than capable of handling a myriad of digital forensic operations. Without needing to install any other piece of software on a Windows machine, a full investigation can be done on the machine with the use of the built-in PowerShell 5. Then when the PowerForensics module is added into the mix, the operations become simpler and simpler but more powerful. This chapter began by giving the reader context and basics to using PowerShell 5 and PowerShell 6+. Then the chapter showed the reader that by using PowerShell an investigator can gather all necessary information, image drives, search over binary, and more. An entire book could probably be written about leveraging PowerShell from the perspective of digital forensics. For now, though, understand that this "old" technology still packs a lot of punch and would do well in any tech sleuth's arsenal.

References

TechThoughts, "PowerShell History and Current State" youtube.com. www.youtube.com/watch?v=nQTZRJjcuE4&ab_channel=TechThoughts (accessed April 18, 2023).

Microsoft, "What is PowerShell?" learn.microsoft.com. https://learn.microsoft.com/en-us/PowerShell/scripting/overview?view=PowerShell-7.3 (accessed April 18, 2023).

Microsoft, "Get-Process" learn.microsoft.com. https://learn.microsoft.com/en-us/PowerShell/module/microsoft.PowerShell.management/get-process?view=PowerShell-7.3 (accessed April 19, 2023).

Microsoft, "PowerShell Commands" learn.microsoft.com. https://learn.microsoft.com/en-us/PowerShell/scripting/PowerShell-commands?view=PowerShell-7.3 (accessed April 19, 2023).

Server Space, "Windows CMD Commands Cheat Sheet" serverspace.us. `https://serverspace.us/support/help/windows-cmd-commands-cheat-sheet/` (accessed April 19, 2023).

MSP 360, "PowerShell vs Command Prompt: a Comparison" serverspace.us. `www.msp360.com/resources/blog/PowerShell-vs-cmd-the-difference-explained/#:~:text=Neither%20of%20them%20is%20a,%3B%20they're%20just%20additions.&text=Another%20difference%20is%20that%20CMD,be%20used%20for%20direct%20manipulation` (accessed April 19, 2023).

Microsoft, "About Command Syntax" learn.microsoft.com. `https://learn.microsoft.com/en-us/PowerShell/module/microsoft.PowerShell.core/about/about_command_syntax?view=PowerShell-7.3` (accessed April 19, 2023).

Microsoft, "Get Member Command" learn.microsoft.com. `https://learn.microsoft.com/en-us/PowerShell/module/microsoft.PowerShell.utility/get-member?view=PowerShell-7.3` (accessed April 19, 2023).

Tech Genix, "PowerShell Core" techgenix.com. `https://techgenix.com/PowerShell-core/` (accessed April 19, 2023).

Interview Bit, ".NET Core vs .NET Framework" interviewbit.com. `www.interviewbit.com/blog/net-core-vs-net-framework/` (accessed April 19, 2023).

Microsoft, "PowerShell Get Command" learn.microsoft.com. `https://learn.microsoft.com/en-us/PowerShell/module/PowerShellget/install-module?view=PowerShellget-2.x` (accessed April 19, 2023).

PowerShell Gallery, "PowerShell Gallery Forensics Search" PowerShellgallery.com. `www.PowerShellgallery.com/packages?q=forensics` (accessed April 19, 2023).

PowerShell Gallery, "PowerShell Forensics 1.1.1" PowerShellgallery.com. `www.PowerShellgallery.com/packages/PowerForensics/1.1.1` (accessed April 19, 2023).

Aiello, Joey (January 11, 2018). "PowerShell Core 6.0: Generally Available (GA) and Supported!". PowerShell Team Blog. Microsoft. Archived from the original on June 11, 2018. Retrieved April 19, 2023.

PowerForensics Read the Docs, "PowerShell Forensics 1.1.1 Documentation Invoke-ForensicDD" powerforensics.readthedocs.com. `https://powerforensics.readthedocs.io/en/latest/modulehelp/Invoke-ForensicDD/` (accessed April 19, 2023).

PowerForensics Read the Docs, "PowerShell Forensics 1.1.1 Documentation Get-ForensicsNetworkList" powerforensics.readthedocs.com. `https://powerforensics.readthedocs.io/en/latest/modulehelp/Get-ForensicNetworkList/` (accessed April 19, 2023).

PowerForensics Read the Docs, "PowerShell Forensics 1.1.1 Documentation Get-ForensicEventLog" powerforensics.readthedocs.com. `https://powerforensics.readthedocs.io/en/latest/modulehelp/Get-ForensicEventLog/` (accessed April 19, 2023).

PowerForensics Read the Docs, "PowerShell Forensics 1.1.1 Documentation Get-ForensicTimeline" powerforensics.readthedocs.com. `https://powerforensics.readthedocs.io/en/latest/modulehelp/Get-ForensicTimeline/` (accessed April 19, 2023).

Test Your Knowledge

A few questions are provided here to aid you in testing your knowledge before you proceed.

1. What operating systems does PowerShell run on?

   a. Windows

   b. MacOS

   c. Linux

   d. Depends on the version of PowerShell

2. Why does the following cause an error: Write-Host 'Hello, World!' | Get-Member?

   a. Write-Host requires the -Object parameter.

   b. Get-Member should come before Write-Host 'Hello, World!'.

   c. Write-Host explicitly prints the ToString() method of the passed object to string, leaving no object in the pipeline.

   d. Write-Host is missing certain required parameters. See Get-Help Write-Host -Full.

3. Which of the following operations are possible with Get-Child?

   a. Get a list of files and subdirectories in the current folder.

   b. Get a list of files and subdirectories in the current folder, recursively.

   c. Access registry hives to check on various keys, given appropriate access.

    d. A and B.

    e. A, B, and C.

4. What does the $_ do in the following command: Get-Command
| Where-Object { $_.Name -like '*Write*' } | Select-Object
-ExpandProperty Name?

    a. It represents the current object that is being processed in the pipeline.

    b. Unnecessary syntax for an old technology.

    c. Helps the Where-Object bypass certain required parameters with a lambda expression.

    d. It is incorrect syntax, and this command would fail with an INVALID SYNTAX error.

5. What is a way that we can further extend the abilities of PowerShell for our own needs or the needs of others in the field?

    a. Publish a custom module to the PowerShell Gallery for any PowerShell users to be able to download.

    b. Use C#/C++ to write libraries for PowerShell.

    c. Pull down the PowerShell Core GitHub repository, create a new Git Branch locally, make modifications/add features, create a pull request, and make lasting changes to PowerShell Core.

    d. All of the above.

CHAPTER 10

Web Browser Forensics

Victoria Balkissoon
Chuck Easttom, Ph.D., D.Sc.

Introduction

Think about the last time you used the Internet, whether on your phone, a laptop, or tablet. In all likeliness, it probably was just a few short moments ago. Since the birth of the Internet, there has been no slowing down with its growth in number of users and their usage. As of January 2023, there are over five billion users of the Internet. The Internet has introduced several different services right at users' fingertips, all housed and available through different web browsers. Users are constantly accessing the Internet and its provided services with ease through browser applications available on practically all devices. Because of the wide range of uses for web browsers and their wide range of capabilities, they are a particularly predominant application for cybercrimes, especially those that are geared toward the stealing of confidential and sensitive information of users for financial gain.

Anyone that has used the Internet has probably used a few different web browsers to do so. The market share of web browsers is currently split with various web browsers, although Google Chrome holds the majority of the share with over 63% of it. Other predominant browsers include Microsoft Edge and Firefox when considering the market shares. In this chapter, we will go into detail on these three browsers in terms of forensics, from discussing data storage to log file locations and contents. While there are a number of similarities between these differing browsers in terms of usage and even forensics, there are also differences which will be discussed.

© Chuck Easttom, William Butler, Jessica Phelan, Ramya Sai Bhagavatula, Sean Steuber, Karely Rodriguez, Victoria Indy Balkissoon, Zehra Naseer 2024
C. Easttom et al., *Windows Forensics*, https://doi.org/10.1007/979-8-8688-0193-8_10

A trend you have probably noticed in this book is the emphasis on the forensic tools that can assist us with evidence retrieval and analysis. NIST or the National Institute of Standards and Technology's Computer Forensic Tools and Techniques Catalog offers various web browser forensic tools, some of which will be covered in this chapter in detail.

In this chapter, we will cover the following:

- Web browser forensics and its artifacts

- Google Chrome, Microsoft Edge, and Firefox forensics

- Tools for web browser forensics

- Challenges in web browser forensics

What Is Web Browser Forensics?

On a daily basis, individuals utilize web browsers extensively, whether it is for professional means, online shopping, social media, checking their email, and more. Web browsers provide us a window into the Internet which delivers a plethora of services at users' fingertips. The unfortunate fact of the users of web browsers is that the majority are unaware of the amount of information and data that is collected about their whereabouts on the Web. Sure, many of us have cleared our cookies and cache from the History tab, trying to eliminate our searches and site visits. Other times, we have even used an incognito window from the start, avoiding history storage from the get-go. We fail to realize that there is much more to the history tab when it comes to tracking our movements on the Web. Web browser forensics uncovers the specifics of what is stored and how it can be accessed in order to uncover even the smallest details which can be pertinent to a forensics case. With the continued growth of the Internet and its usage, there is no doubt that this subfield of digital forensics is highly important and here to stay, only to become more predominant in the future. As you dive into this chapter, consider your own usage of the Web and the browsers you use primarily.

As stated prior, this subfield of digital forensics is not only extremely important due to the heightened use of web browsers but because of what information that can be obtained from these browsers to be used in forensic cases. Web browser forensics play a crucial role in digital investigations helping investigators, forensics analyst, law enforcement, and other authorities trace the activities of a user through providing them with the capabilities to establish timelines of the user's activities, reconstruct the activities, reveal patterns in the user's activities, and much more. This is especially important for a number of different cases such as online fraud, intellectual property theft, and other cybercrimes, especially those for personal financial gain.

The process of conducting web browser forensic analysis is very much similar to the main process and analysis conducted in other subfields of digital forensics. This process includes acquiring data, files, and images of the individual's device, preserving the authenticity and integrity of the data collected through a chain of custody, then using a number of varying tools and even manual examination to analyze and formulate timelines, specific details, and conclusions based on the inspection of evidence. Later in this chapter, there will be a discussion on various digital forensic tools that can be used for web browser forensic analysis; some of these tools will be specific to certain portions of the data collected from browsers and even be specifically for a certain browser, while others will be more generalized. It is important to note while reading this chapter and portion on tools to understand not only what can be collected using these tools but also the connections between evidence that can be found and conclusions that can be drawn from analyzing the evidence collected. Like any other forensic analysis process, the most impactful results are those that not only collect the data but combine it to formulate greater set of evidence that uncovers details and trends beneath the surface.

There are a vast number of web browsers available on the market, varying by platforms, popularity, and more. In this chapter, we will focus on three of the major web browsers used by the global population: Google Chrome, Microsoft Edge, and Mozilla Firefox. You will notice as you read this chapter there are a number of similarities in the artifacts produced by these browsers, while they differ slightly in other aspects, including the location of these artifacts within their browser, organization of data, and differing functionality in features related to browser forensics such as private/incognito mode. We will start with the basics of web browsers and artifacts before diving into the specifics of each, followed by web browser-specific digital forensic tools. The chapter will also highlight some challenges that are present in the world of web browser forensics.

Web Browser Terminology

Before diving into the artifacts produced by web browsers and the different pieces of data and information that can be collected from the various browsers that will be discussed in this chapter, there are specific terms that are important to understand. The most important of those encompasses this entire chapter. So, what is *web browser forensics* defined as?

First, let me provide you with my own definition of web browser forensics:

A specialized sub-field of digital forensics focused on examining web browsers, the content they store and how they are used by individuals to gather user information and track user activities in order to crack cybercrimes or enhance the evidence collected for other digital forensics related crimes.

To further enhance your understanding, the following is another definition provided in the paper "Web Browser Forensics for Detecting User Activities" in the *International Research Journal of Engineering and Technology*:

Browser forensic is mainly used for analyzing things like browsing history and general web activity of a pc to check for suspicious usage or content that has been accessed. This also refers to monitoring traffic on a web-page and analysis of LOG files from server to get actual information about [the] targeted machine.

Knowing the provided definitions is important to understanding web browser forensics at the surface level. The following are additional important words of terminology related to web browser forensics that will greatly enhance your understanding as we move further into the chapter:

- **History**: A record of the URLs visited by a user along with the date and time of each visit.

- **Cookies**: Small blocks of information sent from a web server to a web browser to be stored, allowing the sites to remember your device and pertinent information such as login info, preferences, etc.

- **Cache**: A form of temporary storage that holds copies of images, web pages, and other resources to enhance the browsing experience in terms of speed by minimizing fetching of resources.

- **SQLite Database**: A serverless, zero configuration, transactional SQL database engine that is self-contained.

- **Incognito/Private Browsing**: A mode provided by web browsers which allows users to browse the Web without permanent traces of their activities being left behind.

- **Extensions/Add-ons/Plugins**: Additions to browsers which enhance its functionality. It can potentially cause traces of the users' information to be stored.

- **Form Data**: Any data entered by a user on web forms.

- **Session Data**: Any information in regard to active browser sessions, including timings, accounts logged in, and open tabs.

- **Bookmarks**: Saved links to websites for the user to access at a later time more easily.

- **Downloads**: Varying files obtained from sites and copied to your local device for personal use.

- **User Agent**: A text string sent to a website's server from the browser to identify the browser and its version as well as the operating system that the browser is running on.

- **URL**: Uniform Resource Locator, a web address used to locate resources on the Internet.

The preceding terms are some of the basic terms that appear often in our discussion of web browsers and web browser forensics. It is vital that we understand what each of the terms mean as most are building blocks to our evidence uncovered in web browsers for forensic cases. Additionally, others of these terms also refer to the configuration and storage used by web browsers which also prove to be important when understanding how data is stored on browsers and where information can be found. Not only is understanding terminology essential to formulating your basis for web browser forensics but it is also critical to be familiar with basic file locations and file structures on different operating systems as much data can be uncovered in browser folders on the system; this will be discussed later in the chapter.

Let's dive into the meat of this chapter starting with the basic discussion of web browser artifacts. This will be a more detailed follow-up to this terminology section which will not only discuss different web browser artifacts but also examine how these assortments of artifacts play a role in forensics and cracking important cybercrimes.

An Overview: Artifacts of Web Browsers in Forensic Cases

In the previous section, you were acquainted with multiple pieces of terminology related to web browser forensics. The majority of these terms were specific artifacts that can be extracted and analyzed from web browsers. Now, it is time to discuss the role that these artifacts play in digital forensic cases.

Within any cybercrime or even normal crime, searching for evidence left over by web browsing activity can prove to be fruitful. It is a critical component of digital forensic investigations since almost every movement an individual performs while using a web browser leaves a trace on their computer, which in turn can lead to information about a suspect's search for crime methods, information collected through the browser for the crime, and how their crime was hidden.

The artifacts retrieved such as cookies, download lists, history, and cache from a suspect's computer can be analyzed using a multitude of methods which can produce important bits of information that can be vital to a forensics case. These artifacts can be analyzed for keywords used by the suspect in search engines, the websites visited including their time of access and how frequently they were accessed, and much more. The mere fact about this analysis though is that it must be conducted for multiple browsers for the suspects as typically users tend to utilize multiple browsers or at least have access to multiple browsers on their devices. But the correct manner to do so is not to perform different analyses on each web browser, nor is it sufficient enough to investigate a single log file per browser as evidence can be divided across several files.

In order for the most effective extract, examination, and analysis on web browser artifacts to be performed for the greatest benefit in a digital forensics case, it is essential that the following are performed:

1. Extraction of substantial information related to digital forensics and web browser forensics, such as user activity, search words, cached data, and more.

2. Decoding of encoded words at specific URLs.

3. Recovering deleted information from the web browsers – it is typical suspects delete log information in order to destroy evidence.

4. Timeline analysis includes determining the time zone of the suspect's activity.

5. Integrated analysis of multiple web browsers.

The presented steps are instrumental in obtaining digital evidence from browsers and understanding all pieces when put together to formulate bigger pictures among an individual's usage of browsers as evidence for forensic cases. In order to execute these steps, it is vital to have a sound understanding of where these artifacts can be accessed within each individual browsers and the other intricacies that exist in them which can be of use in digital forensic analyses. This will be explored in the next section of this chapter.

Specific Web Browsers and Forensics

The browser market is composed of various browsers with a varying share of users for each. The most popular browser is Google Chrome, holding approximately 63% of the market. Besides Apple's Safari which holds about 20% of the market, all other browsers compose less than 10% of the market each. This includes the two other browsers we will be covering in this chapter: Microsoft Edge and Mozilla Firefox. Edge composes about 5% of the market share with Firefox having almost 3% of it as well. This section discusses in detail these three browsers in the light of digital forensics, looking into data that is stored, where this data can be found, and more. When considering these three major browsers, you will notice there are many similarities in the forensics of these browsers, while there are also differences that can be identified. It should be noted that extensions to browsers can be malicious. It is a good idea to only add extensions that you truly need and that have been widely reviewed.

Google Chrome

Google Chrome is a top-tier web browser used by more than half of the population of Internet users. The Google Chrome web browser stores data in several formats, one of which is in an SQLite format that makes data accessible in files that can be viewed and examined using an SQLite database viewer. One of the main database files filled with a plethora of data is the History file. The History database file provides a large window into the user's whereabouts in the browser, including user browsing information such as terms searched, downloads, URLs visited, and more. The database file is composed of nine tables with thirteen indices, views, and triggers.

Each of the tables contained in the database file provides different sets of data and extensive information about the usage of the browser. For example, the Keyword Search Terms table provides information like the term along with the lower term, the Keyword ID, and the URL ID. On the other hand, the URLs table provides a list of URLs visited by the user in the browser alongside a title, ID, visit count, type count, favicon ID, last visit time, etc. There are a plethora of database files and plenty of tables such as Logins, Favicons, Cookies, and more filled with insightful information about how the Google Chrome browser is utilized.

In addition to the database files provided by Chrome, there are also various JSON files that are generated and stored by the browser which can be used for analysis. For instance, the bookmarks saved by the user within the browser are stored in the "Bookmarks" JSON file, while the Preferences JSON file stores the Chrome Browser Settings. The fact that the files are in JSON format makes them easy to read and analyze by forensic investigators. Figure 10-1 shows some of the contents of the Preferences. json file. You can see that there is a plethora of settings that can be set and altered by the user that is contained in the JSON file, including the window size and placement, how often history is cleared, whether the bookmarks bar is used, and more. If you view your Preferences.json file for your Google Chrome system, you will even see trails of websites visited through the app banner property that is set in the JSON as well. This is a particularly useful piece of information for forensic investigations when trying to find sites visited.

```
},
"bookmark_bar": {
  "show_on_all_tabs": false
},
"bookmark_editor": {
  "expanded_nodes": [

  ]
},
"browser": {
  "app_window_placement": {
    "_crx_epffkfffophpagfbbklffindaiconkmc": {
      "bottom": 969,
      "left": 0,
      "maximized": false,
      "right": 1280,
      "top": 25,
      "work_area_bottom": 981,
      "work_area_left": 0,
      "work_area_right": 1680,
      "work_area_top": 25
    },
    "_crx_okcomgheggaimnfgjggeopkjbbbfgodi": {
      "bottom": 980,
      "left": 22,
      "maximized": false,
      "right": 1222,
      "top": 25,
      "work_area_bottom": 985,
      "work_area_left": 0,
      "work_area_right": 1680,
      "work_area_top": 25
    }
  },
  "clear_data": {
    "browsing_history": true,
    "cache": true,
    "download_history": false,
    "time_period": 4
  },
  "default_browser_infobar_last_declined": "13206939052125877",
  "has_seen_welcome_page": true,
  "last_clear_browsing_data_tab": 1,
  "window_placement": {
    "bottom": 1002,
    "left": 8,
    "maximized": false,
    "right": 654,
    "top": 111,
    "work_area_bottom": 981,
    "work_area_left": 0,
    "work_area_right": 1680,
    "work_area_top": 25
  }
```

Figure 10-1.   *Preferences.json contents from Google Chrome*

Chrome also uses files to store its cache. It utilizes three different types of files: an index file ("index"), several data files ("f_#####"), and a number of separate data block files ("data_#"). The cache of the browser stores images, scripts, stylesheets, and more of recently visited sites. It is another useful stop into the look of a user's usage. There are even tools which assist solely with the analysis of cache files like Chrome Cache View from NirSoft. Chrome Cache View allows investigators to explore cached files and extract information about them including their content type, URL, file size, last modified datetime, etc. The tool even allows investigators to preview the cached content as well.

Aside from the various storage files utilized by Chrome, there are other places within the browser that can be useful places to find data for investigations or even just explore in general which can uncover info about a user. Within Google Chrome and other browsers that we will discuss in this chapter, there are developer tools. The developer tools have several different tabs that can offer information that may be useful during forensic investigations. Figure 10-2 displays the "Application" tab of the Chrome Developer Tools; you will notice in the image that various pieces of information are provided, and there is more to be uncovered. The "Application" tab provides references into the local storage, cookies, cached storage, indexed database, and more within the browser.

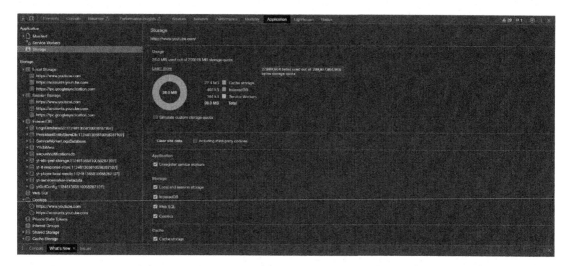

Figure 10-2. *The Application tab of Google Chrome's Developer Tools*

Clicking each of the listed items in the Storage section when on a particular site will uncover all stored information in the various types of storage in Chrome for that site. For instance, Figure 10-3 provides a look into the Local Storage of Google Chrome for YouTube.com. You can see in the image that each key-value pair provides useful info about the data contained, the creation data, and expiration. Information as such can be decoded and utilized to map a timeline of the users' whereabouts on the site and other sites as well.

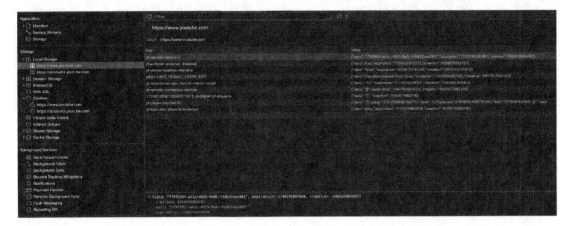

Figure 10-3. *Presentation of values from Local Storage in Developer Tools*

The developer tools of Chrome prove to be another useful and insightful portion of Google Chrome in the digital forensics process as well.

So, after all of the data presented that is captured by Google Chrome during browsing, you may be wondering if incognito mode in Chrome is truly private. The fact is that it is. Incognito mode within the Google Chrome browser does not log any browsing or downloaded histories. Moreover, it does not support the storage of cookies as once the private browsing mode is left, all generated cookies are disposed of.

Just like the browser itself, Google Chrome does a fantastic job of capturing a plethora of information during its usage. The piles of information as discussed in this section can be analyzed using numerous tools such as Chrome Cache Viewer mentioned and other tools to be discussed later in this chapter, providing a deep insight into valuable evidence for investigators.

Microsoft Edge

The newest browser that will be discussed in this chapter is the Microsoft Edge web browser released in 2015 as part of Microsoft's Windows 10 release. The browser was originally known as "Spartan" and has become a "universal" Microsoft application, replacing the original Window's browser, Internet Explorer (IE). Originally, Edge was built with Microsoft's own proprietary browser engine, EdgeHTML, and their Chakra JavaScript engine, but as of late 2020, Edge was rebuilt and released as a Chromium-based browser, making it very much similar to Google Chrome.

Prior to its transition to being a Chromium-based browser, Edge followed Internet Explorer 10, storing history records in Extensible Storage Engine (ESE) database format, an ISAM (index sequential access method) data storage technology developed by Microsoft, instead of Index.DAT files that were originally used as storage by the legacy Internet Explorer. But with its shift to Chromium, it no longer uses the ESE database format either. Since version 79 of Microsoft Edge and higher, its storage follows that of Google Chrome.

As discussed with Google Chrome, Edge uses SQLite databases, JSON files, and the three specified file types for storing its cache. Table 10-1 highlights these file types and their information in relation to important browser artifacts.

Table 10-1. *Artifacts of Microsoft Edge and Their Storage Location*

Artifact	Storage
Bookmarks	Stored in the "Bookmarks" JSON file.
Browser Settings	Stored in the "Preferences" JSON file.
Cache	Stored using an index file ("index"), a number of separate data files ("f_######"), and a number of data block files ("data_#").
Cookies	Stored in the "Cookies" SQLite database within the "cookies" table.
Downloads	Stored in the "History" SQLite database within the "downloads" and "downloads_url_chains" table.
Favicons	Stored in the "Favicons" SQLite database, within the "favicons," "favicons_bitmaps," and "icon_mapping" tables.
Logins	Stored in the "Login Data" SQLite database within the "logins" table.
Searches	Stored in the "History" SQLite database within the "keyword_search_terms" table. Its corresponding URL information is stored in the "urls" table.
Session Data	Stored in the "Current Session," "Last Session," "Current Tabs," and "Last Tabs" files.
Site Settings	Stored in the "Preferences" JSON file.
Thumbnails	Stored in the "Top Sites" SQLite database, within the "thumbnails" table.
Website Visits	Stored in the "History" SQLite database, within the "visits" table. Its associated URL information is stored in the "urls" table.

As you can tell from the table and the discussion in the previous section of this chapter, Microsoft Edge and Google Chrome have basically the same structure in storage of their cache, data, and files, making the analysis process extremely similar between the two. It is so similar that even Chrome-specific tools can be utilized on Edge files. For instance, to decrypt stored passwords from the "logins" table, ChromePass by Nirsoft can also be used with Microsoft Edge to decrypt its stored passwords.

All of the files mentioned in Table 10-1 can be found at the following folder in your Windows system:

C:\Users\<username>\AppData\Local\Microsoft\Edge\User Data\Default

Knowing where to access the files is vital to the forensic analysis process; you will also see a Google Chrome folder in the Local folder that will present a similar file structure before you uncover its files like these as well.

Another important source of information can arise from one of the top features of the Microsoft Edge browser; though not mentioned in the prior section, this is also a lesser-known feature that is offered by Google Chrome. A Progressive Web Application allows you to "install" any website on your device as a web application. This is a feature offered by Edge. There is an executable named msedge_proxy.exe which gets the application ID along with the profile directory and runs an application shell which serves as a static template to load dynamic content from the URL that is necessary to recreate the site from the provided URL. This is all described in the manifest. This manifest file is located under the "Extensions/<App_ID>" subfolder within the Default folder in the previously provided location. This is the same folder that contains the source code of newly added extensions, each of which has its own subfolder named by the unique ID. It can also be located within the "Web Applications" folder as seen in Figure 10-4. The information and data contents contained in the manifest file can prove to be useful in the content analysis of Edge files for the forensic process. Figure 10-4 shows example contents in the Manifest folder from Microsoft Edge.

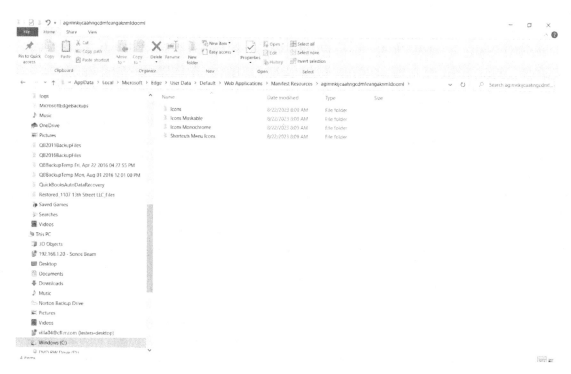

Figure 10-4. *Manifest content files from Edge's Progressive Web Application*

A discussion that will occur later in this chapter is about the importance of considering aspects of networking in the light of a forensic tool. It is also important to consider it within the light of the browsers themselves. Another attribute of the Edge browser is that it utilizes WebRTC or "Web Real-Time Communication" for real-time communication (audio, voice, video) without the need for external applications and plugins. From the data collected through WebRTC, certain particular bits of information such as IP addresses and connections can be obtained, which can also be valuable in the forensic process, shedding light on the communications within the browser and leading to other sources that should be looked into extensively as well that could have played a role in the cybercrime in question.

Microsoft Edge also offers an incognito/private browsing mode that does not give users a completely invisible online presence. When a user utilizes incognito mode through the Edge browser, Edge does not store the browsing history, cookies, or any temporary files locally to the user's device, which makes tracking the user's online activities and actions a bit challenging for forensic investigators. Despite this, information is left behind in other locations that can be useful such as within the user's network activity. IP addresses and DNS queries are continued to be captured by networking tools despite the use of incognito mode, providing insight into a user's whereabouts online. Additionally, some user-friendly features continue to function as normal within privacy mode that can help capture information as well. Despite not saving browsing history in incognito mode, Edge continues to store any bookmarks and downloads initiated within the mode locally, leaving behind traces of information even during its usage. It also does not save the usage of extensions, which can also leave traces of data behind. Even data stored in the computer's RAM from the browser during browsing in this mode can also prove to be useful. So far, in our discussions of incognito and privacy modes provided by these browsers, there is truly no complete privacy that leaves users untraceable, a big win for the forensics world.

Overall, the Microsoft Edge browser is basically a sibling to Google Chrome when considered in the light of digital forensics – from the storage files, use of an SQLite database, ability to use the same forensic analysis tools on both, and more. Having knowledge of either of the browsers will assist with the other. The evolution of Microsoft Edge from its predecessor, Internet Explorer, to becoming a Chromium-based application like Google Chrome proved to be a very fruitful and useful development in the digital forensics' world.

Mozilla Firefox

Mozilla Firefox, simply known as Firefox, is the oldest browser of the three browsers discussed in this chapter. Initially released in 2002, the browser served as basis and inspiration for other web browsers developed in the future such as Google Chrome which was built with free software components from Firefox. In turn, when it comes to useful forensic artifacts present in these browsers, there are similarities.

For instance, as mentioned in the "Google Chrome" section prior, Chrome utilizes an SQLite database; Firefox does the same to record log files and browser information. Firefox stores the majority of its information in a total of 12 individual SQLite files, each corresponding to varying functions like sites visited, cookies, web searches, and more. Table 10-2 provides brief descriptions of each of the 12 SQLite files used by Firefox.

Table 10-2. *SQLite Files Used by Firefox*

Firefox Log File	Description
content-prefs.sqlite	Used to set preferences for the browser and content settings which persists throughout the session alongside the browsing history. It contains three tables which provide information about the visited sites.
chromeappsstore.sqlite	Stores info related to a search engine.
extensions.sqlite	Contains seven different tables which store information about the different extensions installed in the Firefox browser.
webappstore.sqlite	Stores information about the software methods and protocols used in a web browser while also containing information about the different web storage types. The data in this file remains even after the clearing of cookies and history by the user.
places.sqlite	Maintains records of all websites visited, files downloaded, and bookmarks.
downloads.sqlite	Located within the "moz_downloads" table, this file stores all information about past downloads such as sources, time of download, destination, etc.
addons.sqlite	Stores all of the information in regard to browser add-ons within the table in this file, including the version number, name, creator, number of downloads, etc.
permissions.sqlite	Stores site permissions (Adobe Flash, allowing pop-ups, etc.) in a table named "moz_hosts."
cookies.sqlite	Stores all info related to browser cookies.
signons.sqlite	Contains user credentials (username and password) in their encrypted forms alongside other information such as last use and times of creation.
formhistory.sqlite	Stores all of the data for filling out web forms and web searching including search keywords.
search.sqlite	Contains a list of all available search engines that the Firefox browser can use.

When considering the database files listed in Table 10-2, some of the files can be extremely beneficial and impactful in providing useful data related to a user's actions within the Firefox browser, which can be important pieces of evidence for forensic cases. For example, the "places.sqlite" and "downloads.sqlite" files provide lists of sites visited and downloads obtained along with their specificities. Information as such can be used to establish an individual's whereabouts on the Web in an organized and timeline fashion. Furthermore, it can be used to understand the data and information collected by these individuals, a primary motive of cybercrimes. Other files listed, though they won't seem as directly useful, still provide insight into the browser that the user is handling such as "search.sqlite."

In the forensics process, it is just as important to understand the tools and techniques used as it is to understand the evidence gathered from it. Firefox has such a strong emphasis and reliability on SQLite databases that there are even SQLite viewer extensions built into Firefox that can be utilized to analyze its own SQLite files quickly and easily. Figure 10-5 shows the SQLite Manager extension when the "places.sqlite" file is imported into the manager. The default query when a new sqlite file is imported into the application delivers a list of all of the tables that exist in the file including the schema for each of the tables listing the key names and data types that correspond with each.

Figure 10-5. *Output of querying the places.sqlite file from Firefox for its tables*

This can then be used to further analyze the files. Using the table names, other queries can be written to see the actual data stored in these tables as well. Figure 10-6 illustrates this as its query is written to select all of the available columns of the moz_ places. In the case of the output, an id column and url column are provided which are sites visited within the browser. This is part of the process that forensic analysts conduct for browsers like Firefox and Google Chrome to find and extract useful information for their forensic cases.

Figure 10-6. *Query output of the moz_places table from the places.sql file in Firefox*

It is important to note that finding the location of the sqlite files stored by the Firefox browser can be easily obtained for this process through going to the "Help" menu in Firefox and selecting "More Troubleshooting Information" which will take you to the current profile's directory page; there, an "Open Folder" button is available, which takes you to all important storage files for Firefox.

As discussed in prior browser sections, understanding a browser's private mode is also fruitful in browser forensics. Mozilla Firefox provides a private mode that allows users to surf the Web without the storage of any info about the pages and sites they visited. But there's a catch! The private mode in the Firefox browser does not make the user incognito from the websites, ISPs, and networks, in turn, giving way for forensic evidence to be obtained from private browsing as users of the browser can continue to be tracked.

Web Browser Forensic Tools

Recognizing the evidence that can be collected from web browsing is one of the most significant parts of a digital forensic investigation. However, a digital forensic investigation is not limited only to the collection of evidence and logs. The next step in the process is analysis in which investigators begin to reconstruct web browser events and activities. According to a search in the NIST Computer Forensics Tools and Techniques Catalog, there are several tools that can be used for web browser forensics. The site lists 12 tools specifically, but there are an abundant more available on the market as well. There are several browser-specific tools and others that are independent, serving different functionalities and features that in combination can provide the necessities for a particular investigation. This section provides brief overviews of several different tools useful for web browser forensics.

OSForensics

To start off the discussion of digital forensic tools useful for browser forensics, OSForensics is a more generalized tool that has specific capabilities that can be useful to web browser forensics and how browsers work from a forensics point of view. OSForensics has web browser–specific capabilities such as its basic web viewer which can be used with various browsers as the application provides multi-browser support. The web viewer has the ability to load pages from the Web and save screen captures of the pages. This is a particularly useful feature for digital forensic cases in which the capturing of information as both for evidence and explanation such as in forensics reports is imperative. The feature can also be configured to capture web pages from a specific list of URLs specified by the users as well as a subset of linked pages. While capturing these screens, it also has the ability to even extract and save embedded videos from these pages.

Screenshots of web pages are not the only information that can be captured by OSForensics, it also provides the ability to capture web browser activity from users, including usernames, passwords, cookies, browsing, and download history:

- **Browser History**: The tool can help recover URLs, timestamps, titles, and other important and relevant information to sites visited by users in popular web browsers.

- **Cookie Analysis**: OSForensics assists with the retrieval of information from and analysis of cookies stored in web browsers providing insight into preferences, login credentials, and user sessions.

- **Autofill and Form Data Analysis**: The tool can extract autofill data and information entered into web forms. This information can include important information for cases including search queries and personal information related to the user and its victims.

- **User Profile Identification**: OSForensics can assist with the identification of user profiles within different web browsers. This can aid with attributing specific artifacts to specific users.

- **Cache Examination**: The application can help with the examination of cached web content, including images to reveal details about the websites visited and other online activities.

An additional feature in OSForensics that also assists with browser forensics is its SQLite database browser. As mentioned previously, many of the major browsers use SQLite databases to store information; OSForensics houses an SQLite viewer to view, analyze, and obtain information from the browsers' database files quickly and easily.

OSForensics is a powerful tool in the field of digital forensics and provides a series of features that are specific to its subfields including web browser forensics.

Belkasoft Evidence Center

The Belkasoft Evidence Center supports a number of browsers including the three major browsers discussed in this chapter. It runs solely on the Windows operating system. It is a quick, easy-to-use application that can be particularly useful for web browser forensics as it provides an SQLite viewer like OSForensics but also has additional features included. The Belkasoft Evidence Center's SQLite tools also support the recovery of corrupted and incomplete SQLite databases. Additionally, it also has functionalities to restore cleared history files as well as deleted records. Since many popular web browsers utilize SQLite databases as well as history files, these capabilities are particularly useful in forensic analyses in which data has been corrupted or lost. In addition to recover and SQLite viewing, with regard to web browser forensics, it can also extract information from volatile memory. This includes in-private browsing and cleared browser histories, making it a powerful analytics tool for web-based data.

ChromeAnalysis Plus

Similar to the mentioned Chrome Cache Viewer, another recognized Google Chrome-specific forensics tool is ChromeAnalysis Plus. ChromeAnalysis Plus also provides cache analysis, an important feature considering the dependency of Chrome on cache and the amount of useful data that is stored in it. It also provides functions to extract bookmarks, cookies, logins, downloads, favicons, search terms, visited sites, and more, enhancing the history usage retrieval process. The capabilities this software tool provides make it another powerful and useful tool when investigating with the most widely known browser, Google Chrome.

PasswordFox

One of the major difficulties during the extraction process of a digital forensics case is overcoming password-protected information that are behind closed doors through login credentials. PasswordFox, a Firefox-specific tool developed by Nir Sofer, overcomes this issue through providing investigators with the capabilities to retrieve login credentials that are saved by the Firefox browser. This application is an easy-to-use and portable program that does not need to be installed and can be transported via portable devices, making it a go-to software tool during forensic investigations involving the Firefox browser.

By default, PasswordFox retrieves records that are related to the current user profile selected and being utilized in the running Firefox browser but also provides the configuration to select another profile that was utilized on the browser for analysis and data extraction as well. Using the application, information specifically related to the website, username, password, password strength, Firefox version, and more can be extracted and exported to various different file types including TXT, XML, HTML, and CSV. This is an important aspect as reports play a vital role in the investigation process as well.

Internet Evidence Finder (IEF)

As discussed earlier in this chapter, the artifacts are the most important when conducting a forensic analysis on web browsers. The Internet Evidence Finder or IEF tool places major emphasis on just that. The IEF tool searches for Internet-related artifacts on a disk or in a file located on the device and parses them out into readable formats. It even supports processing artifacts such as Facebook chats, Hotmail, Messenger chat, and more. Being able to process social media artifacts greatly enhances the investigation process as the online presence of most individuals and Internet users can be tied to social media accounts. Moreover, it allows for flexible analysis, permitting users to point the tool to specific files or areas you want to search, allowing for both broad and specific analyses for and within web browser–specific content.

The Web Browser Forensic Analyzer (WEFA)

The WEFA provides support for analysis of the Internet Explorer, Firefox, Chrome, Safari, and Opera web browsers. It is an effective web browser forensics analysis tool that extracts online user activity, URL parameters, search words, and more. But its major feature which distinguishes this tool from the others covered in this section is its decoding function. The Web Browser Forensic Analyzer has a decoding function for when the search words are encoded in unknown characters or a foreign language. The decoding capability can uncover motives of illegal actions, another extremely useful piece of evidence and information in digital forensics cases.

Furthermore, as mentioned, integrated analysis of multiple browsers at a time is an important part of the process of a web browser and digital forensic investigation. WEFA provides integrated analysis for five major browsers within various time zones, making it a strong suit in tools for web browser analysis.

Wireshark

When you think of analyzing web browsers, the tool Wireshark probably doesn't come to mind, although the Internet is all about network connections. Wireshark is a powerful network protocol analyzer that can be utilized in the web browser forensics investigation and analysis process also.

In the context of web browser forensics, Wireshark can be used to analyze network traffic generated by web browsers. The tool captures network traffic which can then be dissected to gain insight into the user's online activities, including data exchanges, websites visited, and more. Understanding which sites have packet exchanges on the device's network can lead analysis to more places to inspect and be on the lookout for. It can uncover patterns within the traffic that may be of interest and usefulness as well.

Wireshark can help uncover details like HTTP requests and responses, cookies, URLs, user agents, and more. This information can be extremely valuable in digital forensics investigations. By examining network packets, analysts can reconstruct a user's online interactions and potentially identify malicious activities or unauthorized access in which they are attempting. All of which can be used to formulate the bigger picture of the suspect's activity.

Each of the tools presented in this section, both from the NIST catalog and other known popular tools, presents a vast toolset of features and functionalities that when combined together can significantly enhance the forensics investigation process for web browsers. Whether they are specific to a single browser or a multi-browser tool, each of these tools has specified features that play on certain niches of each browser that assist with revealing much more than surface-level data and information from these browsers.

Challenges of Web Browser Forensics

Like everything else, there are challenges that exist within the field of web browser forensics. With the evolution and development of technology and browsers themselves, some of these hurdles are becoming more and more predominant.

Considering the information presented in this chapter and the discussion of the various browser forensic data, tools, and techniques, the fact that there are numerous browsers that exist for usage at once is a major challenge of web browser forensics. As we saw, there are many similarities between these browsers, but there are also differences in terms of file locations, data storage methods, private modes, etc. Analyzing multiple browsers in an integrated fashion with all of these differences can be challenging for forensic investigators. As mentioned earlier, some specific features like incognito mode in certain browsers can make the recovering of user activity difficult.

Enhancements and evolution are no stranger to the technology field, and while they typically are for the greater good, when it comes to the field of digital forensics, it can pose some difficulties. When it comes to browser forensics, browsers are frequently updated which makes staying on top of all of the data locations, formats, methods of encryption, privacy features, and more a difficult task. Being able to analyze data quickly and effectively from these browsers requires being in the know constantly. Furthermore, the move to the cloud is a whole new ballgame. With many browsers storing data on cloud-based services, accessing the data requires varying forensic techniques from the basics. Much of this data, especially those on cloud-based services, also have heightened security such as encryption alongside compression for the purpose of storage and performance. This makes both extraction and analysis more challenging.

Features that enhance user experience and security also pose obstacles when it comes to the forensic analysis process. These features include cross-device synchronization and two-factor authentication. Considering cross-device synchronization, data can be divided among different devices and services which can cause pieces of it to be overlooked and makes the task of formulating cohesive evidence more difficult. While two-factor authentication and other modes of enhanced security and protection add extra layers to data access making extraction more difficult as well.

Related to security and privacy, the incognito mode provided by all browsers is popular, known and used by a significant number of users. Its features can also pose some challenges to forensic investigators despite its good intentions to keep users safe, private, and secured. The fact that in private mode the majority of browsers, browsing history, cookies, and temporary files are not stored leaves little local traces of evidence for forensic investigators to obtain for information about the user's activity. This leaves investigators resorting to network analysis, extraction of data from RAM, and other more intensive actions to find leads in their investigations.

These are a handful of the hurdles and challenges that can be encountered within the field of web browser forensics. Though difficulty may be added, there are methods, tools, and techniques that in combination can be effective to overcome these challenges to obtain useful information and data and examine them effectively. It is important to utilize critical thinking when conducting digital forensic investigations, and web browsers demonstrate the necessity for it.

Conclusions

In this chapter, you learned about web browser forensics starting at a birds-eye view, taking a look into general artifacts that can be found in all browsers and their significance to digital forensic cases before zooming into the specifics on each in terms of three major web browsers on the market today: Google Chrome, Edge, and Firefox. It is important to recognize useful sources of data when conducting digital forensic investigations such as those presented in the discussion of artifacts in this chapter. It is also a significant part of the forensic analysis to understand where these artifacts are located, how they can be extracted, and how in combination they can make a large piece of evidence and help draw more enhanced and complex conclusions when analyzed together. The process of analyzing all artifacts obtained highly depends on the tools that are used during the analysis process and the extraction process as well.

Much like the other chapters in this textbook, you also learned about numerous important tools applicable to web browser forensics. It was clear that some of these tools emphasized specifics of the individual browser it was for, while others provided generalized features for all the browsers individually and sometimes all at once. The highlighting of various tools was followed by a discussion of challenges associated with the field. Though not small in quantity, it is not impossible to overcome many of the challenges that are faced within the subfield of web browser forensics. With the increasing usage of the Internet, the hope is you find the information presented in this chapter applicable for years.

References

Bencherchali, N. (September 20, 2019). *Web browsers forensics*. Medium. https://nasbench.medium.com/web-browsers-forensics-7e99940c579a

Jadhav, M. R., & Meshram, B. B. (2018). Web browser analysis for Detecting User Activities. *International Research Journal of Engineering and Technology (IRJET)*, *05*(07), 273–279.

Mahaju, S., & Atkison, T. (2017). Evaluation of Firefox browser forensics tools. *Proceedings of the SouthEast Conference*. https://doi.org/10.1145/3077286.3077310

Oh, J., Lee, S., & Lee, S. (2011). Advanced evidence collection and analysis of web browser activity. *Digital Investigation*, *8*, S62–S70. https://doi.org/10.1016/j.diin.2011.05.008

Test Your Knowledge

The following questions are provided here to aid you in testing your knowledge before you proceed.

1. Which browser holds the largest portion of the market share for web browsers?

    a. Microsoft Edge

    b. Safari

    c. Google Chrome

    d. Firefox

2. Where are the database files for Google Chrome located?

    a. In the "Default" subfolder of the Google Chrome folder of the system

    b. Directly in the Google Chrome folder of the system

    c. In the "Browsers" folder on your system

    d. None of the above

3. How many tables compose the database file of Google Chrome?

    a. 12

    b. 9

    c. 10

    d. 5

4. What type of database is used by Firefox to record information? Is it the same used as Google Chrome?

    a. An SQLite database. No, it is not.

    b. An SQLite database. Yes, it is.

    c. A MongoDB database. Yes, it is.

    d. A PostgreSQL database. Not, it is not.

5. What is contained in the chromeappsstore.sqlite file in Firefox?

    a. All information related to browser cookies

    b. Information about the protocols and software methods used in
        the browser

    c. Info related to a search engine

    d. All information in regard to browser add-ons

6. True or False: Microsoft Edge and Google Chrome both use SQLite
    databases, JSON files, and a combo of index files, data files, and
    data block files to store their cache.

    a. True

    b. False

7. Where can you easily find the location of the SQLite files stored by
    the Firefox browser?

    a. Within the developer tools in Firefox.

    b. In a Firefox folder located in the "Documents" folder of the user's
        profile on their local machine.

    c. "Help" ➤ "More Troubleshooting Information"

    d. These files cannot be accessed by the generalized user.

8. When conducting a search in the NIST Computer Forensics Tools
    and Techniques Catalog for web browser forensic–specific tools,
    how many tools are listed?

    a. 80

    b. 12

    c. 20

    d. 35

9. OSForensics is an extremely useful tool in the digital forensics
    field. It has several features that can be useful for web browser
    forensics specifically. In this chapter, what is one major feature for
    the web browser of OSForensics mentioned?

    a. It can take screenshots of web pages from a specified list of URLs
        and also save embedded videos from the site.

    b. The application can log in to user social media sites and retrieve
        all account information.

    c. It can replicate a user's activity on a particular browser for a
        specified time period.

    d. None of the above.

10. Why does the updating of browsers pose a challenge to the field of
    web browser forensics?

    a. Updates require new knowledge of the location of data files, their
        formats, and more, requiring the forensic analyst to continuously
        stay up to date for the most effective analysis.

    b. It disables most capabilities for a short period of time, causing a
        downtime in the investigative process.

    c. It does not pose any challenges.

    d. Every time the browser is updated, all data files and cache are fully
        deleted, leaving no record for analysis.

CHAPTER 11

Windows Email Forensics

Chuck Easttom, Ph.D., D.Sc.

Introduction

Messages can become quite important in any forensic investigation. Retrieving and analyzing email may confirm, or refute, claims made by a party in a court case. Email forensics is a branch of digital forensics that focuses on the investigation and recovery of evidence from email systems and services. This field is particularly relevant in the context of computer science and cybersecurity. Key aspects of email forensics include the following:

Email Analysis: This involves examining the contents of emails, including headers, body, and attachments. Investigators look for clues such as the origin of the email, the path it took through the Internet, and any alterations made to the content.

Header Analysis: Email headers contain valuable information like IP addresses, email servers, timestamps, and routing paths. Analyzing these headers can help trace the email's journey from the sender to the recipient, which is crucial in identifying the source of the email.

Server Log Analysis: Email servers maintain logs that record details about email transactions. These logs can provide insights into the sender's location, the time the email was sent, and any attempts to access the email account unauthorizedly.

Recovery of Deleted Emails: Often, crucial evidence lies in emails that have been deleted. Forensic experts use specialized tools to recover these deleted emails from the server or the user's device.

© Chuck Easttom, William Butler, Jessica Phelan, Ramya Sai Bhagavatula, Sean Steuber, Karely Rodriguez, Victoria Indy Balkissoon, Zehra Naseer 2024
C. Easttom et al., *Windows Forensics*, https://doi.org/10.1007/979-8-8688-0193-8_11

Authentication and Integrity Checks: This involves verifying the authenticity of an email and ensuring that it has not been tampered with. Techniques like checking digital signatures and analyzing metadata are used for this purpose.

Legal and Compliance Issues: Email forensics must be conducted in a manner that is legally compliant, ensuring that the evidence collected is admissible in court. This includes maintaining a chain of custody and using forensically sound methods.

Malware and Phishing Analysis: Investigators also look for signs of malware or phishing attempts in emails, which can be part of cybercrimes like fraud or identity theft.

Email forensics can be crucial in investigating various types of cybercrimes, including fraud, identity theft, and unauthorized access. Email analysis can play a role in counterterrorism efforts, where it's used to track communications and uncover plots. In the corporate world, email forensics can be used for internal investigations, compliance audits, and in litigation matters.

Understanding Email

From a user perspective, sending an email is a simple task. However, the process involves multiple protocols, software applications, and file types. While many forensics tools will provide you the information needed for investigation, to be a truly effective investigator you will need to understand how email works. In the following subsections, you will learn the essentials of email.

Email Protocols

Network protocols are used to manage network traffic. There are specific protocols related to email that you should be very familiar with. Perhaps the most basic protocol is SMTP (Simple Mail Transfer Protocol); it is used to send emails and operates on network port 25. The original SMTP standard was RFC 772 and was published in 1980. It was meant to replace sending messages by FTP (File Transfer Protocol). RFC 722 has long since been outdated. RFC 2476 defined message submission, and RFC 2554 defined SMTP authentication. These were introduced in 1998 and 1999. SMTP itself only deals with text-based files. So, a standard was developed for binary file attachments. That standard is known as MIME (Multipurpose Internet Mail Extensions). An SMTP transaction consists of three command/reply sequences:

- MAIL command, to establish the return address (i.e., the return path), the reverse path, the bounce address, and the sender.

- RCPT command is used to establish a recipient of the message. This command can be issued multiple times if the email has multiple recipients. One RCPT command for each recipient.

- DATA to signal the beginning of the message text; this is the actual content of the message, rather than its envelope. The DATA consists of a message header and a message body separated by an empty line.

The basic process of email is that a mail client, also called a mail user agent (MUA), sends a message to an email server, or mail submission agent (MSA), using SMTP on port 25 (though port 587 is also used today and was formalized by RFC 6509). The MTA (mail transfer agent) will use DNS (Domain Name System) to find the mail exchange (MX) record for the email recipient domain. Then the MTA can send the message on to its destination MTA. The receiving MTA hands the message off to a mail delivery agent (MDA) for delivery locally.

SMTPS or Simple Mail Transfer Protocol Secure takes SMTP and secures the transmission with TLS (Transport Layer Security). At one time, SSL was used, but SSL was rendered obsolete with the introduction of TLS in 1999. SMTPS uses port 465.

POP or Post Office Protocol is used to receive email. The version that has been used for many years now is version 3, usually just called POP3. POP3 listens for email on port 110. If it is encrypted with TLS, then it will listen on port 995. The first version of POP, POP1, was published in 1985 as RFC 918. POP3 was introduced with RFC 1988 in the year 1988. It has been revised with RFC 1939 and RFC 2449. There was a proposal for POP4, but it has been dormant with no work done in many years.

Internet Message Access Protocol (IMAP) is the newer method for retrieving emails. It was first defined by RFC 9051 and works on port 143. If IMAP is encrypted with TLS, then it will usually be assigned port 995. IMAP has several advantages over POP, one being that with POP the client usually connects to the email server only when retrieving messages. With IMAP, the client can stay connected to the email server and actively download messages on demand.

Email File Types

Email is stored in different file formats. With Microsoft Outlook, the user's mailbox on a local computer is stored in a file with a .pst extension. The pst extension is an acronym for *personal storage table*. This is in contrast to .ost files, offline storage, which synch with the .pst file, but cannot be directly opened with Microsoft Outlook. Individual Outlook emails are stored in an .msg format. When using Microsoft Exchange, the email on the Exchange server is stored in an .edb database. EDB is an acronym for Exchange database. Microsoft Outlook also uses the .ics file for its Internet calendar.

Microsoft Outlook is not the only email option. Many other vendors, including Apple Mail, use the .mbox extension rather than the .pst. The .mbox denotes a mailbox. Many email clients will use the .eml extension rather than the .msg. The .eml extension simply means email. The following quote from the Library of Congress may help explain .eml and .mbox files (Library of Congress, 2023):

> EML, short for electronic mail or email, is a file extension for an email message saved to a file in the Internet Message Format protocol for electronic mail messages. It is the standard format used by Microsoft Outlook Express as well as some other email programs. Since EML files are created to comply with industry standard RFC 5322, EML files can be used with most email clients, servers and applications. See IMF for a description of the message syntax.

> EML files typically store each message as a single file (unlike MBOX which concatenates all the messages from a folder into one file), and attachments may either be included as MIME content in the message or written off as a separate file, referenced from a marker in the EML file.

Email Standards

RFC 2822 is a standard that specifies a syntax for text messages that are used in Internet email. It supersedes RFC 822, "Standard for the Format of ARPA Internet Text Messages," updating it to reflect current practices and incorporating incremental changes that were specified in other RFCs. Key aspects of RFC 2822 include

Format of Email Messages: It specifies the syntax for text messages that are sent using the Internet email system. This includes the structure of message headers and the body of the message.

Header Fields: The standard defines various header fields used in an email, such as `From`, `To`, `Cc`, `Bcc`, `Subject`, `Date`, and others. These headers are used to convey information about the sender, recipient, date/time of the message, and other metadata.

Addressing: It outlines the format for email addresses and how they should be interpreted.

Date and Time Specification: RFC 2822 provides a specific format for date and time in email headers, which is important for ensuring consistent timestamping across different systems.

MIME Integration: While RFC 2822 itself does not define the Multipurpose Internet Mail Extensions (MIME) standards, it is designed to be compatible with MIME, which allows emails to include non-text elements like attachments.

Line Lengths and Wrapping: The standard specifies that lines of characters in the message should be a maximum of 78 characters long and provides guidelines for how longer lines should be broken or wrapped.

Character Sets: It allows for the use of different character sets in email messages, although it primarily deals with ASCII text.

Quoted-Printable and Base64 Encoding: For binary data and text in character sets that are not easily represented in 7-bit ASCII, RFC 2822 works in conjunction with MIME standards that define quoted-printable and Base64 encodings.

SPF or Sender Policy Framework is defined in RFC 7209, and it is an email-authentication standard that protects organizations against impersonation. An attacker may use a company's domain and brand name to send fake messages to their customers. These phishing emails seem authentic enough to convince the customers and make them fall for an Internet scam in the company's name. This will harm a company's brand credibility and damage its public image. SPF can be imagined as a safelist of trusted domains of a company from where authentic communication can originate.

RFC 3864 describes message header field names. Common header fields for email include

- **To**: The email address and optionally name of the message's primary recipient(s)

- **Subject**: A brief summary of the topic of the message

- **Cc**: Carbon copy; send a copy to secondary recipients

- **Bcc**: Blind carbon copy; addresses added to the SMTP delivery list while remaining invisible to other recipients

- **Content-Type**: Information about how the message is to be displayed, usually a MIME type

- **Precedence**: Commonly with values "bulk," "junk," or "list"; used to indicate that automated "vacation" or "out of office" responses should not be returned for this mail, for example, to prevent vacation notices from being sent to all other subscribers of a mailing list

- **Received**: Tracking information generated by mail servers that have previously handled a message, in reverse order (last handler first)

- **References**: Message-ID of the message that this is a reply to

- **Reply-To**: Address that should be used to reply to the message

- **Sender**: Address of the actual sender acting on behalf of the author listed in the From

RFC 3798, titled "Message Disposition Notification (MDN)," is a standard that defines a mechanism for email senders to request and receive notifications about the disposition of their sent messages. It was published in May 2004 by the Internet Engineering Task Force (IETF) (`www.rfc-editor.org/rfc/rfc3798`). Key aspects of RFC 3798 include

> **Purpose of MDNs**: Message Disposition Notifications are used to provide the sender of a message with information about how the message was handled after it was delivered, such as whether it was read, deleted without being read, or if any processing errors occurred.

Requesting MDNs: The standard specifies how an email sender can request an MDN from the recipient. This is typically done by including specific headers in the email, such as `Disposition-Notification-To`, which indicates the email address to which the MDN should be sent.

MDN Format: RFC 3798 defines the format of the MDN itself, which is sent as a new message from the recipient's mail user agent (MUA) to the original sender. The MDN contains information about the disposition of the original message.

Automatic and Manual Responses: The standard allows for both automatic responses (generated automatically by the recipient's email client) and manual responses (where the recipient explicitly chooses to send or not send an MDN).

Privacy Considerations: RFC 3798 acknowledges privacy concerns related to MDNs. Recipients might not want to send MDNs for various reasons, including privacy or security. The standard allows recipients to decide whether to send an MDN.

Failure Reporting: In addition to reporting successful message dispositions, MDNs can also be used to report failures in processing the message, such as encountering a virus.

The Disposition field indicates the action performed by the reporting MUA on behalf of the user. This field must be present. The syntax for the Disposition field is

```
disposition-field =
        "Disposition" ":" disposition-mode ";"
        disposition-type
        [ "/" disposition-modifier
        *( "," disposition-modifier ) ]
disposition-mode = action-mode "/" sending-mode
action-mode = "manual-action" / "automatic-action"
sending-mode = "MDN-sent-manually" / "MDN-sent-automatically"
disposition-type = "displayed"
            / "deleted"
```

```
disposition-modifier = "error"
        / disposition-modifier-extension
disposition-modifier-extension = atom
The disposition-mode, disposition-type, and disposition-modifier may be
spelled in any
 combination of upper and lower case characters.
```

The following disposition modes are defined:

```
"manual-action"         The disposition described by the disposition
                        type was a result of an explicit instruction
                        by the user rather than some sort of
                        automatically performed action.

"automatic-action"      The disposition described by the disposition
                        type was a result of an automatic action,
                        rather than an explicit instruction by the
                        user for this message.
```

```
"Manual-action" and "automatic-action" are mutually exclusive.  One or
the other must be specified.
```

Understanding the standards will help you to understand the information you receive in an email header. Viewing headers is easy, but interpreting them requires knowledge of email standards.

Viewing Headers

There are two ways to view an email header in Outlook. Both start with highlighting the message. The easiest method is to open the message by double-clicking, then select *File* and *Properties*, as shown in Figure 11-1.

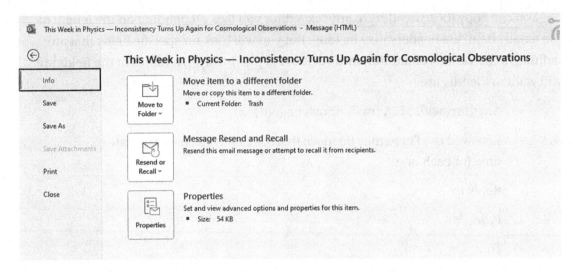

Figure 11-1. *Step 1 in viewing Outlook headers*

At the bottom of properties, you will see *Internet Headers* as shown in Figure 11-2.

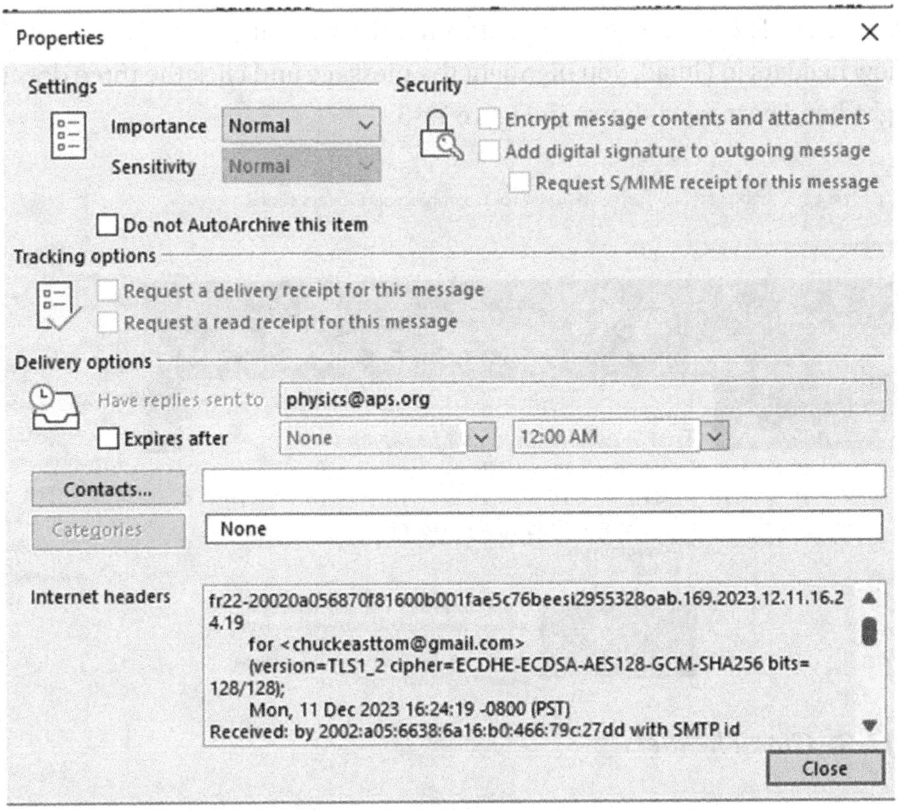

Figure 11-2. *Step 2 in viewing Outlook headers*

You can copy those headers to any text editor you like. Depending on the length of the email chain, the headers may be long. But you will look for specific fields that are defined in the various email standards discussed previously. Examples of the fields you will want to identify are

- Anything with MTA (mail transfer agent)
- Received by. There may be more than one of these, note the date/time for each one.
- Reply to
- From
- To
- Message-ID
- Mailer

Additionally, you will want to note any items that seem relevant from the standards you have studied. This may include disposition-field or manual-action.

To view headers in Gmail, you highlight the message and click the three dots in the upper right-hand corner, as shown in Figure 11-3.

Figure 11-3. *Gmail headers*

Next, you select Show Original, and you will see the headers as shown in Figure 11-4.

Original Message

Message ID	<567c5593-4922-4439-904a-cec3164ee41c@dfw1s10mta164.xt.local>
Created at:	Mon, Dec 11, 2023 at 6:24 PM (Delivered after 1 second)
From:	Physics Magazine <physics@aps.org>
To:	chuckeasttom@gmail.com
Subject:	This Week in Physics — Inconsistency Turns Up Again for Cosmological Observations
SPF:	PASS with IP 13.111.63.126 Learn more
DKIM:	'PASS' with domain aps.org Learn more
DMARC:	'PASS' Learn more

Download Original   Copy to clipboard

```
Delivered-To: chuckeasttom@gmail.com
Received: by 2002:a05:6638:6a16:b0:466:79c:27dd with SMTP id gj22csp2328549jab;
        Mon, 11 Dec 2023 16:24:20 -0800 (PST)
X-Google-Smtp-Source: AGHT+IFf+cESIy7W0aygspF+O0OXG3eZZMc2Z1k1IQ4kvcRpCDwbfGXKA16JDXFbE+/oX538f0OP
X-Received: by 2002:a05:6870:6387:b0:1fb:75a:6d17 with SMTP id
t7-20020a056870638700b001fb075a6d17mr6546466oap.62.1702340659876;
        Mon, 11 Dec 2023 16:24:19 -0800 (PST)
ARC-Seal: i=1; a=rsa-sha256; t=1702340659; cv=none;
        d=google.com; s=arc-20160816;
        b=MVNXZDdLVTOjKyMjRYZoi0ZlpJ6ez8posz3sQCVPQlfBeDtaAl2yTm1zyl6BzOCQ3Y
         Jg7vx+v1fOeTMWaMrGCGFhGL+BaexJlCZcSwJt0LzZMNxzVrXvRLekJvNpnMwpOmLxf3
```

Figure 11-4. Show Original

As you can see, the headers are at the bottom, and there is a convenient Copy to clipboard button. For other email services, you can usually find instructions on how to locate the headers with a simple Internet search.

Email Forensics

In addition to manually reviewing headers, there are a number of forensic tools that help you to analyze email. First, you must keep in mind the legality of searching email. If an email message resides on a sender's or recipient's computer or other devices, the

Fourth Amendment to the US Constitution and state requirements govern the seizure and collection of the message. Determine whether the person on whose computer the evidence resides has a reasonable expectation of privacy on that computer. The Fourth Amendment requires a search warrant or one of the recognized exceptions to the search warrant requirements, such as consent from the device owner. If you are in Europe, you should consult GDPR privacy requirements.

With OSForensics, you select Email Viewer from the Workflow menu as shown in Figure 11-5.

Figure 11-5. *Launch OSForensics Email Viewer*

Then click that button. You will be presented with a dialog box to locate any email file you wish to examine; this can include entire mailboxes such as Outlook .pst files. This is shown in Figure 11-6.

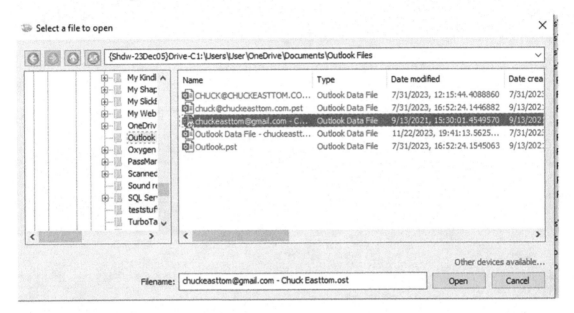

Figure 11-6. *Find email files*

You will then see something like what is shown in Figure 11-7. In this image, there is intentionally no email shown for privacy reasons.

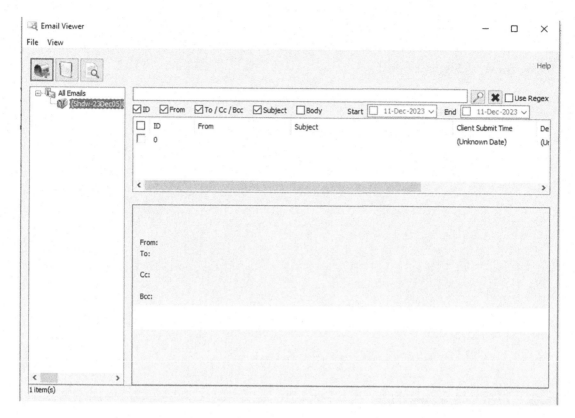

Figure 11-7. *View emails*

Autopsy has a button at the top named Communications, as shown in Figure 11-8.

Figure 11-8. *Autopsy Communications*

When you select that, you are presented with a window showing all communications in the disk image you have loaded. This is shown in Figure 11-9. In this case, no actual images are shown due to privacy concerns.

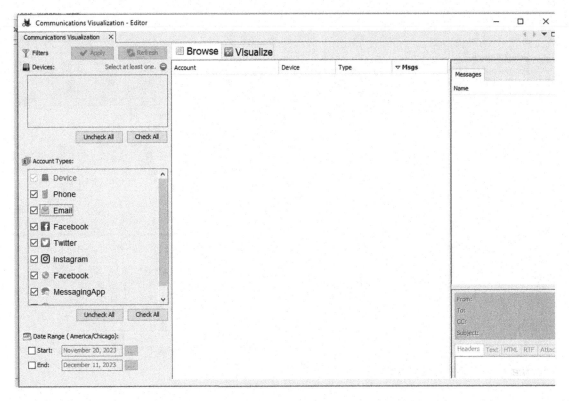

Figure 11-9. *Autopsy Communications viewer*

OSForensics and Autopsy are only two common forensics tools. Most forensics tools that allow you to analyze a Windows disk image will have some tool for analyzing email files.

Kernel OST Viewer will allow you to review OST files and even convert them to PST files. The first step is just to navigate to the OST file in question. This is shown in Figure 11-10.

Figure 11-10. *OST Viewer*

The Wizard then walks you through the process. It is simple, but, depending on the OST file, could take time. You can see the next step in Figure 11-11.

Figure 11-11. *OST Viewer step 2*

Some data is redacted in Figure 11-11 for privacy reasons. However, in addition to converting an OST to a PST, the OST Viewer is also able to recover deleted emails. This makes it an important tool for forensics. The tool is not free, but is also not particularly expensive with licensing ranging from $49 per year to $299 per year, from www.nucleustechnologies.com/page/buy-ost-pst-recovery.php.

The Message Header Analyzer is a website https://mha.azurewebsites.net/ that allows you to paste in a message header and get an analysis. This is shown in Figure 11-12.

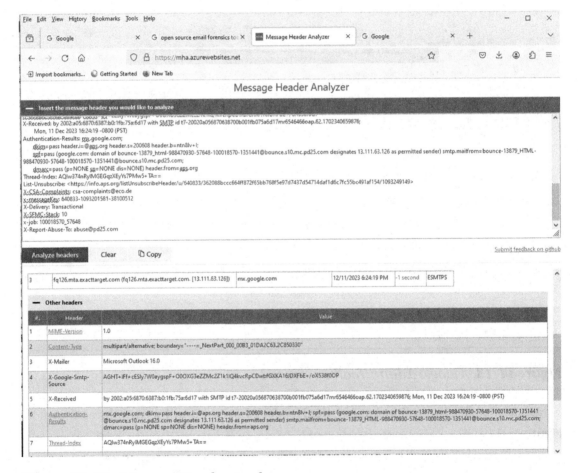

Figure 11-12. *Message Header Analyzer*

This is simply automating what you can do manually by simply referring to the various email standards discussed earlier in this chapter.

Google Admin Toolbox has a similar utility found at `https://toolbox.googleapps.com/apps/messageheader/`. It also has instructions on how to retrieve the headers and how to interpret them. This is shown in Figure 11-13.

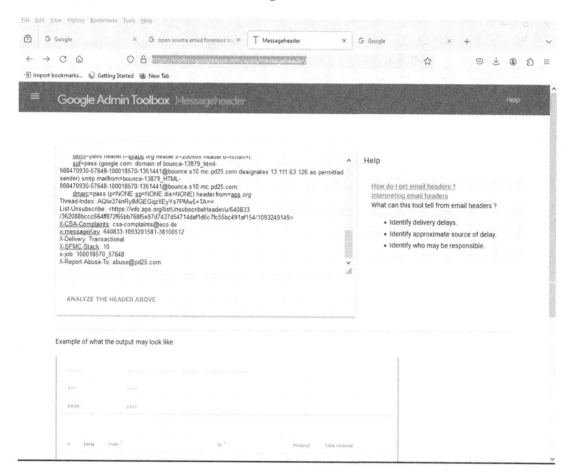

Figure 11-13. *Google Admin Toolbox screen 1*

Once you click the option Analyze the Header Above, you will see results as shown in Figure 11-14.

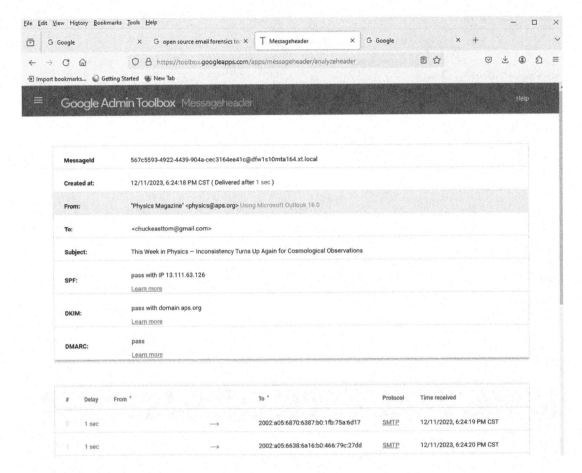

Figure 11-14. *Google Admin Toolbox screen 2*

The site DNS Checker also will analyze the header, but it will attempt to identify the source of the email, as shown in Figure 11-15.

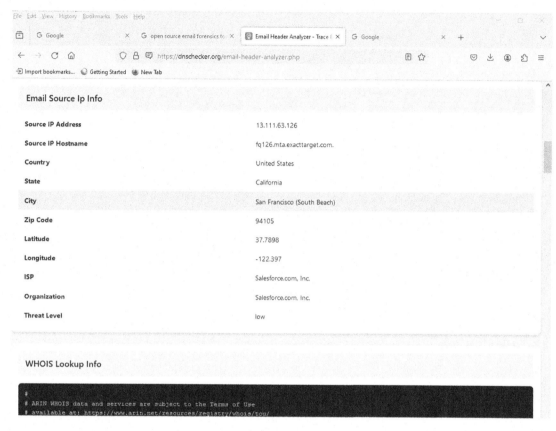

Figure 11-15. *DNS Checker*

Outlook PST Viewer does indeed have a free version, but also commercial version for $69 and $129. This is from www.systoolsgroup.com/. You simply point the tool to a .pst file, and it will scan it, as can be seen in Figure 11-16.

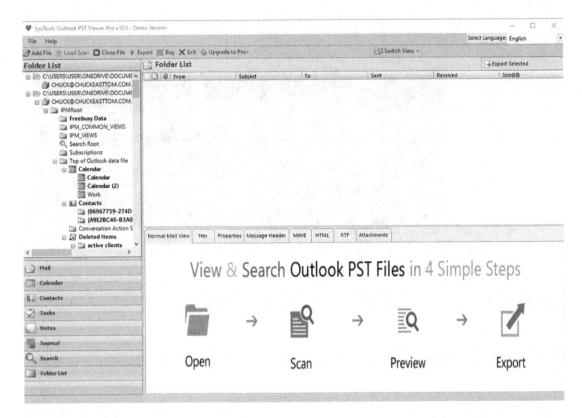

Figure 11-16. *Outlook PST Viewer*

This software can also recover deleted emails, as shown in Figure 11-17.

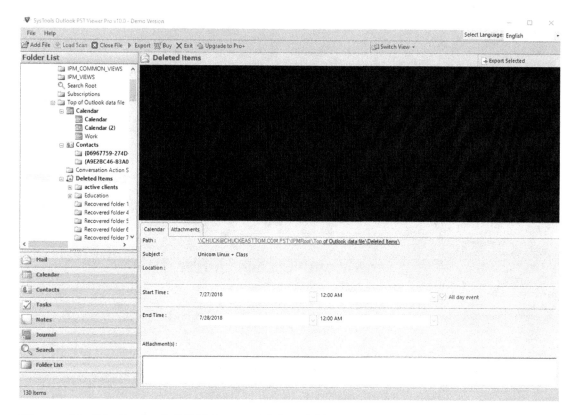

Figure 11-17. *Outlook PST Viewer – deleted file recovery*

Information is redacted from Figure 11-17 for privacy reasons. As you can see, there are a wide variety of tools and techniques to facilitate your analysis of email forensics.

Ediscovery

In addition to criminal investigations, email forensics is a major part of ediscovery. Electronic discovery is the process of producing evidence that is stored electronically. Often, this occurs in administrative and civil investigations. Essentially, it is an extension of traditional civil discovery rules into ESI (electronically stored information). ESI includes emails, word processing documents, spreadsheets, web pages, etc. – any data that can be stored electronically. This will frequently involve email.

In all civil litigation, one needs to first establish who is liable. That is just a legal term meaning *who is responsible*. It is entirely possible to have joint liability. Civil cases usually begin with what is called a tort. A tort is short for a tortious act, and it is an act that causes someone harm. That harm can be physical or financial. The harm may even be accidental, through negligence. The person accused of committing the tort is referred to as the tortfeasor.

Electronically stored information, or *ESI*, includes any data that is stored electronically such as emails, web pages, word processing files, spreadsheets, and databases. The volume of ESI is generally exponentially greater than paper information, and it may be located in multiple places. A single paper memorandum may be stored on the computer hard drives of the document's creator, reviewers, and recipients; on the company server; on laptops and home computers; and on backup tapes.

Conclusions

Email forensics can be an important part of both civil and criminal investigations. In this chapter, we have covered email standards, file types, and protocols. We have also reviewed how to interpret email headers as well as multiple tools to aid you in email forensics.

References

Library of Congress (2023). Sustainability of Digital Formats: Planning for Library of Congress Collections. Retrieved from `www.loc.gov/preservation/digital/formats/fdd/fdd000388.shtml`

Test Your Knowledge

1. What part of an SMTP transaction determines the recipient of the message?

   a. Receiver

   b. Received-by

   c. RCPT

   d. Destination

2. Which component performs the actual DNS lookup to find the recipient?

    a. MTA

    b. MUA

    c. MDA

    d. MXA

3. Port 995 is usually used with what protocol?

    a. Encrypted SMTP

    b. POP3

    c. Encrypted POP3

    d. Encrypted IMAP

4. Which file extension denotes an individual Microsoft Outlook email:

    a. .pst

    b. .ost

    c. .eml

    d. .msg

5. What would you look for in an email header to find something that was explicitly instructed by the user?

    a. Action-intentional

    b. Manual-action

    c. Disposition-manual

    d. Disposition-intentional

CHAPTER 12

Microsoft Azure and Cloud Forensics

Chuck Easttom, Ph.D., D.Sc.

Introduction

Cloud computing is a ubiquitous service and thus is important for digital forensics. Microsoft has its own cloud offering, Azure, with a number of services and features. This chapter will begin with an overview of cloud services, then move specifically into Azure cloud. There are many services available through cloud computing, including Software as a Service (SaaS), Platform as a Service (PaaS), and Infrastructure as a Service (IaaS). Software as a Service (SaaS) is a software distribution solution that delivers specific applications in a virtualized manner. The software is licensed to the end user on a subscription basis and hosted centrally by the licensor. This type of software is often referred to as on-demand software. A brief description of each of these will be helpful. Software as a Service (SaaS) provides access to some specific software via a cloud. Platform as a Service (PaaS) is a cloud service that provides access to operating systems. It allows the users to access a fully configured, patched, and updated version of the desired platform. Infrastructure as a Service (IaaS) is a cloud computing service that provides at least part of a network's infrastructure, such as servers, in a virtualized manner. IaaS is generally used in virtual environments. There are numerous variations such as

- Security as a Service (SECaaS or SaaS)
- Knowledge as a Service (KaaS)
- Data as a Service (DaaS)

375

© Chuck Easttom, William Butler, Jessica Phelan, Ramya Sai Bhagavatula, Sean Steuber, Karely Rodriguez, Victoria Indy Balkissoon, Zehra Naseer 2024
C. Easttom et al., *Windows Forensics*, https://doi.org/10.1007/979-8-8688-0193-8_12

- Mobile Backend as a Service (MBaaS)

- Artificial Intelligence as a Service (AIaaS)

- Content as a Service (CaaS)

These are typically specialized variations of PaaS, IaaS, and SaaS. And based on current trends, one should expect to see many other variations and names in the coming years. But this still begs the question of what, precisely, is a cloud? The National Institute of Standards and Technology (NIST) defines cloud computing as "a model for enabling convenient, on-demand network access to a shared pool of configurable computing resources (e.g., networks, servers, storage, applications, and services) that can be rapidly provisioned and released with minimal management effort or service provider interaction."

The NSA offers a more detailed definition of cloud computing (NSA, 2020):

- Cloud architectures are not standardized, and each Cloud Service Provider (CSP) implements foundational cloud services differently. Understanding a CSP's cloud implementation should be part of a customer's risk decision during cloud service procurement. Cloud architectural services are common to most clouds:

- **Identity and Access Management (IdAM)**: IdAM refers to controls in place for customers to protect access to their resources as well as controls that the CSP uses to protect access to back-end cloud resources. Secure customer and cloud back-end IdAM, both enforcement and auditing, is critical to protecting cloud customer resources.

- **Compute**: Clouds generally rely on virtualization and containerization to manage and isolate customer computation workloads. Serverless computing, the dynamic allocation of cloud compute resources to run customer code, is built upon either virtualization or containerization, depending on the cloud service.

- Virtualization is a cloud backbone technology, not only for customer workloads but also for the cloud architecture itself. Virtualization is an enabling technology that provides isolation in the cloud for both storage and networking. Virtualization typically implements and secures internal cloud nodes.

- Containerization is a more lightweight technology that is commonly used in clouds to manage and isolate customer workloads. Containerization is less secure of an isolation technology than virtualization because of its shared kernel characteristics, but CSPs offer technologies that help address containerization security drawbacks.

- **Networking**: Isolation of customer networks is a critical security function of the cloud. In addition, cloud networking must implement controls throughout the cloud architecture to protect customer cloud resources from insider threat.

- Software-Defined Networking is commonly used in the cloud to both logically separate customer networks and implement backbone networking for the cloud.

- **Storage (Objects, Blocks, and Database Records)**: Customer data is logically separated from other customer data on cloud nodes. Security mechanisms must exist to ensure that customer data is not leaked to other customers and that customer data is protected from insider threat.

Cloud Types

Cloud computing solutions are often categorized by how the cloud is intended to be used, its customer base. Cloud delivery is often categorized as private, public, or hybrid:

- A **private cloud** is one used specifically by a single organization without offering services to an outside party.

- A **public cloud** is one that offers infrastructure of services either to the general public or a private group or organization.

- A **hybrid cloud** is one that combines elements of both private and public clouds. Hybrid clouds are essentially private clouds with limited public access. These are often utilized for solutions in which several organizations have to share cloud access, such as a consortium of several organizations devoted to common security issues.

It is also often the case that a given customer might use more than one cloud provider. This can be done for various reasons, but the two most common are described here:

- **Multicloud**: Multiple different cloud vendors are used heterogeneously. This mitigates dependency on a single vendor. Cloud assets (applications, virtual servers, etc.) are hosted across multiple different public clouds. One can also include private clouds in the architecture.

- **Polycloud**: Polycloud is similar to multicloud, but in this case, the different public clouds are being utilized not for flexibility and redundancy but rather for specific services each provider offers.

High Performance Cloud is another category. This is the use of cloud services for high performance computing. Such HPC applications would normally require clusters of computers or a supercomputer. There are several companies including Amazon Web Services that offer HPC cloud computing. This is commonly used in mathematically intense operations.

Related to cloud computing is fog computing. This is an architecture that uses edge devices for processing, sometimes called fogging or fog networking. Fog networking is often used in IoT. The National Institute of Standards and Technology in March 2018 released NIST Special Publication 500-325, Fog Computing Conceptual Model, which defines fog computing as a horizontal, physical, or virtual resource paradigm that resides between smart end devices and traditional cloud computing or data center.

Cloud Connectivity and Security

Connectivity to a cloud or other virtual resources is often accomplished over traditional network connections. This means users can use a computer on a network and access cloud-based resources through traditional network media. Given that clouds aggregate data, it is necessary to pay particular attention to security in a cloud. Two cloud-based security standards include ISO 27017, which is a cloud security standard, and ISO 27018, which is a standard for privacy of customer data in a cloud.

ISO 27017

ISO 27017 is guidance for cloud security. It does apply the guidance of ISO 27002 to the cloud, but then adds seven new controls:

- **CLD.6.3.1**: Agreement on shared or divided security responsibilities between the customer and cloud provider.

- **CLD.8.1.5**: Addresses how assets are returned or removed from the cloud when the contract is terminated.

- **CLD.9.5.1**: This control states that the cloud provider must separate the customer's virtual environment from other customers or outside parties.

- **CLD.9.5.2**: This control states that the customer and the cloud provider both must ensure the virtual machines are hardened.

- **CLD.12.1.5**: It is solely the customer's responsibility to define and manage administrative operations.

- **CLD.12.4.5**: The cloud provider's capabilities must enable the customer to monitor their own cloud environment.

- **CLD.13.1.4**: The virtual network environment must be configured so that it at least meets the security policies of the physical environment.

ISO 27018

ISO 27018 is closely related to ISO 27017. ISO 27018 defines privacy requirements in a cloud environment, particularly how the customer and cloud provider must protect personally identifiable information (PII). Microsoft has an online resource regarding Azure and ISO 27018 (Microsoft, 2023b).

FedRAMP

This is an acronym for Federal Risk and Authorization Management Program. It is a US government program for standardizing cloud security.

Key aspects of FedRAMP include

Standardization: FedRAMP provides a standardized approach to security assessment, authorization, and continuous monitoring for cloud services. This helps ensure that all cloud services used by federal agencies meet consistent security requirements.

Security Assessments: Cloud service providers (CSPs) that want to work with federal agencies must undergo a rigorous security assessment conducted by a third-party assessment organization (3PAO). This assessment is based on the FedRAMP security requirements, which are derived from the NIST (National Institute of Standards and Technology) Special Publication 800-53.

Authorization: After a cloud service has been assessed, it must be authorized by a federal agency or the Joint Authorization Board (JAB), which includes representatives from the Department of Homeland Security (DHS), the General Services Administration (GSA), and the Department of Defense (DoD). Once authorized, the cloud service is deemed to have met the necessary security requirements and can be used by federal agencies.

Continuous Monitoring: FedRAMP also requires continuous monitoring of authorized cloud services to ensure they maintain compliance with the FedRAMP security requirements. This involves regular reporting, vulnerability scanning, and other security oversight activities.

Reuse of Authorizations: One of the key benefits of FedRAMP is the "do once, use many times" framework. Once a cloud service is authorized through FedRAMP, other federal agencies can leverage the same authorization, significantly reducing the time and cost associated with security assessments.

NSA Cloud Security

The NSA offers guidance on cloud security (NSA, 2020). Some of the NSA's primary recommendations are given here:

- While not a base component of cloud architectures, encryption and key management (KM) form a critical aspect of protecting information in the cloud.

- While CSPs are generally responsible for detecting threats to the underlying cloud platform, customers bear the responsibility of detecting threats to their own cloud resources.

- **Incident Response**: CSPs are uniquely positioned to respond to incidents internal to the cloud infrastructure and bear responsibility for doing so. Incidents internal to customer cloud environments are generally the customer's responsibility, but CSPs may provide support to incident response teams.

- **Patching/Updating**: CSPs are responsible for ensuring that their cloud offerings are secure and rapidly patch software within their purview but usually do not patch software managed by the customer (e.g., operating systems in IaaS offerings). Because of this, customers should vigilantly deploy patches to mitigate software vulnerabilities in the cloud. In some cases, CSPs offer managed solutions in which they perform operating system patching as well.

Multicloud Security

In addition to specific recommendations from standards, there are some general security concepts for multicloud security that are published by the Cloud Security Alliance (Cloud Security Alliance, 2022):

> **Create Cloud Policies, Standards, and Security Baseline**:
> Before even embarking on the cloud journey, establish policies and standards specific to cloud environments. Baseline security configurations need to be established for every cloud platform the organization is intending to use. Ensure that these baselines are enforceable via an automated process to help reduce manual intervention, thereby reducing risk.

Establish Visibility Across Your Cloud Estate: When the organization has a mix of hybrid and multicloud models, unified visibility across all infrastructure, including on-premise and cloud, becomes a challenge. Under the shared responsibility security model, make sure that you know what your organization's responsibilities are. Establish tooling for the appropriate amount of visibility across the multicloud estate.

Implement Automated Tooling capability to detect misconfigurations and auto-remediate via cloud security posture management (CSPM). Automation in this area is key as the human-based approach is error-prone and not scalable.

Drive Secure CI/CD Pipeline: Automation is a must-have when it comes to cloud deployments. This is not only for the ease of deployments but also for embedding security directly into the build stage. The application teams should not have direct access to the cloud assets to make deployments. Rather, everything needs to flow from the secure CI/CD pipeline. Everything that gets into the pipeline needs to be scanned from the security point of view before releasing into production.

Microsoft Azure

As this book is devoted to Windows forensics, most of our discussions will focus on the forensics of Microsoft products. Now that you have a general understanding of cloud computing, it is necessary to delve deeper into Microsoft Azure.

Microsoft Azure, also known as Azure, is a cloud computing service created by Microsoft for building, testing, deploying, and managing applications and services through Microsoft-managed data centers. It provides a range of cloud services, including those for computing, analytics, storage, and networking. Users can pick and choose from these services to develop and scale new applications or run existing applications in the public cloud. Key features of Microsoft Azure include

Computing Services: Azure provides virtual machines, containers, and serverless computing environments. It supports a range of operating systems, programming languages, frameworks, databases, and devices.

Storage Solutions: Azure offers scalable cloud storage for both structured and unstructured data. It also provides persistent, durable storage services for virtual machines and a scalable object storage for data objects.

Networking Capabilities: Azure includes a variety of networking features like Azure Virtual Network, which allows users to create private networks, and Azure ExpressRoute, which provides private network connectivity to Azure services.

Database Services: Azure supports relational databases like Azure SQL Database, nonrelational databases like NoSQL, and big data through Azure Synapse Analytics.

AI and Machine Learning Services: Azure provides a suite of AI and machine learning services, including Azure Machine Learning Service and Azure Cognitive Services, which allow users to build and deploy AI and machine learning models.

Internet of Things (IoT): Azure IoT Hub and other related services enable users to connect, monitor, and manage billions of IoT assets.

Developer Tools: Azure DevOps services provide collaboration tools for software development teams, including high-performance pipelines, free private Git repositories, configurable Kanban boards, and extensive automated and cloud-based load testing.

Security and Compliance: Azure has a strong commitment to security and compliance, offering a wide range of built-in security features and compliance certifications.

Hybrid Cloud Capabilities: Azure facilitates hybrid cloud environments, allowing businesses to integrate on-premises data and apps with cloud services.

Marketplace: Azure Marketplace offers a wide range of third-party applications and services that are optimized to run on Azure.

Figure 12-1 shows the landing page for Microsoft Azure.

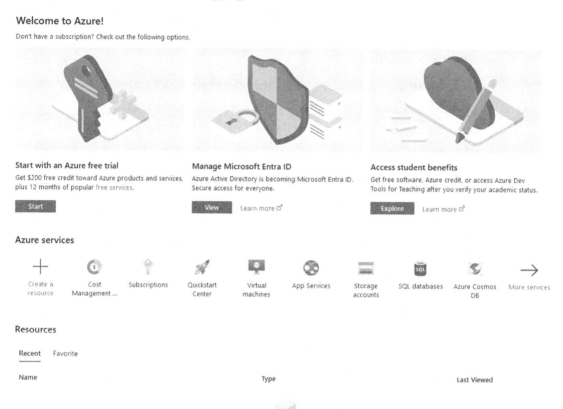

Figure 12-1. *Microsoft Azure*

The tenant is the centerpiece of Azure. An Azure tenant represents a single instance of Azure Active Directory, or Azure AD, which is Microsoft's cloud-based identity and access management service. In the context of Microsoft Azure, a tenant is essentially a dedicated and secure instance of Azure AD that an organization receives and uses when it signs up for a Microsoft cloud service such as Azure, Microsoft 365, or Dynamics 365.

Key aspects of an Azure tenant include

> **Identity Management**: The tenant serves as a central identity service that manages users, groups, and the identities used to access cloud services.

> **Isolation**: Each tenant is isolated from other tenants, ensuring that each organization's data and access policies are kept separate and secure.

Single Sign-On (SSO): Azure AD in the tenant enables single sign-on to multiple applications, both cloud-based and on-premises.

Subscription Management: An Azure tenant can be associated with one or more Azure subscriptions. These subscriptions are used to manage billing, resources, and permissions.

Service Administration: The tenant contains the Azure AD instance where administrators can set security policies, manage user roles, and configure integration with other cloud services.

Integration with Other Services: Tenants can be integrated with other Microsoft services and third-party applications, allowing for a seamless workflow across different platforms.

Custom Domains: Organizations can add their custom domains to the Azure AD in their tenant, allowing users to have identities that are familiar and aligned with the organization's domain naming conventions.

Multitenancy: In scenarios where service providers manage resources for multiple clients, each client can have its own tenant, ensuring data segregation and security.

Cloud Forensics

Cloud forensics, the process of applying digital forensic practices to cloud computing environments, presents unique challenges compared to traditional digital forensics. These challenges arise primarily due to the nature of cloud computing, which is characterized by distributed data processing, multitenancy, and the dynamic allocation of resources. Here are some of the key challenges:

Data Distribution and Localization: In cloud environments, data can be distributed across multiple servers and geographic locations. This makes it difficult to identify and collect relevant data for forensic analysis, especially when dealing with different jurisdictions and legal frameworks.

Multitenancy: Cloud servers often host data from multiple clients (tenants). Ensuring that the investigation process does not compromise the privacy and integrity of other tenants' data is a significant challenge.

Chain of Custody: Maintaining a clear and secure chain of custody for digital evidence in the cloud is complex. It's challenging to establish a clear audit trail when data is transferred across different systems and jurisdictions.

Lack of Control over Infrastructure: In cloud environments, clients typically do not have control over the underlying infrastructure. This limits the ability to conduct certain types of forensic activities, like capturing live memory or disk images.

Encryption: While encryption is essential for securing data, it also poses a challenge for forensics. Encrypted data requires decryption before analysis, and obtaining decryption keys can be difficult, especially if they are managed by the cloud service provider.

Dynamic Nature of Cloud Computing: Cloud environments are highly dynamic, with virtual machines and containers being created and decommissioned frequently. This can lead to the loss of potential evidence if not captured in time.

Legal and Regulatory Challenges: Different countries and regions have various laws and regulations regarding data privacy, cross-border data transfer, and lawful access to data. Navigating these legal complexities while conducting investigations is a significant challenge.

Resource Scaling and Elasticity: The scalable nature of cloud services means that resources can be rapidly scaled up or down. This elasticity can lead to difficulties in identifying where data resides at any given time.

Forensic Tool Effectiveness: Traditional forensic tools may not be effective or applicable in cloud environments. There is a need for specialized tools and techniques to handle the nuances of cloud architectures.

Incident Response and Real-Time Analysis: Conducting real-time analysis and incident response in a cloud environment is complicated due to the distributed nature of services and data.

NIST 800-201

As of 2023, the National Institute of Standards and Technology has released NIST Special Publication NIST Special Publication 800-201 (NIST, 2023). This is an initial public disclosure, and it may change as NIST gets more input. The document is an excellent read for anyone performing cloud forensics. The document begins by outlining the challenges in performing cloud forensics. As this standard is still a work in progress, it is worth reading, but does not provide clear steps on how to conduct cloud forensics.

OSForensics

With OSForensics, you can create a cloud image. The first step is to locate the cloud imager shown in Figure 12-2.

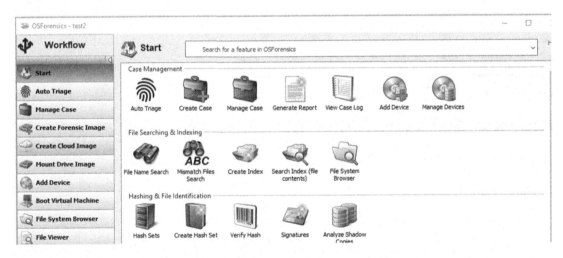

Figure 12-2. *OSForensics cloud imager*

For this example, I chose Microsoft OneDrive, as shown in Figure 12-3.

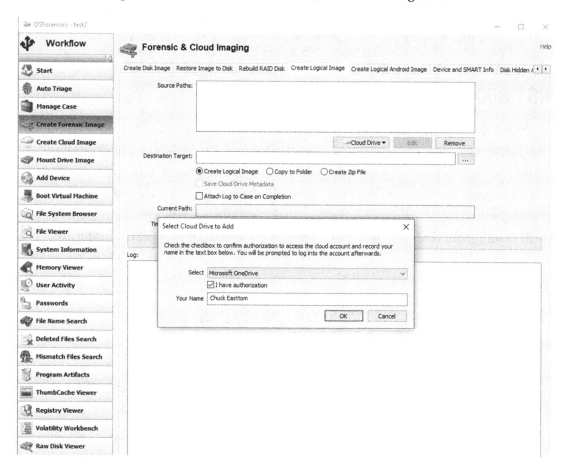

Figure 12-3. *Accessing OneDrive*

You will be directed to the login screen to log in to the cloud resource, as shown in Figure 12-4.

Figure 12-4. *Logging in to Microsoft OneDrive*

For security reasons, I have redacted the username. Assuming you have the proper credentials and login before the system times out, the browser will show the screen depicted in Figure 12-5.

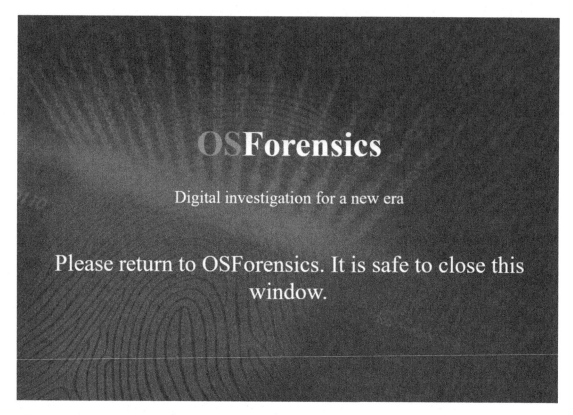

Figure 12-5. *OSForensics cloud connection*

At this point, OSForensics will create a logical image of the cloud drive that you can then examine as you would any other image.

FTK

FTK Imager does not, as of yet, have a cloud imaging solution. However, FTK Imager has always had the option of making a logical image of any folder. If you are on a computer connected to any cloud resource, including Microsoft OneDrive, you can create an image of that folder. This is shown in Figures 12-6 through 12-9.

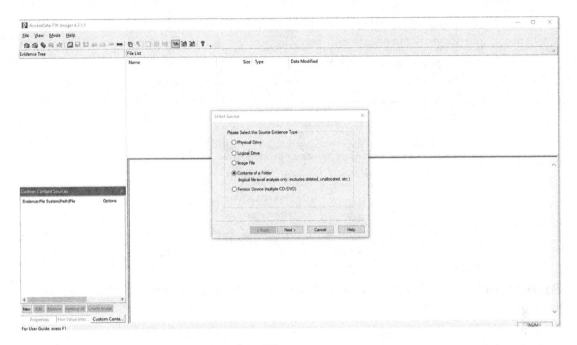

Figure 12-6. *Folder imaging with FTK*

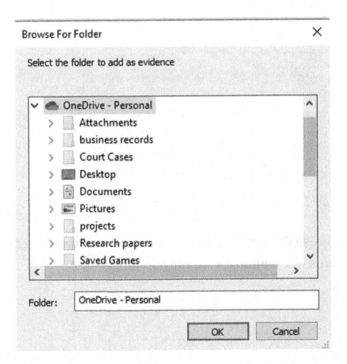

Figure 12-7. *Folder imaging with FTK – choose the folder*

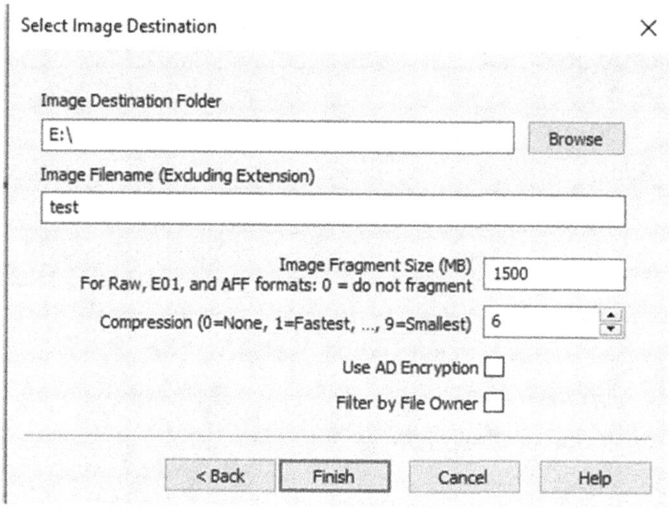

Figure 12-8. *Folder imaging with FTK – choose the destination*

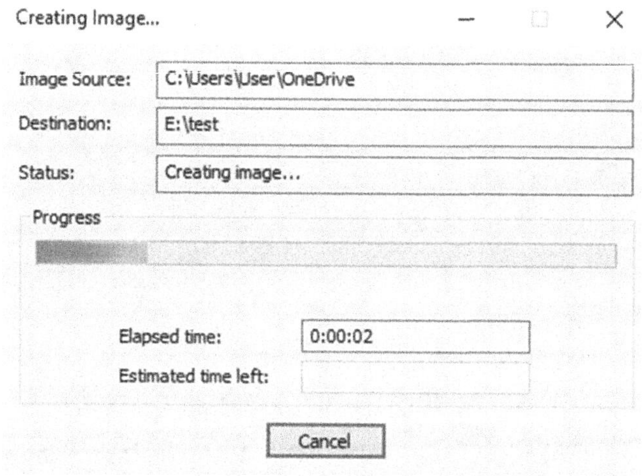

Figure 12-9. *Folder imaging with FTK – start imaging*

A folder image is usually not ideal for functions such as retrieving deleted files. But in the case of cloud forensics, it may be your only option.

Azure Forensics

Microsoft provides guidance on how to conduct forensics in Azure (Microsoft, 2023). The instructions Microsoft provides are repeated here.

The system and organization controls (SOC) team uses a discrete Azure **SOC** subscription. The team has exclusive access to that subscription, which contains the resources that must be kept protected, inviolable, and monitored. The Azure Storage account in the SOC subscription hosts copies of disk snapshots in immutable blob storage, and a dedicated key vault keeps the snapshots' hash values and copies of the VM's Bitlocker Encryption Keys (BEKs).

In response to a request to capture a VM's digital evidence, a SOC team member signs in to the Azure SOC subscription and uses a hybrid runbook worker VM in Automation to implement the Copy-VmDigitalEvidence runbook. The Automation hybrid runbook worker provides control of all mechanisms involved in the capture.

The Copy-VmDigitalEvidence runbook implements these macro steps:

1. Sign in to Azure by using the system-assigned managed identity for an Automation account to access the target VM's resources and the other Azure services required by the solution.

2. Create disk snapshots for the VM's operating system (OS) and data disks.

3. Copy the snapshots to the SOC subscription's immutable blob storage and in a temporary file share.

4. Calculate hash values of the snapshots by using the copy on the file share.

5. Copy the obtained hash values and the VM's BEK in the SOC key vault.

6. Clean up all the copies of the snapshots except the one in immutable blob storage.

This is a general outline and does not presuppose access to any specialized forensics tools.

Conclusions

Cloud forensics presents challenges that standard PC forensics does not. Accessing the data and imaging it is itself a challenge. Furthermore, the cloud might be storing data in other legal jurisdictions, thus creating legal complications. However, one can successfully extract forensic data from a cloud resource and analyze said data to locate evidence.

References

Cloud Security Alliance (2022). Multi-Cloud Security. Retrieved from `https://cloudsecurityalliance.org/blog/2022/02/17/multi-cloud-security/`

Microsoft (2023). Computer forensics chain of custody in Azure. Retrieved from `https://learn.microsoft.com/en-us/azure/architecture/example-scenario/forensic`

Microsoft (2023b). ISO/IEC 27018:2018. Retrieved from `https://learn.microsoft.com/en-us/azure/compliance/offerings/offering-iso-27018`

NIST (2023). NIST 800-201. Retrieved from `https://nvlpubs.nist.gov/nistpubs/SpecialPublications/NIST.SP.800-201.ipd.pdf`

NSA (2020). Mitigating Cloud Vulnerabilities. Retrieved from `https://media.defense.gov/2020/Jan/22/2002237484/-1/-1/0/CSI-MITIGATING-CLOUD-VULNERABILITIES_20200121.PDF`

Test Your Knowledge

1. What technology is best used for isolating customer workloads?

    a. Virtualization

    b. Containerization

    c. Hybrid clouds

    d. Polyclouds

2. Which cloud solution is used specifically for individual services offered by different cloud providers?

    a. Polycloud

    b. Multicloud

    c. Hybrid cloud

    d. High performance cloud

3. What standards govern privacy in a cloud?

    a. ISO 27018

    b. ISO 27017

    c. NIST 800-201

    d. HPC

4. What is the centerpiece of Microsoft Azure?

    a. Subscription

    b. Active Directory

    c. Tenant

    d. Identity Management

CHAPTER 13

Data Hiding Techniques in Windows

Karely Rodriguez, karely.m.rodriguez.galvan@Vanderbilt.Edu

In the realm of digital forensics, investigations face the challenge of unraveling the intricate web of data hiding techniques employed by individuals who seek to conceal their personal information as a safeguard in the case of a criminal investigation. As the need for data protection grows, individuals adopt various methods to safeguard their data from prying eyes. This chapter explores three prominent approaches used to safeguard data: leveraging built-in Windows security features, concealing and transferring data through steganography techniques, and exploiting the unused allocated space commonly known as slack space. As we discuss these methods, a sampling of tools related to each topic will be presented. The tools include both open source and proprietary solutions, which are advantageous for having an arsenal of tools that aid in the process of a thorough and detailed investigation. This chapter also provides an overview of modern algorithms and other demonstrations throughout. Insight is also provided on how these methods or similar tools could be troublesome for digital forensic investigators, as tech-savvy individuals seeking to hide illicit activity may also utilize these tools.

The field of digital forensic science allows experts to identify and carefully analyze the various techniques employed by suspected criminals to conceal their illicit activities through the use of advanced data hiding techniques. Algorithms and automated tools continue to shape the landscape of digital forensics by bringing new approaches and methods to effectively investigate suspects. By understanding these techniques, investigators can uncover hidden information that may be crucial to putting forth important evidence. Therefore, it is essential for investigators to have a thorough understanding of advanced data hiding techniques to contribute toward serving justice.

© Chuck Easttom, William Butler, Jessica Phelan, Ramya Sai Bhagavatula, Sean Steuber, Karely Rodriguez, Victoria Indy Balkissoon, Zehra Naseer 2024
C. Easttom et al., *Windows Forensics*, https://doi.org/10.1007/979-8-8688-0193-8_13

This chapter delves into the intricacies of Windows encryption, steganography, and slack space, which are all common methods utilized by perpetrators to obscure their digital footprints. By gaining a thorough understanding of these techniques, digital forensic experts can successfully uncover evidence that may have otherwise remained hidden. Windows encryption is a built-in feature that offers its users defensive countermeasures which investigators may need to bypass. Steganography refers to the art of concealing information within files, such as images and audio, that appear inconspicuous. Lastly, slack space is the allocated but unutilized wait-space area of a cluster. By considering these topics, digital forensic investigators uncover instances of digital deception, ultimately facilitating criminal investigations. This leads to the delivery of justice and ensures that those responsible are held accountable for their actions. Digital forensic investigators must be familiar with a comprehensive and variable range of available techniques and options to effectively pursue their investigative strategy.

In this chapter, we will cover the following:

- Windows encryption

- Steganography

- Slack space

- NTFS

Why Study Data Hiding Techniques?

In today's digital landscape, criminals who find themselves in custody and facing trial may feel a false sense of confidence that the use of advanced data hiding techniques will result in little evidence being uncovered that can be utilized against them. These individuals had confidence in the measures they took while committing the crime, going to great lengths to conceal their tracks and leaving no stone unturned. As a digital forensics expert, you play a vital role in unraveling their elaborate schemes and exposing the truth. In this chapter, we will dive into the intriguing world of advanced data hiding techniques.

Windows Encryption

Clearly, encrypting data is one way to hide it from a forensic examiner. You will need to have some general working knowledge of Windows encryption to perform Windows forensics.

What Is Windows Encryption?

Windows provides features to protect the private information of system administrators and users. Over the years, Windows has added new ways for systems to be protected. While this is certainly a general public good, these tools can add an additional layer of challenges for digital forensic investigators. We will provide an overview of Windows BitLocker and Encrypted File System.

Must-know terms and definitions:

- **NTFS (New Technology File System)**: Windows file system, offering better performance, security, and larger file size support. It's crucial for forensic investigators working with BitLocker-encrypted volumes to extract evidence and analyze metadata.

- **Volume**: A file system volume is a logical unit within a disk volume formatted with a specific file system, like NTFS in Windows, representing the organization of files and directories on the storage medium.

BitLocker Drive Encryption

BitLocker, also known as BitLocker Drive Encryption, is a comprehensive data protection module integrated into the Windows operating system. It provides full-disk encryption to safeguard personal data, including all data stored on the Windows operating system volume. By employing BitLocker, users can encrypt system partitions, data partitions, and removable storage media to ensure protection against potential data leakage risks arising from loss, theft, or improper disposal of PC hard disks. BitLocker is a proprietary program developed by Microsoft. It offers sufficient security for most computer users who want to protect their data in cases of unauthorized access to their personal drive. It is worth noting that closed source code applications, like BitLocker, may raise concerns among extremely security-minded individuals as the source code cannot be audited for potential backdoors (Microsoft, 2023). Nonetheless, due to its widespread availability in many versions of Windows, we will discuss how to use BitLocker and leverage its encryption capabilities for enhanced data protection.

Activating BitLocker on Windows

BitLocker offers two types of encryption:

- **BitLocker Drive Encryption**: Encrypts local partitions, including the Windows partition

- **BitLocker To Go**: Encrypts removable storage drives like external hard disks and USB flash memory

BitLocker provides a simple encryption process on Windows systems.
To activate BitLocker on a machine running Windows 11, follow these steps:

1. Open the Settings window by clicking the Start menu and selecting "Settings."

2. In the Settings menu, choose "System" and then click "Storage."

3. Under the "Storage" settings, select "Advanced storage settings" and then click "Disks and volumes."

4. Locate the drive that contains the volume you want to encrypt and click its properties.

5. At the bottom of the properties page, click "Turn on BitLocker."

6. A menu will appear, select "Turn on BitLocker" again, and choose "Device encryption."

7. To back up the recovery key, select one of the options provided, such as "Save to your Microsoft account," "Save to a file," or "Print the recovery key," and click "Next."

To activate BitLocker To Go on a machine running Windows 11, follow these steps:

1. Connect a USB flash drive to your device.

2. Open Settings, go to "System," and click "Storage."

3. Under "Storage," select your USB flash drive and click "Properties."

4. Enable BitLocker To Go encryption by checking the "Use a password to unlock the drive" box, entering and confirming your password, and saving the recovery key.

5. Choose "Encrypt used disk space only" and select "Compatible mode."

6. Click "Start" to begin the encryption process.

7. Once the encryption is complete, click "Close" to finish.

The BitLocker encryption mechanisms may vary slightly on different versions of Windows.

BitLocker utilizes the AES encryption algorithm with a 128-bit or 256-bit key and the Full Volume Encryption Key (FVEK), which is 64 bytes (Tan, Zhang, & Bao, 2020). In both cases, the AES encryption key utilizes a bit length to encrypt and decrypt a block of messages (BitLocker Drive Encryption Security Policy, n.d.).

Architecture and Components

BitLocker has several components; highlighted here are the most important components to be aware of.

TPM Chip

A TPM (Trusted Platform Module) is a special chip used by services like BitLocker Drive Encryption, Windows Hello, and others, enabling the device to support advanced security features. It securely creates and stores cryptographic keys and ensures the integrity of your device's operating system and firmware, confirming that they have not been tampered with. Typically, the TPM is a separate chip on the motherboard; however, since the release of TPM version 2.0 in 2016, manufacturers have the capability to integrate the TPM directly into their chipsets. You can use additional authentication methods if your computer doesn't have a TPM. Even without a TPM, BitLocker can still be utilized by storing encryption keys on a USB drive. It is crucial to emphasize that the absence of a TPM should not lead digital forensic investigators to overlook the potential use of BitLocker for hiding information. Additionally, the computer's firmware, which is a type of software, should support TPM or USB devices during startup. If these features are unavailable, you can check with your computer manufacturer for a firmware update to enable them.

In addition to its role in encryption, the TPM chip also performs an authentication check on your computer's hardware and firmware. If it detects unauthorized changes, your PC will boot in a restricted mode to determine potential attackers. For example, if an attacker tries to change your hard drive or add an extra hard disk to copy data from your computer, the TPM chip will restrict the hard disk's use and prevent potential attacks. This feature adds an extra layer of security to your system. It is worth noting that BitLocker was introduced in Windows Vista, and starting from Windows 8.1, BitLocker is automatically enabled, providing users with convenient access to data encryption (Tan, Zhang, & Bao, 2020).

Key Components

BitLocker encryption involves several components that work together to ensure data security. The encryption process involves the use of various keys, including volume and protector keys which can be encrypted using BitLocker. The BitLocker driver integrated into the Windows OS manages encryption and discretion of the data in a drive. Encryption keys play a pivotal role, with the volume key serving as the main key for encrypting and decrypting data on the drive, while protector keys secure and unlock the volume key (Tan, Zhang, & Bao, 2020). Protectors, such as TPM, PIN, password, and recovery key, serve as authentication methods to unlock the encrypted volumes (BitLocker Drive Encryption Security Policy, n.d.). The TPM is a hardware component that securely stores encryption keys and enhances security by performing cryptographic operations. The TPM key in BitLocker adds an extra layer of protection by verifying the integrity of the boot components and utilizing its private key to decrypt the encrypted VMK (Volume Master Key). Additionally, a recovery key, generated during BitLocker setup, is a backup to access encrypted drives if other protectors are unavailable (BitLocker Drive Encryption Security Policy, n.d.). BitLocker To Go extends encryption functionality to removable storage devices like USB flash drives, safeguarding data even when connected to different computers.

Recovery Keys

BitLocker makes the encrypted drive unrecoverable without the necessary authentication of the recovery password or key during recovery mode. The BitLocker recovery key is a 48-digit numerical password that serves as a unique identifier. It acts as a backup method to unlock the system drive in situations where BitLocker cannot verify the authorization to access the drive. BitLocker recovery keys are crucial in accessing encrypted data in certain scenarios. In the absence of a TPM, a recovery key is required to unlock the system drive during the boot process. This key serves as an alternative authentication method and ensures authorized access to the encrypted data. In the case where a TPM is present, the recovery key may only be needed if certain circumstances arise, such as forgetting the password or encountering issues during the boot process. However, it is important to store the recovery key securely should it be required to decrypt the drive and regain access to the encrypted data. Recovery keys safeguard users to recover their encrypted systems and should be carefully managed to maintain data integrity and accessibility.

Recovering BitLocker Data

Repair-bde

Microsoft provides a command-line tool called Repair-bde which can assist in recovering data from BitLocker-protected drives, including instances where the drives have been damaged or failed. Digital forensic investigators may benefit from Repair-bde, which repairs errors and corruption in BitLocker-encrypted volumes, ensuring access to crucial encrypted evidence during data recovery. Though originally designed for system administrators and users who have trouble with their BitLocker-encrypted drives, Repair-bde supports digital forensic investigators in various ways. It enables access and recovery of encrypted data from seized devices and assists in decrypting BitLocker-protected drives linked and uncovering pertinent information. Read about this tool and download it at `https://learn.microsoft.com/en-us/windows-server/administration/windows-commands/repair-bde`.

BitLocker encryption plays a crucial role in protecting sensitive data and is essential for digital forensic investigators. Understanding the encryption process, recovery key mechanisms, and authentication methods enables investigators to handle encrypted drives and retrieve valuable evidence effectively. This knowledge empowers investigators to assess suspects' security practices, identify vulnerabilities, and employ appropriate strategies to access encrypted data (BitLocker Drive Encryption Security Policy, n.d.). It also ensures the preservation of data integrity, evidence, and compliance with legal and ethical obligations throughout the digital forensic process. Proficiency in BitLocker encryption equips investigators with the necessary tools and insights to overcome encryption barriers and uncover vital evidence in their investigations.

BitLocker vs. Encrypted File System

BitLocker and the Encrypted File System offer different approaches to encryption. While BitLocker is used to encrypt entire drives and their contents, the Encrypted File

System operates at a lower volume level. With EFS, users have the flexibility to selectively choose specific files and folders for encryption, allowing for more granular control over the encryption process. Using both BitLocker and EFS, users can benefit from an additional layer of protection, adding more security if an unauthorized person were to bypass BitLocker.

Encrypted File System

The Encrypted File System (EFS) is an encryption and authentication mechanism introduced as a built-in technology in Windows 2000. EFS facilitates transparent encryption and decryption of files in an NTFS volume. EFS encrypts files and directories at rest in the file system. In an encrypted folder, the contents remain protected even if they are moved or copied to another location. Further, if a new file or subfolder is added to the encrypted folder, it will automatically inherit the encryption properties. When a directory is encrypted, all files within it are automatically encrypted as well, ensuring the protection of the folder's contents, which include subfolders and files. EFS uses symmetric and asymmetric key cryptography for the encryption and decryption process. Symmetric key algorithms such as Advanced Encryption Standard (AES) and Triple Data Encryption Standard (3DES) are used to generate a per-file random key, known as the File Encryption Key (FEK). This FEK is used to encrypt and decrypt the file's contents. There are several options available to encrypt files using EFS, including the Windows User Interface and the cipher command-line tool. The cipher tool provides various options for creating and managing EFS-encrypted files.

Encrypting a File or Directory

1. Right-click the file and select "Properties."

2. On the "General" tab, click "Advanced."

3. Check the box that says "Encrypt contents to secure data."

4. Enable "EFS (Encrypting File System)."

5. A prompt will appear, asking what you want to do. Choose either "Encrypt the file and its parent folder (recommended)" or "Encrypt the file only." If you choose the first option, the parent directory will be encrypted as well.

6. After encryption, a padlock icon will appear on the file.

Steps to back up the file certificate and key:

1. After encrypting the file or directory, a notification will appear, saying "Back up your file encryption." If this pop-up does not appear, you can retrieve the certificate by searching for "Internet Options" in the control panel.

2. Select the "Content" tab and click "Certificates."

3. In the new window, select the relevant certificate.

4. Next, click "Export."

5. Whether selecting the pop-up or going through the Internet options, the "Certificate Export Wizard" will appear.

6. In the wizard, select "Export all extended properties" and "Enable certificate privacy."

7. In the dialog box, create and confirm your password.

8. Click "Next," and you will be prompted to browse the file explorer to select a destination for the file.

9. Name the file and save it as a .PFX.

10. Click "Save," and the certificate will begin exporting.

Architecture and Components

It is important to understand the architecture of Windows EFS as having deeper knowledge of the feature may aid in successful access to the encrypted target file.

User Profile

The EFS encryption process is initiated and managed in the Windows user profile which defines the environment for a user after entering their account. The user profile contains all of the respective user's encryption certifications and those certificate's privacy keys

Encryption Certificate

The EFS certificate file is commonly stored in the "%APPDATA%\Microsoft\
SystemCertificates\My\Certificates" directory, serving as a vital link between the user,
the EFS key-pair, and the encrypted file. Deleting the certificate file renders EFS-
encrypted files inaccessible. You can create a new EFS certificate and key-pair using the
cipher /k command for subsequent file encryption. To apply the new key-pair to already
encrypted files, utilize the cipher /u command. The thumbprint, a unique identifier
derived from the certificate's contents, is stored in the registry at HKCU\SOFTWARE\
Microsoft\Windows NT\CurrentVersion\EFS\CurrentKeys (Ramshankar, 2021) and
viewable with the cipher /Y command. This thumbprint provides a distinctive reference
to the certificate. When a new certificate is created, the old certificate becomes obsolete,
and the new certificate is used for subsequent encryption operations. It's stored in the
user's certificate store, a part of their user profile, ensuring new encrypted files utilize the
new certificate.

File Encryption Key

The File Encryption Key (FEK) is a randomly generated symmetric key that is uniquely
associated with each file. It provides fast encryption and decryption operations for large
file sizes and is encrypted using the public key from the EFS encryption certificate. The
encrypted key is then stored in the file's metadata. The key-pair certificate, created
upon initiation of the EFS process at the user level, plays a vital role in the encryption
process. Subsequent files encrypted by the same user can utilize the same public key
to encrypt the FEK, while the private key is used for decrypting the FEK. EFS supports
key-pair generation using both RSA and ECC algorithms. The key-pair file consists of
three elements: public key properties, private key properties, and an export flag. The
public key properties are stored in plain text, ensuring easy access when needed. On the
other hand, the private key properties and export flag are securely stored as DPAPI (Data
Protection Application Programming Interface) blobs, ensuring that only authorized
users have access to the private key. This robust key-pair structure ensures the security,
integrity, and controlled access of the encryption process.

Data Recovery Agent

An optional component that can be configured to enable data recovery if a user loses
access to their EFS-encrypted files is the Data Recovery Agent (DRA). The DRA's own

encryption certificate is added to the recovery policy of the system. The certificate contains a private key capable of decrypting files that were encrypted by others. The Data Recovery Agent (DRA) enhances data protection by enabling authorized entities to recover EFS-encrypted files in case of user access loss, ensuring data availability and integrity. When it comes to recovering EFS-encrypted files, utilizing the built-in agent-based recovery feature is the simplest and most effective approach. This feature involves configuring a recovery agent, which plays a crucial role in the recovery process by encrypting the FEK with the agent's public key and adding it to the $EFS stream (Ramshankar, 2021). This ensures that the recovery agent possesses the necessary access and capabilities to decrypt the FEK and successfully recover the encrypted data whenever it is required. By leveraging this agent-based recovery feature, digital forensics experts can effectively examine and analyze EFS-encrypted files, leveraging their knowledge and expertise in the field to aid in the investigation and recovery process.

Recovery Agent Policy

EFS encryption employs the RSA algorithm as the default with a 2048-bit key. When using RSA, the key-pair file is created in the "%APPDATA%\Microsoft\Crypto\RSA\" directory. The EFS Recovery Agent Policy is instrumental in an Active Directory environment as it defines the configuration settings and rules for DRAs. These agents, authorized users or groups, are capable of decrypting encrypted files as part of the recovery process. Managed through Group Policy (Openspecs-Office, 2018), this policy ensures the enforcement of security measures and safeguards data integrity. This specification outlines a range of group policy settings, including enabling/disabling EFS and defining file recovery policies. Administrators have the flexibility to fine-tune the functionality of EFS according to their environment's specific security requirements, guaranteeing the protection and integrity of encrypted files.

Metadata

EFS-encrypted files have additional metadata that is stored alongside the file's content. The metadata is related to the encryption processes and includes which FEK was used to decrypt the file, what EFS certificates were used, information about the encryption certificates associated with the file, and other file-related details such as file attributes, timestamps, and encryption-related flags.

EFS Artifact Examination

Understanding EFS is essential for experts to identify EFS-encrypted files during the investigation process. Encrypted files often contain valuable evidence and being able to recognize them allows investigators to reprioritize their examination process to deploy appropriate decryption efforts. Additionally, knowledge of EFS artifacts is crucial in comprehending how encryption impacts file recovery efforts, enabling experts to navigate and overcome potential challenges in the decryption or recovery process.

EFS0.LOG

When a file is encrypted, the EFS creates a file called EFS0.LOG, which documents the events that occurred during the encryption process. Once the encryption process is complete, the EFS0.LOG is automatically removed. This log file is owned by SYSTEM and lives within the NTFS system volume where the file selected for encryption resides. Utilizing data carving tools, a digital forensic investigator may be able to retrieve the EFS0.LOG file from the system volume (Ramshankar, 2021). This file may not provide useful information, or it could contain information about the encrypted file including the file paths, timesteps, and access history. The access history may contain information about the user, date, and timestamps which can be utilized for establishing or verifying a timeline. Investigators may be able to find correlations and validate the authenticity of other artifacts such as user activity logs to identify discrepancies that may be present.

EFS0.TMP

Another temporary file, known as EFS0.TMP, is created and owned by the SYSTEM when a file is selected to be encrypted. This temporary file contains a copy of the plain text of the file. Once the encryption is completed, this file is removed. Due to the contents of the plain text file being copied, a minimum available size that is greater than or equal to the original file size is required in order for this temporary file to be contained within the volume. Essentially, the EFS0.TMP file is an extracted plain text replica of the original file. Prior to the release of NTFS 3.1, it was possible to retrieve the EFS0.TMP file with the plain text contents. However, this vulnerability has been addressed by always overwriting the EFS0.TMP with null bytes. As a digital forensic expert, it is important to note the version of the device's NTFS system being investigated. It may be possible to retrieve the contents of the EFS0.TMP file at the state in which it was an exact plain text replica of the file prior to encryption with tools like Sleuth Kit, should the NTFS system be old enough.

NTFS $LogFile

The NTFS $LogFile known as the NTFS transaction log is a binary file that serves as an event log. It records changes and operations performed in the NTFS volume. The $LogFile is used for system failures in order for the NTFS system to reliably recover. An entry is written in the $LogFile when an MFT resident file is encrypted under the DeleteAttribute operation (Operation Code: 0x06). The entry contains the plain text content of the MFT resident file. It is possible to retrieve this plain text content from the DeleteAttribute operation (0x06) and the DATA attribute type (0x80) (Ramshankar, 2021). However, it is also very possible that the entries in the $LogFile have been overwritten during normal file system operation. This approach is also limited to the resident plain text files that are subsequently encrypted.

DPAPI Blob

When digital forensic investigators obtain the password for a system, they may be able to decrypt an EFS file by extracting the private key from the DPAPI blob. The passcode can be utilized to generate a pre-key used to decrypt the Master Key file. The Master Key is a symmetric key used to decrypt the DPAPI blob (Grafnetter M., 2020). The Master Key files live in the %APPDATA%\Microsoft\Protect directory. The private key from the DPAPI blob can be utilized to decrypt the encrypted FEK, which once unlocked can be used to decrypt the EFS-encrypted file.

"Efsm" Pool Tag

It may be possible to retrieve the FEK (File Encryption Key) used for decrypting the corresponding EFS-encrypted file from the kernel memory. Inside the non-paged pool region of the kernel memory, investigators may be able to identify the FEK through the "Efsm" pool tag (EFS driver). The EFS FEKs are written to the Efsm pool object during the encryption of a file. Take note that when the host restarts the system, these Efsm pool objects will be lost, meaning this may not be a viable option by the time the digital forensic expert acquires the machine for investigation. If investigators are able to get the FEK, they must then determine which encrypted file can be decrypted with this key, as all encrypted files have their own FEK.

Encryption Tools

Even though Windows offers built-in encryption tools, there are many open source tools that can be accessed easily for free. It is important for digital forensic investigators to understand a multitude of encryption approaches, and they can be combined together to offer additional layers of security that will need to be bypassed during an investigation. We will cover VeraCrypt, which offers disk encryption like BitLocker, as well as QuickCrypto, which encrypts individual files like EFS does.

VeraCrypt

VeraCrypt has fully replaced TrueCrypt, a tool that had similar functionality; in fact, VeraCrypt utilized the old TrueCrypt code and has solved many of the once-popular tool's vulnerabilities. VeraCrypt is an open source disk encryption tool and provides cross-platform compatibility. Algorithms that VeraCrypt offers, including AES, Serpent, and Twofish, can be used individually and combined. VeraCrypt advertises plausible deniability through hidden volumes and hidden operating systems; this poses challenges in proving the existence of encrypted data. Hidden volumes are indistinguishable from random data, while hidden operating systems create concealed encrypted environments within regular ones. This complexity hinders forensic investigations, requiring advanced techniques like memory analysis and data carving to uncover evidence within VeraCrypt volumes. This tool can be found at `www.veracrypt.fr/en/Downloads.html`.

QuickCrypto

QuickCrypto is advertised as secure and offers easy-to-use strong encryption. It allows many files to be kept securely within one encrypted file volume, where files can each be accessed easily. Users may utilize Blowfish, AES, Serpent, or Twofish encryption algorithms for file and volumes. Single and multiple files, folders, subfolders, passwords, and emails can be secured without a file type limitation as it encrypts text, video, picture, document, and audio file types, which includes those on USB and hard drives. QuickCrypt adheres to cryptographic standards for key derivation and cipher block chaining for confidentiality. Systems that have been encrypted with QuickCrypt will pose an additional challenge for digital forensic investigators. QuickCrypt can be downloaded at `http://quickcrypto.com/download.html`.

Encryption Analysis Tools

FTK Imager and Encase are two widely recognized and accepted tools for encryption analysis. They are crucial in digital forensics investigations since they allow investigators to analyze encrypted data and extract valuable evidence.

FTK

FTK Imager, a widely used digital forensic analysis tool, enables digital forensic investigators to identify, navigate, and access the content of EFS-encrypted files. With FTK Imager, digital forensic analysts can recover metadata and analyze the content within an integrated digital forensic environment (Kessler, 2015). The tool supports the imaging of encrypted drives, including those protected with EFS, allowing the creation of digital forensic images that retain the encrypted state of the data for further analysis that may contain supporting evidence for the investigation. FTK Imager allows investigators to be able to image a live system and conduct support keyword searching within EFS-encrypted files. Digital forensic investigators can navigate the file system, view metadata, access file contents, and analyze the EFS encryption attributes. To inquire about downloading FTK Imager, visit `https://go.exterro.com/l/43312/2023-05-03/fc4b78`.

EnCase

EnCase, provided by OpenText, offers EFS decryption functionality; investigators can examine and extract information related to EFS certificates. EnCase also offers functionality specifically designed to identify EFS-encrypted files within a digital forensic image or live system, making it easier to identify relevant encrypted data. Encase can also generate complete reports on EFS-encrypted files and associated metadata. Knowing how to use EnCase for EFS certificate analysis, encrypted file identification, and reporting is crucial for successful digital forensic investigations. Like FTK Imager, EnCase supports users in the decryption of EFS-encrypted files, allowing access to potentially important information such as metadata and file attributes. Inquire about EnCase at `www.opentext.com/products/encase-forensic`.

Steganography

Steganography is a methodology whereby someone may hide evidence on a digital device. Therefore, it is important for any forensic analyst to have an understanding of this topic.

What Is Steganography?

Steganography aims to ensure that a message remains undetected even if the medium is intercepted. Various techniques can be employed to hide and protect information without immediately raising suspicion. The term "steganography" originates from the Greek words "steganos" and "graphein" which together mean "hidden writing" or "covered writing" (Sushil & Shahi, n.d.). In the pre-digital era, people would hide and transmit messages by sealing them in vessels or using creative mediums during times of war. For example, in both World Wars, messages were concealed in knitted materials or embroidered on silk to transmit critical information to allies across enemy lines. By intentionally manipulating stitches or adjusting the number of knitting gauges, a hidden message could be conveyed. This technique closely resembles line shifting, which can be applied to digital files today (Fairbairn et al., 2023). Proficiency in steganography techniques relies on a deep understanding of computer systems.

Must-know terms and definitions:

- **Payload**: The data intended for covert communication. Payload and secret will be used interchangeably.

- **Cover**: The file to undergo alterations for the purpose of concealing the payload.

- **Carrier**: The file that contains the payload. The steganographic [medium type] will also be used to describe the carrier where the medium types are image, audio, video, and text.

- **Embedding**: The process of hiding the payload in a cover file. This process will alternatively be referred to as encoding.

- **Extraction**: The retrieval of the payload from a steganographic file. Also referred to as decoding.

Steganographic Process

Steganography is the process of concealing secret information within a digital media file such as a text, image, or video file in which the hidden data is not visible to the human eye. The process begins with an initiating party who supplies an initial secret message, a secret key, and an original medium of their choosing to undergo an encoding process to produce a nearly identical replica known as the carrier file. Upon inputting the sent steganographic carrier medium and the correct secret key into a corresponding steganographic decoder, the receiving party will be able to retrieve the embedded secret message, as demonstrated in Figure 13-1.

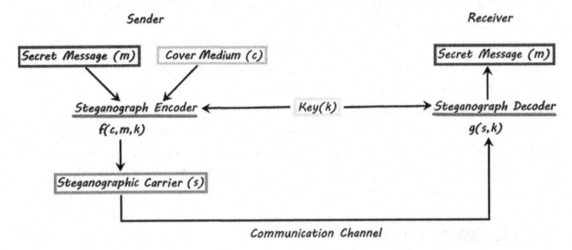

Figure 13-1. *Visual representation of the general steganographic process*

Steganography Domains

Steganography algorithms typically fall into two domain types, spatial domain and transform domain. These domains apply to video, audio, and image steganography.

Spatial Domain

Spatial domain methods directly alter the medium's binary data to conceal the hidden message. This approach allows for easy implementation and direct manipulation of raw data that is organized in a spatial layout. When manipulating images, this steganography technique modifies the pixel values in place. When the medium is a video, the spatial domain is represented by individual frames; in the simplest terms, a frame is a still image with the same pixel properties of a typical image. Additionally, information can be hidden across multiple frames or within the video's temporal characteristics. In audio steganography, the hidden information is encoded within the waveform of the audio data, such as if the amplitude or phase of the audio were altered. The spatial domain is thus referring to the structure of the audio waveform as the raw data.

Transform Domain

Transform domain methods provide an alternative representation of the medium's data. It is the process by which various mathematical processes are applied to the spatial domain, effectively transforming the data into the frequency domain. As a mathematically intensive and complex process, the intricacies involved in reaching the frequency domain are outside of the scope of this chapter. While a high-level overview is provided here, I encourage readers to delve deeper into the specifics of the transform domain as it offers fascinating insights and may be a rewarding learning experience. Alterations in the transform domain are difficult to detect, are robust in preserving the embedded payload, and result in lower distortion effects. The classifications of various transform domain algorithms fall under the following three categories: the Discrete Cosine Transform, Discrete Wavelet Transform, and Discrete Fourier Transform (Surana, 2017).

Discrete Cosine Transform

The Discrete Cosine Transform (DCT) transforms the spatial domain into the frequency one through application of cosine functions. To better understand the idea behind the frequency domain, consider an image of a tree. Areas of the image that have high frequencies are convoluted with fine details, such as the individual leaves which are lost when a person gazes upon the entire image. These areas are the target for embedding payload in many DCT-based algorithms. Low frequency areas are the most noticeable part of an image like the more prominent branches and the tree trunk. These areas draw the most attention; however, some algorithms do still embed data in low frequency areas.

Discrete Wavelet Transform

Both the Discrete Wavelet Transform (DWT) and DCT operate by breaking down an image into high and low frequency components. However, DWT and DCT enter the frequency domain by applying different functions; DWT employs a series of wavelet functions rather than cosine functions. The impact of using wavelet functions captures not just the frequency domain like in DCT but also the spatial one. Two advantages of DWT are space-frequency localization and multi-resolution decomposition (Tushara, 2016), allowing for a focused examination of different frequency sub-bands and scales.

Discrete Fourier Transform

The Discrete Fourier Transform (DFT) technique is more commonly used in audio steganography.

Each signal is broken down into their sinusoidal frequency components to determine the strength of the overall signal; this allows to identify the prominence of each component in the signal. Depending on the DFT algorithm variation, certain signals will be selected for the payload embedding process. Because the alterations are happening in the frequency domain, the steganographic output contains imperceptible data that is quite difficult to detect in the time domain. The time domain is the representation of signals prior to entering the transform domain.

Types of Steganography

The medium types that will be covered are image, video, audio, and text steganography.

Image

Of the various steganography methods and techniques, image steganography stands out as one of the most commonly exploited. By manipulating the smallest units of a digital image, known as pixels, imperceptible messages can be concealed. Due to this vast amount of data, manual analysis by investigators becomes impractical and time-consuming. Furthermore, the subtle variations and patterns in pixels are only discernible at a microscopic level. Therefore, digital forensic investigators heavily rely on advanced software applications and algorithms specifically designed for identifying hidden data, detecting inconsistencies, and uncovering manipulations. Expertise in image analysis plays a vital role in extracting concealed information, detecting tampering, and drawing meaningful conclusions from the extensive pixel data present in digital images.

It is important to understand the structure of pixels. Pixels are made up of three 8-bit values ranging from 0 to 255 that represent a combination of red, green, and blue (RGB) values. Each value represents the amount of light; 0 is represented by black, meaning there is 0 light, and 255 is represented by white or the maximum light value. Each RGB combination creates a unique color. The quality and level of detail in an image are determined by its pixel count, which can reach millions or even billions. This is shown in Figure 13-2.

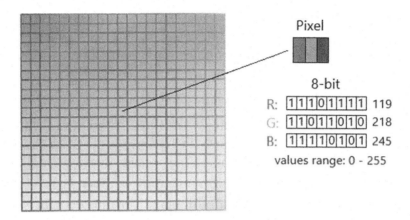

Figure 13-2. *Visualization of pixel composition*

Least Significant Bit

The least significant bit (LSB) technique is used in the spatial domain to manipulate the 8-bit RGB pixel values by modifying the rightmost bit. This rightmost bit represents the value 2^0 or 1. For example, the binary value 11111111 corresponds to the decimal value 255. By changing the rightmost bit to 0 (11111110), the decimal value becomes 254. The difference between these 8-bit values is only one. This minimal difference is why the rightmost bit is known as the least significant bit. As each pixel is composed of an 8-bit value for each of the RGB values, there are three least significant bits which will be replaced by a subsection of the payload (Surana, 2017). The color of the original RGB pixel value is perceived as identical to that of the altered pixel value, resulting in minimal impact on the overall appearance of the image. The differences are imperceptible to the naked eye, as illustrated in Figure 13-3.

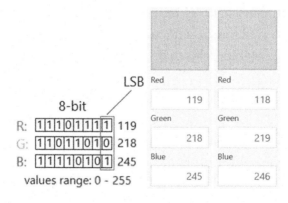

Figure 13-3. *Highlighting the least significant bit and its impact at the pixel level*

Other Common Algorithms

Some of the common algorithms include pixel value differencing, F5, and bit-plane complexity segmentation; however, there are many other algorithms and variations that exist.

Pixel Value Differencing

In pixel value differencing (PVD), the payload is determined by reviewing the difference between two consecutive pixels which are selected for embedding the data. By carefully selecting the pixels and modifying their values based on the secret message, the hidden information can be encoded within the image while maintaining a visually similar appearance. This is a spatial domain technique.

F5

The F5 image steganography algorithm is a transform domain technique incorporating matrix encoding of the secret message. This method follows JPEG compression techniques (DCT and quantization) to reach the frequency domain for the encoding process. The algorithm produces a shuffling key based on the secret key, which generates the pseudo-random path for shuffling DCT coefficients. F5 relies on shuffling to achieve permutation straddling. The purpose of permutation straddling is to uniformly scatter the image alterations from the payload encoding process throughout the cover image. By following the matrix encoding algorithm, the payload is encoded into the nonzero DCT coefficients, which results in the least amount of changes in the overall image. F5 completes the JPEG compression step and promptly uncompresses the image to output the final steganographic image. The F5 algorithm is known for being resistant to statistical attacks (Westfeld, 2001).

Bit-Plane Complexity Segmentation

Bit-plane complexity segmentation steganography (BPCS) is a technique that takes advantage of the 24-bit color depth in images to increase the storage capacity for hidden data. Complex areas in the bit planes of the image are replaced with the payload; this technique can be applied not only to images but also to other types of digital files and signals. Because BPCS considers the complexities of the bit plane when embedding the payload regardless of their spatial arrangement, BPCS can be considered as a hybrid approach of both the spatial and transform domains.

Audio

Audio steganography embedding methods conceal a message in recorded audio. The following methods outlined, in some cases, pair with the Human Auditory System (HAS) to ensure that the sender's message cannot be heard within audio signals by a casual listener. Information can be concealed within common audio formats such as WAV, AU, and MP3 audio files. Steganophony is a term under the audio steganography umbrella which involves hiding information within recordings of the human voice. This is ultimately to ensure that the original audio quality is concealing a message that is imperceptible to the human ear.

Effective audio steganography requires data to be embedded in a manner that is unable to be picked up by the human ear, which is sensitive to frequencies between 2000 and 500 Hz and can detect noise at 20 to 20,000 Hz. This may vary from person to person. One strategy is taking advantage of louder sounds present, which can mask quieter sounds due to the relatively small differential range of the HAS. Another includes taking advantage of the fact that the HAS cannot detect the absolute phase of a sound but can perceive the relative phase between different sounds and audio signals to conceal data. Audio phase refers to a point in time within a sound wave. The sound waves are the vibration of air, and what we're hearing are changes in air pressure. Though the HAS has a large range of dynamic sound, meaning it can perceive a wide range of sound intensities (Djebbar, 2012), it is still possible for people to effectively hide messages without raising suspicion.

Parity Coding

Parity coding is a more robust technique for hiding data inside digital audio files, where each region's parity bit is matched with the corresponding hidden message secret bit. When a match occurs, the encoding within the region will occur utilizing the same parity bit values. If they do not match, the LSB of one of the samples in the region is flipped. Because alterations occur directly on individual audio samples, this classifies as a spatial domain method.

Phase Coding

Phase coding is an audio steganography technique that involves replacing the phase of the original audio segment with a reference phase representing the hidden data. In simpler terms, it encodes the payload by introducing phase shifts in the phase

418

spectrum of a digital signal. This encoding method ensures that the hidden data remains imperceptible in terms of signal-to-noise ratio, making it inaudible. This technique operates in the Discrete Fourier Transform (DFT) domain.

Echo Hiding

Echo hiding is a robust technique that ensures higher security and offers a high data transmission rate. In this method, secret data is concealed within a sound file by inserting an echo signal into a discrete signal. The echo signal acts as a carrier for the hidden data, providing increased robustness compared to previous methods that relied on noise induction. Echo hiding is categorized as a spatial domain technique.

Spread Spectrum

The spread spectrum technique is a very robust technique utilized in military communication. It involves spreading secret data over multiple frequency bands in the transform domain (Chanu, 2012). This data is difficult to detect, particularly because of the low signal-to-noise ratio in each frequency band. Even when sections are removed, the data can still be recovered; the only way to fully terminate the data is to destroy the carrier signal.

There are two commonly used spread spectrum techniques in steganography.

Direct Sequence Spread Spectrum

Direct sequence spread spectrum (DSSS) is a pseudorandom spreading sequence, also known as the spreading code, that is utilized to modify the original payload. This code, when combined with the carrier signal, spreads the energy of the payload across multiple frequencies increasing its resilience to interference and making it difficult for unauthorized recipients to detect. The hidden message can then only be extracted when a receiver is equipped with the correct spreading code. This property of DSSS ensures the security and confidentiality of the hidden information, limiting access to intended recipients.

Frequency Hopping Spread Spectrum

Frequency hopping spread spectrum (FHSS) is a technique that offers effective protection against interference by synchronizing the sender and receiver to the same frequency hopping pattern. This pattern involves rapidly changing the carrier signal across a predetermined sequence of frequencies. Unauthorized recipients would face the challenge of deciphering the specific frequency hopping pattern in order to intercept the transmitted payload.

Video

Various methods, including the previously discussed LSB method, can be used to conceal files or data using video files as steganographic carriers. The information is concealed within common digital video formats such as MP4, MPEG, and AVI. Video files contain a series of images, audio, and other data, sharing attributes with audio and image formats. Regardless of the method, it is important to be aware that video files will be much larger. Therefore, there is more opportunity to hide information. These formats also include specific elements like audio channels, pixels, and frame rates which are unique to video files.

Embedding Methods

Video steganography is divided into four embedding methods, intra-embedding, inter-embedding, pre-embedding, and post-embedding.

Intra-embedding

In this method, the sender will embed the payload within individual frames of the video; it is also known as frame-based or frame-level embedding. This can simplify the embedding process and reduce complexities as a frame is merely a still image. Intra-embedding allows for each frame to contain its own isolated hidden message. This is a spatial domain method.

Inter-embedding

Inter-embedding refers to taking the temporal relationships between frames into account when distributing the payload across multiple frames. The objective is to modify frames in a manner that maintains consistency and ensures a video sequence remains cohesive. This is a much more complex method compared to the other video embedding techniques and is classified as a transform domain technique.

Pre-embedding

Pre-embedding methods involve manipulating the raw video data in either the spatial or transform domains. The sender embeds the payload into the video stream before compression. The receiver can decode the compressed video using a video "coder-decoder" or codec to extract the hidden message. This pre-embedding technique is independent of the specific video coding process and allows for various message-hiding methods. However, the use of video codecs may result in some loss of the hidden message, making extraction and detection more challenging and less efficient.

Post-embedding

Post-embedding methods involve manipulating and hiding a secret message within the compressed video bitstream, that is, the digital representation of video data. This allows for direct embedding and extraction without the need for complete decoding and re-encoding of the entire video content. The technique maximizes the use of existing hardware resources and does not significantly impact the video compression codec system. However, due to compressed bit rate constraints, the amount of data that can be embedded is limited. The embedding of the payload can occur in the spatial or transform domains (Liu, 2019).

Text

Throughout history, hidden messages have been exchanged through tangible non-digital mediums, making it a primary channel for steganography. Even in the digital age, text steganography remains a popular technique for concealing messages. By leveraging the structure and properties of digital text files, individuals can utilize various methods to hide data. These methods include adjusting text font settings, exploiting spelling errors, and manipulating text layout. Text documents, appearing ordinary, provide a camouflage for illicit activities and data transmission without raising suspicion from authorities.

There are three main techniques for concealing data within digital text files: format-based steganography, randomized and statistical methods, and linguistic-based strategies. Understanding these techniques is crucial for digital forensic investigators. By studying text steganography, investigators can develop strategies to detect and uncover hidden messages within digital text files (Nihad, 2017). It is important to note that while text steganography has limited usability in digital data hiding due to its low redundancy, it remains historically significant for concealing small messages and codes.

Format Based

Format-based methods involve manipulating how text is displayed in order to conceal hidden messages. Manipulating the display of text-based information with the express goal of seamlessly blending hidden messages in order for the text to remain inconspicuous to an unintended recipient is known as format-based steganography. As the name entails, the secret communication is presented in the format of the text within a document (Surana, 2017). Manipulation methods that will be expanded on later include utilizing vertical or horizontal shifts of the text, taking advantage of the white space, and strategically presenting information by manipulating the look of characters.

Line-Shift Coding

This method involves utilizing the format settings in a word processor to shift the vertical space between lines of text. The different lines of text that are shifted up or down can represent a 1 or 0 to communicate a message to the intended recipient. Utilizing shifts that are only a fraction of an inch results in difficult detection without a detailed inspection.

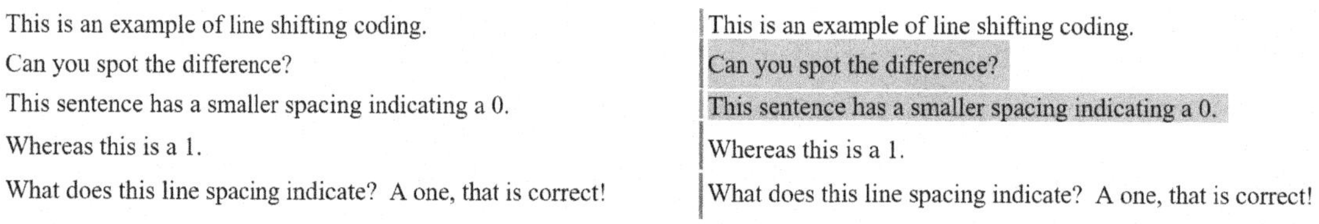

This is an example of line shifting coding.
Can you spot the difference?
This sentence has a smaller spacing indicating a 0.
Whereas this is a 1.
What does this line spacing indicate? A one, that is correct!

This is an example of line shifting coding.
Can you spot the difference?
This sentence has a smaller spacing indicating a 0.
Whereas this is a 1.
What does this line spacing indicate? A one, that is correct!

Figure 13-4.   *Example of line-shift coding*

Word-Shift Coding

This method involves deciphering the hidden text by determining whether a word is shifted horizontally to the left or right and by how much. Just as with line-shift coding, the movements when utilizing word-shift coding are very minimal in order to avoid revealing to an unintended recipient that there is a message hidden within a given text. These shifts are just enough for those in the know to identify what shifts are representing a 1 and what is a 0.

White Space Manipulation

Everything in a text document can be manipulated to hide a message, including the white space itself. By strategically utilizing spaces, tabs, and line breaks, binary representing codes can be embedded within a document without being quickly detected. White space manipulation can go unnoticed by a document reader, while the spacing within words is serving a deeper purpose. This is shown in Figure 13-5. Notice that there are extra blanks; these are used to hide additional data.

This is an example   of white space   manipulation.
Hidden code:10010110

Figure 13-5. *Example of white space manipulation*

Random and Statistical Generation

Random and statistical generation is a text steganography method that hides payload within text by leveraging randomness and statistical patterns. It involves analyzing the frequency distribution of words or characters in the text and replacing certain elements with binary counterparts to encode the hidden message. This technique exploits the natural statistical properties of the text, such as word length and the frequency of characters appearing, making the encoded message less noticeable to readers. For example, if "e," "t," and "a" are the most frequent characters within a text, the binary values 0, 1, and 01 can be assigned to them, respectively, to create a hidden code.

In the phrase "create a hidden code," the binary code decoded would be 0110 01 0 0.

Linguistic Based

Linguistic-based methods involve manipulating language and its presentation to convey one message on the surface while hiding another beneath. It's important for investigators to recognize that a seemingly coherent text with no apparent formatting changes should not be dismissed without further examination. A hastily composed narrative riddled with spelling mistakes, jargon, and acronyms could potentially hold crucial information essential to a case (Nihad, 2017).

Synonym Replacement

Synonyms are words or phrases that have similar or identical meanings. In the context of text steganography, synonyms can be used to hide a message within the overt text, which refers to the visible text in a document that acts as a cover for the hidden message. For instance, a seemingly ordinary instruction to "run to the store and pick up milk, eggs, and sugar" could conceal the actual directive of "raid the supply lines."

Acronyms

Acronyms are handy collections of letters or a word that can serve as a mnemonic device for remembering organization names, procedures, and much more in everyday communication. These are used everywhere from informal communication to all over government websites; it's impossible not to run into them. Utilizing the previous example, let's say the narrative is about going to the store and running to get milk, eggs, and sugar. If the investigator sees

> Bobby, I completely forgot to tell you to run to the store and pick up milk, eggs, and sugar. AFAIR there should have been a note along with the to-do to prepare for your interview with the AAD. I hope to learn how that goes well, leave me a text as I'm going to be AFK most of the day.

in this case, the overt text communicates:

AFAIR: As Far As I Remember

AAD: American Academy of Dermatology

AFK: Away From Keyboard

while the hidden messages could be

AFAIR: A Frontal Assault Is Readying

AAD: Attack at Dawn

AFK: All Facilities Known

Deliberate Misspellings

Manipulating the presentation of words is an effective way for a hidden message to evade detection by automated surveillance mechanisms. Strategic keyword masking can be achieved through intentional misspelling of words, generating Unicode characters, and using words that closely resemble the original keyword (Sushil & Shahi, n.d.).

For example, the intentional writing of "boomb" instead of "bomb."

The next example replaces characters with Unicode homoglyphs, characters that closely resemble ASCII values. The Unicode homoglyph characters are configured to quickly reveal the hidden message "Loot them."

LoOking f0rward To THe wÉekend, Megan

To better see it:

LoOking f0rward To THe wÉekend, Megan

Taking advantage of this technique is simple and does not require expertise; for this reason, it can be exploited rather easily.

Steganography Tools

Familiarizing yourself with the wide selection of powerful open source tools whether free or with a free trial aids digital forensic experts in their investigation. The following selections presented are popular tools but do not represent the full range of available tools for people to access and use. Though there are many techniques one can use to attempt to deceive investigators, those skilled in these tools can effectively analyze and extract hidden information that can serve as significant evidence in any case (Sushil & Shahi, n.d.). The tools presented here are free or have a limited trial; they are comparable to counterparts that require purchase.

OpenStego

OpenStego is a simple steganography tool. This open source tool was written in Java and is offered as a JAR (Java Archive) file, which will require you to have the Java Runtime Environment (JRE) installed on your machine. A secret message can be concealed within image file types BMP, GIF, JPEG, JPG, PNG, and WBMP. The output file will have the BMP extension. OpenStego employs password encryption to secure your data and ensures its concealment within the image file. OpenStego offers AES 128 and AES 256 encryption algorithms. You can click the Downloads tab to install OpenStego at `www.openstego.com/`

These steps taken to hide a text file with an added layer of encryption into a JPEG image go as follows:

1. Click the "Hide data" tab under the "Data hiding" section. Browse for the message file you want to conceal, the cover to serve as the carrier, and the path name of the file destination. See Figure 13-6.

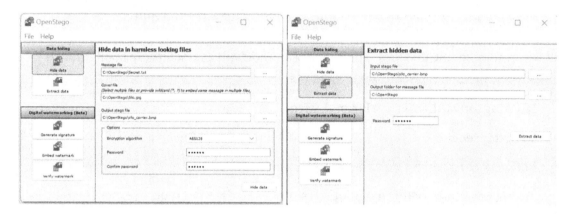

Figure 13-6. *Hiding and extracting data with OpenStego*

2. In the drop-down menu, select the encryption algorithm to add an extra level of security and provide your chosen passwords. Click the "Hide data" button to output the steganographic carrier image. You can see a visual comparison of the cover and carrier in Figure 13-7.

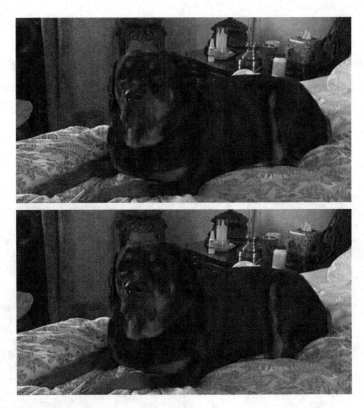

Figure 13-7. *Cover image (top) and OpenStego steganographic carrier image (bottom)*

3.   To extract the hidden data under the "Data hiding" section, ensure
the tab "Extract data" is selected and browse for the carrier output
from step 2. Provide the destination path for the output message
file. Enter the password and click "Extract data."

Hide'N'Send

Similar to OpenStego, this tool provides straightforward functionality and offers
encryption of the hidden text file before embedding. Hide'N'Send utilizes modern
steganographic algorithms, specifically F5 and LSB. Encryption options include AES,
RC4, and RC2. The encryption key is derived from the user's password using hash
functions such as RIPEMD, SHA-512, or MD5. You can download it at https://hide-n-
send.soft32.com/.

QuickStego

QuickStego is an image steganographic tool released by QuickCrypto. QuickStego features a user-friendly interface and displays the selected image and a textbox for composing a message and provides an indication that the selected image contains a concealed message. This tool supports JPG, JPEG, GIF, or BMP formats. You can download and find more information at `http://quickcrypto.com/free-steganography-software.html`. This is shown in Figure 13-8.

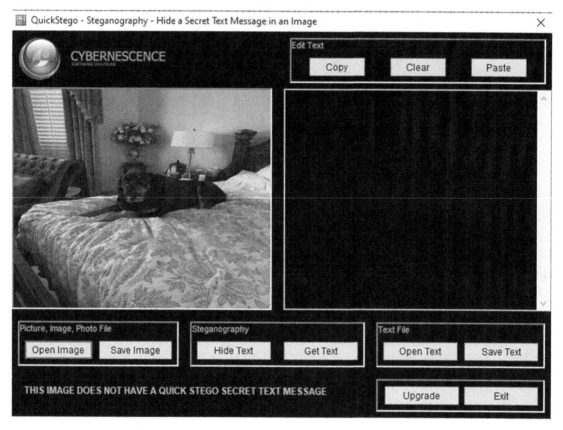

Figure 13-8. *QuickStego GUI display*

DeepSound

DeepSound offers a user-friendly interface where one can hide audio files in MP3, WAV, CDA, and other file formats. It provides advanced features and supports various encryption algorithms such as AES, RC4, and RC2 for secure message encryption. The tool utilizes sophisticated steganographic techniques, including F5 and LSB algorithms, to embed the hidden message seamlessly into the audio file. DeepSound also features an Audio Converter Module, which enables users to convert audio files between various formats such as FLAC, MP3, WMA, WAV, and APE. Download this tool from `http://jpinsoft.net/deepsound`.

1. Click "Open carrier files" and browse for your desired audio file that will serve as the cover. Next, select "Add secret files" and choose the audio file to be embedded.

2. By clicking the "Encode secret files" tab, a window for output options will appear. To add an optional layer of encryption with a password, select the checkbox labeled "Encrypt secret files (AES 256)." This will enable the password input boxes (see Figure 13-9). Finally, click "Encode secret files." You can see this in Figure 13-9.

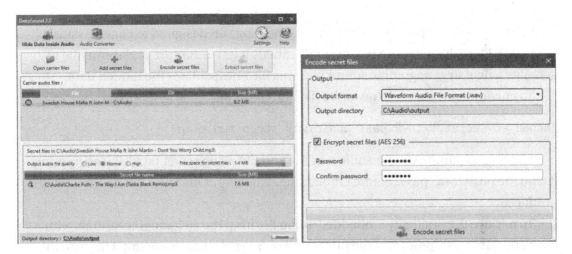

Figure 13-9. *DeepSound GUI – cover and secret audio file selected (left) and configuring encoding options (right)*

3. To extract the previously hidden audio file, click "Open carrier files" and select the output file that was created within your file system in step 2. Notice the file is added under the "files" header in blue rather than green. Immediately, an "enter password" dialog box opens. With the correct password, you will see the previously embedded audio file listed under the "Secret file name" header. You can see this process in Figure 13-10.

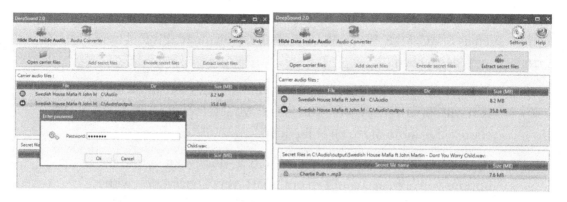

Figure 13-10. *Password validation window (left) and extraction of secret audio file (right)*

MP3Stego

MP3Stego is a simple-to-use command-line program designed to conceal data within MP3 files. It encrypts a text file and embeds it into a compressed sound file to generate a new steganographic sound file. This file encapsulates the hidden data.

To encode a message into an audio file, the command goes as follows:

```
encode -E secret.txt -P pass audio.wav stego_audio.mp3
```

MP3Stego compresses the audio.wav file and hides the secret.txt file by encrypting it with the password "pass" before embedding. The output file stego_audio.mp3 is then produced.

To retrieve the originally embedded audio file from the steganographic one, with the same password "pass", and the previously outputted stego_audio.mp3 file, run the following command:

```
decode -X -P pass stego_audio.mp3
```

The file stego_audio.mp3 is uncompressed into a new file named stego_audio.mp3. pcm, then it extracts the hidden message. The message at this point will need to be decrypted with the password to finally output the hidden message into stego_audio.mp3. txt. You can download MP3Stego from `www.petitcolas.net/steganography/mp3stego/`.

OpenPuff

OpenPuff offers a user interface that provides the capability to hide messages and documents within multiple files. It supports various carrier types, including images, audio, flash, and video formats such as 3GP, MP4, MPG, and VOB. The tool imposes a file size limit of 256MB on the secret file. OpenPuff uses advanced encryption techniques, including symmetric encryption, data scrambling, and data whitening to encrypt your secret file. With OpenPuff, you can distribute a document across several files, with each file containing a portion of the secret document. All files will be necessary to recover the complete hidden file.

Things to keep in mind: OpenPuff can be rather complex, as it requires three passwords and three files from a selection of mediums. The file that the user desires to conceal must be smaller than the cover file. If the file being concealed is larger than the cover file, additional cover files need to be added to embed the hidden file across them. Download OpenPuff at `https://openpuff.en.lo4d.com/windows`.

Here are the steps to hide and unhide files using OpenPuff:

1. Click the "Hide" button on the main screen to access the next window.

2. In the first section, enter three different passwords.

3. In the second section, select the carrier file(s) from your file system. Remember the carrier file(s) must be larger than the cover file. You can select multiple carrier files to meet the size requirements.

4. In the top-right section, choose the cover file you want to hide.

5. Click the "Hide Data!" button to initiate the hiding process.

To unhide the hidden data

1. Go back to the main window and select the "Unhide" button. This will take you to a window similar to when you first hid the file.

2. Enter the three passwords in the same order as before.

3. Select the cover files in the same order as before.

4. If all matches, click the "Unhide!" button to uncover the hidden file.

The process is shown in Figure 13-11.

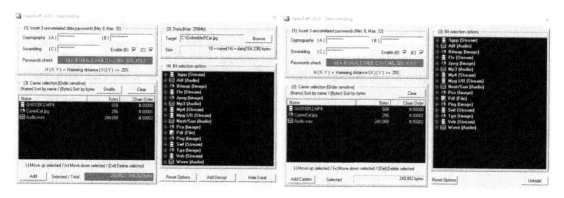

Figure 13-11. *OpenPuff GUI – Data Hiding window (left) and Data Unhiding window (right)*

IronGeek

The hidden code "Loot Them" discussed previously was created with IronGeek which is a simple and free online tool that any person can access to embed a code in minutes. The website can be accessed at `www.irongeek.com/homoglyph-attack-generator.php`.

Begin by entering a phrase or sentence to modify. As characters are entered, columns presenting different homoglyphs will appear below:

1. Modify the letters needed to write out the hidden code by selecting similar looking homoglyphs in the appropriate columns. You may need to scroll horizontally to see all of the columns that appear. This is shown in Figures 13-12 and 13-13.

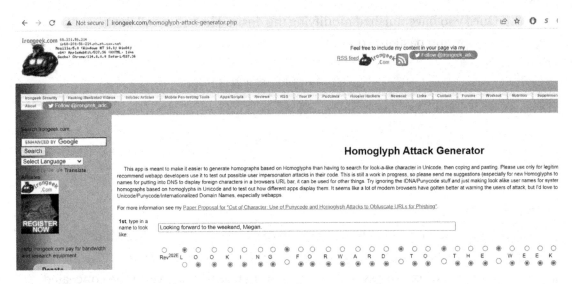

Figure 13-12. *IronGeek Homoglyph Attack Generator home page*

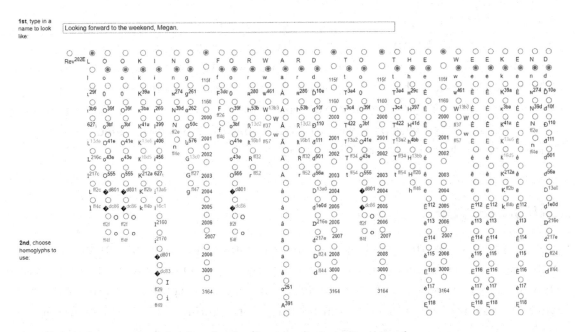

Figure 13-13. *Homoglyph substitution options in IronGeek*

2. Once you have finished modifying the desired letters, scroll down
    to copy and paste the output.

This one is for testing linking:

3rd, Output will
be something
like this:

LoOking f0rward to the weekend, Megan

This one is so you can copy & paste:

LoOking f0rward to the weekend, Megan

SNOW

The SNOW program conceals messages in ASCII text by appending white space to the end of lines, making the hidden message invisible to casual observers. The program also provides optional compression and encryption features to protect the concealed message further. Compression is achieved using a Huffman encoding scheme optimized for English text, which can typically result in 25–40% compression. The home page shares that SNOW is thematically consistent because the encryption algorithm utilized by SNOW is called ICE (brrr...). A 64-bit block cipher operates in 1-bit cipher feedback (CFB) mode. This encryption mode ensures strong security, even when encrypting different messages with the same password. If a message exceeds the available text space, empty lines can be appended to accommodate the overflow. The SNOW program, which stands for Steganographic Nature Of WhiteSpace, can be downloaded from `https://darkside.com.au/snow/index.html`.

Steganalysis

The process of uncovering covert communication, hidden messages, and malicious activities through steganalysis requires thorough investigation and attention to detail. However, it can be a challenging process for digital forensics experts to determine whether files have been subjected to steganography techniques. Activities such as data exfiltration, information theft, or the dissemination of sensitive content can be revealed through steganalysis. Investigators must apply different steganalysis methods depending on the medium and steganography techniques being analyzed, making use of advanced algorithms designed to identify patterns or anomalies, statistical analysis, file format analysis, and visual inspection.

When investigators are manually searching drives, they are doing so with the express purpose of finding inconsistencies that may indicate the presence of steganographic content. One such strategy is carefully observing metadata. The created date and last-modified date are both essential pieces of information. The created date is the date when the file was created on the device and not when it was originally created. An example of an inconsistency could arise from a downloaded MP3 file; if the last-modified date is newer than the created date, it may have been edited using music software or possibly indicate steganography manipulation and should be investigated. Other details, such as inconsistent file sizes like a 4MB picture in a collection of 2MB pictures, can also reveal file manipulation as steganographic images tend to bloat in size as a by-product of processing from steganography tools. Paying close attention to even seemingly minor details is crucial for detecting anomalies and inconsistencies that could lead to compelling evidence. Being detail-oriented is key.

Detection Tools

Detection tools aim to identify hidden data within digital media types. By utilizing these tools, digital forensic investigators can analyze potential steganographic content that may contain crucial evidence of illicit communication or activities. These tools feature techniques such as statistical analysis, visual inspection, and pattern recognition which support investigators in discovering anomalies and potentially valuable insight for an investigation.

StegSpy

StegSpy is a tool that detects steganographic information embedded within images, audio files, and other media formats. This includes a wide variety of file types such as JPEG, PNG, BMP, MP3, and WAV, among many others. StegSpy is capable of identifying both the specific program used, such as Invisible Secrets, JPHideandSeek, Masker, etc., and the start location of the hidden content within the file. Download at `www.spy-hunter.com/stegspy`.

StegSpy did detect the OpenStego carrier image (Figure 13-14) but misclassified the tool detected as Hiderman. When a Hide'N'Send F5 steganographic image was tested on StegSpy, it failed to detect the image as containing a secret message. Using StegSpy is simple:

Step 1: Launch the StegSpy application and select the "Run" button. This will prompt you to select the desired file from the directory and that is it. You can see this in Figure 13-14.

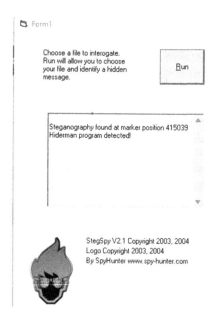

Figure 13-14. *Successful detection of steganographic image utilizing StegSpy*

StegoHunt MP

Many detection tools have severe limitations, have been deprecated, or lack maintenance. WetStone Technologies' StegoHunt, on the other hand, is a well-composed and developed tool. The tool requires extra steps to obtain; however, it may be worth pursuing as it is a standout tool from its up-to-date website, features, and detailed walk-through tutorials. These tutorial videos can be found at `https://video.wetstonetech.com/video-categories/stegohuntmp/`.

Users must go through an inquiry page in order to obtain a free ten-day trial as well as purchasing. StegoHunt MP can generate reports in html and csv file formats which includes algorithms likely used to conceal the hidden data and which files may be steganographic in nature. The analysis includes different statistical tests, depending on the carrier file's medium. Supported file types include image formats (JPEG, BMP, GIF, PNG, TIFF, PCX), audio formats (WAV, MP3, M4A), video formats (M4V, MOV, MP4, AVI, FLV, MPG, ASF), container formats (7z, ZIP, TAR), Microsoft Office files (OLE, .docx, .pptx, .xlsx, etc.), and PDF files. This tool helps extract files hidden within other files and conducts decrypt attacks on the discovered concealed messages. It also improves statistical analysis checks to reduce false positives and improve accuracy. WetTechnology offers a suite of three software: StegoHunt along with StegoAnalyst and StegoBreak. The former is utilized to detect steganography image and audio files, while the latter offers decryption capabilities. Inquire and review details of the suite at www. wetstonetech.com/products/stegohunt-steganography-detection/.

While no steganography method or tool is perfect, the effectiveness of steganalysis tests varies based on the steganographic tool used, with some tools being more efficient in concealing information than others. An additional layer of challenge is always present when suspects employ hidden data techniques.

Statistical Analysis

By exploring statistical analysis techniques, digital investigators can gather insight as to whether there is embedded data or not. However, in this process, files are not decrypted, only analyzed for the plausibility of the need to attempt retrieval of concealed information (Surana, 2017). These techniques streamline the investigation process as they provide supporting evidence for which files to review more closely, saving the investigators from needing to review every file present in a system.

Chi-Square

The objective of the Chi-Square test is to assess the level of randomness introduced to an image from a potential embedding of a secret message. By performing a Chi-Square analysis, investigators can quantify the disparity between frequency distributions in the image and compare it to the expected level of randomness. By partitioning an image into isolated blocks and examining the pixels within each block, the frequency calculation of each pixel value is calculated. The obtained frequency data is then compared using an appropriate statistical model to determine the presence of hidden data. If the difference is significant enough, then it is more likely than not to contain an embedded message.

Residual Based

This technique focuses on observing the statistical property of calculated image residuals to draw a prediction on the possibility of embedded hidden data. The image in question is processed through a statistical model for the purpose of creating an image with pixel values that may be close to the original cover image values; this is merely a prediction of the cover image. The residuals are calculated by the differences between values in the image being reviewed and the image prediction. The final statistical analysis involves measuring the mean, variance, deviations, or spatial dependencies among the residual values. If the results are significant enough, hidden data is probable.

Histogram Based

Separate histograms are developed from the frequencies of the pixel values in each RGB channel that make up the image in question. Digital forensic investigators can analyze the distributions presented for patterns and anomalies. Essentially, if there is embedded data in the image, then the distributions could reflect this.

Deep Learning

Deep learning techniques are being applied to the world of steganography and steganalysis; research in Convolutional Neural Networks (CNNs) and Generative Adversarial Networks (GANs) are working toward achieving more effective results in hiding and uncovering hidden data. CNNs find patterns, learn and recognize features, and exploit spatial relationships, making them effective for detection of steganographic carriers. Several CNN models proposed for steganalysis are Xu-Net, Ye-Net, Yedroudj-Net, SR-Net, Zhu-Net, and GBRAS-Net. GANs are known for performing well in generation tasks and, thus, are best suited for generating steganographic images (Subramanian, 2021). Notable proposed GANs for steganographic purposes are SS-GAN, StarGAN, and StegaStamp. Research has demonstrated advances in improved detection accuracy, feature extraction, and correct binary classification in steganalysis (Tabares-Soto et al., 2021). Furthermore, deep learning models efficiently handle large volumes of data at an accelerated rate compared to existing methods and techniques. As deep learning models continue to develop their capacity to be trained, the existing complexities and challenges of detection, extraction, and decrypting for the purpose of digital forensic analysis will become more streamlined and further empower digital forensic investigators to put forth accurate, timely, and compelling evidence.

Slack Space

What Is Slack Space?

Consider a vehicle's fuel gauge, a display that allows the driver to evaluate at a quick glance how much gas is remaining. In relation to slack space, we can draw a parallel between the segmented display of a fuel gauge and the concept of slack space in a computer system. The display on the fuel gauge informs the driver how much gas is currently contained in the gas tank, just as the file size indicates how much of the allocated cluster it occupies. What is important here is the unused capacity of the gas tank; there is more space that can be utilized just as there is more space that can be utilized in a file cluster but is not presently being utilized. This unused space can be exploited to hide information.

With an understanding of what slack space is, it is critical for one to understand why it is important in order to achieve a thorough investigation. When suspects store files on a machine, there can be intentional and unintentional usage of any slack space which a digital forensic investigator may utilize to uncover hidden information or gather valuable file fragments as evidence. By comparing the logical and physical ends of files, slack space analysis can reveal intentionally concealed information, files that have been modified or tampered with, and manipulated timestamps. Communication logs, encrypted messages, and other forms of covert channels which give details about the suspected person(s) and their activity may be found (Nihad, 2017). Slack space can be advantageous as remnants of deleted files may still reside in slack space; this means that while suspects may have intended for files to be lost, an investigator may be able to recover data by reconstructing the fragments of deleted files. Users can unintentionally create data within the slack space, and this depends on their actions and system behavior. What this means is data in slack space does not necessarily indicate malicious activity. It does, however, require some deeper analysis. Furthermore, utilizing advanced carving techniques can allow an investigator to piece together fragments of files that were not fully overwritten. Slack space is demonstrated in Figure 13-15.

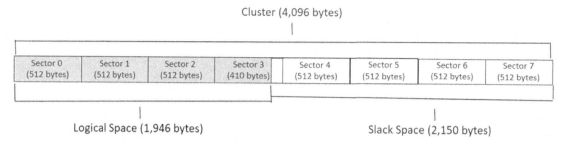

Figure 13-15. *Visualizing file allocation and slack space in the cluster structure*

Must-know terms and definitions:

- **Sector**: The basic unit of data storage on a Windows hard disk. Modern systems utilize a larger sector size of 4096 bytes, also referred to as 4K or 4KB sectors, as opposed to the 512-byte sectors found in traditional systems.

- **Cluster**: A unit of allocated space within a hard disk for data storage. It is a logical grouping of sectors.

- **Hard Disk**: A hard disk is the physical data storage device in a machine that is segmented into clusters of a particular size. The size typically ranges from 4KB to 64KB.

- **Slack Space/File Slack**: The unused allocated space between the logical end of a file and the physical end of a file. Alternatively, file slack can be used interchangeably to describe this leftover space within a cluster. We can calculate the size of slack space by assessing the unallocated or unused storage within a cluster.

Calculating Slack Space

In the realm of hard drives, files are organized within clusters that span multiple sectors. Data is stored in sectors, which are the smallest units of data. Each sector holds a fixed amount of information. Clusters are logical groupings of sectors; only one file can be stored within a cluster. Files can span multiple clusters based on their size and the system's allocation. Each cluster allocated to a file, regardless of its utilization, belongs entirely to that file (Mulazzani, 2013). The sizes of clusters and sectors vary across different machines, making it crucial to look up their sizes when calculating slack space.

When saving a file to the hard disk, it occupies one or more clusters, depending on its size. Smaller files may occupy just one cluster, while larger files may span multiple clusters (Nihad, 2017). By understanding the relationship between files, clusters, and sectors, we gain insight into how data is organized and stored on a hard drive. This knowledge is fundamental in calculating slack space and effectively utilizing the available storage capacity.

Hard Disk Cluster and Sector Sizes

To determine the unused allocated slack space of a file, you can utilize the Windows Command Prompt to find the cluster and sector sizes:

1. In the Windows search bar, type in "Command Prompt."

2. Right-click "Command Prompt."

3. Click "Run as administrator."

4. Run the following command in the terminal window where "C" will be the letter corresponding to the hard disk in question (the command is shown in Figure 13-16):

   ```
   fsutil fsinfo ntfsinfo C:
   ```

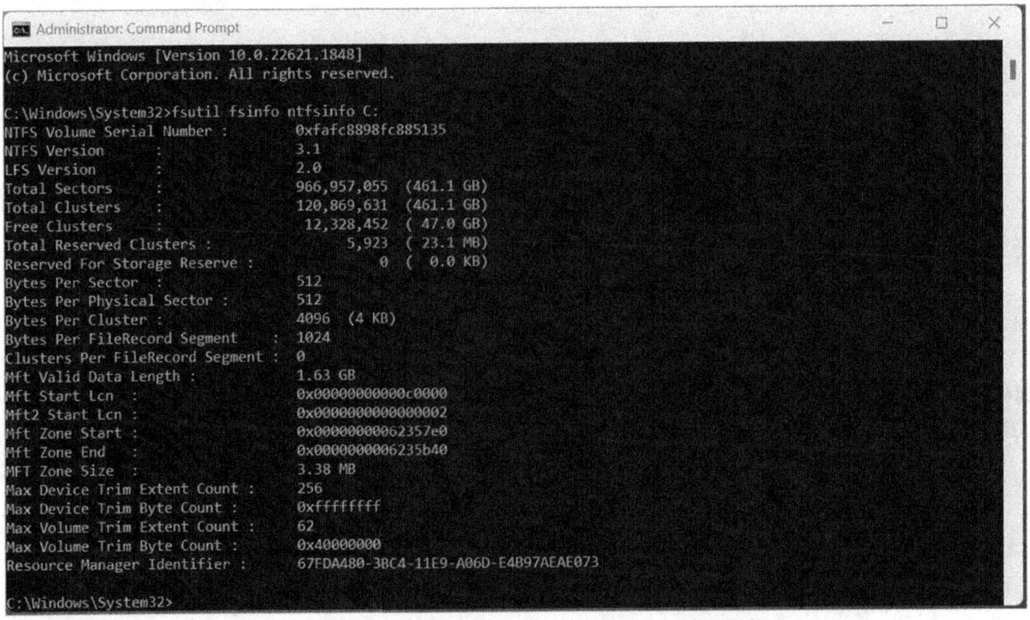

Figure 13-16. *Cluster and sector sizes displayed within the Windows Command Prompt*

Figure 13-16 presents the command result, highlighting key information in yellow. The highlighted information draws your attention to the sector and cluster sizes. These values are essential for calculating the slack space of a file.

This system's cluster sizes are 4096 bytes, while each sector is 512 bytes. We can determine the number of sectors a cluster spans by dividing 4096 by 512, resulting in eight sectors.

File Slack Calculation

In this example, we will calculate the slack space for a single file. The process is similar for folders, where you would need to calculate the individual slack space for each file and sum them together to determine the total slack space in the folder.

For this exercise, I have a .png image file named Slack_Space_Decoy_File. png located within a folder with a file size of 550,070 bytes. This is demonstrated in Figure 13-17.

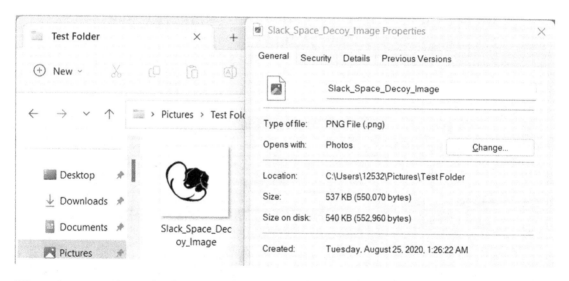

Figure 13-17. *Sample decoy image with file size and total size allocated on disk displayed*

To calculate the slack space, we need to determine how many clusters the file occupies and then calculate the unused space within the last cluster.

Given that the cluster size is 4096 bytes and the file size is 550,070 bytes, we can now proceed with the calculation.

First, let's calculate the number of clusters occupied by the file:

Number_of_clusters = ceil(*file_size / cluster_size*)

where ceil() is a function that rounds up to the nearest whole integer.

Number_of_clusters = ceil(550,070 / 4096) = ceil(134.259765625) = 135 clusters

Next, we calculate the total space occupied by the file:

Total_space_occupied = *number_of_clusters_allocated* × *cluster_size*

Total_space_occupied = 135 × 4096 = 552,960 bytes

As you can see, the resulting size of 552,960 total bytes occupied on the disk aligns with the "Size on disk" displayed under the image properties, as shown in Figure 13-17. Finally, we calculate the slack space:

Slack_space = *Total_space_occupied – file_size*

Slack_space = 552,960 – 550,070 = 2890 bytes

Therefore, the slack space for the file is 2890 bytes. This indicates that the last allocated cluster for this file contains 2890 bytes of unused allocated space.

In terms of sectors, we can calculate the unutilized space as

Unused_sectors = *Slack_space / sector_size*

Unused_sectors = 2890 / 512 = 5.64 sectors

In other words, there are 5.64 sectors out of 8 of unused slack space.

Hiding Data in the Slack Space

Having determined the available slack space in the preceding exercise, I have prepared a text file that will represent the information a suspect is attempting to hide. After walking through this process, we will later utilize an open source tool to detect this hidden file.

Working with our Slack_Space_Decoy_Image.png file from Figure 13-17 as our container file for the hidden data, we will go through the process of hiding a text file in the slack space. Recall this image has a slack space of 2890 bytes. It is important that the intended hidden file does not exceed the available slack space. The file we have prepared is a text file named Hidden_File.txt with a file size of 2641 bytes. This is shown in Figure 13-18.

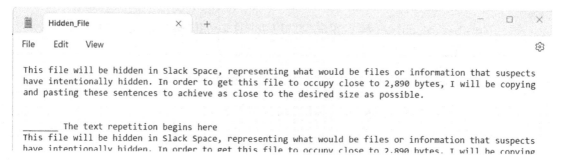

Figure 13-18. *Contents of Hidden_File.txt*

Next, combine the files by appending the text file to the end of the image file. This can be achieved by the Windows CMD command:

```
copy /b image.jpg+message.txt concealed.jpg
```

- "image.jpg" represents the name of the container decoy image file.

- "message.txt" represents the name of the text file that you want to hide.

- "concealed.jpg" is the name you want to give to the resulting combined file.

The "/b" flag is used to indicate binary mode, which treats the files as binary when concatenating them without any additional processing.

Ensure that the image file and text file are in the same directory as the open command prompt or provide the full file paths if they are located elsewhere. You can see this in Figure 13-19.

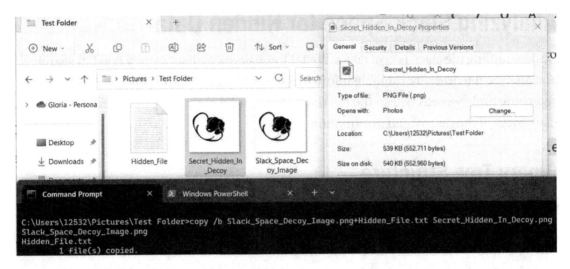

Figure 13-19. *CMD command appending text file to the end of the decoy image, output image showing no visual difference from decoy, and image file size displayed under properties*

Concatenating the text file data to an image does not directly affect the visual appearance of the image. You can see this is true in Figure 13-19. Also, notice how the resulting image Secret_Hidden_In_Decoy.png has a file size of 552,711 bytes; that is compared to the 550,070 bytes file size of the original Slack_Space_Decoy_image.png image. Both images still occupy exactly 552,960 bytes on the disk.

It may not be the case where the metadata updates, especially when combining files with other automated tools; one clear indicator that something is being concealed within slack space is when the file size does not align with its metadata. Some fields of the metadata that can be tampered with or removed include timestamps, author information, and geolocation data, thus making it more challenging to detect hidden files. Modifying the metadata is as simple as running a powershell terminal command with administrator privileges or utilizing open source tools to achieve this for you. As a digital forensic expert, remaining vigilant and being attentive to the metadata is critical as it can provide important insights in an investigation.

People seeking to conceal information that could be compelling evidence against them will attempt to avoid drawing attention to their hidden files. Be aware that suspects will aim to fabricate inconspicuous file locations or place potential evidence within directories with legitimate purpose. Further attempts to cover their tracks include deleting all reminisce of old hidden text and decoy image files. Scripts may even be created to automate this entire process in one step with tools like Python.

Analyzing Slack Space for Hidden Data

Understanding file slack is crucial for digital forensic specialists as they need to search and analyze it to identify valuable information to document their findings. This involves searching for keywords within the file slack space and determining the relevance and usefulness of the discovered information.

Binary Tree Structure

Quick searches of the entire hard disk for hidden files such as documents and logs can be conducted by utilizing full-text indexing techniques. One such technique that can be employed is a binary-tree structure which enhances investigative efficiency by organizing and visualizing the hierarchical relationships between files and directories during digital investigations. Searching terms such as names, identifiers, sensitive information, and specific file types associated with the case significantly streamlines the research process when investigating slack space. FTK Imager allows investigators to build a binary tree-based dictionary from a drive image. Remember, adhering to legal and ethical guidelines is essential for selecting appropriate keywords and operating within established boundaries.

Data Carving

Recovering deleted or fragmented files from unallocated space, which includes any slack space, is done by utilizing file carving techniques and tools. Investigators may be able to identify and uncover these file fragments through using hints, such as file headers, in the investigation process. The data carving techniques can identify file boundaries and will search for specific file signatures, headers, or footers that match identified patterns (Suresh, 2020). The "carved out" scattered file fragments and remnants, which some users may unintentionally leave behind in the slack space, can be pieced together to reveal hidden information. Tools that perform data carving include FTK Imager, Autopsy, and the several tools offered by X-Ways Forensics.

Hexadecimal View

Like data carving techniques, hexadecimal view allows investigators to identify file boundaries allocated in the disk. The hexadecimal view visually allows for navigation of the disk, including the slack space, at a low level. Each byte is converted and presented as a two-digit, base-16, hexadecimal value. The numeric and alphabetical values range from 0–9 and A–F. Digital forensic experts can detect unusual patterns or anomalies that may indicate hidden or altered data in slack space, including steganographic content, remnants of deleted files, or other concealed information. Autopsy, WinHex, and FTK Imager offer a hexadecimal view.

Analytic Tools

We will dive deeper into the previously mentioned tools within this section and conclude our slack space demonstration.

FTK Imager

FTK Imager provides image preview, metadata analysis, and hexadecimal view, which aids in identifying any anomalies or hidden information within the image. Image preview allows investigators to view an image's file system structure and contents without mounting it or examining files individually (Kessler, 2015). It displays information in a binary-tree structure that streamlines digital forensic investigations. Regarding metadata, it also provides information about file creation, modification, and access times giving valuable insights into possible intentional use of slack space. It can also generate a hexadecimal view of files for analysis and identification of hidden or encrypted data within each file. Inquire about download at `https://go.exterro.com/l/43312/2023-05-03/fc4b78`.

WinHex

X-Ways Forensics offers a wide range of digital forensics tools; WinHex is one of their free tools. This tool is a hexadecimal editor, allowing investigators to inspect the raw byte-by-byte data. This tool is available at `www.winhex.com/winhex/hex-editor.html`.

You may recall the data hiding example in Figure 13-19 where we produced Secret_Hidden_In_Decoy.png, which contains the appended Hidden_File.txt (Figure 13-18). Recall the produced image had no visual impact.

In Figure 13-20, WinHex was utilized to provide visibility of the entire contents of Secret_Hidden_In_Decoy.png. The interface allows digital investigators to distinguish the boundaries of the logical end of the image file and the start of an appended text data living in the slack space.

After opening WinHex, you can analyze files in the main window by following these steps:

1. In the menu bar, select "Tools" followed by "Open Disk...."

2. Select the hard disk you want to freely browse (you can see this in Figure 13-20).

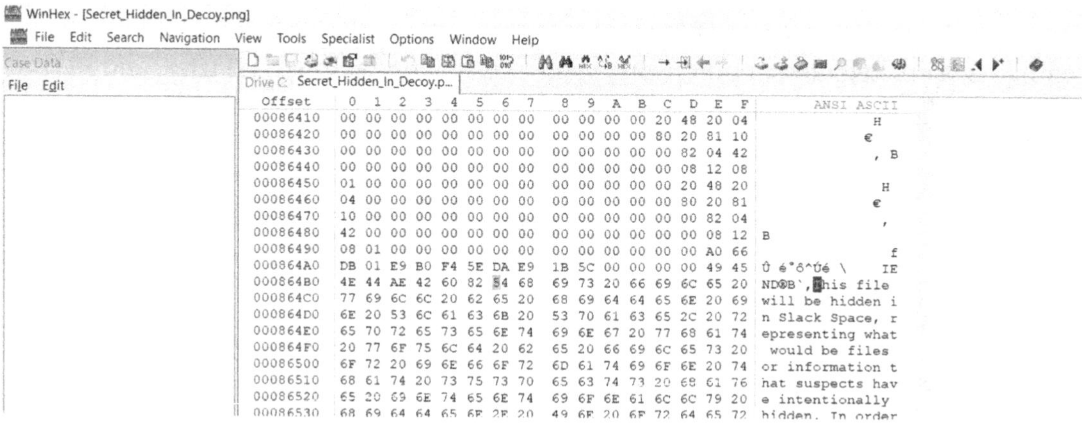

Figure 13-20. *WinHex analysis of Secret_Hidden_In_Decoy.png exposing the hidden text in the slack space*

Autopsy

Autopsy is another tool that can be utilized for data carving, keyword searches, file type analysis, and file metadata examination. Autopsy provides insights into file types, file origins, and potential manipulations that may have occurred. Keyword search features allow investigators to identify relevant evidence or hidden information, enhancing their ability to uncover hidden data and conduct comprehensive analyses. It is worth noting that Autopsy integrates the power of another program, Sleuth Kit, while offering an extended selection of tools and a user-friendly user interface. You can inquire about downloading at `www.autopsy.com/download/`.

Conclusions

This chapter explored various aspects of advanced data hiding techniques and their relevance in digital forensics. Skillful digital forensic investigators possess expertise in a variety of methods and tools to analyze systems and uncover hidden information. It is crucial to consider the methods employed by individuals attempting to hide information, such as deployed Windows encryption features, generating steganographic content, and utilizing slack space. The presented tools and techniques provide a sample collection for both illicit activities and digital forensic investigations. A thorough and detailed search is the responsibility of the digital forensics expert.

To become skilled investigators, a profound understanding of uncovering hidden information, analyzing altered files, and conducting digital investigations is essential. By reviewing various steganography algorithms and developing an understanding of the limitations of steganalysis, we can strengthen our ability to successfully retrieve crucial evidence in the future. Remaining informed of new tools as well as staying up to date with deep learning research will allow forensic investigators to become early adopters of emerging technologies that have shown to be promising. By doing so, they can ensure that they are equipped with the necessary knowledge and expertise to tackle even the most complex investigations. Empowered with this comprehensive knowledge, investigators navigate the intricate world of data hiding, ensuring the integrity of digital evidence.

As digital forensic professionals, continuous learning and adaptation to technology's ever-changing landscape are vital. Embracing the concepts explored in this chapter provides a solid foundation to confidently pursue methods to uncover hidden data. By equipping ourselves with the acquired knowledge and skills, we better prepare to tackle the challenges in digital forensics, staying at the forefront of this evolving field. This journey deepens our understanding of data hiding techniques' significance in digital forensics, enabling us to investigate hidden information, uphold justice, and ensure the integrity of digital evidence. Let us boldly apply our knowledge and skills to make a difference in the world of digital forensics.

References

BitLocker Drive Encryption Security Policy (n.d.). Retrieved from https://csrc.nist.gov/csrc/media/projects/cryptographic-module-validation-program/documents/security-policies/140sp1053.pdf

Chanu, Y. J., Tuithung, T., & Manglem Singh, K. (2012). A short survey on image steganography and steganalysis techniques. In 2012 3rd National Conference on Emerging Trends and Applications in Computer Science (pp. 52–55). IEEE. https://doi.org/10.1109/NCETACS.2012.6203297

Djebbar, F., Ayad, B., Meraim, K. A., et al. (2012). Comparative study of digital audio steganography techniques. Journal of Audio, Speech, and Music Processing, 25. https://doi.org/10.1186/1687-4722-2012-25

Fairbairn, L., Lanthier, M., & Tworek, H. (2023). A New Arena of War: Knitting Needles in Action in Great Britain (pp. 1939–1945). https://open.library.ubc.ca/media/download/pdf/52966/1.0433579/5

Grafnetter M. (March 24, 2020) #CQLabs – Extracting roamed private keys from active directory. CQURE Academy. https://cqureacademy.com/blog/extracting-roamed-private-keys

Kessler, G. (2015). Steganography for the computer forensics examiner. Retrieved from www.garykessler.net/library/fsc_stego.html

Liu, Y., Liu, S., Wang, Y., Zhao, H., & Liu, S. (2019). Video steganography: A review. Neurocomputing (Amsterdam), 335, 238–250. https://doi.org/10.1016/j.neucom.2018.09.091

Microsoft (June 2023). BitLocker overview – Windows Security. Microsoft Learn. https://learn.microsoft.com/en-us/windows/security/operating-system-security/data-protection/bitlocker/

Mulazzani, M., Neuner, S., Kieseberg, P., Huber, M., Schrittwieser, S., & Weippl, E. (2013). Quantifying Windows File Slack Size and Stability. Advances in Digital Forensics IX, AICT-410, 183–193. https://doi.org/10.1007/978-3-642-41148-9_13

Nihad Ahmad Hassan, & Rami Hijazi (2017). Chapter 4 – Data Hiding Under Windows® OS File Structure. In Data Hiding Techniques in Windows OS (pp. 97–132). Elsevier Inc. https://doi.org/10.1016/B978-0-12-804449-0.00004-X

Openspecs-office (September 12, 2018). [MS-GPEF]: Group policy: Encrypting file system extension. Developer tools, technical documentation and coding examples | Microsoft Docs. https://docs.microsoft.com/en-us/openspecs/windows_protocols/ms-gpef/14d3fd83-7537-41a2-af39-8e52c19ef0e3

Ramshankar, R. (January 27, 2021). A Forensic Analysis of the Encrypting File System, SANS Institute. www.sans.org/white-papers/40160/.

Subramanian, N., Elharrouss, O., Al-Maadeed, S., & Bouridane, A. (2021). Image Steganography: A Review of the Recent Advances. IEEE Access, 9, 23409–23423. https://doi.org/10.1109/ACCESS.2021.3053998

Surana, J., Sonsale. A., Joshi, B., Sharma, D., Choudhary, N. (2017). Steganography Techniques. International Journal of Engineering Development and Research, 5(2), 989–992. www.ijedr.org/papers/IJEDR1702167.pdf. ISSN: 2321-9939

Suresh Kumar Shetty, B., & Shetty H, P. (Eds.) (2020). Digital Forensic Science. IntechOpen. doi: 10.5772/intechopen.78450

Sushil, V., & Shahi, A. (n.d.). Review paper on image steganography. Retrieved July 11, 2023, from http://ijariie.com/AdminUploadPdf/Review_paper_on_image_steganography_ijariie18563.pdf

Tabares-Soto, R., Arteaga-Arteaga, H. B., Mora-Rubio, A., Bravo-Ortíz, M. A., Arias-Garzón, D., Alzate-Grisales, J. A., Orozco-Arias, S., Isaza, G., Ramos-Pollán, R. (2021). Sensitivity of deep learning applied to spatial image steganalysis. PeerJ Comput Sci, 7, e616. https://doi.org/10.7717/peerj-cs.616

Tan, C., Zhang, L., & Bao, L. (2020). A Deep Exploration of BitLocker Encryption and Security Analysis. In 2020 IEEE 20th International Conference on Communication Technology (ICCT) (pp. 1070–1074). IEEE. https://doi.org/10.1109/ICCT50939.2020.9295908

Tushara, M., & Navas, K. A. (2016). Image steganography techniques using discrete wavelet transform. IJIREEICE. Retrieved from https://ijireeice.com/wp-content/uploads/2016/07/nCORETech-38.pdf

Westfeld, A. (2001). F5—A Steganographic Algorithm: High Capacity Despite Better Steganalysis. In Information Hiding (pp. 289–302). Springer Berlin Heidelberg. https://doi.org/10.1007/3-540-45496-9_21

Assessment

1. What is the most common method of hiding data in an electronic file?

    a. Echo hiding

    b. Encrypts individual files or folders

    c. Encrypts whole hard drives

    d. LSB

2. When using steganography, what is the term for the type of media (video, image, etc.) that you are hiding data in?

    a. Carrier

    b. Cover

  c. Embedding

  d. Host

3. What is an FEK?

   File Encryption Key

4. Where are the EFS certificate files stored?

   a. In the user's personal certificate store

   b. In the DPAPI blob

   c. In the hexadecimal view

   d. In the NTFS volume

5. What is steganography?

   a. The study of detecting hidden data

   b. The process of hiding data within mediums

   c. The analysis of file metadata

   d. The encryption of data

6. Which is the most common and simple spatial domain steganography algorithm?

   a. F5

   b. Chi-Square

   c. DCT

   d. LSB

7. Which is not a common statistical steganalysis technique?

   a. Chi-Square

   b. Residual based

   c. Frequency hopping

   d. Histogram based

8. Which one is a text-based steganography technique?

    a. Random and statistical generation

    b. Spread spectrum

    c. Inter-embedding

    d. Parity coding

APPENDIX A

Volatility Cheat Sheet

The basic format for running a volatility command is: volatility-version.exe commandname -f filepath -profile=profilename

To learn more about a plugin volatility-version.exe commandname -h

Profiles volatility_2.6_win64_standalone.exe --info. If this provides you a list of profiles you can use for memory analysis, then all is working well.

Running processes PSlist volatility_2.6_win64_standalone.exe pslist -f memdump. mem --profile=Win8SP0x64

DLL's DLLList volatility_2.6_win64_standalone.exe dlllist -f memdump.mem --profile=Win8SP0x64

Windows Services syscan volatility_2.6_win64_standalone.exe svcscan -f memdump.mem --profile=Win8SP0x64

Drivers modscan volatility_2.6_win64_standalone.exe modscan -f memdump.mem --profile=Win8SP0x64

Users and privileges getsids volatility_2.6_win64_standalone.exe getsids -f memdump.mem --profile=Win8SP0x64

Processes psscan volatility-2.6.standalone.exe psscan -f C:path\tovolatility\dump. bin --profile=Win8SP0x64

Processes as a tree pstree volatility-2.6.standalone.exe pstree -f C:path\tovolatility\ dump.bin --profile=Win8SP0x64

Injected code malfind volatility-2.6.standalone.exe malfind -f C:path\tovolatility\ dump.bin --profile=Win8SP0x64

User hashes hashdump volatility-2.6.standalone.exe hashdump -f C:path\ tovolatility\dump.bin --profile=Win8SP0x64

Registry hives hivelist Processes hivelist volatility-2.6.standalone.exe psscan -f C:path\tovolatility\dump.bin --profile=Win8SP0x64

© Chuck Easttom, William Butler, Jessica Phelan, Ramya Sai Bhagavatula, Sean Steuber, Karely Rodriguez, Victoria Indy Balkissoon, Zehra Naseer 2024
C. Easttom et al., *Windows Forensics*, https://doi.org/10.1007/979-8-8688-0193-8

APPENDIX B

Registry Cheat Sheet

General Registry Information

The Registry is organized into five sections referred to as *hives*. Each of these sections contains specific information that can be useful to you. The five hives are described here:

- **HKEY_CLASSES_ROOT (HKCR)**: This hive stores information about drag and drop rules, program shortcuts, the user interface, and related items.

- **HKEY_CURRENT_USER (HKCU)**: This hive is very important to any forensic investigation. It stores information about the currently logged-on user, including desktop settings and user folders.

- **HKEY_LOCAL_MACHINE (HKLM)**: This hive can also be important to a forensic investigation. It contains those settings common to the entire machine, regardless of the individual user.

- **HKEY_USERS (HKU)**: This hive is very critical to forensics investigations. It has profiles for all the users, including their settings.

- **HKEY_CURRENT_CONFIG (HCU)**: This hive contains the current system configuration. This might also prove useful in your forensic examinations.

© Chuck Easttom, William Butler, Jessica Phelan, Ramya Sai Bhagavatula, Sean Steuber, Karely Rodriguez, Victoria Indy Balkissoon, Zehra Naseer 2024
C. Easttom et al., *Windows Forensics*, https://doi.org/10.1007/979-8-8688-0193-8

Hive Registry Path	Hive File Path
HKEY_LOCAL_MACHINE \SYSTEM	\winnt\system32\config\system
HKEY_LOCAL_MACHINE \SAM	\winnt\system32\config\sam
HKEY_LOCAL_MACHINE \SECURITY	\winnt\system32\config\security
HKEY_LOCAL_MACHINE \SOFTWARE	\winnt\system32\config\software
HKEY_LOCAL_MACHINE \HARDWARE	Volatile hive
HKEY_LOCAL_MACHINE \SYSTEM \Clone	Volatile hive
HKEY_USERS \UserProfile	Profile; usually under \winnt\profiles\user
HKEY_USERS.DEFAULT	\winnt\system32\config\default

Specific Keys
ComDlg32

The ComDlg32 key in the Windows Registry stores configuration settings and other information related to these common dialog boxes. This can include things like the last directory accessed, user preferences for viewing files (such as list view or detail view), and other state information that Windows uses to provide a consistent experience across different uses of the dialog boxes: HKEY_CURRENT_USER\Software\Microsoft\Windows\CurrentVersion\Explorer\ComDlg32.

MUICache

Each time that you start using a new application, the Windows operating system automatically extracts the application name from the version resource of the exe file and stores it for using it later in a registry key known as the "MUICache." MUI is a technology in Windows that allows for the interface of an application to be displayed in multiple languages. This is particularly important in environments where computers are used by speakers of different languages.

HKEY_CURRENT_USER\SOFTWARE\Classes\Local Settings\MuiCache

Wireless Networks

HKEY_LOCAL_MACHINE\SOFTWARE\Microsoft\Windows NT\ CurrentVersion\
NetworkList\Nla\Wireless

Another key that is of interest can provide information regarding the specific
network cards:

HKEY_LOCAL_MACHINE\SOFTWARE\Microsoft\Windows NT\CurrentVersion\
NetworkCards\

DHCP information:

HKLM\SYSTEM\CurrentControlSet\Services\Tcpip\Parameters\Interfaces\{GUID}

Malware Analysis

Run keys:

HKEY_CURRENT_USER\Software\Microsoft\Windows\CurrentVersion\Run
AppInit_DLLs:

HKEY_LOCAL_MACHINE\SOFTWARE\Microsoft\Windows NT\CurrentVersion\
Windows\AppInit_DLLs

Applications

This key provides a list of all applications registered on the computer. The key is found at
HKEY_LOCAL_MACHINE\SOFTWARE\RegisteredApplications.

- Kazaa has data in the key HKCU\Software\Kazaa

- Morpheus stores data at HKCU\Software\Morpheus\GUI\
  SearchRecent

- **WinRAR**: \HKEY_CURRENT_USER\SOFTWARE\WinRAR\
  ArcHistory

- **TurboTax**: \HKEY_CURRENT_USER\SOFTWARE\Intuit

- **Adobe**: \HKEY_CURRENT_USER\SOFTWARE\Adobe\Adobe
  Acrobat\DC\AdobeViewer

- **Bitcoin Wallet**: \HKEY_CURRENT_USER\SOFTWARE\Bitcoin\

- **Installed Products**: \HKEY_CURRENT_USER\SOFTWARE\ Microsoft\Installer\Products

- **Mozilla Plugins**: \HKEY_LOCAL_MACHINE\SOFTWARE\ MozillaPlugins

- **Uninstalled Programs**: HKLM\Software\Wow6432Node\Microsoft\ Windows\CurrentVersion\Uninstall\

Page File Management

This is a very interesting key. Normally, the Windows Page File is not cleared when a computer shuts down. Many people, even those quite proficient, are not aware of this fact. This allows a skilled forensic investigator to find evidence in that Page File. However, by using this registry key, one can change that:

HKLM\SYSTEM\CurrentControlSet\Control\Session Manager\Memory Management

BAM/DAM

The Background Activity Moderator (BAM) and Desktop Activity Moderator (DAM):

HKEY_LOCAL_MACHINE\SYSTEM\CurrentControlSet\Services\bam\state\ UserSettings\

Shared Folders

There may be cases where you wish to know what shares a computer has. This is found in the registry at HKLM\System\ControlSet001\Services\lanmanserver\Shares.

TypedPath

Windows Registry keeps information regarding when a user types in a path in Windows Explorer. That is found at \HKEY_CURRENT_USER\SOFTWARE\Microsoft\Windows\ CurrentVersion\Explorer\TypedPaths.

USB Information

The registry key HKEY_LOCAL_MACHINE\System\ControlSet\Enum\USBSTOR lists USB devices that have been connected to the machine.

SYSTEM\MountedDevices allows investigators to match the serial number to a given drive letter or volume that was mounted when the USB device was inserted.

The user who was using the USB device can be found here:

HKCU\Software\Microsoft\Windows\CurrentVersion\Explorer\MountPoints2

The vendor and product ID can be found here:

SYSTEM\CurrentControlSet\Enum\USB

Another important key is

SYSTEM\ControlSet001\Enum\USBSTOR{VEN_PROD_VERSION}{USB serial}\

The values for this are

0064: First connection

0066: Last connection

MRU

The Most Recently Used list can show items that have been used recently:

HKCU\Software\Microsoft\Windows\CurrentVersion\Explorer\ComDlg32\
LastVisitedMRU

ShellBags

ShellBag entries indicate a given folder was accessed, not a specific file.

This entry can be found at HKCU\Software\Microsoft\Windows\Shell.

User Assist

Windows User Assist is a feature within the Windows operating system that tracks and records the frequency and time of application usage.

This key can be found at

HKEY_CURRENT_USER\Software\Microsoft\Windows\CurrentVersion\Explorer\ UserAssist

Prefetch

Prefetch files contain the name of the executable, a Unicode list of DLLs used by that executable, a count of how many times the executable has been run, and a timestamp indicating the last time the program was run. This can be found at HKEY_ LOCAL_MACHINE\SYSTEM\CurrentControlSet\Control\Session Manager\Memory Management\PrefetchParameter.

Mounted Devices

HKEY_LOCAL_MACHINE\SYSTEM\MountedDevices: This information can be useful to a forensic examiner as it shows any connected storage device has been recognized by the operating system.

AutoStart Programs

Those locations are

HKLM\Software\Microsoft\Windows\CurrentVersion\Run

HKLM \Software\Microsoft\Windows\CurrentVersion\RunOnce

HKLM \Software\Microsoft\Windows\CurrentVersion\Runonce

HKLM \Software\Microsoft\Windows\CurrentVersion\Policies\ Explorer\Run

HKLM \Software\Microsoft\Windows\CurrentVersion\Run

The key HKLM\Software\Microsoft\Windows\ CurrentVersion\Run

Index

A

Acronyms, 260, 354, 379, 423, 424
Active Directory (AD), 5, 14, 384, 385, 407
Advanced Power Management (APM), 158
AmCache, 198–200
Artifacts, 233
    browser extensions, 151
    RDP, 147
    timeline events, 147, 149, 150
    WER, 146, 147
Autopsy, 57, 97–99, 101, 102, 448
    recovers deleted files, 113, 114
    scanning user activity, 115, 116
    uncovering user activity, 115
    user activity, 116, 117

B

Background Activity Moderator (BAM),
       196, 197, 460
BitLocker, 40, 41, 399–404, 410
BitLocker Drive Encryption
    activating on Windows, 400
    components, 402
    definition, 399
    recovering data, 403
    recovery keys, 402, 403
    TPM, 401
Bit-plane complexity
       segmentation steganography
       (BPCS), 417
Boot sequence

definition, 38
POST, 39, 40
warm/cold boot, 39

C

cacls command, 27
Certmgr, 37–38
Chi-Square test, 437
chkdsk command, 26
Cloud computing, 375
    connectivity/security, 378, 379
    FedRAMP, 379–382
    NSA, 376, 377
    types, 377, 378
Cloud forensics
    Azure forensics, 393
    challenges, 385–387
    definition, 385
    FTK Imager, 390–392
    NIST 800-201, 387
    OSForensics, 387, 389, 390
Cloud Service Providers (CSPs), 376,
       380, 386
Cloud services, 375, 376, 378, 380, 385
ComDlg32, 182, 458
Command-line interface (CLI), 274, 285
Committee on National Security System
       (CNSS), 47, 48, 63
Computer forensics, 45–51, 341
Computer memory
    distinct hierarchy, 232
    RAM, 232

463

© Chuck Easttom, William Butler, Jessica Phelan, Ramya Sai Bhagavatula, Sean Steuber,
Karely Rodriguez, Victoria Indy Balkissoon, Zehra Naseer 2024
C. Easttom et al., *Windows Forensics*, https://doi.org/10.1007/979-8-8688-0193-8

Printed in the United States
by Baker & Taylor Publisher Services